City & Guilds

7103 Diploma
NVQ/SVQ
Technical Certificate

ood & Beverage Service

2nd Edition

Series Editor: **Pam Rabone**

Holly Bamunuge • **Graham Edwards** • **Joyce Nutley**

Levels 1 & 2

Part of Pearson

Heinemann is an imprint of Pearson Education Limited, a company incorporated in England and Wales, having its registered office at Edinburgh Gate, Harlow, Essex, CM20 2JE. Registered company number: 872828

www.heinemann.co.uk

Heinemann is a registered trademark of Pearson Education Limited

Text © Pearson Education Limited 2008, 2010

First published 2008; this edition 2010

14 13 12 11 10
10 9 8 7 6 5 4 3 2 1

British Library Cataloguing in Publication Data

A catalogue record for this book is available from the British Library.

ISBN 978 0 435027 19 3

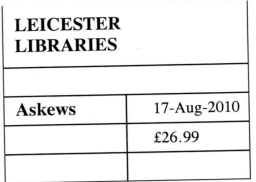

Designed and typeset by Kamae Design, Oxford
Illustrated by Asa Andersson and Kamae Design
Cover design by Siu Hang Wong
Printed in Spain by Graficas Estella

Acknowledgements

The publisher would like to thank Marcus Wareing for providing the Foreword, Judi Strain for the Functional Skills mapping, and Paul Meikle Janney for additions to Chapter 18.

The authors and publisher would like to thank the following individuals and organisations for permission to reproduce photographs:

p.v:©Comstock/Alamy; pp.2, 8: Alamy; p.3:Black Star/Alamy; pp.15, 213:Center Parcs; p.16:Wimpy International; p.17:Camelot Theme Park; p.22:David Crausby/Alamy; p.25:David Templeton/Alamy; p.27:Aramark UK; p.51:©Chris George/Alamy; p.52:©Joe Fox/Alamy; p.103:©Keith Morris/Alamy; p.110:©Pearson Education Ltd; p.111:©ACE STOCK LIMITED/Alamy; p.112:©Lynne Siler Photography/Alamy; p.134:©WoodyStock/Alamy; p.140:©PhotoDisc/Photolink; p.142:©Pearson Education/Jules Selmes; p.168:©PhotoDisc/Cole Publishing Group/Bob Montesclaros; p.210:Anthony Collins/Alamy; p.232:©Ingolf Pompe 63/Alamy; p.233:©Jeff Greenberg/Alamy; pp.245, 261–3, 313, 322–5, 335–41, 365:©Pearson Education Ltd/Oliver Beamish; p.248:©PhotoDisc; p.252:©Fresh Food Images/Photolibrary; p.272:©Comestock; pp.282, 290:©Justin Kasezthreez/Alamy; p.283:©Image Source, ©Rough Guides/Alamy; p.287:©Peter Titmuss/Alamy; p.312:©John Rensten/Alamy; p.329:©WR Publishing/Alamy; p.354:©Vannellbob/Alamy; p.355:©Jack Carey/Alamy, ©Tricia Toms/Alamy; p.356, top:©Jeff Greenberg/Alamy; p.357:©Image Source; p.358:©Andreas Keuchel/Alamy; pp.380–1, 386, 394–5, 417, 443–6, 452, 455, 458–60, 488, 491–2, 495, 497, 501–2, 504, 505, 512:©Mark Bassett; p.392:©Elvele Images/Alamy; p.398:©Urban Zone/Alamy; p.416:©Pearson Education Ltd; p.419:©PhotoDisc/John A. Rizzo; p.420:©JupiterImages/BananaStock/Alamy; pp.445(2nd from top), 459(3rd from top), 535:©Bon Appetit/Alamy; p.459(bottom):©Elba Photo Agency/Alamy; p.463:©Digital Vision; p.471:©Frank Tschakert/Alamy; p.478:©Rob Walls/Alamy; pp.522, 530:©Pearson Education Ltd; p.523:©Arco Images/Alamy; p.524:©Holt Studios International Ltd/Alamy; p.526:Yuri Arcurs/Shutterstock; p.527:©Christopher Nash/Alamy; p.528:ifong/Shutterstock; p.529:©Brian Buckley/Alamy; p.534:©iStockphoto/Jason Boeselager; p.536:©Charles Stirling/Alamy; p.539:©Ian M Butterfield/Alamy; p.540:©Amana Images Inc/Alamy; p.545:©Dominic Whiting/Alamy

Every effort has been made to contact copyright holders of material reproduced in this book. Any omissions will be rectified in subsequent printings if notice is given to the publishers.

The authors and publisher would like to thank The Vegetarian Society for their kind permission to reproduce the seedling symbol on page 223.

Websites

There are links to relevant websites in this book. In order to ensure that the links are up to date, that the links work, and that the sites are not inadvertently linked to sites that could be considered offensive, we have made the links available on the Heinemann website at www.heinemann.co.uk/hotlinks. When you access the site, the express code is 7193P.

KT-442-685

Contents

Foreword

Congratulations! You have now embarked on one of the most rewarding and challenging careers there is – hospitality. Going to college and working towards a City & Guilds qualification is the best start you can get. But don't think the learning ends when you get your certificate, it's just the beginning!

My career with food started when I was 16 at Southport Technical College. More than 20 years later, I am just as passionate about food and still learning and adding to my basic training from all those years ago.

Since I started cooking the world of catering has changed. Chefs are better known, there are more cooking shows on TV and diners have greater knowledge of food than ever before. What an exciting time to be joining the world of hospitality with so many opportunities across the industry.

I continue to be inspired by food and the ingredients. In the kitchen our food development never stands still, we are constantly trying new dishes, testing and tweaking until we reach perfection. However, very few guests visit restaurants solely to taste the food; they are looking for an experience where service plays just as important a role as the menu. At The Berkeley we spend just as much time looking at ways to improve our levels of service in the dining room as we do our menu.

Successful restaurateurs need to understand and offer the whole package, which means understanding the consumer, learning to manage a team, handling finances, but most of all learning to be hospitable. The guest experience begins the moment the telephone rings until the moment the guest leaves the dining room, and of course the effect it has on their decision to return!

Hospitality is a great industry to work in. It doesn't matter where you start from, if you have determination with ability and you are prepared to work hard and grab every opportunity to learn, the future will be bright for you. In the kitchen or in the dining room the roles are hugely demanding but equally hugely satisfying.

This City & Guilds course is the foundation to your future – my advice, listen to your mentors, keep your head down and work hard, the sky is the limit!

Marcus Wareing
Marcus Wareing Restaurants Ltd
Marcus Wareing at The Berkeley
London

Introduction

This book has been designed with you in mind. Its purpose is to provide:

- the skills and knowledge requirements of the key units for the Level 1 and Level 2 S/NVQ Diploma in Food and Beverage Service (7132)
- the skills and knowledge requirements of the units for the Technical Certificate in Hospitality and Catering (Food and Beverage Service) (7091)
- coverage of key units in the Level 1 Certificate and Level 2 Diploma in Professional Food and Beverage Service (7103-1; 7103-2)
- a reference book for you to use while working towards your qualification and after you have qualified.

You will find a table on page ix which shows you which units are relevant to your study for these qualifications.

The catering and hospitality industry

The catering and hospitality industry is large. There are many roles to choose from and different types of businesses in which to work. The skills and knowledge you will develop while working towards your qualification will be put to good use in the industry.

Your job title and tasks will be defined by which part of the industry you are working in. The table below shows various job roles which you could undertake with a Level 2 S/NVQ qualification and the sort of functions or tasks you will undertake.

Job title	Role	Core functions
Commis Waiter	To assist in the service of food and drinks	Prepare tools and equipment ready for service; help to serve food; help to prepare and serve drinks; contribute to the provision of customer service; minimise waste
Waiter	To serve customers food and drinks and provide customer service	Prepare tools and equipment for the service of both food and drink; provide good customer service; complete food and drink orders accurately; obtain and receive payments; liaise with other staff; minimise waste
Bar person	To serve customers drinks, prepare and maintain all tools and equipment	Prepare tools and equipment for the service of drinks; provide good customer service; complete drink orders accurately; obtain and receive payments; liaise with other staff; deal with problems promptly and efficiently; minimise waste

Figure i.1 Job title and tasks at entry level

When deciding which part of the industry you would like to work in you need to take into account the different roles and functions as well as the hours of work and terms and conditions.

What is an S/NVQ?

An S/NVQ (Scottish/National Vocational Qualification) assesses a person's technical competence to perform a job. It can also form part of a Modern Apprenticeship. The assessment is continual but you will only be assessed when you are competent at a task. NVQs are divided into units. In order to pass a unit you need to fulfil various requirements:

Each unit has a

Unit aim

This explains what the unit is all about and relates the unit content to typical tasks you may carry out.

Learning outcomes

Each unit is then divided into learning outcomes. These outcomes are either about practical skills (tasks) that you need to be able to perform or the knowledge needed to carry out the tasks within your job role.

What you must cover

This details the range of situations/tasks and/or commodities that you need to demonstrate you can cover.

- **Evidence requirements** – details how much needs to be assessed by observation and how much can be covered by other methods of assessment.

How do I gain an NVQ?

The flowchart below summarises the process of gaining an NVQ.
Each stage is discussed in more detail on the next page.

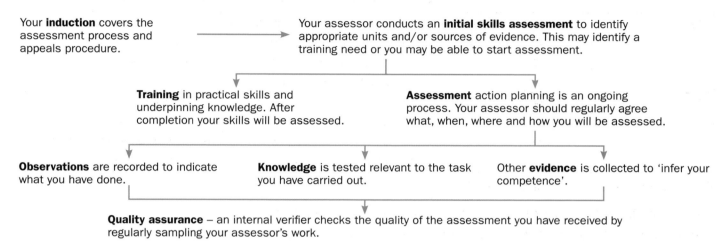

Your **induction** covers the assessment process and appeals procedure.

Your assessor conducts an **initial skills assessment** to identify appropriate units and/or sources of evidence. This may identify a training need or you may be able to start assessment.

Training in practical skills and underpinning knowledge. After completion your skills will be assessed.

Assessment action planning is an ongoing process. Your assessor should regularly agree what, when, where and how you will be assessed.

Observations are recorded to indicate what you have done.

Knowledge is tested relevant to the task you have carried out.

Other **evidence** is collected to 'infer your competence'.

Quality assurance – an internal verifier checks the quality of the assessment you have received by regularly sampling your assessor's work.

Figure i.2 How to gain an NVQ

Induction

You should receive an induction as soon as you start your NVQ. This should include an overview of the assessment process and a detailed explanation of the appeals procedure which you must follow if you meet a problem.

Initial assessment

When you start your qualification you should have an initial assessment. Together with your assessor you will work through the units you have selected to do in order to identify how much knowledge and/or skills you may already have. Your assessor may have a special form to record an action plan so that you are very clear about what needs to happen next.

Training

If your initial assessment identified a training need you will receive training in practical skills and underpinning knowledge before your skills are assessed.

Assessment

Your assessment will be ongoing with your assessor. You should receive assessment plans outlining what you have achieved and what you have to do next.

Observation

Your assessor will observe you carrying out tasks. The outcomes will be recorded in your portfolio.

Knowledge testing

You will be required to answer questions to prove you have the knowledge that underpins your performance.

Other evidence

It may also be possible to collect other evidence including:

○ witness testimonies – from colleagues or managers at your place of work

○ assessment of prior learning or experience – evidence that you may already have some of the skills or experience required by the qualification, e.g. a food safety certificate

○ work product (naturally occurring evidence) – e.g. menus, till receipts, XY readings, food orders, etc.

Your assessor will work with you to decide on the best method of collecting evidence for each unit.

Expert witness

May be used where additional support relating to the assessment of technical competence is required. The expert witness must be abe to demonstrate through relevant qualifications, practical experience and knowledge about your performance.

Professional discussion

Professional discussion is a really good way of providing additional evidence to confirm your competence. It can be used at the start of the qualification to identify your daily tasks or throughout your assessment to fill gaps in your evidence.

Your assessor will work with you to decide on the best method of collecting evidence for each unit.

Your portfolio

All evidence should be placed into your portfolio and will need to be referenced to the NVQ standards. You may be given a paper logbook showing these standards. There are different styles of logbooks depending upon which awarding organisation you are registered with. Alternatively you may be using an e-portfolio such as the ProActive e-portfolio which is linked to the qualification. Your assessor will advise you on whether you will use a logbook or the ProActive e-portfolio.

Who checks my portfolio?

Your assessor will make decisions on your competence and work with you to help you build your portfolio of evidence.

In order to ensure fairness and to monitor the quality of the assessment an internal verifier (quality assurance person) will check the assessor's work regularly. This may be by observing them assessing you or by sampling evidence already collected and logged in your portfolio.

Shortly after you start your NVQ you will be registered with an awarding organisation e.g. City & Guilds. It is responsible for checking the quality of the assessment and internal verification. The awarding body appoints an external verifier to carry out checks before certification.

Apprenticeships & Technical Certificates

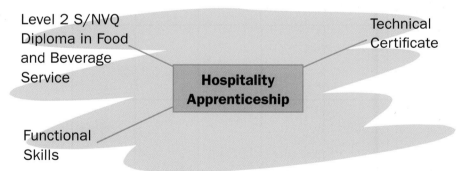

Figure i.3 Qualifications that make up the Hospitality and Catering Apprenticeship

Technical Certificate and Hospitality Apprenticeship framework

Some of the units of this book serve towards making up your Technical Certificate. This is a qualification that you will take as part of your Hospitality Apprenticeship programme. As you work through the units in your Technical Certificate you will have the opportunity to learn, develop and practise the knowledge and skills for employment/or career progression in the Hospitality sector. The Technical Certificate contributes knowledge and understanding towards your S/NVQ Level 2 qualification in Food and Beverage Service whilst containing additional skills and knowledge which go beyond the scope of the S/NVQ.

How this book can help you

Each chapter covers the requirements for the qualifications outlined on p v, so you can use the book to:

○ develop your skills and knowledge for the 'what you must know' sections

○ identify the tools, equipment and ingredients for the practical activities undertaken in the 'what you must cover' and the practical outcomes 'be able to' sections.

The following table lists the qualifications covered in this book and the chapters that relate to them

Qualification	Chapter 1 Investigate the catering and hospitality industry	Chapter 2 Health and Safety	Chapter 3 Teamwork	Chapter 4 Customer Service	Chapter 5 Food safety	Chapter 6 Dealing with payments	Chapter 7 Menu knowledge and design	Chapter 8 Preparing and clearing food and service areas	Chapter 9 Providing a counter/ takeaway service	Chapter 10 Serving food at table
S/NVQ Level 1 Diploma in Food and Beverage Service (7132)			x	x	x	x		x	x	x
S/NVQ Level 2 Diploma in Food and Beverage Service (7132)		x	x	x	x	x		x	x	x
Technical Certificate in Hospitality and Catering (Food and Beverage Service) (7091)		x	x	x	x	x		x		x
Level 1 Certificate in Food and Beverage Service (7103-1)	x	x	x	x	x	x	x	x	x	x
Level 2 Diploma in Food and Beverage Service (7103-2)	x	x		x	x	x	x	x	x	x

Qualification	Chapter 11 Silver service	Chapter 12 Providing a carvery buffet service	Chapter 13 Preparing and clearing drinks service areas	Chapter 14 Serving alcoholic and soft drinks	Chapter 15 Preparing and serving bottled wines	Chapter 16 Cellar work	Chapter 17 Receiving and storing drinks	Chapter 18 Preparing and serving hot drinks	Appendix Workplace skills
S/NVQ Level 1 Diploma in Food and Beverage Service (7132)			x	x				x	x
S/NVQ Level 2 Diploma in Food and Beverage Service (7132)	x	x	x	x	x	x	x	x	x
Technical Certificate in Hospitality and Catering (Food and Beverage Service) (7091)				x					x
Level 1 Certificate in Food and Beverage Service (7103-1)		x	x	x	x			x	x
Level 2 Diploma in Food and Beverage Service (7103-2)		x	x	x	x	x		x	x

Throughout the book there are useful tips and activities that you can use as well as some questions to help test your knowledge and support your learning while you work towards your NVQ. Photographs identify equipment and tools and the sequence of complex practical tasks. Clear illustrations identify the equipment and tools that you will need.

Key features

Look out for the following special features as you work through the book.

 Marcus says — Practical ideas and tips from top chef Marcus Wareing

 Definition — All important words are defined to help you develop your underpinning knowledge.

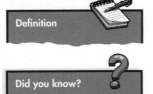 Did you know? — Interesting and useful food and drink service facts.

In the restaurant
In the food service area — These short real-life case studies tell you about the experiences of other people working in the catering industry.

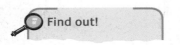 Remember! — Important points to promote good practice and reminders about safe working practices.

 Find out! — These independent research activities help you explore new areas and extend your knowledge.

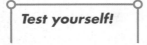 Try this! — Short practical activities for you to try in the classroom. Sometimes they may provide evidence for your portfolio.

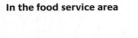 *Test yourself!* — At the end of each chapter there is a set of questions to check your knowledge. These are a useful way of revising the underpinning knowledge for a unit ready for assessment.

1

Investigating the catering and hospitality industry

In this chapter you will cover skills and knowledge in the following units:

- 7103 – Unit 101: Introduction to the catering and hospitality industry

- 7103 – Unit 201: Investigate the catering and hospitality industry

Working through this chapter could also provide evidence for the following Functional Skills at Level 2:

Functional ICT – Finding and selecting information – search engines and queries and AND/NOT/OR, >,<,>=,<=, contains, begins with, use of wild cards; recognise and take account of copyright and other constraints on the use of information; evaluate fitness for purpose

In this chapter you will learn about:

- the structure of the UK catering and hospitality industry

- the main features of establishments within each sector

- the main job roles and responsibilities within the different sectors

- job opportunities in catering and hospitality

- legislation and regulations covering working in catering and hospitality

- the functions of different professional associations

The hospitality and catering industry

It is a great time to join the hospitality and catering industry. Over the last few years it has become increasingly vibrant, exciting and forward-thinking. The importance of the industry is set to increase, helped by London hosting the Olympic Games in 2012. The eyes of the world will be on the UK, looking at the standards we set for catering and hospitality for the event, and beyond.

Did you know?
There are about 1.64 million people employed in hospitality and catering in the UK. This is about 6 per cent of the total working population in the UK.

Structure of the UK hospitality and catering industry

The structure of hospitality and catering reflects the different organisations that make up the industry, and how they relate to each other.

The hospitality and catering industry can be divided into:
○ the commercial sector, and
○ the public service sector.

Commercial sector

The commercial sector covers businesses where accommodation and/or catering are the main source of income, e.g. hotels and restaurants. Those working in the commercial sector provide food, drink and accommodation to UK residents and overseas visitors.

Did you know?
The commercial sector is sometimes known as the profit sector.

Figure 1.1 Fine dining restaurant at the Ritz hotel, Piccadilly, London

Public service sector

In the public service sector accommodation and/or catering are not the main business interest but these services are still needed for customers, staff and visitors. It covers hospitality and catering occupations in non-hospitality industries, e.g. hospitals, residential homes, schools and colleges and the workplace. These services may not be paid for directly by the customer or the customer may pay only part of the cost if the services are **subsidised**.

Hospitality and catering services may be:
○ owned or managed 'in house', e.g. school meals may be managed by the local council, or
○ contracted out to another organisation that provides hospitality (often called a contract caterer).

See Figure 1.3 for more information.

At one time the public service sector was mainly welfare catering, e.g. in hospitals. Contract catering for industry falls within the public service sector but in terms of conditions of service and skills needed by employees it often has more in common with the commercial sector; see page 2.

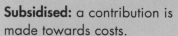

Definition
Subsidised: a contribution is made towards costs.

Did you know?
The Public Service Sector is sometimes known as the Not for Profit Sector or the Cost Sector.

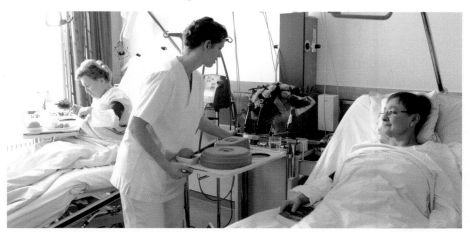
Figure 1.2: Food being served in a hospital

Operations

The hospitality and catering industry provides three main operations:
○ catering
○ accommodation
○ hospitality.

Top marks!
When researching, try to collect different information from different sources, e.g. websites, professional magazines, local guides and advertisements. Find out about national and international companies.

Catering

Catering operations involve preparing, distributing, finishing and serving food and drink. Commercial establishments (such as fast food outlets, cafés, restaurants, motorway service areas, pubs and bars) and public sector establishments (such as school canteens) are all types of catering operation. Catering operations are very diverse and range from a small café run by the owner to a company with a **chain** of restaurants employing hundreds of staff to a specialist caterer contracted to provide food and drink at a football game.

> **Definition**
> **Chain:** when there are a lot of establishments that operate under a particular name, e.g. McDonald's operates a chain of fast food restaurants.

Accommodation

Accommodation operations are about providing somewhere for people to stay. It includes **serviced accommodation** like guesthouses, and **self-catering accommodation** like caravans and chalets. Some accommodation-only functions are similar to those in a catering establishment, e.g. taking reservations and receiving customers. Providing accommodation involves other areas of operation, however, that are different to those of a catering establishment.

> **Definition**
> **Serviced accommodation:** some catering is provided, e.g. bed and breakfast.
> **Self-catering accommodation:** customers cater for themselves.

Hospitality

Hospitality operations provide accommodation, catering and service, e.g. an hotel. These aspects may be divided between departments in a large hotel. In a small family hotel just one or two people are likely to run the whole operation.

See Figure 1.3 for more information.

Types of establishment	Descriptions/examples
Commercial sector	
Hotels	○ Provide food, drink and accommodation ○ Range from low cost with restricted catering to expensive 5-star hotels with full restaurant service, a range of places to eat and 24-hour room-service menu ○ May accommodate conferences ○ Include: independent, owner-run hotels; large chains, e.g. Hilton and Intercontinental; independent consortium, e.g. Best Western; boutique hotels; country house hotels ○ Demand and number/type of staff varies according to quality, reputation and location

Lodges	<ul><li>Provide basic, low-cost accommodation with tea and coffee making facilities</li><li>Usually near motorways</li><li>Minimal staffing, with evening shift usually finishing by 11pm</li><li>High demand with low-cost leisure travellers and people travelling on business</li><li>Standard, modern designs</li><li>Often next to restaurants, e.g. Whitbread's Premier Travel Inn is always next to one of their Brewers Fayre or Beefeater restaurants.</li></ul>
Guest houses	<ul><li>Provide accommodation with a limited range of catering</li><li>Limited hours of service</li><li>Low-cost</li><li>Improving quality has increased popularity</li><li>Run by one person or just a few staff.</li></ul>
Restaurants	<ul><li>Provide food and drink</li><li>Includes independents and chains</li><li>Can be conventional, speciality, themed, e.g. La Tasca tapas bars and restaurants or ethnic, e.g. Chinese food</li><li>Seated dining ranging from those offering quick service to fine dining</li><li>Prices, staffing, opening hours, demand and design vary according to brand, style, quality, location and menu offered.</li></ul>
Traditional cafés	<ul><li>Provide food and drink</li><li>Independent</li><li>Full fried breakfast-style menu with non-alcoholic drinks</li><li>Low-cost in basic surroundings</li><li>Minimum staffing</li><li>Opening hours to suit local hours, often daytime only.</li></ul>
Chain café outlets	<ul><li>More sophisticated international café style, e.g. Café Rouge</li><li>Offer interesting meals and alcoholic drinks</li><li>Opening hours are daytime or day and evening</li><li>Staffing, prices and demand vary according to location, quality and reputation.</li></ul>
Fast food outlets	<ul><li>Limited choice standard menu</li><li>Food to eat in and/or take away</li><li>Low cost</li><li>Little or no waiting</li><li>Some, e.g. local fish and chip shops, open only at lunchtime and in the evening</li><li>Chain outlets, e.g. McDonald's, often have long hours or 24-hour opening</li><li>Mainly low-skilled staff</li><li>Located in areas of high demand, e.g. shopping centres</li><li>Often counter service with multiple till points</li></ul>

Travel and leisure outlets: trains, airlines, coaches	o Standards of catering can depend on type of seat booked, e.g. standard, business or first class o Catering provided at terminals, motorway service stations and on board o Often contract caterers o On airlines, tray service is by airline staff, serving pre-prepared food o Usually only self-service drinks on board a coach, except for executive coaches o Train service varies from refreshments brought round on trolley or purchased in the buffet car, to good-quality meals in the dining car and fine dining on the Orient Express o Demand varies according to length of journey, standard of catering and whether it is included in the cost of travel o Hours are linked to departure and travelling times, often 24-hour opening o Prices and staffing vary.
Travel and leisure outlets: cruises	o Provide accommodation and extensive catering in a wide range of establishments o Very high standards o Opening hours are linked to stopovers, sailing times and type of establishment o Demand is high as food is normally included in the cost of the cruise and passengers have no alternatives while at sea o Large numbers of staff at all levels in kitchen, restaurants, bars, coffee bars, etc. o Staff often employed through an agency o Employ a mix of nationalities.
Tourism and recreation outlets: museums, historic buildings, theme parks, visitor attractions	o Catering should be part of the 'visitor experience' o Frequently fast-food outlets or quick service restaurants o Some have well-known brands o Staffing according to the outlet types o Much use of Catering Assistants to serve prepared or partly prepared food o Large theme parks like Disney have fine dining restaurants o Prices may be slightly more than outside the attraction o Opening hours match those of the attraction o High demand at peak times.
Retail store outlets	o Food courts o Frequently fast-food outlets or quick service restaurants o Some have well-known brands o Staffing according to the outlet types o Much use of Catering Assistants to serve prepared or partly prepared food o Little or no waiting o Opening hours in line with store or shopping centre o Department stores like Harvey Nicholls or Harrods offer a range of high-quality eating establishments.

Event and outside catering	<ul><li>One-off events or functions</li><li>Catering matched to the needs of the event or function</li><li>Range from burger vans at a flower show to VIP catering for corporate clients at a racecourse to a wedding at a private house</li><li>Contract caterers, sometimes with extra staff</li><li>Mobile equipment.</li></ul>
Public service sector	
Employee catering – staff restaurants, cafeterias, directors' dining rooms, catering for business meetings, special events, etc.	<ul><li>Often contracted out to specialist catering companies (also called Food service management)</li><li>Opening hours, menus, design, etc. match the needs of the individual site</li><li>Often the business subsidises costs to provide good-quality low-cost meals</li><li>Demand is high, particularly at remote sites</li><li>Some employers are removing subsidies to reduce costs, which brings employee catering nearer to the commercial sector</li><li>Excellent conditions for many contract catering staff who cater for employees, reflected in job titles, pay, etc.</li></ul>
NHS hospitals	<ul><li>Usually a tray service at set times</li><li>Patients do not pay directly</li><li>Often subsidised, but a low budget per head</li><li>Charged staff meals and catering for visitors normally provided</li><li>Usually open to match main working and visiting hours</li><li>Some or all of these services are often contracted out</li><li>High volume as patients rely on catering provided.</li></ul>
Private hospitals	<ul><li>Meals paid for by patients or their medical insurance</li><li>May be in-house or contracted out</li><li>Staff meals may be subsidised</li><li>Greater flexibility in meal times and better quality meals.</li></ul>
Residential homes	<ul><li>Catering and other services may be provided by the individual home, a direct service from the local authority, or contracted out</li><li>Some subsidisation</li><li>In homes for old people and children this is often the only food residents will have access to</li><li>Usually set times for meals and refreshments, although drinks may be provided on request during the night</li><li>Private residential homes may include catering in the overall charge or make separate charges.</li></ul>

School meals and college canteens	o Catering may be controlled by the individual school, a direct service from the local authority, or contracted out
	o Local authority has a duty to provide a paid meal in school where parents request it
	o Now emphasis on healthier menus, and government guidelines on nutrition
	o Opening hours usually just fit in with school lunchtimes
	o Some schools and college canteens provide breakfast, lunch and refreshments and provide for evening and weekend courses
	o Emphasis on quick service
	o Low/reasonable cost
	o Some subsidies.
Prison services	o Catering may be run by the Prison Service or contracted out
	o Usually set meal times
	o Low budgets for food costs
	o Minimum staffing supplemented by food being prepared by inmates
	o High demand as no alternatives
	o Separate, higher standard catering for prison staff
	o Some innovative schemes, e.g. where inmates are given training and achieve qualifications.

Figure 1.3 Summary of main types of establishment and their characteristics showing the type of operation and the sector to which they belong.

Try this!
Look at Figure 1.3. Note down any types of establishment you have been to as a customer. Which have you been to most and why?

Figure 1.4 A very specialised type of operation: a buffet on a cruise ship

Top marks!
Using a variety of sources will help you to discover different views on featured topics. Comparing these views will help you to investigate the industry as a whole, help to support the points you make and add depth to your work.

Scope of the catering and hospitality industry

In every town you will find many different types of hospitality and catering establishment. The scope of their operations will vary a great deal.

Regional, national, international, multinational, global operations

Many of today's multinational hospitality and catering companies began with just one person opening an establishment which became popular in the local area. Figure 1.5 shows the development stages of a business.

Definition

Local: operates within a small, defined area

Regional: operates within the surrounding local area

National: operates throughout one country

International: operates in more than one country

Multinational: this type of business has a significant proportion of operations abroad

Global: this type of business operates on a worldwide scale.

Business type	Description	Area of operation	Examples
Sole trader	○ A sole trader is self-employed and can start trading immediately, subject to any specific licences ○ A sole trader is responsible for all the liabilities of their business, e.g. debts.	Local	Sandwich bar Café Bed and breakfast
Ordinary partnership	○ A partnership of two or more people has no legal status. It is just a means of linking two or more self-employed people in a simple business structure ○ Partners are personally liable for any debts incurred.	Local/regional	Bistro Take-away Guest house
Private limited company	○ Most small businesses (except sole traders and partnerships) set up as private limited companies ○ The term 'limited' means the company's finances are separate from the personal finances of the owners ○ Shareholders in limited liability companies are not responsible for company debts ○ The company must be registered at Companies House, produce and file annual accounts and returns, pay corporation tax if due.	Regional/national	Restaurant – single/multiple/chain Hotel – single/multiple/chain Contract caterer
Public limited company (PLC)	○ Designed for wider share ownership and can raise much more capital ○ Subject to more controls ○ The company can offer shares to the public, and may also apply to be listed on the Stock Exchange, so that shares can be bought and sold more easily ○ The original owners may have less control of the business, or lose control completely.	Regional/national/international/multinational/global	Large chain of themed restaurants Chain of branded hotels

Figure 1.5 Business development stages

Case study — Pizza Express

Gondola Holdings is one of the fastest growing casual dining groups in the UK and Ireland. It owns the Ask, Zizzi and Pizza Express brands. It employs over 11,000 staff and served 30 million meals in 2005/06. Visit the Pizza Express website. A link has been made available at www.heinemann.co.uk/hotlinks. Just follow the links and enter the express code 7193P. When did Pizza Express start? How did it develop? How many restaurants are there now? In which countries?

Investigate!

Choose a multinational or international hospitality or catering business or brand that interests you. Produce a short fact sheet about the stages in its development and operations. Include brief details about its history and development and present-day operations, e.g. sector, business type, the countries in which it operates, number and range of establishments, staffing. Discuss your findings in a group.

Definition

Enterprise: business. An enterprise is often a small or family business.

Other business types

SMEs

There are lots of SMEs (small, micro and medium-sized **enterprises**) in hospitality and catering. SMEs tend to be more flexible than large companies. Their owners often have new ideas, creativity and a 'can-do' attitude. They need support that is specifically for small businesses, e.g. in the European Economic Area SMEs can apply for special grants and loans. Within the UK there is also lots of help for small or family hospitality and catering businesses, e.g. the UK Environmental Agency's website for SMEs contains guidance for guest houses, small hotels, camping and caravan sites, restaurants, pubs and bars, mobile catering, etc. about meeting environmental legislation. A link has been made available at www.heinemann.co.uk/hotlinks. Just follow the links and enter the express code 7193P.

Franchises

If you have ever bought something to eat or drink at a Wimpy Bar or from Domino's Pizza, then you were a customer in a franchised catering establishment. A franchise is where a company (the

Did you know?

KFC started as a small restaurant at a Kentucky roadside service station. There are now outlets across North and South America, Europe, Asia and Australia. KFC is part of the American based company YUM! Brands Inc, which is one of the largest fast food operators in the world.

franchisor) lets its brand name be used in return for payment. There are strict policies and procedures which must be followed to make sure the brand is protected. Franchising is often used as a way of rapidly expanding a brand.

Size and importance of the hospitality and catering industry

Workforce

As over 80 per cent of the population of the UK lives in England, the vast majority of hospitality and catering employees work in England, followed by Scotland, then Wales and then Northern Ireland. Hospitality and catering employers and staff make important contributions to national insurance and corporation tax and income tax. Figure 1.6 shows that there was an increase in the number of people employed in hospitality and catering between 2000 and 2004, which was followed by a drop in the number of people employed in 2005.

Type of establishment	2000	2004	2005
Hotels	245,000	247,071	238,400
Restaurants	446,300	518,738	513,700
Pubs, clubs and bars	383,100	368,394	333,900
Food and service management	167,000	179,589	178,300
Hospitality services	336,300	402,062	379,900
Other (includes travel and tourism services, gambling, holiday parks, youth hostels and attractions)	255,000	233,261	241,400
Total	**1,832,650**	**1,968,753**	**1,885,600**

Figure 1.6 The number of people that work in each type of establishment from 2000 to 2005. Note that individual sums may not add up to totals for statistical reasons.

Did you know?
One in ten people worldwide now work in the hospitality industry. In the UK, 1.64 million people work in hospitality and catering. Forecasts suggest that by the London Olympics in 2012 an extra 846,000 employees will be needed.

Top marks!
Wide research will help to show you know: what is happening in the hospitality and catering industry at home and abroad, what shapes the industry, and what is predicted for the future.

Number of establishments and total turnover

Look at Figure 1.7. You will see that the number of hotels declined between 2003 and 2005. This is a result of the closure of small hotels and guest houses. The remaining hotels are larger so the number of meals served and the income from food and drink sales has increased. The number of pubs also declined. However, the number of restaurants increased by almost 2 per cent and the number of quick-service establishments also increased. Notice that, in terms of total numbers, the commercial sector is much larger than the public service sector.

Hospitality, catering, leisure, travel and tourism establishments in the UK are estimated to generate over £135 billion a year in sales turnover. Tourism and leisure contribute around 4 per cent to the UK's **GDP**.

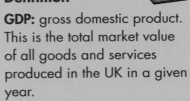

Definition

GDP: gross domestic product. This is the total market value of all goods and services produced in the UK in a given year.

Type of establishment	2003	2004	2005
Hotels	47,725	47,389	47,009
Restaurants	25,954	26,208	26,416
Quick service	29,459	29,496	29,645
Pubs	51,352	51,267	51,046
Leisure	18,869	18,995	19,121
Total commercial sector	**173,369**	**173,355**	**173,237**
Business and industry	20,875	20,839	20,625
Health care	30,926	31,048	31,384
Education	34,663	34,630	34,663
Ministry of Defence	3,078	3,076	3,073
Total public service sector	**89,542**	**89,593**	**89,745**
TOTAL	**262,910**	**262,948**	**262,982**

Figure 1.7 Estimated number of establishments in all hospitality and catering sectors

Try this!

Produce a bar chart to show the number of people working within hospitality and catering in the UK in the last five years.

Produce a pie chart to show numbers of commercial establishments and public service sector establishments in 2005.

Factors affecting the hospitality and catering industry

Inflation

Inflation influences how much spare money customers have to spend on eating out. Low **rates of inflation** have for many years helped keep costs down, which in turn has kept the price of eating out down. Inflation rates began to rise in 2006, which makes it more expensive to borrow money and increases the cost of goods, staff wages, etc. It is therefore likely that selling prices will begin to rise slightly.

Tourism

Tourism is important to the success of many economies around the world. Spending by overseas visitors and UK residents on holiday in the UK is very important to the commercial sector. Almost 30 million tourists visited the UK in 2005 and spent nearly £14,250 million.

In 2005 UK residents took nearly 139 million trips within the UK and spent £22,667 million. The pie chart below shows how this money was spent:

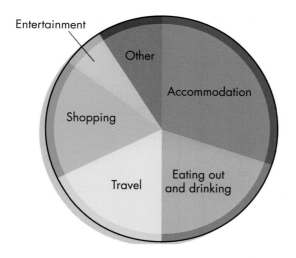

Figure 1.9: How UK residents spent money on UK holidays

Definition

Inflation: increase in average prices. If prices rise there is a fall in the value of money, as people have to spend more money to buy the same items.
Rate of inflation: a measure of how much prices rise (or fall), usually given as a percentage by comparing prices at two points in time.

Figure 1.8: Tourism is very important to the UK economy

Try this!
With a partner discuss why tourism has a big influence on the hospitality and catering industry.

Hospitality and catering establishments
Commercial sector

Hotels and other hospitality providers

Investigate!

Visit the website for the trafalgar hotel in London. A link has been made available at www.heinemann.co.uk/hotlinks. Just follow the links and enter the express code 7193P.

How many guest rooms does it have? What are they like? What is Rockwell Upper? What are the bar's opening hours? What type of food is served at the hotel and at what times? Make an information poster about the hotel.

Case study — Accor international hotel group

In 2006 Accor was the fifth largest hotel operator in the UK with 93 hotels (13,529 rooms). In June 2006 Accor had 480,036 rooms in 140 countries and employed 168,500 staff.

The group began in France in 1967 with the Novotel hotel chain concept, followed by Ibis in 1974 and Formule 1 in 1985. Accor has successfully developed its hotel portfolio to cover all budgets from luxury to low-cost hotels. Accor also owns Wagons-Lits onboard train services, Eurest food service management and the Relais Autoroute motorway restaurants among others.

Accor has lots of employee benefits, e.g. good salaries, annual profit-sharing, a savings plan and stock options, staff training, intern and apprenticeship programmes. Three-quarters of hotel managers got their jobs through internal promotions. Staff can move from country to country if they have the language skills.

A link has been made available to their website at www.heinemann.co.uk/hotlinks. Just follow the links and enter the express code 7193P.

Investigate!

Find a website that is promoting a large, city centre hotel and another that is promoting a small, rural hotel. Compare the two establishments.

Investigate!

Find a website that is promoting a business hotel with conference and exhibition facilities. Now find one that is promoting a hotel aimed at the family holiday market. Compare the two establishments.

Investigate!

Center Parcs is part of the commercial sector and operates holiday villages in the UK, Denmark, Holland, France, Germany and Belgium. About 90 per cent of their staff are employed from the local area, so they are a major contributor to the local economy. Download the Student Information Pack from the website. A link has been made available at www.heinemann.co.uk/hotlinks. Just follow the links and enter the express code 7193P.

Prepare a short talk about Center Parcs. Talk about the accommodation available, the restaurants, staffing and other points that interest you.

Try this!

Worksheet 56

In two minutes, write down as many establishments as you can think of that provide accommodation in your local area. Now categorise them into:

- *commercial sector/public services sector*
- *hotels/guest houses/lodges/residential homes*
- *budget hotels/mid-class hotels/high-quality hotels*
- *restaurant on site, no restaurant*
- *local/regional/national/international.*

Restaurants

The table below shows the top ten restaurant groups in 2006. There are many familiar brand names, but note that the ownership of the brands can change rapidly.

Owner	No. of outlets	Selected brands
Mitchells & Butlers	799	Harvester, All Bar One, Toby
Spirit Group	510	Chef & Brewer, Two for One, Miller's
Gondola	505	Pizza Express, Ask, Zizzi
Restaurant Group	279	Frankie & Benny's, Garfunkel's
Wimpy	250	Wimpy
People's Restaurant Group	235	Little Chef (sold late 2006 – operating problems)
Tragus	162	Café Rouge, Bella Italia
Whitbread	157	TGI Friday's
Greene King	90	Hungry Horse
Nando's	133	Nando's

Figure 1.10: The top ten restaurant groups in 2006

Case study — Wimpy

The Wimpy brand was created in Chicago in the 1930s. It can now be found in many countries. Wimpy has been in operation in the UK since the mid-1950s and has been franchising for over 40 years. Wimpy International Ltd is one of the largest independent chain restaurants in the UK.

Wimpy now has over 270 franchised restaurants and units. Opening hours vary, depending on location, e.g. 24-hour opening in a motorway service station or opening for just a few hours on match days in a football stadium. Staffing varies according to the opening hours and the anticipated number of customers.

There are three types of Wimpy outlet in the UK. What are they? What type of locations are they suitable for? What type of menu do they offer? What support and benefits do franchisees receive?

A link to their website has been made available at www.heinemann.co.uk/hotlinks. Just follow the links and enter the express code 7193P.

Did you know?

'Wimpy' is named after the burger-eating character J. Wellington Wimpy from the cartoon strip *Popeye*.

Did you know?

The British Franchise Association represents franchise companies and promotes good standards. A link to their website has been made available at www.heinemann.co.uk/hotlinks. Just follow the links and enter the express code 7193P.

Travel and leisure

Case study — RoadChef

People who travel by road need to stop from time to time for refreshments, a comfort break and a rest. The RoadChef Coach Support Team help people in the coach travel industry plan routes and pre-book into RoadChef motorway service areas, so the service station is prepared for the coach's arrival.

How many sites do RoadChef have? How many have a Costa Coffee outlet? How many have a Premier Travel Inn? What other services do they offer? What benefits do they offer employees?

A link to their website has been made available at www.heinemann.co.uk/hotlinks. Just follow the links and enter the express code 7193P.

Figure 1.11: Coaches at a RoadChef

Case study — Wagons-Lits

Wagons-Lits trains (part of the Accor Group) have an on-board attendant. They work from a small galley and look after passengers on French Railways' overnight sleepers, making sure everything is clean and in order, and distributing water, breakfasts and other products. Prior experience in a hotel is helpful and the position can lead on to Sleeping Car Attendant and possibly to On-board Services Manager, or back into hotel reception work.

Figure 1.12: Food being served by an on-board train attendant on the Gatwick Express

Try this!

Think of a recent journey you have made. Describe the catering available, e.g. type of food and drink, amount of choice, how it was served, name of brand/catering company.

Tourism and recreation outlets

Case study — Camelot theme park

Camelot is a theme park in Lancashire. There are around 350,000 visitors per year, mainly families and school children. The aim is to serve food quickly as customers want to make the most of their time at Camelot. There is a range of fast food catering units to suit different customers and different locations. They include:

- Wimpy outlets, 2
- Fish and chip shops, 2
- Coffee shop, 2
- Pasta unit, 1
- Ice cream parlour, 4
- Rollover hot dogs, 3
- Hot drinks and snacks units, 2

Groups can book a buffet lunch with the Catering Manager. The Park Manager holds a licence so that alcoholic drinks can be served if requested in advance.

Camelot is open for around 145 days each year. The park opens at 10 a.m. but closes at different times according to the season. The catering outlets have different opening hours to the park based on their location and customer demand. The approach has to be flexible to meet the needs of customers, operate effectively and control costs. Savings are made by reducing opening hours and/or reducing staffing when demand is low.

Except for the Catering Manager, most staff are seasonal and part-time. Students often take on these types of jobs. Camelot's main competitors for staff are the retail trade and local catering outlets. In a typical year the park will employ:

- 70 Catering Assistants
- 6 Team Leaders
- 3 Supervisors
- 1 person in the stores.

Staffing costs use over 25 per cent of Camelot's income. The budgeted income in a recent operating year was £4.5m, with wages of £1.125m. That means, for every £1 the park takes in sales, 25p goes on paying wages and salaries.

Staff receive full training, a free uniform and are given a pass to the park for them and their family. They work on rotas. There are two staff parties each year. In January or February Catering Assistants who have done well will be asked to come back and work for the next season; they often get a promotion and Camelot's policy is to promote from within.

A link to their website has been made available at www.heinemann. co.uk/hotlinks. Just follow the links and enter the express code 7193P.

Catering Manager
in charge of all catering operations

↑

Catering Supervisor
supervises several units

↑

Catering Team Leader
looks after one unit

↑

prepares food and drink, serves customers, cleans

Figure 1.13: Progression route at Camelot

Public services sector

School meals

The main purpose of a school or college is education, but hungry and thirsty students, staff and visitors need suitable on-site catering facilities.

Figure 1.14: Food being served in a primary school

Case study – Hertfordshire Catering

Hertfordshire Catering provides school meals for Hertfordshire Education Authority. They serve 36,000 primary school meals a day and provide catering services to 44 secondary and middle schools. The team of 1,600 staff aim to provide high-quality, tempting and nutritious meals within a fixed budget. The current Head of Catering has extensive experience of the school meals service as a Cook Manager, Area Manager and Business Development Manager. The service sent out 90,000 menu leaflets to parents across the county to launch the new primary menu, which included a nutritional analysis.

> **Investigate!**
> Research a commercial hotel restaurant, themed restaurant, quick service restaurant or fast-food outlet. Find out the opening hours, types of menu, price ranges, number of staff, type of uniforms worn, how the food is served, what it looks like and whether it has a popular brand name. What does it have in common with your college canteen? How is it different? Prepare a short talk.

> **Top marks!**
> Remember to keep a note of all your sources of information, plus copies where appropriate. They can then be checked by you or by someone reading your assignment.

Professional bodies

Professional bodies work within the UK and internationally to promote their members' interests.

Institute of Hospitality (formerly the Hotel and Catering International Management Association)

This is a worldwide professional body for managers and potential managers in the hospitality, catering, leisure and tourism industries. Its purpose is to:

- help members keep up to date with industry issues and developments
- raise standards within the industries, in general and through special schemes like Hospitality Assured, the industry standard for service and business excellence
- help the industries to meet new challenges, e.g. Hospitable Climates, a scheme that shows participating members how to improve energy efficiency
- set recognised educational standards and offer accreditation or endorsement to UK and international study programmes
- provide access to a wide range of services, e.g. discounted and free entry to conferences and seminars, free legal helpline, BIH library and information service.

British Hospitality Association (BHA)

The BHA, incorporating the Restaurant Association, is the UK's national trade association for the hotel, food service and leisure industry. It has been representing the hotel, restaurant and catering industry for 90 years. The BHA's main role is to unite the industry and make its views known to governments across the UK and in Europe. It also aims to lead the industry towards better practices, e.g. Best Practice Forum.

> **Try this!**
> Links to the Institute of Hospitality and BHA websites have been made available at www.heinemann.co.uk/hotlinks. Just follow the links and enter the express code 7193P.

Other major professional bodies

British Institute of Innkeeping: This is the licensed trade's professional body, and promotes good practice within the industry by offering a comprehensive system of training and qualifications for both new and experienced members.

Craft Guild of Chefs: This is the leading chefs' association in the UK, representing members worldwide. Activities include training and demonstrations.

Hospital Caterers' Association: This association exists to promote and improve catering standards and to protect the interests of catering staff within healthcare establishments in the UK. Every year it hosts a national conference as well as seminars, study days and equipment demonstrations.

International Travel Catering Association: This is a forum and representative body for all companies involved in the airline, sea and rail catering industry, plus suppliers of products and equipment.

International Hotel and Restaurant Association: This is a networking and lobbying body for the hotel and restaurant industry around the world. It organises conferences, exhibitions, forums and social events.

Local Authority Caterers' Association: LACA is the professional body representing catering managers in all sectors of local authorities. It organises an annual conference plus events such as National School Meals Week.

National Association of Care Catering: This body promotes good catering standards in care homes, social service environments and meals-on-wheels services.

Top marks!
When you finish a piece of work, check that you have covered everything and given sufficient detail. Giving lots of relevant, current examples helps to show that you have a wide and up-to-date knowledge of the hospitality and catering industry.

Top marks!
Professional bodies like the BHA play an important role within the hospitality and catering industry and will help you to understand it. Professional bodies are an excellent source of information, often summarising information from other key players.

Key influences

Many influences affect the range and style of what the hospitality and catering industry offers.

Media

The past ten years have seen an increased interest in:

- cooking
- different cookery methods
- different types of cuisine
- working in hospitality and catering.

Famous chefs, helped by the media, have raised interest in food and drink, and concerns about unhealthy eating practices. This has prompted many establishments, including hospitals, schools and airline caterers to introduce healthy eating options and to source their ingredients locally.

Social trends

Changes in society have led to:

- fewer families sitting down to eat together
- people having less time to cook
- people not wanting to wait more than a few minutes for food to be cooked and served
- people having more money to spend on eating out and takeaways.

As a result, there is a major demand for fast-food and quick service catering establishments in shopping centres, leisure attractions, airports, stations and other places where customers want food to be served quickly in clean premises and at value for money prices.

Re-generation plans for city centres include leisure facilites, e.g. hotels, restaurants, wine bars, pubs and coffee shops. These often appeal to young people with money to spend. There are a growing number of luxury and/or specialist establishments for customers who are 'cash rich and time poor'.

Globalisation

As a result of globalisation it is now possible to go almost anywhere in the world and see the same branded restaurants, e.g. McDonald's. If you compare cities in the UK you will see that many of them have the same restaurant and coffee shop brands.

Definition

Globalisation: indicates that companies are expanding their operation internationally.

Tourism, culture and fashion

The increase in overseas holidays by UK residents since the 1960s and the influence of ethnic communities has created an interest in other cuisines. The UK now offers a wide range of restaurants where exciting national and ethnic dishes are served, and the increase in competition has improved standards. The presentation of food is better and theatre cooking has been introduced.

Clean, uncluttered furnishings and designs are currently fashionable in restaurants, with out-dated premises being refurbished. Boutique hotels and sushi bars are recent exciting developments.

Figure 1.15: The sushi bar at Harvey Nicholls, Manchester

Legislation and regulation

Regulations and legislation have a tremendous effect on the industry, e.g. nutrition guidelines for school meals. Stricter food hygiene, health and safety and environmental regulations improve standards, but increase costs. The introduction of minimum wage levels in 1999, plus increased rights for part-time staff, significantly increased labour costs throughout the UK, particularly in hospitality and catering.

The ban on smoking in the workplace, which was introduced in July 2007, will affect how premises are designed.

Test yourself!

1 Are these statements true or false?
   a The Public Service Sector is sometimes called the Cost Sector.
   b Hotels and guesthouses are part of the Public Service Sector.

2 Complete the sentence.
   A _____ caterer for employees at an industrial site needs to plan _____ that are suitable for the client.

3 How many people are employed in hospitality, catering, tourism, travel and leisure within the UK?

4 Describe three influences on today's hospitality and catering industry and the impact of each.

5 Draw a chart or table of the structure of the hospitality and catering industry.

Job opportunities in catering and hospitality

The most important people in catering and hospitality are the customers, but without the staff there would be no customers.

Main job roles in catering

Many different types of people choose to work in the industry and there is something to attract almost everyone. By exploring some of the job roles in catering you will be able to see what it is like to work in the industry and the range of career choices available to you.

Level	Role and approximate salary range	Description
Operational ○ members of staff who carry out the day-to-day work ○ may be skilled, semi-skilled or trainees ○ helped by on- and off-the-job training.	Commis Chef/ Assistant Cook/ Trainee £8,000–£16,000	This starting position involves food preparation, basic cooking, and presenting food under supervision. The term 'Commis Chef' is mainly used in a traditional kitchen for fine dining while 'Assistant Cook' is used in the public service sector.
	Cook £9,000–£12,000	A cook helps to prepare, cook and present food. In a very large commercial kitchen there might be cooks to help out in each section. The term 'cook' is often used in public service catering.
	Wine Waiter £12,000	Responsible for serving wine. Able to recommend wines to suit the food the customers have ordered, the occasion and the customer's budget.
	Waiter £8,000–£15,000	Responsible for serving food and drinks. Works closely with the kitchen to make sure that food is served swiftly and appropriately.
Supervisory ○ direct and oversee the operational staff ○ usually started as operational staff and been promoted as their skills developed.	Chef de Partie £14,000–26,000	Runs a section in a large traditional kitchen. In smaller, more modern kitchens may be responsible for preparing, cooking and presenting a range of dishes. Usually in charge of Commis or Trainee Chef(s).
	Head Waiter £13,000–£22,000	Assists the Restaurant Manager and supervises the restaurant staff. Often greets customers and takes orders. If there is no Wine Waiter, will take and serve the wine order.
	Bar Manager £15,000–£27,000	Manages the daily running of the bar(s) and the cellar, orders stock and liaises with suppliers. Oversees the bar staff.

Management	Head Cook/Catering Manager/Cook Manager £19,000+	Number 1 in a public services sector kitchen.
o in charge o make the main decisions o have the most responsibility o will often have worked their way up from an operator, to supervisor, to manager.	Head Chef/Executive Chef £22,000–£50,000+	Number 1 in a commercial kitchen. Manages staff, plans menus, works out the costings, orders stock, plans staff rotas and training, makes sure the kitchen and staff work within the law, ensures standards. (In a large business the Executive Chef will be a separate role above that of Head Chef and in charge of several outlets.)
	Restaurant Manager £16,000–£50,000+	Responsible for running the restaurant, particularly supervising the service and the restaurant staff. Responsible for hiring staff, encouraging food/drink sales, ensuring profitability, customer service. Liaises with Head Chef and customers.
	Catering Manager (£13,000–£35,000+)	A catering expert managing a team, responsible for food production to agreed budgets, menu planning and training. Usually in charge of food production and food service for an establishment. In the public service sector may work in-house for a contract caterer. Often responsible for several catering services or outlets.

Figure 1.16: The main job roles in catering

The owner and manager of a small catering establishment will, in addition to their business responsibilities, probably welcome customers, take orders, serve the wine, work out the bills, cash up, and so on. They are likely to select staff because they are reliable and able to multi-task.

Differences in staff roles and conditions

Kitchen and restaurant staff

Traditionally the kitchen brigade worked behind the scenes and was unlikely to come into direct contact with customers. These days some catering establishments have brought the cooking equipment into the restaurant so the chef can be seen by the customers and may sometimes interact with them. In some Pizza Express restaurants, for example, children are given a chef's hat to wear and can choose their pizza toppings with the help of the chef and the waiters. Similarly, a chef working at a carvery within the restaurant area or a kitchen assistant who also serves at a self-service counter will also meet customers face to face.

Staff who work in the restaurant, e.g. waiters and bar staff, are seen by customers as they are responsible for meeting, greeting and serving them.

Uniforms

Uniforms are normally worn by both kitchen and waiting staff and are often provided by management. The commercial sector and industrial contract caterers for employees tend to have more money to spend on uniforms than the public service sector. Uniforms are designed to be fit for purpose (see Chapter 2 for more information). In some kitchens chefs at different levels wear different styles of uniform. There is more attention to style than there used to be.

Uniforms for waiting staff reflect the type of establishment. They range from the smart formal outfits worn in hotels to casual trousers and polo tops with a black apron worn in contemporary seated restaurants to the overalls worn in a residential home. Managers usually wear formal suits.

Figure 1.17: A waiter in a bistro

Progression

Many top chefs started as kitchen porters, doing the washing-up, cleaning, preparing vegetables and washing salads. This provides good first-hand experience and on and off the job training, with opportunities to study for qualifications such as a Food Hygiene Certificate, NVQ or VRQ.

Another way to progress is to continue on to Higher Education and gain experience through part-time work or work experience placements.

Advanced Business Studies course. P/T job at local hotel. → University course in Hotel and Restaurant Management, with work placement at top hotel resort in the, USA. → Graduate Trainee, e.g. with Aramark UK's one year programme which includes, varied training around the UK, then a permanent post.

Promoted to General Catering Manager at a major industrial contractor in the UK. ← Promotion to Assistant Manager at industrial contractor in the UK.

Figure 1.18 A possible progression route

Management roles

Head Chef in a traditional hotel kitchen

The Head Chef is in charge of the kitchen but still has hands-on involvement in creating and cooking the food. When the Head Chef is absent, the Sous-Chef (Under-Chef) will take charge of the kitchen.

The duties of the Head Chef include:

○ Planning, choosing and writing menus
○ Running the kitchen, in line with company policies and procedures
○ Implementing food safety, health and safety and other practices to meet the requirements of relevant legislation
○ Managing the staff
○ Liaising with the Restaurant Manager and Heads of other hotel departments as required
○ Cooking (depending on the size of the kitchen and number of staff)
○ Costing, ordering stock and storing food
○ Managing gross profits
○ Staff rotas, recruitment and training
○ Making sure that what goes on the plate is of the highest quality.

Head Cook in a residential care and nursing home

Head Cook needed to manage a small brigade, catering for 90 residents plus staff, 3 meals a day, 7 days a week. Overtime is paid at T½ if Sunday is worked.

Applicants must be currently residing in the UK and have authorisation to work in the UK.

Salary: £19,000.

Hours: Rota based on 37.5 hours a week, 5 out of 7 days, 10.30am–6.30pm, 6.30am–2.30pm or 11am–7pm.

Figure 1.19 Job advertisement for a Head Cook to work for a contract caterer providing the catering for a residential care and nursing home in the South East

Rotas are common within hospitality and catering where operations may be seven days a week, and cover long hours, e.g. industrial catering for workers on an oil rig, 24-hour hotel room service, high-demand fast-food outlets or hospital catering for staff.

> **Try this!**　　　　Worksheet 57
>
> **What do you think might be the likely progression routes for:**
>
> 1 A school leaver to Head Cook in a residential home
> 2 A kitchen assistant to Catering Manager in a hospital
> 3 A waiter to Restaurant Manager

Case study — James Blackwell

James Blackwell is a Head Chef at Holroyd Howe, a contract caterer. James says:

'I started as an apprentice working for the Moat House hotel group for one year and then moved on as Commis and Junior Chef de Partie in a one-rosette restaurant. After a further two years I worked in a cocktail bar and restaurant where I was promoted to Chef de Partie. I then moved to Chef de Partie with a golf and country club and worked my way up to Sous-Chef, running the hospitality kitchen and members' restaurant. After three years' experience in hospitality, I moved to work for Holroyd Howe as Sous-Chef in a large private business university. After one year I was promoted to Head Chef and now oversee all food operations in student restaurants, hospitality and private directors' dining. I have been in my current role for three years.'

James describes a typical day at work. 'First I open up the building and meet with my Sous-Chef to give out plans for the day. Then I work on main courses and hand over to the Sous-Chef so I can work on menu planning and costing. Part of my mid-morning will be for client meetings and future planning before I return to the kitchen to oversee lunch service and hospitality. Early afternoon is used for training and developing new ideas within my site and for the company. Two afternoons per week are used for junior training and development. After lunch service is finished I meet again with my Sous-Chef to plan for the evening service and any directors'/hospitality dining. Late afternoon is used for finalising menus and working on current and financial projects in conjunction with my General Manager. Final checks and meetings with evening teams are done and then I meet with all Heads of Departments to debrief on the day's business and the following day.'

Try this!   Worksheet 57

1. *Produce a flow chart to show James's career progression.*
2. *If you have a part-time job or a work placement in hospitality and catering, describe your duties on a typical day.*

Catering Manager

We are seeking a Catering Manager for a healthcare contract in SE London.

You will be responsible for overseeing the catering at this hospital including patient feeding, a staff/visitor restaurant and a coffee shop. You will manage a team of 15. You will preferably have experience of working in a healthcare contract as a Catering Manager. You need to be a good communicator, with an eye for quality, able to give direction and support to all catering staff. You will need to identify areas where the service can be improved and implement initiatives. Financial ability is important as you will need to work within your budget and control costs. Salary: £25,000–£26,000 depending on experience. Excellent benefits.

Figure 1.20 Job description for a Catering Manager in healthcare. Note the variety of hospital catering and outlets for which the Catering Manager is responsible

Restaurant Manager

The benefits of a Restaurant Manager will depend on the type of establishment, sales turnover, whether it is independently owned or part of a chain.

RESTAURANT MANAGER

JOB DESCRIPTION

Job Purpose
To be responsible for the smooth and successful day-to-day running of the restaurant, ensuring satisfied customers and that all financial targets are achieved

Key Responsibilities
- Be the host and communicate with guests
- Organise the restaurant team: their tasks, schedules and information meetings
- Manage the staff: recruitment, training, evaluation and promotion
- Monitor customer service levels
- Ensure the quality of service and service provision
- Maximise restaurant occupancy
- Ensure on-going profitability and have knowledge of financial matters
- Increase restaurant sales.

Qualifications
- 2 years' further education in hotel/food and beverage studies to BTS/HND standard or similar
- Significant experience of restaurant management.

Figure 1.21 Job description for a Restaurant Manager

Case study – Stella Martin

Stella Martin is the Restaurant Manager for a major chain of fast-food restaurants. Stella says, 'I'm responsible for all aspects of running the restaurant, including building sales, training my team, maintaining product quality standards and ensuring the restaurant is profitable. I work with people from a cross-section of society. It's a fun atmosphere and you get through the busy times by everyone working as a team. Restaurant Managers at my company earn £18,000–£24,000, depending on the volume of the site and the location. There's a staff discount scheme, a pension scheme and training and development. I get free meals when I'm on duty, and we get 20 days' holiday, which increases with service.

Try this!   Worksheet 58

Look at the job descriptions, advertisements and case studies. Choose either the roles of Head Chef and Head Cook or Restaurant Manager and Catering Manager. Describe the similarities and differences between their duties, responsibilities and conditions.

Supervisory roles in the kitchen

Chef de Partie

CHEF DE PARTIE JOB DESCRIPTION

Hours: 160 hours per 4-week period. Shifts as per rota. Average 5 days per week

Job purpose

To prepare, cook and present service menu items to agreed standards. To deputise for the senior Chef de Partie in their absence and supervise the unit chefs to maintain the smooth running of the kitchen.

Minimum educational/vocational qualifications:

NVQ 2 in Professional Cookery or equivalent

Intermediate Food Hygiene

1:1 Trainer (either formal qualification or by experience)

Good standard of spoken and written English

Minimum previous work experience

3 years' experience as Chef de Partie in a small establishment or in a more junior position within a large brigade with supervisory and training responsibility.

Responsibilities

Produce a high standard of work to meet company standards and guest satisfaction.

Manage the cost of sales through effective use of the ordering system, stock control, portion control and minimising of food wastage.

Deputise for the Senior Chef de Partie in their absence.

Provide general supervision and coaching to junior staff.

Assist with the production of rotas, sickness and holiday management to ensure optimum staffing.

Work closely with team to create and maintain a good working environment

Work with Senior Chef to create new menu ideas, ensuring that accurate costing and specifications are considered.

Figure 1.22 Part of the job description for a Chef de Partie at Center Parcs

Case study — Mark Symmers

On leaving school Mark started a Youth Training Scheme working in a local hotel and attending college. He then had various chef positions in small restaurants, a hospital and in contract catering sites. He now works as a chef for the UK part of the international contract catering company Aramark.

The order of a typical day is:

- stock take/open kitchen diary
- enter details from invoices in diary, including temperature control readings
- cook hot food, etc. for breakfast
- freshbake for the day, e.g. breakfast scones
- make soups
- prepare and make the special dishes for that day's menu
- have a break
- prepare and cook vegetables for menu
- support hospitality with buffets
- help on servery
- do more paperwork and go through checklists
- clean down
- place orders
- prepare for the next day.

Bar Manager

Experienced Hotel Bar Manager required. Reporting to the Food and Beverage Manager you will be responsible for all Bar Operations within the Hotel and a team made up of a Food and Beverage Supervisor and Bar Assistants.
Job Type: Permanent. **Location:** Midlands.

Main Duties will include:

- To deliver food and beverage service of high standard and in accordance with departmental standards and procedures
- To develop departmental standards and procedures to promote salesmanship, beverage creativity and profit
- To communicate to your superior any difficulties, guest comments and other relevant information
- To deliver daily briefings and attend other meetings as scheduled
- Cellar management
- Stock order
- Financial management control

Who we are looking for: Someone with a Personal License. A minimum of 2 years' experience in Bar Supervision or Management. A confident team motivator with an eye for detail.

About the employer: The employer is a high-quality national hotel group with large conference capabilities. Many opportunities for career progression. Salary: £17,500, free uniform, 20 days' holiday, other benefits

Figure 1.23 Advertisement for a hotel Bar Manager in a large city in the Midlands

Head Waiter

Job Title	Head Waiter
Salary	£16,000–£17,000 per annum
Type	Permanent
Location	Club la Playa, Valencia, Spain
Job Details	Luxury 4* hotel with superb leisure facilities is looking for a Head Waiter. The chosen individual will be enthusiastic and friendly with previous experience as a supervisor and an eye for detail. You will be responsible for the smooth running of your section in a restaurant, training new staff, maintaining high standards of service and reporting to managers. If you are looking for a great career opportunity and an ambitious role, please apply by sending your CV.

Figure 1.24: Job summary for a Head Waiter for a high-quality 4-star hotel in Spain

Try this!

Produce a short talk to give at a careers evening about one of the supervisory jobs described. Include a comparison of that job with a job of the same title in another establishment.

Operational roles

Commis Chef

Case study — Sarah Pettit

Sarah is a chef at a low cost, 2-star hotel in Bristol. She says: 'I am part of the Food and Beverage team in a hotel that is part of a multi-national chain. Although I am a chef, I sometimes work in the bar or the restaurant. This is good because I get to learn about what it takes to run a hotel. The money is OK and it's important to work hard. Once I've worked at the hotel for over a year I'll get a staff discount card that I can used at other hotels in the same chain. My ambition is to work in a 4- or 5-star hotel. I'd like to be the Head Chef of a big hotel.'

This flexible, multi-skilled approach is becoming more and more common in hospitality and catering. It helps to reduce labour costs and also makes work more varied.

Cook

Cooking for 30 children and staff a day catering for lunch and tea. This nursery is seeking an experienced cook, preferably who has worked in a similar environment. Knowledge of allergies would be an advantage.

Satisfactory disclosure from the Criminal Records Bureau will be required. All candidates need to be currently living in the UK and provide proof of identity, eligibility to work in the UK and any relevant qualifications.

Salary: £6.15 per hour. Hours 9.30–4.30 p.m. Monday to Friday.

Figure 1.25 Advertisement for a School Cook for a contract caterer at a nursery school in the South East

A cook in a large secondary school is likely to earn slightly more, probably around £12,500 a year.

The background of staff working with children or vulnerable people must be checked by the Criminal Records Bureau to try to ensure these customers' safety and security.

Waiting staff

Job Description — Hotel wine waiter/waitress

Duties
- Be able to recommend a wine or wines to guests to suit the food they have ordered, the occasion and their budget.
- Ensure the wine is served at the correct temperature, in the correct glasses and with suitable ceremony. Some wines may have to be decanted.
- You may have a role in recommending what wines are included on the wine list.
- Be in charge of selling and serving liqueurs, brandies and other drinks for after the meal, and cigars.
- Liaise closely with other restaurant staff so you are on hand to take drink orders and serve guests at the appropriate time.
- Be responsible for briefing restaurant colleagues on the wine list, so that they promote particular wines and can advise customers.
- Pass the wine check to the restaurant cashier.
- Be knowledgeable about the laws relating to the service of alcohol.

Relevant qualifications
NVQ/SVQ; National Traineeship; Modern Apprenticeship or similar

Progression
You could continue to specialise, and increase your knowledge of wines, or move into a management position in the restaurant or hotel.

Figure 1.26 Job description for a hotel Wine Waiter/Waitress

Working in the UK

Rates of pay normally reflect:

- the level of responsibility of the job
- the number of staff managed or supervised
- the range and difficulty of duties
- the location, e.g. in the London area an extra 'London weighting allowance' is often added to basic rates
- whether unsociable hours need to be worked
- how many hours need to be worked
- the sector, type and size of the establishment
- how successful the establishment is
- the amount of money available for salaries, benefits, etc.
- how the market is doing.

Hourly rates are often advertised for lower-level jobs, particularly within the public service sector. These should be at or above national minimum wage rates. An annual salary is normally advertised for higher level roles within both sectors, and will relate to the hours worked. Large organisations normally have set pay scales, which are looked at each year, and a clear career progression route. Benefits such as free uniforms, staff meals, a pension scheme, a profit-sharing scheme, staff and family discounts add value to pay. When job seeking, it is sensible to compare extras as well as rates of pay. Part-time employees should receive the same treatment as full-time employees.

Waiting staff often rely on tips to increase their income, although these should be declared for tax purposes. Some restaurants pool tips, and then share them between all of the staff. Some restaurants add a service charge to the bill but staff do not always benefit directly from this.

Physical working conditions vary tremendously. They relate partly to how well designed an establishment's kitchen and restaurant are and partly to the attitude of the management. Often large companies set minimum standards which are over and above legal requirements. Many smaller organisations also maintain high standards. Good working conditions are very important in hospitality and catering and are often stressed in job advertisements.

> ### Try this!
> Which of the operational roles described above would you most like to do? Explain what appeals to you about it and why you feel you could be good at it.

Legal requirements and qualifications

In the UK there are laws covering maternity and paternity rights, equal opportunities, working time, paid holidays, national minimum wage, disability and age discrimination, etc. They are designed to protect employees. Hospitality and catering employers and employees also have to take into account the following:

- **The Licensing Act**: People can work in a bar from 16 years of age. To manage a licensed premises, a person must be over 18, hold a Level 2 National Certificate for Personal Licence Holders, apply to their local authority licensing office and have a criminal record check.
- **Employment Equality Age Regulations**: It is against the law to discriminate on the grounds of age unless this is a requirement of other regulations.
- **Criminal Records Bureau check**: Employees and volunteers who work with children or vulnerable adults, e.g. in a school, may be asked to apply for a Criminal Records Bureau check.
- **Work permits**: People who are British, Swiss or from a country in the European Economic Area do not need permission to work in the UK. Special arrangements apply to workers from Romania and Bulgaria. People from other countries need a work permit.
- **Food Hygiene Regulations**: The level of training a food handler needs depends on their job. See Chapter 2 for more information.
- **Health and Safety and Food Hygiene legislation**: This is important for both employers and employees. All staff have a duty to take reasonable care and to notify management if they are ill. Proof of vaccinations or a health check may be required. See Chapter 2 and the Food Standards Agency website for more information. A hotlink has been made available. Access the Heinemann website at www.heinemann.co.uk/hotlinks. Enter the express code 7193P.

Working abroad

UK qualifications and/or work experience are useful when looking for a job abroad. A person who works for an international organisation, e.g. a major hotel chain, may be able to apply to work for that chain in another country. A reputable employment agency can advise on the requirements of a particular country. Some organisations provide accommodation for staff. Membership of a professional body like the Institute of Hospitality (formerly the HCIMA) can help a person to stand out.

Army chefs give a catering demonstration

Case study — Mark Furr

During 22 years of Army Service, I have served in military units worldwide and undertaken a variety of exciting roles within food service.

I trained as a military chef and provided high quality cuisine for Royalty and VIPs as well as providing large volume catering at home and on overseas deployments.

As the principal catering authority to the Commanding Officer of a Logistics Regiment I was responsible for the management and provision of all food service. This involved detailed planning and the co-ordination of complex feeding on overseas operations and routine feeding in-barracks, plus fine dining within military messes. I managed 50 catering staff and supervised multi-activity contracts. I managed a £750,000 annual food budget and ensured rigid compliance with Defence food safety management systems and food safety legislation.

I have reached the pinnacle as a Warrant Officer Class One Chef Instructor and Quality Assurance Co-ordinator. I am currently the Chief Internal Verifier for the Defence Food Services School.

If you want to work in another country you will need to have good job-based and interpersonal skills and at least a basic command of the language. You will need to abide by the laws in that country. There are fewer restrictions for EU nationals wanting to work within the EU. For countries outside the EU a work permit and/or a visa may be required and possibly health checks.

Case study — Jayne Johnston

I spend my winters in France working as a cook for a catered ski chalet company. My duties include menu planning, buying and storing food and drink. I prepare and serve breakfast and a three-course evening meal as well as bake cakes for afternoon tea. In addition, I clean the chalet and eat with the guests.

I earn €100 a week with one full day off, free food and accommodation, a ski pass and insurance plus travel to and from the resort.

My catering qualification and restaurant experience helped me to get the job. You also need to be able to work independently, enjoy company, drive — and love skiing!

Sources of information

There are lots of sources which can inform you about job opportunities in the UK and abroad:

- specialist hospitality and catering careers magazines and websites
- trade magazines, e.g. *Caterer and Hotelkeeper*
- research published by organisations such as *People1st*
- company publications, e.g. annual report, publicity materials and websites
- job centres
- staff recruitment agencies
- local, regional and national newspapers
- information from professional bodies
- libraries, tourist information centres and guide books.

Investigate!

Choose a job role you feel would be suitable for you on finishing your studies. Then choose a job role you feel would be suitable for three years after that. Identify which sector and types of establishments appeal to you. Explain your choices.

Investigate!

Find out about three jobs at either operational, supervisory or management level. One should be in the commercial sector, one in the public service sector and one in non-welfare contract catering. Write a short summary for a trade magazine, comparing the three jobs and the sectors. Look at job titles, levels of authority and responsibility, qualifications needed, progression opportunities, working conditions, uniforms, pay, working hours, legal requirements and benefits.

Test yourself!

1 A waiter is promoted to Head Waiter. To what job role are they most likely to progress next? Explain your answer.

2 What do the initials BHA stand for? Describe the function of the BHA.

3 Are these statements true or false?
   a A Commis Chef's work permit is about to expire. He should discuss the situation with his manager.
   b A Commis Chef strains her back while at the gym. She must report the injury to her manager.

4 Why were regulations introduced covering minimum wages?

Practice assignment tasks

Background information

Imagine you are just about to complete your Diploma in Professional Cookery. You need to consider which part of the industry you would like to work in. You need to think about the structure, scope, size, types of establishment and key influences in the sector.

Task 1

Produce a brief report to:

- Give a description of the term 'hospitality and catering'.
- Summarise the structure of the sector and give examples of different types of operations.
- Include a table with examples of a range of establishments, explaining the features of each.

Task 2

In preparation for an interview produce a PowerPoint presentation to show you understand the:

- key influences in the hospitality and catering sector
- importance of the sector to employment rates and GDP.

Task 3

Using a range of resource material/sources of information (which you must list in the notes) identify a job in a specific sector and briefly describe:

- The main job roles in the chosen environment.
- The key features of each job.
- Legal requirements that may apply in the chosen job role.

2

Health and safety

In this chapter you will cover skills and knowledge in the following units:

- 7132 – Unit 101 (1Gen1): Maintain a safe, hygienic and secure working environment

- 7091 – Unit 151: Safe, hygienic and secure working environments in hospitality

- 7103 – Unit 103: Health and safety awareness for catering and hospitality; and part of Unit 104: Legislation in food and beverage service

- 7103 – Unit 203: Health and safety in catering and hospitality; and part of Unit 204: Legislation in food and beverage service

Working through this chapter could also provide evidence for the following Functional Skills at Level 2:

Functional Maths – Analysing – Recognise 2D representations of 3D objects; find area, perimeter and volume of common shapes

In this chapter you will learn about:

- health and safety regulations that you need to work within

- personal safety and hygiene and how to work and present yourself in a safe and hygienic way

- hazards in the workplace and how to deal with them

- emergencies in the workplace and how to deal with them

- safe working practices and ensuring you work safely

- security procedures

Health and safety regulations

Working in a safe manner

It is important that all workers are able to carry out their tasks without causing any accident or injury to themselves or others (including work colleagues and members of the public). Many years ago injuries at work were quite common, but since the Health and Safety at Work Act 1974 was brought in, most people take much greater care to work in a safe manner. This means there are fewer accidents in the workplace.

The Health and Safety at Work Act gives everyone certain responsibilities. While at work you must:
- take reasonable care of your own safety and the safety of others
- work in the manner laid down by your employer, especially regarding safety
- tell your supervisor if you see anything that you think may be unsafe and could cause an accident.

The Health and Safety at Work Act makes sure that employers do not put their staff in dangerous situations, where they could hurt themselves or others. Under this Act, employers must:
- keep all their staff safe while working
- provide safe equipment, tools and surroundings in which to work
- train staff how to work, clean and maintain equipment they use
- produce a policy document telling everyone how to behave safely
- provide first-aid equipment and help
- keep an accident book and use it correctly.

Laws relating to working safely

The Health and Safety at Work Act is an 'umbrella' act. This means that it includes other important regulations that relate to health and safety.

Regulation	Example
Hazard Analysis and Critical Control Point (HACCP) This system identifies the main risks at important stages of work. Any risks found then need to be made as safe as possible. (This system is particularly important in the hygiene risk assessment of food production.)	The dry store at the back of a restaurant is fitted with five shelves around all the walls, providing storage space from floor to ceiling. There have been several problems with staff trying to take items down from the higher shelves. One staff member nearly overbalanced after climbing onto the lower shelf to reach tins that had been pushed to the back of a higher shelf. The HACCP system was used to identify that this was a safety risk, and a ladder was provided to try and prevent accidents in this area. 
Control of Substances Hazardous to Health (COSHH) Regulations 2002 Identifies dangerous chemicals, e.g. cleaning agents. Chemicals must be labelled accurately. They must be used only after suitable training has been given. The correct protective clothing, e.g. gloves and goggles, must also be used.	A member of the bar staff was provided with a very effective beer line-cleaning chemical. He kept it in a container under the sink in the bar. The barman had been trained how to apply the chemical. While the barman was on holiday, the waiter was told to clean the beer line. He tried to use the same chemical, although he had not been shown what to do. The solution he used was too strong and tainted the fresh keg of beer. This was against the Regulations, as he had not been trained how to use the chemical. 
Reporting of Injuries, Diseases and Dangerous Occurrences Regulations (RIDDOR) 1995 Concerns the reporting of major or fatal injuries to any person in an accident connected with the business where you work. The report must usually be made to the Environmental Health Department of the local council.	A waitress slipped over on a greasy floor while carrying a large tureen of very hot soup. She sustained some nasty burns and had to go to hospital. The accident was recorded in the company's accident book. To comply with RIDDOR, the local council was informed. This resulted in a Health and Safety Inspector visiting the premises to carry out an investigation of how the accident happened.

Manual Handling Operations Regulations 1992 Aims to reduce the number of accidents caused by people moving heavy and awkwardly shaped items while at work. Adequate training must be given and equipment provided to help move items safely (see page 66).	A dinner for 500 guests was going to be held in the exhibition hall of a large conference centre. All the equipment and prepared food needed to be transported from the kitchen to the hall, several hundred yards away. The last time this type of function was held, the staff had to carry all the items on trays and in large containers. Some items were so heavy that two people had to share the load. After the event had taken place, one of the waiters had to have time off work with a strained back. This time, trolleys were provided to move the equipment, and all the staff had received training in lifting heavy items safely to satisfy the Manual Handling Operations Regulations.
Provision and Use of Work Equipment Regulations 1998 Used together with the Prescribed Dangerous Machines Order to make sure people are not injured when they are using machines and other equipment while at work. Before using any type of machinery or equipment, the member of staff must be trained in the correct procedures. If the machine is listed under the Prescribed Dangerous Machines Order, then no-one under the age of 18 may clean, lubricate or adjust it.	A young barmaid was asked to change a keg of draught lager in the cellar. She had not yet been trained how to do this, but thought it should be easy enough. She tried to change the keg without turning off the gas in the cylinder first. The barmaid should not have attempted to change the keg without first being trained to do so safely. This could have resulted in an offence under the Provision and Use of Work Equipment Regulations. 
Fire Precautions Workplace Regulations 1997 Ensures there are suitable measures in place to protect staff and keep them safe in the event of a fire. There should be appropriate fire extinguishers supplied, and a rehearsed evacuation procedure which is regularly checked. (see page 60).	A waiter was cooking a flambé dish at the table. He poured a generous amount of liqueur into the pan and tilted the dish to set it alight. The flame was much larger than he anticipated, and set fire to the low-hanging decorations on the ceiling of the restaurant. The waiter grabbed the nearest fire extinguisher to use it on the fire. The extinguisher was empty. By the time the waiter had located another fire extinguisher, the flames had spread over the ceiling of the restaurant, which had to be evacuated. The fire brigade had to be called to put the fire out. The employer could have been prosecuted under these Regulations because they had failed to maintain the appropriate equipment to extinguish fires. 

Figure 1.1 The different regulations that form part of the Health and Safety at Work Act

Where to find information

It is very important to work in a safe and hygienic way, for several reasons:

○ it avoids injuring yourself or others
○ it is usually quicker and easier
○ it is more professional.

There should be a health and safety representative at your workplace. You should follow any guidelines they give you about safe working practices. If health and safety regulations are not met, you or your employer could be fined and your workplace may be closed down until safety improvements have been made. The fine for not following health and safety law is unlimited. You could also be sent to prison for an unlimited length of time! This means that a serious health and safety problem, such as a major accident, could be very expensive and could give the person responsible a criminal record.

In due course, you will need to know more about health and safety in your workplace. You can:

○ ask your supervisor
○ ask your health and safety representative
○ ask your human resources manager
○ look on the staff notice board.

Figure 2.2 All catering staff need to know the laws on health and safety

Try this!

Try to remember an accident that you saw or one that happened to you.

○ *What happened?*
○ *How many people did it involve?*
○ *What pieces of equipment (if any) were involved?*
○ *Did it involve any of the 'fabric' of the building (e.g. the floor)?*
○ *How was it dealt with?*
○ *Who dealt with it (the manager or head waiter)?*
○ *What did they do?*
○ *Did the accident result in any changes in the area afterwards, e.g. a change in the position of some equipment or a different floor surface being laid?*

Figure 2.3 What is the cause of this accident?

In the restaurant

A student visiting a fast-food restaurant was electrocuted when she accidentally touched a live wire sticking out of a hand-dryer that had been vandalised. The dryer had been damaged at least ten days prior to the accident, but had not been repaired.

Figure 2.4 Negligence can result in serious consequences in the workplace

In the service area

A waiter refilling **flambé** lamps turned into a human fireball when the vapour given off from the fuel ignited around him. The flammable liquid had not been stored properly, the waiter had not been trained properly in this procedure, and there were no suitable fire extinguishers to use nearby.

Figure 2.5 Training is essential in preventing disaster

Definition

Flambé: a French term used to describe cooking at the table in the restaurant and setting fire to the dish using alcohol, to give a few seconds of flame.

Find out!

What year was the Health and Safety at Work Act introduced? If there is a safety problem at work, what is the name of the government organisation that will become involved?

Did you know?

Slips and trips account for more than half of all accidents reported in the catering industry.

Find out!

Make a list of all the potentially dangerous tasks and equipment you may be involved with while at work. These could include, among others: polishing glasses, refilling spirit lamps, lifting full bottle crates, changing beer and gas lines, cleaning beer pipes, filling chafing dishes with hot water, carrying sharp knives, carving at the table, cooking at the table.

Test yourself!

1 Complete the sentences.
The _____ and _____ at Work Act requires all staff to work safely in the kitchen.
All _____ are responsible for the safety of themselves and others.
Staff can find out more information about these Regulations by asking their _____ and looking at the _____.

2 What do these initials stand for?
a HACCP

_____

b COSHH

_____

c RIDDOR.

_____

3 Name two common dangerous occurrences that break the Health and Safety at Work Act.

4 How old must a person be in order to clean a machine listed under the Prescribed Machines Order?

5 Complete the sentence.
The Manual Handling Operations Regulations aim to _____ the number of _____ caused by people moving _____ and _____ shaped items while at _____ .

Personal safety and hygiene

To avoid accidents, you must be alert and able to see ahead to notice any possible danger. The safety of you and your colleagues in a catering kitchen may be affected by:

○ being short of sleep
○ being under the influence of alcohol or drugs
○ having long hair that is not tied back correctly
○ wearing jewellery.

Long hair or jewellery could get caught in machinery or cause hygiene problems by falling into food that is being prepared.

Personal hygiene

Personal hygiene is very important when working in a catering environment. You need to be pleasant to work with (no body odour!) and feel comfortable in the restaurant. Make sure you wash your hair – if it feels sticky and heavy, it will not be pleasant to look at or work with. Clean your teeth regularly – your colleagues will not want to work near you if you have bad breath! Keep your hands and nails clean and in good condition when working directly with food. See Chapter 5 for more information.

Clothing, footwear and headgear

Your uniform should fit correctly and be comfortable to wear. If your shoes are too tight and make your feet hurt, for example, you will not be able to concentrate properly. This could cause an accident if you are carrying glasses, or hot food or drinks.

It is important to wear the correct uniform in the restaurant, not only for health and safety but also to create a professional image. Customers, visitors and other members of staff are impressed by food service staff who are dressed in a clean, smart uniform. Businesses may have 'house rules' regarding correct dress, but all food service uniforms should be comfortable and safe to work in.

What to do if you injure yourself

Despite wearing the correct uniform and working as safely as possible, it is quite likely you will injure yourself at some time while working in a food service environment. The most common injuries are burns and small cuts.

A small cut may be self-treated if appropriate. Wash it, dry it with a clean, disposable cloth or tissue and then cover it with a waterproof blue plaster. Occasionally the cut may need protecting with a **finger stall** over the dressing. If self-treatment is not possible, call a first-aider.

Figure 2.6 Wearing appropriate gloves for a task may help prevent skin problems

Definition

Finger stall: a plastic tube that fits over a dressing (bandage or plaster) on an injured finger to protect it. It is secured by an elastic strap around the wrist.

Did you know?

A first-aider is someone who has successfully studied a first-aid course run by the British Red Cross, St John Ambulance Association or the St Andrew's Ambulance Association. This qualification lasts for three years. After this, the course needs to be retaken.

A small burn may also be self-treated if appropriate. Immediately plunge it under cold running water and hold it there until all the pain has gone. Do not put any type of cream on a burn. A burn should not normally be covered. If it blisters, seek the advice of a first-aider.

Report all injuries to your supervisor and make an entry in the accident book. See page 56, Reporting accidents.

Figure 2.7 Proper attire and behaviour is not just about being professional – it is about safety too

Reporting illnesses and infections

Report any illnesses or infections to your supervisor. An illness may prevent you from working until you are better, on health and safety grounds. Even if you feel quite well, you may be very infectious and risk passing the illness on to your fellow workers or customers.

Illness may be brought on by activities at work, for example a new cleaning chemical may react with your skin and make it sore, itchy or cause a rash. If this happens, your employer may provide you with gloves to wear when you use this chemical in the future.

Figure 2.8 Would you want to eat at this restaurant?

Clothing, footwear and headgear

Hair should be clean, neat and tidy. It should not cover your face and must be securely tied back if below the collar or falling forward as you lean over.

Trousers/skirt should be cotton-mix, loose-fitting for comfort, and allow easy movement. They may have pockets for storing pen and order pad. Skirts that are too short do not look professional and will not protect against spillages. Skirts and trousers that are too long can be a tripping hazard.

Socks/tights should be the correct colour and a comfortable fit without any holes or ladders.

Figure 2.9 The correct presentation

Shirt/blouse should be a cotton-mix material with a high neck and long sleeves to protect the wearer from burns from hot dishes. It should always be clean and in good repair with a full set of buttons.

Apron (if provided) should be made of cotton with strings long enough to tie securely. It may be bibbed, and could have a pocket in the front for storing pen and order pad. It should not be any longer than below the knee, as this would be a tripping hazard. As soon as an apron gets dirty, it should be changed.

Shoes should be comfortable, strong and solid with protected toes. Footwear must have non-slip soles and non-absorbent uppers.

Test yourself!

1 What is the best material from which a restaurant uniform should be made?
  a nylon
  b plastic
  c cotton
  d rubber.

2 Why is a pocket provided in an apron, skirt or trousers?
  a to carry your mobile phone
  b to keep your handkerchief
  c to hold your order pad and pen
  d to keep your hands warm.

3 What is the most important reason why long hair should be tied back?
  a it looks smart
  b it keeps your head cool
  c it allows the customer to see your face
  d it stops you touching your hair when working.

4 What should you do if you feel very tired after work?
  a go to bed early
  b eat a large meal
  c go out with your friends
  d watch more television.

5 What four things should you do if you accidentally cut yourself slightly while at work?

6 What should you do if you burn yourself and a blister forms on the burnt area?

7 What should you do if the skin on your hands becomes itchy and flaky?

8 How often must a first-aid qualification be retaken?

9 Which of these organisations run first-aid courses?
  a Red Arrows
  b Red Cross
  c Red Square
  d Red Aid.

10 Complete this sentence.
  All injuries must be reported to
  _____ _____ and an
  entry made in the _____
  _____.

Hazards in the workplace

Types of hazard

Think of a food service area – what types of **hazard** exist there? Look at the picture below. How many accidents can you see waiting to happen?

Figure 2.10 Spot the hazards in this restaurant

From the picture, you can see there are several types of hazard. They can be grouped according to their causes:

- hazardous substances
- hazardous equipment
- hazardous work methods
- hazardous work area.

Hazardous substances

Any substance that is not in the appropriate place, or is not being used correctly, may become a hazard. In catering, the types of substance that may become hazardous include:

○ cooking oil, which may
   – overheat and catch fire
   – get spilt on a floor and make it very slippery
○ cleaning chemicals, which may
   – be used incorrectly, e.g. not **diluted** sufficiently
   – not be used with the appropriate protective equipment, e.g. goggles and gloves
   – be mixed together and give off dangerous fumes
   – be decanted from a large, labelled container into a smaller, unlabelled container and mistaken for another liquid.

> **Definition**
> **Dilute:** to add extra liquid (usually water) to make the solution weaker.

COSHH

The COSHH Regulations form part of the Health and Safety at Work Act. They are rules controlling substances that are considered hazardous to health. The COSHH Regulations state that:

○ chemicals that may be dangerous to people must be clearly identified
○ those chemicals must be stored, issued and used safely
○ training must be given in the use of these chemicals
○ suitable protective clothing must be provided when using the chemicals.

When using any type of chemical:

○ always follow the manufacturer's instructions carefully
○ never mix one chemical with another
○ never move any chemical from its original container into an alternative one that is incorrectly labelled or has no label at all
○ never use food containers to store a cleaning chemical
○ always store chemicals in the correct place.

In the restaurant

A pub kept some beer pipe-cleaning fluid in an unlabelled, clear glass bottle on the floor. It was placed near the beer pipes ready to use. A new member of staff, who was very thirsty, opened the bottle and drank from it. The liquid was clear and looked like lemonade, but in fact was an extremely strong, caustic chemical. The member of staff suffered extensive burning of mouth, throat and stomach and can no longer eat normally.

Figure 2.11 Never pour a liquid into an unlabelled container

Hazardous equipment

Hazardous equipment may be manual or electrical. Training must be given in the operation of equipment, and the equipment must be checked regularly.

Types of manual equipment include:
○ knives
○ spirit lamps.

Knife care and safety

Poor knife techniques and untidy work methods are often a cause of accidents in the kitchen. Follow the rules below.

○ Store your knives in a specially designed area when not in use, e.g. in a box, case, wallet or on a magnetic rack. Storing loose knives in a drawer can damage the blades and cause injury.
○ When moving knives, transport them in the appropriate box or case. Never leave them loose. This avoids accidents in the workplace. It also stops you getting into trouble with the police when carrying your knives to and from work.
○ When carrying a knife, always point it down and hold it close to your side. Work colleagues can be unintentionally stabbed if this rule is not followed!
○ If passing a knife to a colleague, always offer it to them handle first.
○ Never leave a knife on a work surface with the blade upwards.
○ Never leave a knife hanging over the edge of a work surface.
○ Never try to catch a falling knife – let it come to rest on the ground before you pick it up.
○ Never use a knife as a can opener or screwdriver.
○ Do not use a knife that is blunt or has a greasy, loose or damaged handle. A knife in any of these conditions can easily slip and cause a serious cut.
○ It is recommended that you use colour-coded knives to prevent cross-contamination; see pages 162–163.
○ Only use a knife on a chopping board that has a damp cloth underneath to prevent slippage.
○ When wiping a knife clean after use, wipe from the blade base to the tip with the sharp edge facing away from your body.
○ Never leave a knife in a sink. Wash it and remove it immediately.

Figure 2.12 Knives should be stored carefully

Electrical equipment

Hazardous electrical equipment includes:

○ hotplates
○ coffee machines
○ water boilers.

Rules for operating machinery

○ Always follow the manufacturer's instructions.
○ Never operate machinery if the safety guards are not in place. Many machines will not work unless correctly and fully assembled. However, some older models may work without the safety equipment being fitted (be very careful with these).
○ If the machine will not work properly, seek help from your supervisor.
○ Ensure that the correct attachments are being used on the equipment for the task to be carried out.
○ Never push food against a cutting blade with your hands – use a proper plunger or the handle supplied. (Many chefs have lost fingers by not following this rule!)
○ If using a spoon, do not let it touch any moving parts. If it does, the spoon and the machine will be damaged.
○ Do not use faulty machinery. Label it 'out of order' and unplug it or partly dismantle it so it cannot be used. Report the problem to your supervisor so a repair can be arranged.
○ Do not overload electrical sockets. This may cause a fire or cause fuses to blow, and could affect everybody working in the building.
○ Do not operate electrical equipment with wet hands, or near a sink or any other sources of water. An electric shock could result from this action.
○ Keep your hands away from sharp blades. Wait for them to stop rotating after switching the machine off before starting any other activity, such as cleaning.
○ Make sure the power is disconnected before starting to clean electrical machinery.
○ Do not use machinery if the plug or flex is damaged in any way.

Figure 2.13 An espresso machine could be hazardous if not used correctly

Remember!
Take great care when operating machinery. No-one under the age of 18 may clean, lubricate or adjust a machine if they will be at risk of injury from a moving part.

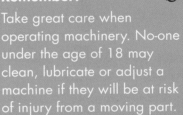

Remember!
Before using any type of machinery or equipment, the member of staff must be trained in the correct procedures. They must be fully instructed about any danger that may arise, and must be supervised adequately by someone with knowledge and experience of the machine.

Hazardous work methods

Many accidents are caused by poor work methods. Before starting work, consider the following points.

- When a range of tasks have to be completed, they should be carried out in order.
- Finish one task before starting the next.
- Assemble all the equipment necessary before starting the task.
- Allow sufficient time and space to carry out the task involved.
- Follow a logical sequence. The flow of work should move one way, e.g. left to right.
- Make sure there are no spillages on the floor. If this happens, it will become slippery and could cause an accident.

Did you know?

If a hard floor is getting slippery during service, you should throw several generous handfuls of salt over the surface. This is a quick, temporary remedy as the salt absorbs the liquid or grease. The floor can then be cleaned properly when there is time.

Figure 2.14 An untidy work area showing hazardous work methods – and how it should be

Hazardous work area

Some areas of the restaurant may not be the most appropriate to work in.

- A food service area might be very crowded with customers, including young children. People could be seated or moving about the restaurant.
- It is easy to collide with other people in a crowded space. This could be very dangerous if you are carrying a pot of hot liquid.
- Floors can get greasy and wet if spillages are not cleared up quickly and thoroughly. Staff walking from the restaurant into the kitchen servery and out again may make the floors slippery.

Did you know?

Heated plates brought out of the kitchen ready for service need to be kept wrapped in a service cloth. As well as keeping them warm, it helps to warn everyone that they are hot.

Reporting hazards

If you see a hazard in your work area that could cause an accident, you should:

1 make the hazard safe, as long as you can do so without risking your own safety
2 report the hazard to your supervisor as soon as you can, making sure no-one enters the area without being aware of the danger.

Two good ways in which you can warn other people about hazards are:

○ block the route past the hazard
○ use a sign.

A sign is usually the best way. Temporary signs may be handwritten if there is no alternative. Many signs involve visual symbols which are best in case people passing the hazard cannot read English. Where signs are in frequent use, e.g. fire exits, they are produced in colours that can be seen by colour-blind people.

Some hazards are temporary so the sign relating to them should also be temporary, e.g. a wet floor sign. Others are there because of the nature of the building, e.g. a low beam may have a permanent sign nearby warning everyone to mind their head.

Commonly used hazard warning signs

A black and yellow sign is used with a triangular symbol where there is a risk of danger, e.g. 'Mind your head'

A red circle with a line through it tells you something you must not do in the area, e.g. 'No smoking'

A solid blue circle with a white picture or writing gives a reminder of something you must do, e.g. 'Shut the door'

A green sign with a white picture or writing is an emergency sign for escape or first aid

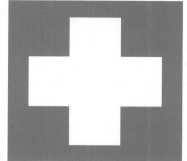

A red sign with white symbols or writing indicates fire-fighting information

> **Definition**
> **Caustic:** a substance that will stick to a surface and burn chemically. It is used for heavy-duty cleaning.

When using chemicals that could harm you, the following signs may be displayed on the container:

Corrosive – could burn your skin

Poison – may kill you if swallowed

Irritant – may cause itching or a rash if in contact with skin

Figure 2.15 The colours of the signs indicate the type of hazard involved

 Find out!
What type of chemicals used in your workplace have these symbols?
What type of protective equipment should you wear when using them?

Reporting accidents

All accidents should be reported to your supervisor. Each accident is recorded in an accident book, which must be provided in every business. The key information that has to be recorded about an accident is the:

- date and time of the incident
- full name and occupation of the person involved
- type of injury
- location of the accident and what happened
- names of any witnesses to the accident
- name and job title of the person completing the report
- time and date the report was made.

Accident report

Details of person involved

Name: _John Smith_____ Occupation: _Waiter_____

Type of injury: _Serious burn_____

Incident details

Location: _Restaurant_____

Date: _20/11/06_____ Time: _19.45_____

Details of witness: _Bob Jones, Samantha Rice, Faye Lemon_____

_____

_____

Description of what happenend:

While handling a pot of boiling water from the hot water boiler, the waiter slipped and spilt the contents on his arm. He sustained heavy burns and was sent to hospital.

Report completed by: _Sarah Jane Smith_____

Job title: _Head waiter_____

Date and time of report: _20/11/06 20.30_____

Figure 2.16 An accident report form

A serious accident has to be reported to the Environmental Health Officer of the local council. This may be done by phone at first and then followed up in writing. A serious accident means: broken bones, loss of a limb or eyesight, electric shock, or any other circumstance that involves the person being kept in hospital for more than 24 hours.

Try this!

Complete a blank accident form describing the following incident.

Beryl Smith, who worked in the wash-up area, came into work on Monday morning as usual. She had just returned from her mid-morning break when she slipped on some grease. This had dripped onto the floor from a pile of unscraped plates left on the side of the table. She fell down, banged her head on the leg of the table and cut her ear. Mr Newman, the waiter, who is a first-aider, treated the cut, which soon stopped bleeding. He made Beryl sit in the office for a while to make sure she had no ill-effects from banging her head. After about 15 minutes, Beryl felt able to carry on with her work. The grease on the floor was cleared up by the kitchen porter while Beryl was being looked after.

Test yourself!

1 Write down four safety points about using electrical equipment.

2 Write down four safety points about knives.

3 What action should you take if you notice each of the following situations:

a The handle of a floor mop has fallen across the corridor, blocking the way. It had been left leaning against the wall.

b Some boxes stacked up on a high shelf are leaning to one side and looking as if they will soon fall down.

c A corner of vinyl flooring has come unstuck and is likely to cause someone to trip over it.

4 Match the signs to the written warnings.
   a Danger _____
   b No entry – restricted area _____
   c Now wash your hands _____
   d Emergency exit _____

i   ii   iii   iv

5 Complete these important safety points, which you must follow when using any type of chemical.
   a Always follow the m_____ i_____ carefully.
   b Never m_____ one chemical with another.
   c Never m_____ any chemical from its o_____ container into an alternative which is i_____ labelled or has no l_____ at all.
   d Never use f_____ c_____ to store a cleaning chemical.
   e Always s_____ chemicals in the correct p_____.

6 There are 12 rules for operating machinery. Write down four of them.

7 Why might it be difficult to work in the following places?
   a A kitchen servery.
   b A crowded restaurant.

Emergencies in the workplace

Types of emergency

Several types of emergency can happen at work. They include:

○ a sudden serious accident or illness of staff or customers
○ the outbreak of a fire that cannot be safely put out
○ a security alert in the building, e.g. a bomb scare
○ the failure of a major system in a building, e.g. power, drainage.

Each of these needs to be dealt with in a different way. The management of the organisation should have systems in place to deal with each of them. Some of these systems may involve certain members of staff being trained in particular skills, e.g. first aid or fire fighting. Other procedures may mean that all staff need to carry out special tasks when a particular type of emergency happens. These procedures need practising every so often, and this is why routine building evacuations take place and alarms are tested regularly.

The main types of emergency can be dealt with in the following ways.

○ **Illness:** trained first-aiders on duty to help with staff or customers who are taken ill or have an accident. Security/door staff trained in calling an ambulance or doctor and escorting them to the medical emergency smoothly, e.g. by holding lifts ready for them and having information about the person concerned available.
○ **Fire:** a thoroughly rehearsed fire evacuation procedure, which can take place quickly and without panic, allowing for all people in the building to be accounted for to make sure they are safe.
○ **Security:** a fully rehearsed emergency procedure to prevent unnecessary disruption to the normal running of the building, but allowing a full evacuation if necessary. Special training of security staff and telephonists in how to deal with suspicious packages or telephone calls threatening explosions.
○ **Supply failure:** depending on the system that has failed, the building may have a back-up system, such as a generator for power, which can take over automatically with very little disruption. Some services, such as the water supply failing or a gas leak, may mean the building has to close until the problem can be put right. Sometimes the area around the building can be affected as well.

Did you know?

Many fires on catering premises have been started by a spark from the stove being sucked up the extraction canopy. When that canopy is dirty and coated with a layer of grease, a fire can easily start. Because the smoke gets sucked up through the extraction system, no-one may be aware there is a fire until it has spread to a dangerous level. Some commercial insurance companies will not insure catering premises unless the kitchen canopy is professionally cleaned very regularly.

Remember!

The thick, toxic smoke that a fire gives off kills and injures people more than the flames. It is very important to keep fire doors closed to stop smoke spreading. Thick smoke can make escape from a burning building impossible.

Remember!

Emergency escape routes must always be kept clear and unlocked. Never leave anything in front of an emergency exit. Most deaths in fires occur because people cannot get out of the building.

First aid

Special courses are run for people who wish to learn how to treat minor injuries and apply techniques that may help to save the life of someone who has been involved in a serious accident or who has become very ill. It is always useful to know what to do in the event of a medical emergency, and if you become a first-aider it gives you skills that you can use at any time. Find out more by visiting the St John Ambulance website. A link is available at www.heinemann.co.uk/hotlinks – just enter the express code 7193P.

Even if you are not a first-aider, there are some basic techniques it is helpful to know about in case there is no-one else around to treat someone who has had an accident.

tweezers

book to record use of equipment

Date	Time	Incident

scissors

bandages of various sizes and types

dressings of various sizes and types (including 'blue plasters' for catering use)

cotton wool

Eye pads

eye pads

safety pins

FIRST AID

Figure 2.17 Contents of a first-aid box

first aid guidance card

What to do in the event of an accident

- Visually make sure the injured person is in no further danger. Do not touch them.
- If there is any machinery involved, immediately turn off the power at the plug or the main switch. This is very important if you think the person may have been electrocuted. Otherwise, if you touch them you will get electrocuted too.
- Contact your supervisor and get the help of a first-aider.

○ If this is not possible:
- telephone 999 (free call – even from a locked phone)
- ask for the ambulance service
- give your telephone number so you can be called back
- give the location of the accident
- describe what has happened and give details of the injuries as clearly as you can
- follow any instructions given over the phone – this may be giving some first aid, getting information from the injured person, or going to a meeting point to wait for an ambulance.

How to treat a casualty while waiting for help

○ Talk to the person and reassure them. If you do not know them, find out their name and where they live. Be kind and considerate.
○ Tell them that help is on the way.
○ If they feel cold, cover them with a blanket or any available clothing. Try not to cover a major burn.
○ Do not move the person unless they are in danger of further injury.

See how to treat a minor cut or a burn on page 9.

Figure 2.18 Reassure the casualty

Emergency procedures and how to follow them

When there is an emergency, it is important that everybody does exactly as they are told and follows the rehearsed procedure. The immediate result of most emergencies is evacuation of the building.

Evacuation procedure

If you have to leave the kitchen as the result of an emergency, remember to do the following:
○ turn off all the power supplies (gas and electricity) – this may mean hitting the red button in a modern kitchen, or turning off all the appliances individually
○ close all the windows and doors in the area
○ never stop to gather personal possessions
○ leave the building by the nearest emergency exit (do not use a lift)
○ assemble in the designated area away from the building
○ answer a roll-call of names so that everyone knows you have left the building safely.

External emergency procedure

If there is an emergency, such as a bomb alert, outside the building, you may have to stop working and take shelter inside. Staff should rehearse for this type of emergency as well as the evacuation procedure. This external emergency procedure should include the following instructions:

○ turn off all power supplies in the kitchen
○ close all the windows and doors in the area
○ do not stop to gather personal possessions
○ gather in a designated safe area, usually in a central stairwell or corridor away from windows, and as close to the middle of the building as possible
○ stay in this area until told to leave by an emergency official
○ answer a roll-call of names to make sure no-one is missing.

A modern kitchen has a red button that turns off power supplies in an emergency.

Fire in the workplace

Fire is very dangerous and can easily become life-threatening. It is very important that you know what to do in the event of a fire. Respect fire and treat it with the utmost caution.

Figure 2.19 A fire can start when an electrical socket is overloaded

Causes of fire in the workplace

Fires can quite easily be started in restaurants, for example by hot plates which are left on for long periods of time. Cooking at the table, especially flambé dishes, can get out of control. There is a large amount of electrical equipment which can develop a fault and start a fire.

How to minimise the risk of fire

Careful work practices and being observant are the main ways of reducing the risk of fire. These good practices include:

○ keeping hot work areas clean of fat and grease
○ never overfilling flambé lamps
○ keeping areas around naked flames clear
○ not cooking at the table under low ceilings and decorations
○ not overloading electrical sockets
○ never leaving electrical appliances on unattended.

In the restaurant

A **smouldering** oven cloth nearly caused a serious fire in a London hotel. One Sunday afternoon, a young chef was very keen to leave work after lunch service. He changed into his outdoor clothes as quickly as he could. Then he threw his chef's whites and cloths into his locker. He did not realise that his oven cloth was smouldering. After a while the fire alarm in the hotel sounded. The sensor board indicated the problem was in the male changing rooms.

On investigation the room was found to be full of smoke with a fire building up inside the young chef's locker. It was put out promptly, which was a good thing as the changing room was located next to the fuel store where tanks of oil were kept.

> **Definition**
> **Smoulder:** to burn slowly with a small red glow and little smoke.

Understand how a fire can start

Fire needs three things to burn. As soon as one is removed, the fire will go out.

○ **Fuel:** fire has to be fed, and will use any substance that will burn, e.g. gas, electricity, cloth, oil or wood. Once the fuel has been used up, the fire will go out.

○ **Oxygen:** fire requires oxygen to keep going. If the source of air is removed, the fire will go out. This is why a fire blanket can put out a fire.

○ **Heat:** fire creates heat. If the heat of the fire is removed, the fire will go out. This is how many fire extinguishers work.

A fire can be put out by:
○ starving it of fuel
○ smothering it by removing air
○ cooling it by taking away the heat.

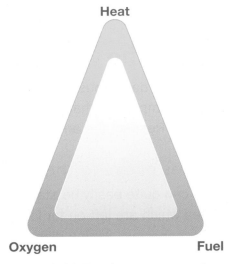

Figure 2.20 The three components that fire needs

The significance of fire alarms

Fire alarms are required in all businesses over a certain size. They save lives and are essential in large buildings. They are required in all businesses that need to have a fire safety risk assessment to operate. See Fire safety laws on pages 64–65.

Fire alarms work by fitting smoke and heat sensors in various parts of the building. When any of these sensors is activated, an alarm sounds. The sensor that has been activated shows up on the control panel, and the area it covers has to be investigated immediately.

Sometimes a sensor may sound the alarm even though there is no apparent reason. This may be due to the system developing a fault. The area covered by the sensor must always be checked, even if nothing is found. A false alarm must never be assumed. If a false alarm continues to occur, then an engineer will be called in to check the system.

Testing fire alarms

To ensure the alarm system is working correctly, it should be tested regularly. Most businesses check their system at the same time every week. This involves:

○ all staff being told when the test takes place, so they know not to evacuate the building

○ the alarm bells ringing on-and-off for a few minutes.

If the alarm sounds at any other time, all members of staff should follow the procedure they have been taught. This usually means leaving the building and assembling in a particular area outside. At the assembly point there is a roll-call (a type of register) to make sure everyone has left the building and is safe.

Some alarms have two stages.

Stage 1: the smoke or fire sensor will set off the first alarm, which sounds briefly. Trained members of staff will then investigate the area. If they can deal with the cause of the alarm, or if it is a false alarm, no further action is taken.

Stage 2: should there be a fire or other emergency, the second stage of the alarm will be activated. This means the alarm will sound continuously and the building will be evacuated. The fire brigade will also be called.

How to deal with a fire

A fire can easily start in a restaurant, so it is important to know what to do if it happens. Sometimes a candle may fall onto a table and start burning the surface. If dealt with immediately, it can usually be put out easily. This is not an emergency. However, if it does not go out and gets bigger it could become dangerous.

If you are going to try to put out a small fire, you need to know which extinguisher to use for which type of fire. If you use the wrong one by mistake it could make the fire much worse.

Once you have used a fire extinguisher, you must let your supervisor know as it has to be refilled as soon as possible. Extinguishers must be checked each year to make sure they are full and work properly.

In some situations it may be appropriate to try to put out a fire that has just started, but you must act speedily!

Situation		Response
A person's clothes catch fire 	FIRE BLANKET PULL	Quickly wrap them in a fire blanket or wet tablecloth (or similar) and lay them on the floor. This excludes air and heat from the fire so it should go out. Do not take off the blanket or tablecloth. Call for a first-aider to attend the scene.
A pan of fat catches fire 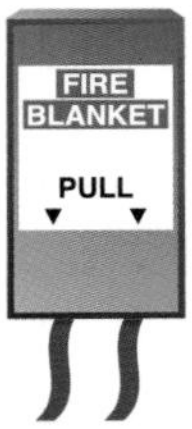	FIRE BLANKET PULL	Turn off the gas or electricity and quickly cover the pan with a lid or fire blanket and leave it where it is. Use an oven cloth if possible to protect your hands. The fire should go out by itself after a few minutes as the air has been removed. **Do not** try to move the pan. **Do not** put water on this type of fire as it will make it much worse immediately.
An electrical appliance (e.g. a blender) catches fire 	CO_2	Turn off the electricity at the plug and use a carbon dioxide extinguisher. This gas cools the fire and removes the oxygen. It does not conduct electricity and is safe to use on electrical machinery. **Do not** use any other type of extinguisher in this situation.

Figure 2.21 Action to take to put out a fire

If a fire starts that cannot be put out easily:
○ raise the alarm by operating the nearest fire alarm, or shouting 'Fire!'
○ follow the procedure as rehearsed in your company fire training.

Fire safety laws

The main fire safety law is the Regulatory Reform (Fire Safety) Order 2005. The Health and Safety at Work Act also contains specific regulations concerning fire precautions at workplaces, and there is also European law relating to fire precautions.

All businesses over a certain size have to have a fire safety risk assessment completed by the owner. The assessment should be reviewed and the premises checked regularly.

The assessment should cover the following:

- the total number of people allowed in the building at any time (one reason why a nightclub has to restrict how many people can enter)
- the use of the premises
- the provision of:
  - fire exits
  - fire doors
  - extinguishers
  - alarm systems
  - emergency lighting
  - signage.

Try this!

Imagine a fire was to break out now.

- **Where is the nearest fire extinguisher?**
- **Where is the nearest emergency exit point?**
- **Where do you have to assemble outside?**

Without asking for help, see if you can answer these questions explaining the procedure your company want you to carry out in the event of a fire.

Afterwards, answer them again with the help of someone who knows the correct answer. Were you right?

Test yourself!

What type of extinguisher would you use for each type of fire?

a Paper in a waste bin.

b A frying pan of burning oil on a flambé lamp.

c An electrical bar blender smoking and starting to burn.

Safe working practices

It is very important that everyone at work tries to work in a safe manner. Many accidents can be avoided if you remember:

- any spillages should be cleaned up immediately
- any slippery surfaces should have warning notices nearby
- no items should be placed in corridors and walkways, for any reason
- to take care when lifting and carrying items
- to use a trolley or sack truck whenever possible to transport large or awkward items
- to get help if you cannot manage to move or clear away an item easily

- to keep your work area clean and well organised
- to plan the movement of all items in advance
- not to rush around the kitchen
- to consider others working around you.

Safe lifting and handling techniques

It is very easy to hurt yourself if you do not know how to lift and move items safely. It is not just heavy items that can cause problems when moving them about.

- Be very careful moving pots containing hot liquids. Do not have them too full.
- When moving hot items, be careful not to burn someone who may be passing by.
- Do not overload trolleys or trucks.
- Always make sure you can see where you are going.
- Stack heavier items at the bottom and lighter items at the top of a pile.
- Do not stack shelves too high.
- Use steps with great care. Have someone hold them at the bottom if possible.

Figure 2.22 Careless handling and lifting can lead to problems

Lifting a heavy object

To lift a heavy object safely needs correct training. Guidelines include:

- keep your muscles relaxed – tense muscles strain easily
- plan what is to be carried to where
- check the route is clear, doors are open, ramps in position, lights on
- get help if the object is likely to be heavier than you can easily handle
- position your feet carefully at either side of the object to keep your balance
- use one hand to support the weight of the item, the other to pull the item towards you – this way your body can take part of the weight
- use your whole hand to lift, not just the tips of your fingers
- do not twist to change direction as you are lifting or carrying
- move your feet in plenty of small steps.

Figure 2.23 Lifting a heavy object safely

Try this!
Try lifting a medium-sized, empty box following the guidelines above to avoid straining yourself.

Security procedures

Security procedures on catering premises are important for a variety of reasons:
- to protect staff, visitors and customers on the premises
- to reduce theft and pilfering
- to help to keep a workplace safe and secure.

Keeping the workplace secure

Key control
- Always follow the correct procedure for issuing and returning keys.
- Never leave keys in locks – replace them in the correct place after use.
- Never lend keys to someone else – make them sign for them as you have done.
- Never leave secure areas unlocked and unattended.

Personal possessions
- Do not take anything valuable to work. If you have to, keep it locked in your locker.
- Respect workplace rules regarding personal possessions.
- Do not take personal bags into your work area – you could be suspected of theft.
- You may be asked by your employer to agree to the right to be searched at random to deter theft.

Visitors and customers

- Challenge politely anyone who is in your area who you do not recognise. 'Can I help you?' is the best way to start.
- If the person says they are waiting for a member of staff, check the name and position of the person they are waiting for. Try to contact that person, while keeping an eye on the stranger to make sure they do not wander off.
- Escort anyone who appears to be lost to the nearest supervisor or manager.

Closedown procedures

- Make sure you check all doors and windows are closed.
- Check that all cooking and preparation equipment is turned off and/or put away.
- Check that all storage areas – fridges, freezers, dry stores and cupboards – are secure.

General observation

- If you see someone behaving suspiciously, tell your supervisor as soon as you can.
- Try to remember what any suspicious person looks like, as well as what they were doing.
- If you see an unattended package and you do not know what it is, do not touch it. Inform your supervisor as quickly as possible.

Property

Lost property

Your workplace should have a procedure for dealing with lost property. It will involve you giving the item to your supervisor and telling them:

- where the item was found
- the date and time the item was found.

If the item you found is not claimed by the owner after a certain period, it may be given back to you. Some businesses put unclaimed lost property into a charity box, or sell it and put the money into a staff fund.

Security when dealing with customers' property

If you have to handle customers' property, you must be very careful. You have a duty to keep the property of others safe and secure. Make sure you record:

○ a description of the item
○ to whom it belongs
○ the date and time it was left with you
○ where it was kept
○ the date and time it was returned to the customer or passed to your supervisor.

This information should help you if there is any query in respect of the property.

Reporting incidents

It is very important that you report anything happening that is out of the ordinary or that you feel is not 'right'. It does not matter if it turns out not to be of concern on this occasion – it could be a very helpful observation for your manager or the police next time.

When you report an incident, you must try to remember as much detail as you can. You may be asked to complete an incident form with the following details, then sign and date it.

○ date, time and place of incident
○ who was involved and what they looked like
○ who saw the incident
○ a description of what happened
○ how long the incident lasted
○ whether anybody was hurt
○ whether there was any damage to property
○ whether the emergency services were called.

Further information
Useful organisations

○ St John Ambulance
○ Health and Safety Executive
○ Royal Society for the Prevention of Accidents
○ Institute of Hospitality.

Find out!
What procedure does your establishment have for dealing with lost property?

Find out!
You can find out more about these organisations by visiting their websites. Links have been made available at www. heinemann.co.uk/hotlinks – just enter the express code 7193P.

Try this!

Study the picture below for three minutes. Close this book and write down all the details that would be needed on an incident form.

Figure 2.24 Can you describe what happened here?

Test yourself!

Give one security procedure for each of the following issues:

a key control
b personal possessions
c visitors and customers
d closedown procedures
e general observation.

3 Teamwork

In this chapter you will cover skills and knowledge in the following units:

- 7132 – Unit 104 (1Gen4): Work effectively as part of a hospitality team
- 7091 – Unit 152: Effective teamwork
- 7103 – Part of Unit 106: Introduction to personal workplace skills

Working through this chapter could also provide evidence for the following Functional Skills:

Functional English – Speaking, listening and communication Level 1 & 2

Functional English – Read and understand a range of texts and write documents to communicate Level 1

Functional ICT – Using ICT Level 1 and Developing and presenting communication information Level 1

In this chapter you will learn how to:

- work effectively as part of a team
- organise your own work
- support the work of your team
- communicate effectively with colleagues and customers
- ask for feedback on what you do well and where you could improve
- contribute to your own development

Effective teamwork

Effective teamwork is vital in the hospitality industry. A good standard of service and production cannot be provided by individuals working alone. A successful meal service depends upon all the staff in the restaurant and kitchen working together to ensure:

o correct timing
o smooth service
o high standard of production
o food served at the correct temperature.

The perfect team will consist of members who:

o are committed to the task in hand
o work together towards a common aim
o are well organised
o communicate openly.

The benefits of working as a team mean that:

o a higher output of work can be achieved for less effort
o people are usually happier working in a group
o responsibility for work and decisions is shared
o team members are loyal to each other
o the workforce is more creative.

Marcus says

Understand the work of your colleagues. Reservations, front of house and the kitchen may all work different shifts and carry out different tasks, but we all work towards the same shared goal – hospitality.

In the food service area

Pat was the manager of a retail store restaurant. Each member of staff was responsible for preparing certain areas of the restaurant and counter every day. Her staff often complained about their colleagues' speed of work. They had to wait for each other on many occasions when using the same pieces of equipment such as glasswashers and polishers. Some staff worked more quickly than others and did not want to be held up. Some staff criticised the cleanliness and presentation of their colleagues' working areas.

Pat decided to restructure the organisation of the restaurant. She put her staff to work in teams, each responsible for a larger section of the restaurant. She also moved the teams around so that they did not prepare the same areas all the time. This meant that the staff had to work together and help each other much more. They organised their use of the equipment better and they stopped criticising each other's standards. They started to share the equipment they used and found they had more time to get their jobs done.

Figure 3.1 The advantages of working in a team

In the café

Jim used to work alone serving food in a small café. He was often stressed in his job and struggled to keep pace with demand at lunchtimes when it was busy. He found he had to start work really early in the morning to make sure everything was ready. Jim found that if he wanted a break or to finish early, he had to work even harder to make up for the lost time.

Jim moved to work at a larger café. He was much happier straight away. There were other people to share the workload, and there was often time to have a laugh and a joke with them. If he wanted a break, others would cover his job so he did not fall behind. He liked being able to help the others if they needed it. As a team, far more customers could be served than if each person worked separately. The group liked to try to sell extra items to all the customers each week. Jim enjoyed the challenge of persuading customers to spend more money. The customers liked Jim and found him friendly and helpful with his suggestions, and sales rose. The owner of the business was very pleased and gave the whole team a bonus payment.

Figure 3.2 Jim preferred working with a team

Working as a team member also has advantages, such as:
- feeling more valued at work
- being able to learn from others
- being able to show others what you can do
- greater job satisfaction
- having the support of others
- benefiting from any team 'perks' – such as a productivity bonus.

Types of team

There are two main types of team that work in the service area of any food service business.
- Formal: a team that is led by the restaurant manager with a deputy and staff running all the areas within the restaurant.
- Informal: a team that is put together at short notice, but may not normally work together.

Formal teams have:
- an appointed leader
- specific tasks to achieve
- clear channels of communication
- clear lines of authority and responsibility.

The diagram (right) shows how a formal team works in a 40-seater restaurant.

A very small catering business will have only a small team. The members of small teams will work very closely together, and eventually will be able to help and deputise for each other in all areas.

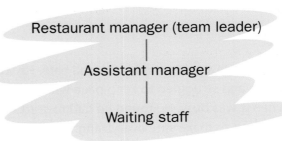

Restaurant manager (team leader)

|

Assistant manager

|

Waiting staff

Figure 3.3 A small food service team in a 40-seater restaurant

Below is a diagram showing the organisation of a formal team in a large restaurant: a conference centre catering for up to 1,000 customers at a time. You can see that the large operation has the restaurant split into a number of teams. Each team has a specific area to look after.

Figure 3.4 A large team in the food service section of a conference centre

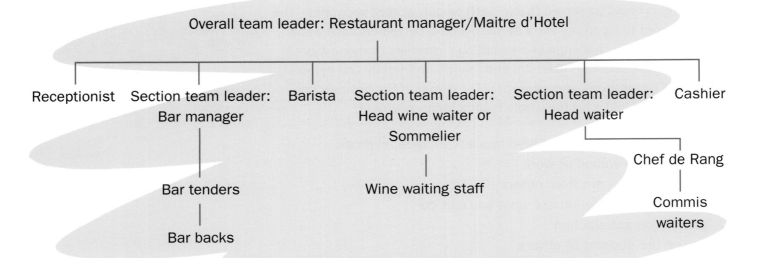

Overall team leader: Restaurant manager/Maitre d'Hotel

Receptionist — Section team leader: Bar manager — Barista — Section team leader: Head wine waiter or Sommelier — Section team leader: Head waiter — Cashier

Bar tenders

Bar backs

Wine waiting staff

Chef de Rang

Commis waiters

Try this!

Draw a diagram of the organisation of your restaurant. Compare it with diagrams of people who work in other types of food service operation. The charts are likely to be quite different because:

○ *some food service areas, such as a small fast-food café, will be very small and employ only a few staff*

○ *some operations, such as an international exhibition centre with conference and banqueting facilities, will be very large and employ many staff.*

In your diagram, is there one team or several small teams?

Think about if and when any informal teams are used in your workplace. What are they used for? Are you involved in any informal teams outside the workplace?

The organisation of an informal team cannot be shown in the same way. An informal team:

○ develops from a particular need
○ exists for a short period
○ may have a flexible structure
○ deals with a particular situation.

Look at Figure 3.4. Normally the staff would work in their formal team structure. However, at service time, if there was a large party to be served, instead of working in teams covering a certain number of tables, all of them might work together serving the whole room together, creating an informal team. Once this service had been completed, the informal team would disband. The staff would return to their formal teams and continue with their work.

Another time when an informal team might be formed is when change is proposed. If a new style of service was to be introduced, managers and supervisors would work together in an informal team to develop a new system to be used. Informal teams may also exist outside the formal workplace. If a member of staff is in hospital, other staff members may become an informal team to organise a schedule of visits and help for that person's family. A group of friends may form an informal team to organise a Christmas or charity event.

Members of a restaurant team

Restaurant manager

Has overall responsibility for all aspects of managing the restaurant including food and drink.

Maitre d'Hotel

Oversees the restaurant, saying what tables need to be set to meet bookings, liaising with restaurant manager and managing the restaurant staff.

Head waiter

Oversees the work of restaurant staff during service, ensuring that customers are served in a timely fashion and dealing with any problems. The head waiter is often the same person as the Maitre d'Hotel, depending on the size of the establishment.

Chef de Rang

A section head waiter – looks after a group of tables or section, depending on the size of the establishment.

Commis chef

Lays up tables, assists the Chef de Rang, serves customers under supervision of Chef de Rang.

Aboyeur

This literally means 'barker'. He shouts the orders in the kitchen and manages the pass, where finished dishes are collected by the waiters, to ensure efficient service.

Sommelier

A specialist wine waiter. In good quality establishments, this role extends to identifying suitable wines for the wine menu, meeting suppliers, ordering stock, and on a day-to-day basis providing customers with detailed information about suitable wines to go with their choice of menu.

Bar tender

Responsible for the setting up of the bar area, restocking of drinks, glasses, garnishes and general tidiness and maintenance of the bar area.

Cocktail bar tender

May be the same person as a bar tender. The role includes: the extent of garnishes and equipment, the knowledge and expertise of mixology of cocktails and, in some cases, the development of new cocktails. They may also advise customers on cocktail choices.

Bar back

Assists the bar tender. May be a trainee. Helps restock drinks during service, supports the pouring of drinks for a group of customers, collects glasses and general help.

Barista

Someone who serves non-alcoholic drinks. They need a good working knowledge of making coffee, tea and chocolate, using specialist equipment. They may also make milk shakes, smoothies, and other soft drinks.

Cashier

Main responsibility is to reconcile orders that have been taken, in order to prepare bills. They deal with customer payments and reconcile the till at the end of service.

Receptionist

The receptionist function is to potentially take bookings depending on the booking service. This may include following up to confirm or remind about online restaurant reservations. They deal on a one-to-one basis with the hosts of larger functions, greet customers, help with looking after customers' property such as coats, and ensuring that the last impression of the customer is the best one.

Roles and responsibilities of team members

All teams must have a leader. Formal teams have an appointed leader, recognised by their job title. They may also be paid at a higher rate than the rest of their team.

An informal group will also have a leader. The leader is unlikely to be appointed, and could change as and when the tasks to be carried out require different strengths.

The success of a team depends very much on the leader. The leader of a team should:
- set a good example
- be respected by all the team members

Try this!
Think of your team leader at work. Do they do a good job? Can you identify what they do to make the team work well together?

- be consistent in decisions made
- encourage, motivate and support team members.

How do team members work together effectively?

A good team member will:

- always be reliable and on time for work
- be organised, work cleanly and methodically
- complete all tasks required within a reasonable time
- help other people to complete their work if necessary
- share information and learn from other team members
- communicate clearly with others.

If a team is working effectively it will:

- complete the required work on time and to a good standard
- be able to learn new skills and techniques easily
- communicate well within the team
- motivate the team members to work harder and be successful
- work to achieve a common aim.

The working day is much less tiring and stressful for everyone if teams work well together.

Organising your own work

When to ask for help

Sometimes, particularly when starting a new job, you may not be sure what to do. Being uncertain about a task can result from:

- not being shown how to do it
- being unsure of the standard expected
- forgetting how to carry out a task
- being uncertain if you have sufficient time to carry out a task properly
- not knowing how to operate equipment necessary to complete the task.

Test yourself!

1 List four benefits of working in a team.

2 Name the two types of team.

3 Give an example of how working in a team can be better than working individually.

Remember!

If you keep asking for help at very frequent intervals, your team members and your supervisor may get fed up with you. Pay attention to help that you are given. Make notes so that you are sure what to do, and have them to hand for next time. Ask questions when the person is helping you, not after they have gone back to their own work. The more you carry out a task, the more confident and skilful you will become.

You need to ask for help whenever necessary, particularly at the start of a new job. If you do not, you could:

- waste materials and time carrying out the task incorrectly
- injure yourself or someone else
- produce a substandard item
- irritate other members of your team who then have to rectify your mistake.

In the restaurant

Paula had just started to work in the banqueting department of a large hotel. The Head Waiter asked her to lay up the tables in a function room for a buffet lunch service. Paula followed the procedures she was used to using in the restaurant where she worked before. She laid out the cutlery and glassware for each cover on the tables. She thought she had done this correctly, and was surprised when she ran out of the correct cutlery before finishing the lay-up. Instead of asking the Head Waiter for advice, she carried on using some non-matching items on the table. When it was nearly time for the customers to arrive, the Head Waiter came into the room and found Paula had laid up cutlery for the wrong menu. All the other food service staff had to rush into the room and put the lay-up right before the customers arrived. The Head Waiter was very cross that Paula had not asked for help as soon as she realised something was wrong.

Figure 3.5 The Head Waiter was very cross

You need to ask for help when:

- you are asked to do something you have not done before
- you are still uncertain about a task you have not carried out very often
- you cannot find something – and have had a thorough look for it
- you have not understood or remembered instructions you have received.

Helping others

Working in a team, you will be encouraged to help each other. Help is invaluable and your team members will always appreciate support. But remember that help should only be given if:

- the assistance has been asked for, or offered – people may get upset if others start to take over uninvited, thinking they are helping

- by helping, the problem will be solved, not made worse
- helping with one problem does not create another – by stopping to help, you may not be able to finish your own preparations on time.

In the bar

Phil had to make 500 kir cocktails for a wedding party that afternoon. He was very proud of the cocktails he could make – the Head Barman said they were some of the best he had tasted. He was running short of time to finish them, but working as fast as he could. Mike decided to help him and started to pour in the blackcurrant liqueur. He did not ask Phil for the correct amount to use in each one. He poured in the ingredient quickly without measuring, as he didn't think there was time to bother with being precise. As a result, there wasn't enough liqueur for all the glasses. Phil had to pour blackcurrant liqueur from one glass to another many times to even up the amounts. This made the glasses very sticky and messy. Phil was very cross with Mike for interfering and spoiling the high quality of his work. Mike could not understand why Phil was so cross – he thought Phil should have been grateful for the help!

Figure 3.6 Why was Phil cross with Mike?

Using your work time effectively

When working in a restaurant, you must have very precise time management. Every food service operation may have up to three deadlines each day – breakfast, lunch and dinner. Customers will not accept any excuse if their food is not served promptly – they will go elsewhere to eat, and probably not come back to your outlet again.

Especially when starting work in a new food service area, or at new premises, you need to be very well organised. To be able to manage your time effectively you must:

- plan out your time to schedule the order of your work
- assemble all the equipment you will need before you start the job
- fill in 'gap' times, when waiting for customers to arrive, with other tasks
- clear and clean as you go – include time for this on your work plan
- include a break in your plan at a suitable time.

Organising your work area

To be able to work efficiently, you must be organised. Part of being organised is planning ahead to make sure you have everything you need for a job before you start. You also need to position the items you are going to use sensibly on your work area.

○ Leave yourself sufficient space to carry out the task.

○ Avoid cluttering your work space with any equipment you are not going to use.

○ Use any shelves that may be above or below your work area. Do not overload shelves or position anything on them that might fall off easily.

○ Include waste bowls or trays on your list of equipment. They should be big enough to hold waste food and paper without overflowing. They should not be so big that they take up too much space on the worktop and cramp the work area.

○ If working with high-risk foods, avoid any risk of contaminating any of the items.

○ Make sure you can work in a safe manner so that you do not endanger either yourself or others (see Chapter 2 Health and safety).

Figure 3.8 In which area could you work more efficiently?

Try this!

At work on a fairly quiet day, test how organised you are!

While you carry out one of your routine preparation jobs, make a note of how many times you have to leave your workplace to fetch items you have forgotten. Time yourself from when you start to get ready until the task is finished.

The next time you have the same job to do, take a few minutes to write out all the supplies and equipment you will need, then get them ready. Time yourself from the start of assembling the equipment to the end of the job, and see if you have saved any time – you should have!

Test yourself!

1 You have been asked to position tables and chairs for a formal dinner in a 'horseshoe' arrangement. You do not understand this term. Should you:

   a ask for help?

   b lay the tables out as you think might be correct?

   c position the tables as they are usually laid out?

   d leave the area in search of a textbook?

2 When starting the lay-up procedure for lunch service, do you:

   a start with the first task on the list and work your way through to the last?

   b start with the most difficult and leave the easiest until last?

   c pick the one you enjoy most to do first, leaving the others until later?

   d decide in advance which is going to take the longest and start with that task, working out a time plan to include the others?

3 You find that you have had to go back to the stores several times for ingredients and equipment for your current task. You could save time and energy by:

   a assembling all the ingredients and equipment together at the start

   b leaving that task until the end of the day, next time

   c asking someone else to collect the items you had forgotten

   d requesting your work area to be moved nearer to the stores.

Supporting the work of your team

To be able to work together as a team, it is important that members:

○ each carry out a fair share of the workload
○ all work to the same standard
○ show consideration to each other
○ communicate effectively with one another.

Figure 3.9 Should these waiters be at work?

Unfair work practices

One problem that can occur when people work in teams is unfair working. Everyone in a team is expected to contribute fairly to the workload of the team. In a food service area there is no choice about how much preparation work has to be completed before service – it all has to be done, otherwise the meal service will be affected.

The reason someone may not be pulling their weight in a team at work could be:

○ they are new at the job and cannot work at the necessary speed yet
○ they are not feeling well
○ they have personal problems, which are affecting their performance at work
○ they are tired
○ they are lazy
○ they are not keen or interested in their job.

New staff members are usually given a period of induction and training when they start a new job. They are not often given a full workload to complete. If they are struggling, the team leader should notice this and assign another team member to help them until they can cope.

Staff who are not feeling well should not come to work. They should contact their employer as soon as possible. This is particularly the case with those employees whose jobs involve handling and serving food. Their illness could be transmitted through the food to other staff or customers (see pages 144–145).

Sometimes staff come to work because they do not want to let their other team members down. If this is the case, the team leader should either send them home or transfer them to duties not involving food handling or serving until they feel better.

Many people have to deal with personal problems outside work. Sometimes this can affect their performance at work. If this is the case, the poorly performing person should be encouraged to see their team leader or someone either at work or outside with whom they can talk about their problem. If nothing is done to help, the person could end up losing their job – which would be an additional problem for them to deal with.

Working in food service is a tiring job (see pages 139–144). If those employed in the industry do not look after themselves properly, they will not be able to continue to do their job well. This can cause them to be persistently late or careless and slow in their tasks. After a while, the rest of their team will not continue to tolerate this.

In the restaurant

Tom started a new job in a busy restaurant. He worked in the main bar area with two other bar staff. Tom found the work quite hard. He was very tired when he got home at the end of his shift, but he still enjoyed going out with his friends after work. Most nights he went out and did not come back until well after 4 a.m. After a few days, he started being late for work. Tom kept oversleeping. At first, the two other bar staff helped him catch up with his preparation so that he was ready for service. Tom liked the help. It meant it didn't really matter if he was late. A couple of weeks went by, then the two other bar staff stopped helping Tom. This meant that Tom could not finish his tasks preparing the bar in time for service. He got into trouble with the Bar Manager and received a formal warning for being persistently late for work.

Why did the two other bar staff help Tom at first? Why did they stop helping him?

Being reliable and considerate to your other team members is very important.

There are also people who do not pull their weight at work because they are not really interested in the job they do. This situation may result in staff:
o being noisy
o being thoughtless
o being inconsiderate
o being annoying
o being careless
o taking shortcuts
o producing work of a poor standard.

This affects other members of the team in a bad way.

Consideration to other team members

Occasionally, members of a team do not get on together or with the team leader, for a variety of reasons. These may include:

○ a personality clash
○ members of the team having different standards and principles
○ individuals not accepting criticism very well.

It may take some time for frictions in a team to settle down. As long as all the team members are considerate and motivated, this should happen eventually. A positive attitude is required from everyone concerned.

Figure 3.10 The wrong way to deal with a problem

Try this!

Beverley had been working in the restaurant for ten years. She enjoyed her job and knew she was very good at it. She maintained high standards, and expected other people to do the same. Beverley did not tolerate fools gladly and she could be very impatient.

Rob started working in the restaurant. It was his first full-time job after completing his college catering course. He did very well at college and won a prize for achievement. He knew he could be very good at his job, and expected to be promoted very soon. Rob did not agree with some of Beverley's work practices. He told her some of the things she was doing were wrong. This infuriated Beverley. She started to resent Rob and felt that she was being made to look foolish in front of the rest of the staff. One day the Restaurant Manager asked Rob to serve the wine at a table of very important guests. Rob collected the wine from the dispense bar, presented it to the customer and started to open it. The cork slipped down into the bottle of wine. Rob was not sure what to do and asked Beverley. Beverley took great delight in telling Rob in a very loud voice that he had ruined the wine and should have known better than to push the cork down into the bottle. She reminded him that there was no more of that particular wine left and told him he would just have sort the problem out himself. Rob swore at Beverley and stormed out of the restaurant.

What approach did Rob have that upset Beverley?

What approach did Beverley have that upset Rob?

If you were the Restaurant Manager, how would you put this situation right?

Figure 3.11 The right way to deal with a problem

Remember!

Never:
○ be rude or swear at anyone
○ be malicious or spiteful
○ take people for granted
○ let your standards slip.

Always:
○ show respect for others
○ be enthusiastic
○ be helpful
○ listen carefully to others.

Communication skills

Being able to work well as a team is possible only if you communicate well. This does not just mean talking to each other. Communication can take different forms, including:

- talking face-to-face
- speaking on the phone
- sending an email
- sending a text message
- writing a message or letter
- body language.

Most communication in the restaurant involves speaking and body language. However, sometimes there is a need to write things down – food and drink orders, stock requisitions, messages for other members of staff.

Talking face-to-face is the most effective method of communication, as both people can see the expressions on each other's faces as well as hear what they are saying. This helps them understand better.

How to communicate effectively

Most people do not listen carefully to what is being said to them. This is where many problems occur. The best way to find out if someone has understood what you have said is to ask them a question about it. Alternatively, you could ask them to repeat back what you have said to them. If you have been telling them how to do something, you could ask them to do it for you.

The catering and hospitality industry is international. You may have to communicate with someone who does not speak the same language as yourself. To ensure they understand what you are trying to say to them you may need to:

- show them what you mean
- draw a picture to help you explain
- get someone who speaks both languages to help you.

Using the phone at work

Speaking on the phone is something we are all used to at home. At work, communication must be precise and accurate. The phone is used at work because you can receive an instant response to a question from someone who is not in the same area.

Figure 3.12 Listen carefully and be precise

When speaking on the phone, you must remember:

- to speak clearly
- not to speak too quickly
- to announce yourself and your position when you answer
- to smile as you speak (it does make a difference!)
- to write down any important information you are given
- to **repeat back** to the caller any important information to ensure it is accurate – particularly important with telephone numbers and menu descriptions and prices, for example.

Always keep a record of the:

- name of the caller
- time of the call
- date of the call
- contact number to return the call.

Sending an email

Sending a business email should be similar to writing a business letter. These are some of the informal rules to observe:

- do not abbreviate or use slang expressions or text language
- always read over the message before you send it, to check it makes sense
- never use all capitals – IT LOOKS AS THOUGH YOU ARE SHOUTING!
- always use a greeting, such as 'Dear Mr Phillips'.

In a food service environment, emails may be sent internally to:

- different departments, about guest requests
- departmental managers, about staffing arrangements and new procedures

or externally to:

- suppliers, about orders
- potential suppliers, asking for prices and delivery information
- service companies, to arrange for engineers to call.

Figure 3.13 Follow the informal rules when sending an email

Writing a message

It is very important when you prepare a message for someone else to read that you:

- write as clearly as possible – print if necessary
- double-check any names and numbers as you write them down
- sign the message with your name and the date and time you wrote it
- leave the message in a safe place, where you are sure it will be seen by the appropriate person as soon as possible.

Figure 3.14 Write messages carefully

Body language

Body language is the way people communicate with each other without using words – instead, they use gestures. It is done subconsciously, without you noticing. You must be aware of the effect body language can have. If you are trying to hide your feelings from someone, be very careful – body language never lies!

Body language differs from culture to culture. If you are working with people from other parts of the world, you need to be aware of this. Examples of this include:

o Japanese people greet each other by bowing very low
o Indian people may move their heads from side to side when they mean 'yes'.

Which method of communication is best to use?

It is important to know which form of communication is best to use on which occasion. As more ways of transmitting information are invented – such as email and text messages – choosing the best method can be difficult.

> **Try this!**
> **Choose the best method of communication for the following examples.**
> o **To get an order to a supplier for delivery the next morning.**
> o **To ask a member of staff to prepare a drink straight away.**
> o **To instruct a member of staff how to garnish a new cocktail.**
> o **To remind a member of staff to start work early the next day.**
>
> *Did your answers cover a range of communication methods? If your answers were exactly the same for each example, think carefully. Could any problem or confusion result from your choice of communication method? Would this affect the service to the customer? Could others in the kitchen have to work harder to put the problem right?*

What do all these situations have in common?

o The Restaurant Manager tells you the new prices for some of the dishes on the menu.
o The wine supplier tells you the new telephone number to be used to place orders.
o The Restaurant Manager asks you to provide a list of the items you need to prepare for the service next week.
o The beer supplier gives you the website address where the up-to-date prices can be found.

○ The Restaurant Manager asks you to submit the hours that you worked last week.

○ You need to carry out the weekly mineral stock-take in the bar.

Each of the six tasks above needs to be recorded in writing. This may involve:

○ typing on a computer
○ filling in a form
○ writing in a notebook
○ jotting down information on a piece of paper.

To be able to carry out all these tasks accurately, it is important to write information down for both yourself and others to use in the future.

Test yourself!

Complete the sentences.

1 Sometimes, members of a team may not _____ _____ _____ because they have personal problems at home.

2 Never:
   ○ be rude or _____ at anyone
   ○ be malicious or _____
   ○ take _____ for granted
   ○ let your standards _____.

3 Always:
   ○ show _____ for others
   ○ be _____
   ○ be _____
   ○ _____ carefully to others.

4 Complete these guidelines for recording a message:
   ○ _____ as clearly as possible – _____ if necessary.
   ○ Double-check any _____ and _____ as you write them down.
   ○ _____ the message with your _____ and the _____ and _____ you wrote it.
   ○ _____ the message in a _____ _____ where you are sure it will be _____ by the appropriate person as soon as possible.

Contributing to your own development

How improving yourself helps your team

As you become settled in your job, you may wish to improve your skills and abilities. This may help you to get promoted in your workplace. It may also enable you to move employment and get a better-paid and more challenging job in the future.

The ways that you can develop your skills and abilities include:

○ attending college on a part-time or full-time basis
○ going on short training courses from your workplace
○ working alongside very skilled craftspeople.

If you improve your own skills and abilities, this will also help your team. The advantages include:

○ productivity for the whole team may improve
○ you can share your skills with your team mates
○ everyone may become more motivated and creative as a result
○ the reputation of the whole team will be improved.

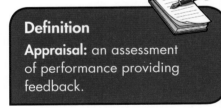

Definition
Appraisal: an assessment of performance providing feedback.

Feedback from others

Feedback is defined as 'information provided about the quality or success of something'. In the workplace, feedback usually takes the form of:

○ customer opinion about the quality of a meal (often from a customer service questionnaire)
○ the result of an **appraisal** of an employee by a supervisor or manager.

Figure 3.15 Feedback may be the result of an appraisal

Feedback will often result in a change or reward, for example:

○ a negative customer comment about a dish may mean it is removed from the menu

○ a positive appraisal may mean an employee is considered for promotion.

Developing and using a learning plan

A learning plan is a useful way of organising your development. As you progress in your job, you may improve your skills and abilities on a formal basis – such as a college course. You may also learn different skills in your everyday work.

A learning plan can help you in two ways:

○ it can help you to plan out a career path

○ it can help you organise any formal learning you are undertaking.

Planning out a career path

If you are ambitious and want to own your own catering business or manage a large food service operation, you will need a high level of technical knowledge as well as good business and management skills. To obtain these skills, you may need to study several courses. A learning plan will help you map these out so that you take the right courses in the most suitable order – either full-time or part-time. You need to match these courses with appropriate jobs at the right level to help you develop your skills.

It is useful to have the help of a careers advisor when using a learning plan in this way.

Formal learning

If you are already studying a course, a formal learning plan can be very useful. It will:

○ help you order the reading and coursework that you need to complete

○ allow you to set realistic targets to achieve these stages in your studying

○ help to train you in time management

○ help you to keep your learning on track so that you can achieve your ambition.

What you need to set up a formal learning plan

You will need a diary and a notebook. In the notebook you will need to record:

o your long-term aims – what you want to achieve finally
o your short-term aims – the achievements you need to fulfil your long-term aims
o the formal short-term aims that may be set for you by your workplace or college, such as passing your Personal Licenceholder examination, or completing a project on different types of beer.

In the diary, set yourself some realistic target dates such as:

o the date you have to take your Personal Licenceholder examination
o the date by which you should start revising for the examination
o the date you should hand in your project
o a series of dates by which you should have various sections of your project researched, prepared and produced.

By planning your learning in this way, you are giving yourself the best chance of fulfilling all your ambitions. You are also demonstrating to your employer and others that you can be organised, conscientious, focused and reliable. By completing the learning experiences, you will acquire knowledge and skills that will help you later in life.

Test yourself!

1 Name three ways in which you could improve your work performance and further your career.

2 What could happen if you had a bad appraisal interview with your manager?

3 What do you need to set up a formal learning plan?

4 Providing customer service

In this chapter you will cover skills and knowledge in the following units:

- 7132 – Unit 103 (1Gen3): Maintain customer care
- 7132 – Unit 201 (2Gen1): Give customers a positive impression of yourself and your organisation
- 7091 – Unit 253: Giving customers a positive impression
- 7103 – Part of Unit 104: Legislation in food and beverage service; and part of Unit 106: Introduction to personal workplace skills
- 7103 – Part of Unit 204: Legislation in food and beverage service; and part of Unit 211: Principles of customer service in hospitality, leisure, travel and tourism

Working through this chapter could also provide evidence for the following Functional Skills at Levels 1 and 2:

Functional English – Speaking, listening and communication Level 1 & 2

Functional English – Writing documents to communicate information

In this chapter you will learn how to:

- create a positive impression
- establish effective relationships with customers
- respond appropriately to customers
- communicate information to customers

Creating a positive impression

One of the most important parts of looking after customers in a food service situation is the welcome they receive at the door of the establishment. The first impression that a customer has lasts a very long time. If they are disappointed by the greeting they receive at the entrance to a restaurant, customers will look very carefully at their surroundings, food and service to see if these aspects may not be very good either. A positive greeting can encourage your guests to relax and start to enjoy themselves. Customers will sense that they will be well looked after, and will not worry that something will go wrong.

Figure 4.1 A warm welcome is very important

There are many different types of food service operation – and all of them involve dealing with customers. If you are the restaurant manager of a top-class establishment in London, you will be expected to have impeccable personal presentation and excellent social skills, and to be able to provide faultless service to celebrities, VIPs and the general public. If you are a food service assistant behind a counter in a motorway service station, you will need to be clean and smart in appearance, have good manners, be very polite and have plenty of patience. The members of the public you will be serving will be hungry, thirsty, tired and uncomfortable after travelling long distances.

Did you know?

A VIP is a 'very important person' who needs tactful and diplomatic service at all times.

Did you know?

Motorway service stations have to be open 24 hours a day, every day of the year.

How can you create a good impression when first meeting customers?

A genuine smile

If you smile at someone, usually they will smile back. Smiling makes everyone feel better. Remember – when you smile, you should be able to reveal a set of shining white teeth. If you do not look after your teeth and mouth you will not be able to do this. You need to keep your teeth clean and your breath fresh.

Figure 4.2 A genuine smile makes your voice sound sincere

A neat uniform

Most food service staff are issued with a uniform, or asked to wear clothing of a certain style and colour when at work (see page 8).
It is important that all clothing worn for work is:

- clean (no marks or stains; fresh-smelling)
- well pressed (not crumpled; ironed after washing)
- in a good state of repair (no buttons missing, frayed collar, hem hanging down)

Remember to check your uniform in plenty of time before you need to wear it again so that you can make sure it is in the best condition.

You also need to wear your uniform with pride so that your posture is upright and confident.

A clear speaking voice

If you are used to speaking mostly to your friends and family, you may find that you need to speak differently to members of the public. People may not be able to understand you if you mumble and run your words together, which a lot of families and close friends do when chatting together. You may also be using slang expressions, which the general public may not understand or appreciate. If you cannot be understood by customers, confusion and bad feeling can result on both sides.

It is always possible that customers arriving at the door of the restaurant may not be from the same country as you. They may have trouble understanding the local language. In various parts of the country, people pronounce words in different ways, and also use different names and expressions. Visitors to the area may not understand these terms.

Remember!
You need to be polite and courteous at all times.

Did you know?
People in Scotland and Ireland call a 'turnip' the vegetable that English people term a 'swede'.

You may have come from a different country to work in the restaurant. You may speak with quite a strong accent, which your customers may not be able to understand at first. It is important that you speak clearly, and not too quickly, particularly when speaking for the first time to people you do not know. Be careful to use words that can be understood easily by everyone.

If a customer does not understand what you are talking about, try to use as many visual guides as you can to help. If you are taking a food order, you may need to show them your order pad and pen to indicate what you are trying to do. Referring to photographs of dishes and bringing samples of drinks to the table may also be helpful in this situation.

Positive body language

As well as greeting your customers enthusiastically and giving a generous smile, you must also make sure that you welcome them with your body posture as well (see page 95). You may be giving out signals to people indicating that you do not really want to see them, without realising it. Be careful – your body never lies! Non-verbal communication is as important as verbal communication. When greeting your customers, make sure that you:

- make eye contact with them (don't look above or past them)
- turn and face them fully as you meet them (that way they know you really want to speak to them, and if they lip-read they can understand what you are saying)
- use your arms to encourage guests into the area (do not hold your arms across your body).

Remember!
If you have non-English-speakers arriving at your establishment, they will appreciate it if you can find a member of staff who can speak to them in a language they can understand.

Find out!
Keep an up-to-date note of all the languages spoken where you work, with the names of who can speak them.

Find out!
Do you know any ingredients that have more than one name?

Remember!
People who are hard of hearing can understand what you are saying more easily if you speak clearly while looking directly at them, so that they can use lip-reading to help them.

Remember!
When dealing with customers, or waiting to serve or clear the next course, you should never:
o play with your hair
o look at your watch
o yawn
o bite your nails
o fidget with your jewellery
o sneeze without using a handkerchief.

Figure 4.3 Staff appearance and behaviour is all-important

Did you know?
Lip-reading is a technique of being able to identify spoken words by looking at the shapes made by the mouth of the person who is talking.

Body language is the way people communicate with each other without using words – instead, they use gestures. It is done subconsciously, without you noticing. If you are trying to hide your feelings from someone, be very careful – body language never lies!

Try this!
Look at the faces below and decide what feeling or mood you understand from each one. Note that the only features that change are the eyebrows and mouth, which shows how expressive they are.

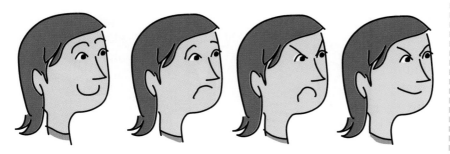

Figure 4.4 Facial body language

Try this!
Look at the stick people below, and decide what they are saying from the movements of their bodies. You can be quite sure of their meaning – but remember, no words are being spoken.

Figure 4.5 Body language can speak louder than words

Definition
Body language: communication that takes place between people from the movements of their body and facial expressions.

Try this!
Ask a friend to cover their ears so they cannot hear. Stand directly in front of them, and describe an item from a menu to them. Then ask them to repeat back to you what you said.

Did you know?
Out of what we communicate to each other:

o 70% is transmitted by body language
o 20% by tone of voice
o 10% the words that we use!

Figure 4.6 Look at how the body language matches the greeting here

97

In the restaurant

Prasad is busy taking an order from a seated guest when another customer comes up to him. If he continues taking the order, the second customer will think they are being ignored and start to feel angry. If he completely stops what he is doing and gives them all his attention, the first guest whose order he is taking will be the one feeling ignored and angry. He can't win! Or can he?

He needs to acknowledge the second customer in some way – by looking up and smiling at them, for example. It may be appropriate to say 'please take a seat and I'll be with you in a moment', and then return to the first guest. He should apologise to them for the interruption, and finish taking their order. The second guest will know that he has noticed them and will give them his full attention as soon as he can. They will wait more patiently and feel happier.

Be careful – if you do not deal with waiting customers in the correct order they can get upset very quickly.

Figure 4.7 Always deal with customers in the correct order

What is the best greeting for customers?

What you say when you first meet a customer may vary. If you are greeting them as they come through the door, you may wish to welcome them to the restaurant. It is always best to start with 'Good morning, afternoon or evening' as appropriate. You should use the terms 'Sir' and 'Madam' if you do not know the names of the guests. You may need to find out if there is a table reserved in advance for the customers. To do this, you will have to ask for the name in which the booking has been made. From then on you can address this person by their name – 'Mr Smith', for example. Some establishments will ask you to find out and then use the name of the guests, even if they have not made a prior reservation. If you think you will not remember the name of the customer, you need to keep a note of it on your order pad with the table number.

> **Remember!**
> Never use the first name of a customer unless they expressly ask you to.

Receiving a group of people

When you are receiving a group of people who will be sitting together, you need to check how many people are in the party so you can seat them at a table of the appropriate size with the correct number of seats. Some customers may prefer a particular table, for example in the corner or by a window. If their visit to the restaurant is for a particular occasion, customers may have made special arrangements for their meal. There may be a cake with candles provided if it is a birthday party; place-cards put out in advance to indicate where people should sit; particular table decorations such as balloons, candles and photographs may have been supplied in advance. It is very important that these customers are seated at the correct table! Even if a party has pre-booked, it is advisable to check the number of guests arriving – the final number can often change at the last minute and the table layout may need adjusting.

Marcus says

Communication is the key to good customer service. Make sure you understand the needs of each guest and then share this information with the relevant members of the team. Mistakes can always happen but handling them well and finding solutions can often result in very satisfied and loyal guests.

Receiving single diners

People eating on their own should be treated carefully. They should be offered a table at the side of the restaurant rather than in the centre, where they may feel vulnerable. If they are dining alone they may have brought a book or newspaper to read, and space should be made for this on their table. People dining alone also may want to chat to you. It is important to converse politely with them, but not for so long as to affect the service you offer both them and the other diners. You may need to excuse yourself occasionally so that you do not neglect the other customers.

Figure 4.8 A single diner should be looked after carefully

Receiving guests in other situations

If you are working in a hotel serving breakfast, it may be appropriate to greet your guest with a cheery 'Good morning' (Sir, Madam or their name if possible), and then ask 'Did you sleep well?' as you guide them to their table. If they mention to you that their sleep was disturbed in some way connected to the hotel, it is important that you let your supervisor know. Such problems could include noise from the hotel corridors, a rattling air-conditioning system, or disturbance from an adjoining room. If this information is passed on to your supervisor and then to the appropriate manager in the hotel, the problem can be investigated so future customers are not disturbed in the same way.

Did you know?

Any comments about food, service or surroundings made to you by customers are termed 'feedback'. Many establishments like to know about any type of feedback – both good and bad – so that they can improve the experience for their customers and encourage them to return.

99

If you are seating customers at a table and you get the impression that they are not very comfortable, ask them if they are happy where they are sitting. You may get the impression they are not comfortable if they take a while to get settled when they sit down. They may keep moving the chairs to slightly different positions at the table, and look around at other tables to see if they appear more suitable. As long as you have a spare table, suggest they might prefer to move to an alternative. Even if they do not move, they will be happy to have been offered the choice and will appreciate your concern. (For the importance of body language, see page 97.)

Figure 4.9 As long as you have a spare table, offer customers the opportunity to move

If you are meeting customers for the first time, and they have already been seated by another member of staff, you would greet them according to the time of day and then follow your organisation's policy. This could include introducing yourself to them, and involve you explaining how the service is organised. You may have to invite the guests to go over to a buffet and collect their choices of food themselves. If a buffet service is not involved, you will need to offer the menu to the customers and describe any special dishes that are on offer during that particular service. Do be very careful to get the detail of the ingredients in the dishes correct – customers will not be pleased if they order an item and then find it contains something that they don't like, or – even worse – to which they are allergic! (See Helping your customers decide, pages 102–103.)

Figure 4.10 Always make sure you are accurate when taking an order

The wow! factor

If the customers have visited the restaurant before, it is always very impressive if you can greet them by name – e.g. 'Good evening Mr and Mrs Patel, how nice to see you again.' Your customers will also be impressed by your attention to detail if you are able to remember their preferred choice of **aperitif**, food or wine. The effect

> **Definition**
> **Aperitif:** a drink served either in a bar or restaurant before a meal is served.

created by giving the customer this type of service is sometimes called the 'wow!' factor, as it gives them a pleasant surprise. Some organisations keep records of customers' preferences to remind staff and enable them to impress customers in this way.

> ### Try this!
>
> **With your work colleagues, make a list of your regular customers, and between you try to remember as much as you can about them. This may include their favourite table, preferred meal, usual drink, common topics of conversation, or aspects of the food and service they have commented about in the past.**

The best time to take the order

It is usual to offer guests a drink as soon as they sit down at a table for service. This often takes place just after the greeting, and the first order should be taken from a female in the party, if appropriate. Make sure you approach the table with the correct items ready to take a drinks order, and ensure you know the range of drinks on offer (the beers on draught, the range of fruit juices available, and so on). You must know if any of the items are out of stock before you take the order. The customer will not get a good impression if you have to return to the table after taking the order to tell them they cannot have their choice. If you are not sure you will remember which items are out of stock, or the selections available, write them down on a notepad that you keep with you during the order-taking process. After a while, you should find that you are able to remember this information without having to refer to your notes.

Figure 4.11 Make sure you find out all the choices available in advance

> ### Remember!
> When taking an order, if a particular dish will take longer than the others to prepare, make sure the guest is aware of this. If the restaurant is very busy and the food is taking longer to come out of the kitchen than usual, let the customer know that there could be a slight delay.

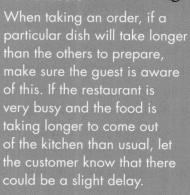

Guests will need time to look at the menu and make a decision – but not too long! Read their body language to see if they could be ready to order. When you have been working in food service for a while, you should be able to tell when your customers have made a decision. They often put the menus down on the table and may settle back in their seats a little. They will either start chatting with the other members of their party, or look around the restaurant to see what is happening around them. At that point it would be appropriate to go up to the table to find out if they are ready to order. Be careful not to interrupt if they are talking, wait patiently at the side of the host or organiser of the party until the conversation has finished. If you have another urgent task to carry out, it may be necessary to leave the table for a few more minutes so that you have time to take the order carefully. Rushing this key process may lead to mistakes being made, which could cause problems later on in the service.

Figure 4.12 Don't leave customers too long before taking their order

Figure 4.13 Is it appropriate to take the order at this table now?

Taking a wine order

If the restaurant has a licence to serve alcohol, there may be a wine list to present. It is sometimes quite difficult to decide to whom the wine list should be offered. The wine list should be presented to the organiser of the party, or the person who made the booking. They may choose to pass the wine list on to another member of the party. It is important to remember to present the wine for service and tasting to the person who placed the order.

Helping your customers decide

Many customers know exactly what they want to order from the menu. Guests may have a favourite dish, or they may have been to the restaurant before and have decided in advance what they would like to eat and drink. Sometimes customers may have difficulty making a choice themselves, and ask for your help. To be able to advise customers you need to make sure that you:

○ know the ingredients, cooking methods and approximate preparation times of all the dishes on the menu
○ have up-to-date information about which dishes are still available and which have sold out
○ understand the basic guidelines of menu planning
○ are able to find out, or already know, the food likes and dislikes of the customer
○ can find out if the customer has any special considerations, for example they may have a limited time for their meal.

Remember!

If you can't answer a question about the menu, one of the members of staff on duty will be able to. Make sure you inform the customer that you will find out the answer for them, and ask your supervisor straightaway. If your supervisor is not available, ask the most suitable person you can find (such as the chef in the kitchen or the restaurant manager).

Did you know?

A well known fast-food business used to have a set service time for meals. If the meal was not provided within four minutes of the order being placed, the customer received the meal free of charge.

Some restaurants have 'daily specials' on the menu, and encourage their staff to sell them to the customers. These dishes consist of ingredients the chef wants to use up, and will make more profit for the organisation. It is important that you make your customers aware of these items by describing them in an appealing and accurate way. Take care not to 'push' these items too much when telling customers about the menu. If you keep mentioning them, your customers could become suspicious and be put off ordering them.

Working under pressure

In the catering industry there are three main mealtimes – breakfast, lunch and dinner. People also use coffee bars, tea shops and cafés for snacks and beverages at all times during the day. There will be plenty of occasions when food service staff have to deal with several customers all wanting attention at the same time. This requires skill and organisation – and, above all, professional customer service.

In some forms of food service, a great deal of coordination with the kitchen takes place. When a table service restaurant is very busy, each member of staff will have a series of tasks to complete that can involve a large number of customers. These tasks will all have to be completed within a very short period. The service involves the efficient transportation of food and drinks to customers. Both food and drink must be served while they are the correct temperature and at their best appearance. This can only be achieved if they are collected from the kitchen at exactly the time the items are ready, and served to the guests immediately. This takes very careful

Figure 4.14 The 'daily specials' board may display additional menu choices

timing and excellent teamwork between the staff in the kitchen and restaurant. Usually customers are served in the order in which they are seated in the restaurant, but sometimes this may not apply. Reasons for customers to be served out of order might include:

○ if a customer is slow to decide on their choice

○ if the dish chosen has a longer preparation time

○ if the kitchen staff have had a problem, such as a piece of equipment not working correctly

○ if the restaurant staff have had a problem, such as a dish being dropped in transportation.

Figure 4.15 In some forms of food service, a great deal of coordination with the kitchen takes place

If you find that you have a large number of customers to deal with suddenly, you may need to excuse yourself from the customer you are dealing with and contact your supervisor for some help. To stop briefly and ask for help in this way is much better than delaying all the customers waiting for service.

Figure 4.16 If you suddenly become very busy, call for help to avoid keeping customers waiting

It is sometimes difficult to remain polite and respectful to customers when you are very busy at work and have a large number of demanding guests. Every customer in the establishment expects good service and wants to feel they have received good value for money from their dining experience. They are not interested in how busy you might be with other guests, or any problems that may exist in the kitchen. Neither are they concerned about the other guests in the restaurant, who all want the same standard of food and service as themselves. It can be challenging to remaining calm, organised and polite in these circumstances, but there is no reason to be otherwise. Guests can become extremely upset if a member of staff is rude to them. Such actions can create a good deal of bad feeling, and having to deal with such an incident means that service is delayed even more for other customers.

Bidding farewell

It is very important to look after customers from their arrival through to their departure. Once a guest has finished their meal and paid their bill, it is easy to forget about them and concentrate on other customers. While the guest is unlikely to need as much attention at this stage of their visit, it is very important to continue to look after them. This could include such actions as getting their coats from the cloakroom as they start to leave the table; and opening the restaurant door for them to go through while wishing them 'goodnight' or 'goodbye' and hoping to see them again. Try to use their name in the farewell so that they feel you are treating them as an individual, not just another customer. Even if you are busy looking after another party of customers when some of your guests get up to leave, it is important that you acknowledge them, thank them for their custom and say goodbye to them. This is the last impression the customer takes away from a restaurant, and it will stay with them.

Figure 4.17 Always acknowledge customers who are leaving

Test yourself!

1 State three ways in which a customer can be made to feel welcome.

2 Two customers sitting at a table are having a serious discussion. You need to take their food order. What do you do?
   a Interrupt them by saying 'Excuse me, I have to take your order now'.
   b Ignore them for the next 20 minutes so they can finish talking.
   c Go up to the table and start coughing to gain their attention.
   d Observe them every few minutes to catch when they pause in conversation.

3 When you are dealing with a customer and another guest tries to attract your attention, you should ignore them: true or false?

Responding appropriately to customers

It is essential in customer service to be able to respond correctly and quickly to the needs of guests. This requires concentration, organisation, experience, and being able to interpret guests' behaviour. It is very important not to become distracted when delivering customer service. Distraction can be caused by:

○ members of staff who try to attract your attention not realising you are busy

○ other customers who may stop you and request immediate service

○ equipment such as the telephone ringing or buzzers from the kitchen indicating that food is ready to serve.

Some of these distractions, such as other customers and food being ready in the kitchen, are very important and may need immediate attention. You will need to decide if you can suspend your current task and deal with these issues, or whether you should pass word on to your colleagues or supervisor that these items need attention. This is known as **prioritisation**. Making the correct decision in these circumstances is not easy, and will only come from experience – each situation is different.

Try this!

Ganesh is a waiter in a popular restaurant on a busy Saturday night. He is on his way into the kitchen with an order he has just taken. A customer indicates that he would like to speak to him. Ganesh stops and the customer asks for a jug of water. Ganesh knows that if he does not get the order into the kitchen quickly, his customer will have longer to wait for his meal to be served. The bar, where he should go to collect a jug of water, is situated on the opposite side of the restaurant from the kitchen. What should he do?

Figure 4.18 What should Ganesh do?

Try this!

Paul is a waiter in a fashionable tapas bar. The Friday lunchtime service is very busy. He is about to collect a plate of hot food from the kitchen to take out to a customer. Joe, another waiter on duty, calls over to ask Paul to give him a hand putting some more clean plates into the hotplate. What should he do?

Figure 4.19 What should Paul do?

Try this!

Krishnan is a waiter in an ethnic restaurant, where dishes of food are taken from the kitchen to the customer's table and kept hot on heated stands. As he is coming out of the kitchen carrying a tray of three hot dishes, he trips. The meals spill out of the dishes over the tray. The restaurant is very busy, and Krishnan's customers have been waiting a long time for their meals. What should he do?

Figure 4.20 What should Krishnan do?

Try this!

Either stand and observe a service when you are not working, or arrange to eat a meal in a busy restaurant and see if you can spot customers' needs before the serving staff on duty. If any of the staff have to say 'no' to the customer (for example, if a dish is not available), notice if they manage to turn a negative into a positive by recommending something similar.

Anticipating guests' needs

One way of giving impressive customer service is by being able to provide service to the guest before they have to ask for it. This can greatly increase the 'wow!' factor (see pages 100–101). To be able to anticipate accurately, it is necessary to know your job thoroughly, be very organised, and be able to **empathise** with your guest. A simple example is when a person stops at a table to talk to some guests who they obviously know very well. If they continue talking for some time, it may be appropriate to offer the standing person a chair so that they are more comfortable. This may result in the person being asked to join the party, and could increase the sales in the restaurant!

Definition

To **empathise** is to be able to imagine that you are the guest and try to think what they will need next – before they do.

107

Try this!

A guest enters a restaurant from the street. Outside, it is raining heavily. The guest is wearing a very wet jacket and carrying a half-closed umbrella dripping with water. Pascal, the restaurant manager, is ready to greet her at the door. What would be the best action for Pascal to take first?

Figure 4.21 What should Pascal do?

Try this!

A mother with a baby in a pram and a toddler clinging on to her arm struggles into the self-service café. Selina is a food service assistant who is clearing and wiping tables. She is just about to go on her break. What should she do?

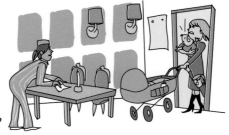

Figure 4.22 What should Selina do?

Timing of service

It is very important to be able to time the service of each table of guests correctly. A restaurant may be full of customers, and they may all have been served every course of their meal at exactly the same time intervals. If the customers were asked at the end of their meal if the timing had been appropriate, they probably would not all agree. This is because people eat out for a variety of reasons, such as:

○ celebration – birthday, anniversary, achievement
○ business – entertaining important clients, launching new products
○ social – getting to know each other better on a personal level
○ convenience – eating lunch when away from home, for example at work or shopping.

Due to these different reasons for dining, people want to spend different amounts of time in restaurants. A person leaving their workplace at lunchtime may only have half an hour available to eat, and will need quick service. A business meal has the topic of business as its priority, and has to be very carefully timed. No business customer will want to be interrupted in important discussions to be asked if they want their main course served. Neither will they want their guests kept waiting if they are ready for their dessert.

A celebration may be more relaxed, and the timing a little more flexible. If a party is having a meal and then moving on elsewhere to continue the evening, there may be a time constraint. Intimate tables of two people may prefer a long, leisurely service while the couple chat together, and they will not want to be rushed.

To gauge the timing of service required is quite a skill, and needs to be correct for the customers to enjoy their meal fully. It requires tactful questioning where appropriate, and very careful observation of body language (see pages 96–97). The cooperation of the kitchen in achieving the correct timing of service for all the courses is essential. Getting this type of timing correct improves with experience.

Figure 4.23 People eating at lunchtime may only have a very short time to eat

Try this!

Suggest the general speed of service required for the following types of customer, and give the reasons why:

- *a family with three young children eating out in the half-term holiday*
- *a group of elderly ladies out for lunch*
- *a company director taking a new client out for a meal*
- *a group of professional people out to celebrate a birthday, with taxis booked to take them home.*

Some catering establishments specialise in large groups of people eating together as part of an event. The event may be for business or pleasure. These functions require very careful timing of service to ensure the kitchen has all the food ready at the correct time. Each course is usually served to the whole party at the same time, so that all the guests can start and finish the meal together. This means the speed of service for the whole function can be affected by a delay in serving any one table. It is important that the service and clearing of each course starts at the same time on all the tables throughout the room. Some establishments with very large rooms use a system of traffic lights, so that all the staff can see when they should start serving or clearing the next course.

Figure 4.24 Large establishments may use a system of traffic lights

Understanding customers' needs

Most visitors to food service establishments are there because they want something to eat and drink. However, hunger and thirst may not be the main reason for coming to your premises. Think of the additional reasons your customers have for eating out. They could include:

○ meeting friends
○ passing by
○ attending a celebration/sporting event
○ visiting relations
○ staying away from home.

The reason for a customer's visit can affect their needs while you are looking after them.

> ### Try this!
> **What special considerations might the following customers appreciate when eating out?**
> ○ *A person visiting a sick relative in a nearby hospital.*
> ○ *A couple having a pre-theatre meal in the early evening.*
> ○ *A group of friends meeting up together after a long time.*
> ○ *A party celebrating a win at the races.*

You should be able to appreciate that there is a great deal involved in offering good customer service – more than just putting food and drink in front of the guest. Different customers have different priorities at different times.

Sometimes guests will make requests that seem rather strange. These might include:

○ wanting to eat their dessert with a teaspoon, even though it is served on a plate
○ having a large cup for their after-dinner coffee, rather than the traditional small **demi tasse**
○ asking for food to be served in a bowl, rather than on a plate.

All requests will be made for a reason, even if it may not be apparent at the time. Some reasons might be personal preference (e.g. eating dessert with a teaspoon). Other reasons might be more necessary – a partially sighted person can eat more easily from a bowl rather than a plate.

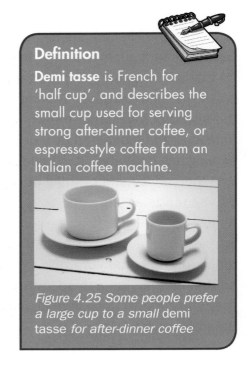

Definition

Demi tasse is French for 'half cup', and describes the small cup used for serving strong after-dinner coffee, or espresso-style coffee from an Italian coffee machine.

Figure 4.25 Some people prefer a large cup to a small demi tasse *for after-dinner coffee*

Serving children

Many restaurants in the UK are criticised for how children are looked after when families visit them for a meal. When eating outside the home, children have different needs, according to their age and background.

Babies and infants

Figure 4.26 It is important to serve families with children as quickly as possible

These children will not be very mobile, and will be unlikely to eat even a half-sized portion of food. They may eat food brought with them by their parents, or your establishment may provide baby food. The range of baby food available is unlikely to be on the menu, and you will need to find out what can be provided by asking your supervisor or the chef. Your organisation should have suitable seating provided for young children – usually high chairs, which should be designed to prevent the child being able to climb or fall out of them. When providing a high chair for a child, always check that:

○ the chair and table fitment are very clean
○ the chair is correctly assembled.

There are health and safety issues involved in ensuring such equipment is safe: see page 252.

Toddlers and primary school-age children

This age range tend to be impatient and not want to sit still for very long. They are too big for high-chair seating, but may still be a little small for the standard chairs in the establishment. Your organisation may provide booster cushions or something similar to raise the height of the young person on their chair, so that they can reach the table to be able to eat their meal. These children are likely to have dishes from a children's menu, or your establishment may offer half portions from the full menu. Usually a parent will choose what the child has to eat. It is very important that children's meals are served as quickly as possible. This age group tend to feel hungry very quickly, and are also very impatient and easily distracted. If their meal does not arrive promptly, they may forget about eating and prefer to play. A toddler is unlikely to be able to sit still while the rest of their family eat a three-course meal. However, if they are allowed to run around the establishment they may cause an accident, hurting themselves and other guests or staff. Most restaurants that expect young children as guests have some entertainment for them. This usually takes the form of crayons, colouring books, jigsaw puzzles and other table toys. Games should be given to children when they are becoming restless (for example if there is a wait for the food to arrive), but will be most successful if given to the child when they have finished eating. Other points to remember when serving children include:

○ have extra napkins to hand

○ provide food on small plates

○ provide a teaspoon, and no other cutlery with which children could injure themselves

○ provide a plastic tumbler for the child to drink from, maybe with a straw

○ provide a bread roll or equivalent if the child has to wait for the food to be prepared.

Looking after people with disabilities

Under the Disability Discrimination Act 2005, it is illegal not to do the best you can to assist disabled people who arrive as customers at your establishment. You may also have colleagues working with you who have a disability of some sort. Remember – disabled people are not only those restricted to using a wheelchair to move around. Disabled people include:

○ those who are hard of hearing, partially sighted or blind

○ those who have a physical problem that limits them in moving around and using their arms and legs

○ those who have mental problems that affect how they communicate and live in society.

Wheelchair-users

Some people are able to get out of a wheelchair and sit on the chair provided. In this case, the wheelchair needs to be moved out of the way while the guest has their meal, and brought out for them when they are ready to leave. Other guests may be completely wheelchair-bound, and a clear space must be left at the table to allow them to manoeuvre the wheelchair

Figure 4.27 Wheelchair-users need plenty of space around them

into position, and to allow staff and guests to pass easily behind them. Remember, wheelchairs have handles, and some have wheels that are quite wide and take up a good deal of room. Other important points to remember include:

○ do not lean or hang onto a wheelchair

○ when talking to a person in a wheelchair, put yourself at their level – crouch or kneel down for short periods, or sit down if appropriate

○ do not assume wheelchair-users need pushing, but ask if they need any help – many wheelchair-users can manoeuvre themselves very well

○ do not leave a wheelchair in a busy area or on a slope, as the occupants could be pushed or knocked by other people or their bags – if a wheelchair is left on a sloping floor without the brake on, the result could be very unfortunate.

Partially sighted or blind people

Some guests may be able to see a little, others not at all. When dealing with people whose vision is poor, it is important to give them a commentary. This will include an introduction of who you are and how you are going to help them. Your commentary should also include:

○ where you are taking them in respect of steps, etc. – allow them to take your arm, but do not push or pull them

○ identifying yourself and anyone with you

○ when serving food, describing what and where the items are, in terms of a clock face

○ telling the guest about any hot plates as you put them on the table.

Figure 4.28 Always explain the menu fully to a blind or partially sighted person

Other physical disabilities

Some people may have limited movement in both arms and legs. Where this is severe, their enjoyment of a meal may be affected. If you have a guest who cannot hold a knife and fork to eat, or a glass to drink, you may need to offer some additional help. You will need to observe the guest very carefully at first, so that you can offer help tactfully. If they have a carer with them, in some circumstances it may be more appropriate to ask them what assistance the guest likes to have when dining out – but ensure that you don't talk over the disabled person as if they weren't there.

○ Check whether a disabled guest wants their food cutting up for them before you do so. Have it done in the kitchen, and recreate the shape of the dish as far as possible before it is served.

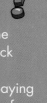

Did you know?

Describing the meal on the plate in the terms of a clock face can help blind and partially sighted guests. Saying such things as 'the breast of chicken is at 12 o'clock, the carrots at 3 o'clock and the chips at 7 o'clock' can enable the customer to eat their meal more easily.

- Have a supply of straws for people who may not be able to use cups and glasses conventionally. Be very careful with hot liquids – they feel much hotter if they are consumed through a straw.
- Position the side plate, glass, fork and spoon on the mobile side of the guest so they can reach them easily.
- Find out if the disabled person will be able to manage more easily with a bowl rather than a plate – or the other way round.
- Have a supply of paper napkins to hand in case of spillages, etc. Clear any used napkins promptly. It may be appropriate to provide a small basket to collect these in during the meal.
- Do not fill glasses more than one-third full, so the guest will not spill the contents when using them.

Make sure the carer who is with the disabled person has excellent service and needs to help the disabled person as little as possible during the meal – it may be the only time they get a break from these tasks.

Providing good quality of service

How happy a guest is when they leave your establishment will depend totally on how well their needs have been met. If you have been able to look after them really well, they will be very happy. Happy customers:
- tell a few friends, family and colleagues about their experience
- often return to repeat the experience
- spend more money at your establishment.

Unhappy customers:
- tell many friends, family and colleagues about their experience
- seldom return to the same place
- may refuse to pay for poor food and service.

Providing good quality of service will involve sticking to your own organisation's policy regarding specific standards of operation. These will vary from establishment to establishment. They could include:
- every new customer at the restaurant entrance should be greeted within 30 seconds of arriving
- no customer should wait more than two minutes to be served
- customers having coffee should be offered a 'top-up' at least twice.

Providing feedback to customers' comments

All responses from customers in respect of their time spent in the establishment are important and should be listened to carefully. Where customer feedback is good, it should be passed on to others – just as it should be if it is bad. A customer may make a passing remark on their way out at the end of their meal: 'Thank you, I enjoyed my meal very much', or they may say 'the service was rather slow this evening'. Both comments can be fed back to the appropriate person – one giving praise to encourage the staff who looked after that table, the other for investigation as to why the service had been slow to that particular table. By acting on initial comments in a positive way, systems and procedures should improve and hopefully the negative comments will not be received again.

It is also necessary to act in the same way about comments overheard between customers, such as: 'The toilets are round the corner but be careful, the floor is slippery' or 'It's difficult to see where to park in the car park, the lines are very faded'.

Try this!

In your establishment, how would you respond to the following comments?

○ *It was rather draughty where I was sitting.*
○ *The vegetables were rather cold this time.*
○ *I could have eaten a bit more than that!*
○ *It was rather dark in the corner where our table was.*
○ *The sauce with the chicken was very salty.*
○ *The wine was cold.*
○ *It was very noisy where we were sitting.*
○ *My wife was upset by the conversation on the next table.*

Some customers' comments may not be made verbally. As you become more experienced in your job, you should be able to spot happy and unhappy customers from the way they behave, before they say anything to you at all!

Figure 4.29 Unhappy...

Figure 4.30 ...and happy customers

Try this!

What impression would you gather about the following situations, and what might you do about each one?

o *The customers at a table keep looking around, trying to catch the eye of a member of staff.*
o *The customers have finished eating, but there is a large amount of food left on their plates.*
o *All the customers get up to leave the restaurant before the meal has finished.*
o *The customers are laughing and joking with each other and eating their meal.*
o *A customer asks for their jacket, which they wear while continuing with their meal.*
o *The host of a party is standing up, pouring wine for the rest of the party.*
o *A table of two people who obviously know each other very well are not speaking to each other.*

Providing accurate information

Accuracy is very important in food service. As well as the importance of giving accurate information to customers as part of quality service, it is also necessary to do this to stay within the law. There are four main areas of the law where accuracy is essential.

o Health and safety – you should not agree to carry out any unsafe practices that may endanger your customers, other members of staff or yourself. This might mean, for example, having to refuse a guest's request to light fireworks inside the restaurant as part of a birthday celebration.

o Weights and measures – if a glass of wine is offered to the customer, it should be served in a legal measure of either 125 or 175 ml – no other amount. A listing on a menu of a 12 oz rump steak indicates the raw weight prior to cooking, and it should be correct.

o Licensing regulations – a 16-year-old cannot buy an alcoholic drink with a meal in a restaurant. However, if they are accompanied by a person over the age of 18 who buys them a beer, cider or glass of wine, they are allowed to drink it with their meal.

o Trade descriptions – great care should be taken to describe the dishes on the menu accurately. If you describe a salmon dish as garnished with lobster mousse and the chef has changed it to a crab mousse, this is a mistake under the Trades Descriptions Act. Another breach of this Act would occur if you described sole fillets as fresh when they had been frozen.

Figure 4.31 You are responsible for helping keep your customers safe

- It is essential to have full knowledge of the menu on offer in your establishment, and what special requests can and cannot be met. If all the items are made on the premises, it is usually easier to prepare something different for a customer, such as leaving an ingredient out of a dish if requested.
- Particular care is needed when describing dishes to customers. It has always been important to describe them accurately, but in view of the increasing numbers of people allergic to certain ingredients, it is essential to know the composition of a dish. It would be most unfortunate if a customer became ill or even died as a result of having a dish misdescribed to them.

Find out!

Can you give the alternative names by which these items are known?

scallions   egg plant   zucchini   dhal (or daal)   okra

calabrese   maize   cilantro   papaya   pimento

Dealing with customer incidents

A variety of incidents may happen where you are working. Some may be caused by actions of the food service staff. Others may have nothing to do with either yourself or your workplace, but may affect the enjoyment of the customers who are dining there. In either case, they have to be dealt with quickly and carefully. It is important not to make the situation worse rather than better! For some incidents you will have guidelines set for you at work – but these will not be able to cover every eventuality.

When you have to deal with an incident of this sort, it is difficult to know what to do first. There can be quite a commotion and sometimes a variety of different people can become involved. The method of dealing with most incidents is as follows.

Identify any danger – this may involve:
- removing broken glass
- turning off any dangerous equipment
- removing any potentially dangerous items (such as knives) if necessary
- calling the emergency services.

Did you know?

Some people have a very violent reaction to eating peanuts, and can die in minutes. Although a dish may not include the nuts themselves, peanut oil may have been used in making the dish, or powder from the nuts may have come into contact with some of the other ingredients. This can happen in bakeries, and great care is needed with these items.

Remember!

Some ingredients have more than one name – peanuts are also called 'groundnuts', and you need to know both names when describing dishes to international guests.

Try this!

What would you do in the following situations?

o *You spill some sauce onto a customer's clothing as you are serving it to them.*

o *A customer knocks a glass onto the floor and it shatters over a wide area.*

o *A customer telephones to say they have lost an earring while dining in the restaurant earlier.*

o *The last customer to leave the restaurant finds that their coat, left in the cloakroom, has been taken by someone else and the remaining coat does not belong to them.*

o *A customer is taken ill in the restaurant.*

o *A fight between two drunken passers-by breaks out in the street just outside the restaurant window.*

o *A rather unkempt person, who is shouting loudly, enters the restaurant.*

o *A passer-by is sick just outside the restaurant entrance.*

o *A child runs into the restaurant from outside, screaming loudly.*

o *A nicely dressed couple enter the restaurant and announce to you they are from the Environmental Health Department.*

o *A customer who has had too much to drink is pestering another guest sitting at a different table.*

o *A female customer comes back from the toilets not having noticed the bottom of her dress at the back is caught up in her belt.*

Keep your customers comfortable and undisturbed as much as possible – this may involve:

o offering a damp, clean cloth to allow mopping of spillages on a customer's clothing

o covering up any evidence of spillage on the table with a napkin or tablecloth

o moving customers to another table

o temporarily closing or locking the restaurant door and leaving a member of staff on duty beside it

o seating a guest and taking details of lost property.

Dealing with unsafe incidents and security risks

If the incident involves issues of health and safety, you must deal with them very carefully. Under the Health and Safety at Work Act, you and your employer have a legal responsibility to keep customers, visitors and other members of staff safe in your workplace (see pages 40–42). Your organisation should have a health and safety accident procedure to follow in any situation where an accident has happened or an unsafe situation has occurred. This may involve filling in an accident form or writing a report (see page 56).

The types of incident that may happen in a food service situation could include:
○ a customer slipping over on a wet floor
○ a customer cutting their mouth by finding a sharp object in their food.

Figure 4.32 Accidents must be dealt with very carefully

In some areas, at certain times, it is necessary to pay particular attention to security alerts. Occasionally restaurants are targets for terrorist bomb attacks. Restaurants may also be targeted by thieves, and have cash and alcohol stolen from them. If you notice any unusual activity by customers or members of staff, it is important to report it to your supervisor (see page 69). This also applies to any bags of any sort which have been left unattended for any period of time. Your organisation should have a security procedure in which everyone should be trained, and which everyone should follow.

Remember!

When dealing with any type of incident:
○ remain calm, polite and helpful
○ get help as soon as possible if necessary
○ try and remember as much as possible about any serious incident and write notes down about it as soon as you can
○ if there was an accident involved, this record may take the form of an accident form (see page 56).

Dealing with drunken guests

People who have had too much to drink can be very disruptive. They can talk very loudly, lose control of their actions, and become angry very easily. When dealing with a guest you suspect is under the influence of alcohol, you should:
○ respond very quietly and politely to the guest
○ **not** argue with the drunken customer – even if they want to argue with you
○ get the help of a supervisor, preferably one who is the opposite sex to the drunken customer.

A drunken man may well become more aggressive if a male member of staff tries to deal with him. He tends to be more controllable if spoken to tactfully by a female member of staff. A woman who has too much to drink will usually respond better if dealt with carefully by a male member of staff.

Figure 4.33 People who have had too much to drink can be very disruptive

Dealing with unhappy customers

It is not always possible to keep all your customers happy all the time. It is highly likely you will have to deal with some unhappy customers at some stage. Your customers may be unhappy for a variety of reasons. You need to try and find out the cause of their disappointment as tactfully as you can. If at all possible, you must then try and make the situation better. Unfortunately, if a customer is unhappy while they are in your establishment – even if it is nothing to do with the restaurant – they will associate their unhappiness with the location and will be unlikely to return.

You can often tell if your customers are unhappy by how they behave, even if they do not say anything to you. Signs of unhappy customers might include the following.

Figure 4.34 Couples who do not talk to each other and look miserable

Figure 4.35 Customers not finishing the food on their plate

Figure 4.36 Customers looking around trying to gain the attention of a member of staff

Figure 4.37 Customers leaving the restaurant before they have finished their meal

Some customers' problems can be easily put right. If they are not happy with certain aspects of their meal experience, you should be able to remedy this quickly. By spotting a problem early and dealing with it effectively, you can turn an unhappy customer into a happy one. If this is done successfully, you may find you have returning guests who will tell others how well they were treated in having their concerns put right so quickly.

Sometimes customers may be rude or bad-tempered; they may have had too much to drink. They may have work or personal stresses that come out when they are talking to you. Even though a customer may be quite nasty and unpleasant to you, try not to take it personally. Many customer service staff look on their job as a form of acting. When they put on their uniform to start working, they take on a professional 'role'. This helps them to feel protected against personal comments, and they are able to be polite and pleasant no matter what the customers may say to them.

Formal complaint-handling

Sometimes you can't put a situation right, and the customer will remain unhappy. They may decide to make a complaint. There is a set approach to dealing with a customer complaint, and you will be told how to deal with the situation by your supervisor where you work. You may be able to give the customer a free drink, or replace a dish with which they are not happy. Some establishments always want any complaint to be handled by a supervisor.

Dealing with a complaint

○ Allow the customer to tell you why they are not happy. Do not interrupt. Make sure the customer can see that you are listening very carefully to what they are saying.

○ Say how sorry you are to hear that they aren't happy with the situation. Don't make excuses or blame another member of staff. Never argue with the customer. They are not happy, whatever the reason, and it is up to you to try and start to put the situation right.

○ Ask any questions necessary to clarify the situation. Try to keep these to a minimum or the customer may feel as if they are being interrogated. Keep calm and remain polite at all times.

> **Try this!**
> Which of the problems in Figures 4.34–4.37 do you think you could put right? How would you go about it? Remember – you may have to be very tactful and diplomatic in some cases. You may not be able to solve all of them – but at least you can try!

Use the customer's name if possible – if not then make sure you use 'Sir' or 'Madam'. Thank the customer for bringing the matter to your attention. This must be said with sincerity to show the customer you care about the situation.

o Ask the customer how they would like the situation put right. This may be something really straightforward and easy for you to do. If it is something you are not allowed to do, then you will need to get the help of your supervisor.

o Explain to the customer what you intend to do next in respect of their complaint. If you are going to pass the situation over to your supervisor, say what you are going to do, and why. If you are able to do what the customer has asked, then tell them so. Never offer to do or provide something you will not be able to. That will only make the situation worse. If you are offering a replacement dish, always check that it is available before you confirm to the customer that is what you are going to get for them.

o If there is any sort of delay in providing the promised replacement, make sure you keep the customer informed of progress – for example, 'your replacement main course will be ready in five minutes'. Once the dish has been re-served, make sure you check after a couple of minutes that it is satisfactory. If it is not, offer to change it again. Remember to provide fresh cutlery as necessary before serving the dish.

Find out!

Make sure you know the limits of your authority in the event of a customer issue. Are you entitled to:

o offer customers a free drink?
o offer customers free food?
o refund customers money off their bill?
o offer to pay for the dry cleaning of damaged customer clothing?

Test yourself!

1 How would you deal with a young child eating with their family in a restaurant?

2 What must you remember when looking after a wheelchair-bound customer?

3 Why might a customer ask for their meal to be served in a bowl?

4 How can you tell that a customer is unhappy (without asking them)?

5 List the main steps in handling a customer complaint.

Communicating information to customers

In your job, you will spend a good deal of time giving customers all types of information, from ingredients in a dish to directions to the toilets. How effectively are you able to do this? Do you leave customers confused and unhappy? Or are you able to communicate clearly and give the guests a really good impression of how helpful and professional you can be? You will know if you have given enough information to a customer by their reaction. If they smile, nod and thank you, then they are happy. If they frown and shake their head a little, or look fed up, then you need to help them further (see pages 96–97).

Handling customer enquiries

All questions asked by customers must be answered politely and clearly. If you have not heard or understood the question, you need to ask the guest to repeat their enquiry: 'Could you repeat your question please' or 'Would you mind saying that again please?' might be appropriate phrases. If you still cannot understand the guest after a second attempt, then you should ask them to wait a moment and ask a colleague or supervisor to help you. It is important to stay and listen to how the questions are answered, if you can, so that you will know what to say and do next time.

Figure 4.38 A customer may wish to arrange a special meal or plan a party to be held at your establishment

123

Sometimes a guest enquiry may be more complicated. A customer may wish to arrange a special meal or plan a party to be held at your establishment. If the question involves something you know needs another member of staff to answer, and may take a few moments to sort out, you need to let the guest know that this is the case. If the guest is able to wait, they should be seated in a convenient place and kept informed of what is happening until the member of staff who can help them has arrived. It may be the policy of the organisation where you work to offer them a complimentary drink while they are waiting. If they are not able to wait, then a name and telephone number should be taken and the guest should be contacted as soon as possible by the appropriate person.

> **Remember!**
> A **beverage** usually indicates a non-alcoholic drink, often hot, such as tea or coffee.

Dealing with different types of information

Confidential information

In some food service jobs, you may be serving customers in private situations. You may be serving a meal in the bedroom of a hotel, or attending to a celebrity in a private dining room. You may see actions or overhear conversations that are personal to the guests. In these situations, you have a duty of confidentiality to the guests and must not tell anyone what you have seen or heard. The only exception to this is if you are asked for information by the police. Such an enquiry will normally be made through your supervisor, and the member of the police must show you their identification.

> **Definition**
> **Confidential:** private or personal.

It may not be appropriate to divulge the names of other guests to enquirers. You need to be guided by the policy where you work. It is highly unlikely that you would be allowed to speak to members of the press or give out any information about guests at your establishment. Another aspect of confidentiality involves methods of payment. If, as part of your job, you have to deal with customers' credit cards, you are required to keep any knowledge of card numbers completely private. The same applies should you have occasion to notice a customer inputting their security number into a credit card-processing handset.

Figure 4.39 In some food service jobs you can be serving customers in private situations

Sometimes you may be asked questions about the performance of the business where you work. Owners of establishments that may compete with yours may send their staff or friends in to ask questions. They will try to find out information that may help them steal some of your customers. You may also be asked about security procedures – such as when cash is taken to the bank, or who holds the keys to the safe. You should not give out any information of this nature about your workplace to anyone. By doing so, you may help cause an incident of theft, fraud or loss of business, and could get into trouble. Be careful – it is easy to give out little bits of information in general conversation that can be pieced together to be used by people who wish to cause harm where you work.

Figure 4.40 Be careful – it's easy to give out little bits of information in general conversation

Non-confidential enquiries

It is a sign of good customer service if you can answer most questions a guest may ask, and be able to find out the answer to those you cannot. Customers can sometimes ask some quite unexpected questions, but usually they concern:

○ the facilities in the restaurant
○ local facilities
○ planning future visits to the restaurant.

It is essential that you are accurate in your answers.

Try this!

Test your knowledge of your workplace – can you answer all the following questions about it? If you can, well done! You know a great deal about where you work. Now test your colleagues to see if their knowledge is as good as yours. If you have not been able to answer all the questions, make sure you find out the answers you don't know as soon as you can.

o *What are the opening times of your establishment?*

o *What day(s) do you close (if any)?*

o *What type of food is served in your establishment?*

o *What type of menu is offered?*

o *What types of food service are available (e.g. buffet, silver service, gueridon)?*

o *What is the largest number of customers that can be seated around one table at your establishment?*

o *Are there any extra charges made when dining at your establishment?*

o *Which areas may guests need to be directed to in your establishment?*

o *How can a guest get a taxi home from your establishment?*

o *Where is the nearest place they can stay overnight?*

o *What are the local attractions in the area?*

o *How can guests arrange for a bouquet of flowers to be provided?*

o *Can your establishment provide a birthday cake?*

o *Can the guest have their table decorated with balloons?*

o *Does your establishment provide place cards? What about specially printed menus?*

o *Can your establishment be used by people in wheelchairs? What about Braille menus?*

o *Can your establishment provide baby food?*

o *Does your establishment have a high chair?*

o *Can your establishment cater for special diets?*

o *What types of credit card does your establishment accept?*

o *Can a guest pay by cheque at your establishment?*

Definition

Gueridon service means food partially prepared or cooked within the restaurant itself, on a little trolley table beside the guest's table.

Promoting facilities

Part of looking after customers may include encouraging them to use all the facilities available in your establishment. This may mean guiding guests to the bar area for a pre-dinner drink, or offering coffee in a separate lounge area at the end of their meal. If customers ask about bringing a number of guests with them, it may be appropriate to show them any private dining rooms or other function areas your establishment may have. In the summer, this may include patio or barbeque areas, gardens or marquees. Some restaurants also offer outside catering facilities, where meals can be served at the customer's choice of venue. Other establishments may offer a take-away service as well as dining '**in house**'.

If you work in a large establishment, such as a hotel, there may be a range of facilities you can promote in addition to food service. Your customers may be interested in seeing the decor in the guest bedrooms, the spa and leisure facilities, and any banqueting facilities.

Figure 4.41 It may be appropriate to show customers around your establishment

Definition

In house means on the premises.

How much can you help?

Even though you may be very keen to help a customer as much as you can, it is important to know when to hand a situation over to a colleague. Some questions may need decisions making that you should not take. In some organisations, all staff are trained to deal with most procedures; in larger operations, more tasks are allocated to specific members of staff. Depending on where you work, you may have to pass a guest's request on to a colleague if it involves such things as:

○ making a reservation
○ requesting a special dish
○ dealing with a complaint
○ dealing with a payment problem.

It is important to stay within the role of your job and deal with circumstances for which you have been trained, if at all possible.

Figure 4.42 You may have to pass a guest problem on to your supervisor

Keeping customers informed

It is very important to remember to tell customers about any situations that may affect them. You do not have to go into detail, and should not blame anyone for a situation. If a customer is likely to have to wait longer than expected for a dish to be served, they should be informed that there is a delay. If their request means that another member of staff has to become involved, they should be told to whom their enquiry is being passed on.

Remember – dealing with customers is an essential part of food service. If there were no customers, there would be no-one to serve the food to! You will find it easier to provide good customer service if you naturally enjoy talking to people and helping them. However, you can still be very good at customer service even if you are rather shy and quiet, as long as you have plenty of practice. Everyone can get better at their job by experience and observation – and the area of customer service is no exception.

Test yourself!

1   Give one example of confidential information that you may come across in your workplace.

2   Give an example of non-confidential information that you may come across in your workplace.

3   State five pieces of information you may need to provide for a customer visiting your establishment.

4   Name three occasions when it may not be possible to help a customer in your workplace.

Acknowledgements

This chapter has been completed with the assistance of:

Hayter, R. (1998) *Bar Service*. Macmillan, Basingstoke, in association with the Hospitality Training Foundation, Ealing, London.

Bullied, A., Ritchie, C. and Roberys, T. (1993) *Serving Food and Drink in the Bar*. Stanley Thornes, Cheltenham.

5

Food *safety*

In this chapter you will cover skills and knowledge in the following units:

- 7132 – Unit 204 (2Gen4): Maintain food safety when storing, holding and serving food
- 7091 – Unit 252: Food safety in catering
- 7103 – Unit 102: Food safety in catering; and part of Unit 104: Legislation in food and beverage service
- 7103 – Unit 202: Food safety in catering; and part of Unit 204: Legislation in food and beverage service

Working through this chapter could also provide evidence for the following Functional Skills at Level 2:

Functional ICT – Developing, presenting and communicating information – apply a range of editing, formatting and layout techniques to meet needs, including text, tables, graphics, charts, graphs or other digital content

In this chapter you will learn how to:

- identiify the causes of food poisoning and how to avoid it
- recognise good and bad practices in personal hygiene
- report and handle illnesses and infections
- identify correct cleaning procedures and practices
- identify pests and signs of infestations and describe correct pest management and control methods
- store items correctly and undertake stock control
- hold hot and cold food for service
- identify food safety procedures

Food poisoning

What is food poisoning?

If food is not stored, prepared and held correctly during service, it may become a **hazard**, and those who consume it may become very ill or may even die. This is why there are many laws and regulations controlling the provision of food. In the catering industry, this puts a great responsibility on all employees whose job involves food preparation and service.

Food poisoning is caused by eating food contaminated with harmful **micro-organisms** (e.g. **bacteria**). These micro-organisms need food and water to survive. They have to multiply to a dangerous level to make a person ill. Food poisoning symptoms are usually fairly mild and short-lived.

A food-borne disease is passed on by the micro-organisms that cause illness being present in food or water. Food-borne diseases cause severe illnesses, which can kill. Bacteria or viruses causing food-borne diseases such as typhoid and hepatitis can make people very ill, even when they are present in only small numbers. Bacteria causing food-borne diseases do not become harmful only after multiplying in the food; they are very dangerous by themselves. Some of the symptoms of food poisoning and a food-borne disease are very similar.

Definition

Hazard – something that could be dangerous.

Figure 5.1 Bacteria can multiply very quickly

Symptoms of food poisoning

The main symptoms are:
○ abdominal pain
○ diarrhoea
○ vomiting (being sick)
○ fever.

Other symptoms that may occur include:
○ abdominal cramp
○ difficulty in breathing
○ nausea (feeling sick)
○ flu-like symptoms
○ rashes
○ convulsions (fits).

The time between consuming food and experiencing symptoms can be as little as one hour, or as long as 70 days!

If you are suffering from food poisoning, the doctor will want to know what your symptoms are, and how much time passed from the consumption of any suspect food to the symptoms appearing. This information often gives the first indication of the type of bacteria responsible for the outbreak. To find out the exact cause of food poisoning, a **faeces** sample will have to be taken and sent to a laboratory for analysis.

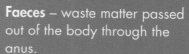

Definitions

Faeces – waste matter passed out of the body through the anus.

Excrement – any solid waste matter passed out of the body.

Pathogen – an organism that causes disease.

People at risk from food poisoning

The majority of people who suffer food poisoning will have some very unpleasant symptoms for a few days and will feel rather weak and uncomfortable. They should make a full recovery within one to two weeks. Unfortunately, some sectors of the population may have a more severe reaction to the condition and need hospital treatment. Some people may even die from severe symptoms. Those most at risk are:

○ babies and young children
○ pregnant women and nursing mothers
○ the elderly and infirm
○ those already suffering from an illness or medical condition.

Some of those most at risk from food poisoning may be found:
○ in hospitals
○ in children's and old people's homes
○ attending medical centres.

Any confirmed outbreak of a food-related illness causes severe problems for a business. Reports in newspapers and on the television and radio will stop many people from visiting a restaurant or take-away outlet. Many catering firms that have had an outbreak of food poisoning have had to close down, so the staff lost their jobs.

Causes of food poisoning

The most common cause is consuming a large number of the types of bacteria that cause illness. Other possible causes include:
○ chemicals
○ viruses present in some types of food (e.g. shellfish)
○ moulds
○ physical contaminants.

Micro-organisms

Bacteria

Bacteria are **micro-organisms**. They cannot be seen with the naked eye, and cannot be tasted or smelt if they are on food.

Bacteria multiply by splitting into two. They can do this every 20 minutes. This means that after a few hours, a small amount of bacteria can have multiplied many times. When there are about one million **pathogenic** bacteria per gram of a portion of food eaten, food poisoning can occur.

Pathogenic bacteria

The bacteria that cause food poisoning are called pathogenic bacteria. Figure 5.2 shows common types of pathogenic bacteria.

Pathogenic bacteria	Where they come from
Salmonella	Raw meat and poultry, eggs and milk, pets, insects, sewage
Staphylococcus aureus	Human body (skin, nose, mouth, cuts, boils), milk
Clostridium perfringens	Human and animal **excrement**, soil, dust, insects, raw meat
Clostridium botulinum	Soil, raw meat, raw, smoked and canned fish
Bacillus cereus	Cereals (especially rice), soil, dust

Figure 5.2 Types of pathogenic bacteria

Food-borne micro-organisms

Food-borne diseases are caused by micro-organisms that are found in food and water, but do not depend on them to survive. This makes these micro-organisms different from pathogenic bacteria. Only a small number of these micro-organisms are needed to cause illness. Figure 5.3 shows where food-borne diseases come from.

> **Definitions**
> **Bacterium (pl. bacteria)** – a single celled micro-organism.
> **Dysentery** – a food-borne disease causing mild to severe diarrhoea and fever. It can be fatal.
> **Micro-organism** – a very small life form, which cannot be seen without a microscope.
> **Organism** – any living animal or plant.

Food-borne micro-organisms	Where they come from
Campylobacter	Raw meat and poultry, milk, animals
Escherichia coli 0157 (E. coli)	Human and animal gut, sewage, water, raw meat
Listeria	Soft cheese, **unpasteurised** milk products, salad, pâté
Shigella dysenteriae (bacillary dysentery)	Water, milk, salad, vegetables
Salmonella typhi and Salmonella paratyphi (typhoid/paratyphoid)	Food or water contaminated by human faeces or sewage

Figure 5.3 Sources of food-borne micro-organisms

Spores

Some bacteria can form **spores**. A spore is a form of protective coating in which the bacteria can survive being cooked, dried and treated with cleaning chemicals. They cannot multiply when in this state, but when the conditions become more suitable, they start multiplying again.

Conditions for bacterial growth

Bacteria multiply when they have ideal conditions to grow. These are listed below.

- Food – bacteria multiply on food, particularly protein-based food, e.g. meat, fish and dairy items.
- Moisture – bacteria thrive in moisture, but cannot survive in food preserved by drying, salting or adding sugar.
- Warmth – bacteria prefer body temperature, but they are also happy at room temperature. In the fridge or freezer they do not die, but become **dormant**, so they do not multiply. High temperatures of over 70°C for more than three minutes will kill most bacteria.
- Time – in the best conditions, the fastest time in which a bacterium can multiply is ten minutes. The average time for most bacteria is 20 minutes.
- Oxygen – some bacteria need oxygen to multiply, others prefer no oxygen. There are also types of bacteria that multiply regardless of whether there is oxygen or not.

High-risk foods

As Figures 5.2 and 5.3 show, several types of food may harbour the dangerous bacteria that can cause food poisoning. These are known as high-risk foods.

- They are mainly ready-to-eat foods, which will not be cooked further (cooking can make food safe to eat).
- They involve mixing and processing several ingredients. This increases the preparation time at room temperature. Time and temperature are needed by bacteria to multiply.
- Some dishes involve breaking down and mixing surface tissue with internal muscle. This happens with minced meat, poultry and fish. Few bacteria are found within the muscle, and when this is cooked in a large piece (e.g. chicken breast) the bacteria on the outside surface are killed quickly. If the meat is minced, the outside surfaces – which contain more bacteria – are mixed in with the muscle areas.
- Some ingredients are sourced from high-risk areas, e.g. seafood from contaminated water.

> **Definitions**
> **Pasteurised** – has been heat treated.
> **Unpasteurised** – has not been heat treated.
> **Spores** – cells produced by bacteria and fungi.
> **Dormant** – not active or growing.

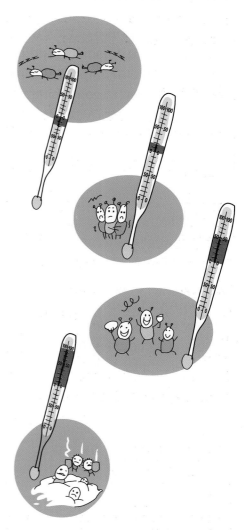

Figure 5.4 The effect of temperature on bacteria

The most common high-risk food categories include:

○ cooked meats and poultry, plus pâtés and spreads made from these ingredients
○ meat stews, gravy and meat stock-based soups and sauces
○ milk, cream and eggs – particularly items that involve raw or lightly cooked ingredients, including artificial creams and custards
○ shellfish and seafood, including prawns, mussels and oysters, both raw and cooked
○ cooked rice that is not used immediately.

Viruses

A virus is a germ that causes disease. Viruses are even smaller than bacteria. Viruses multiply after they are eaten, so only a few of these tiny micro-organisms are needed to cause illness. The most common food that can cause viral poisoning is shellfish, which may have been grown in contaminated water and not correctly cleaned before consumption. Viruses can also be passed from person to person via poor personal hygiene, for example not washing your hands after using the toilet.

Moulds

Moulds are multicellular organisms that will grow on food of all types – sweet, salty, acid or alkaline. They grow most quickly at a temperature of 20–30°C, but can also grow slowly at temperatures as low as –10°C. Mould spores survive in the air, so even if they are destroyed by cooking, it is virtually impossible to prevent them existing on food. Some moulds produce **toxins** that cause food poisoning symptoms, and also may cause cancer. Moulds present on cereals, nuts, herbs, spices and milk can produce toxins in this way. Other moulds produce chemicals that are toxic to bacteria and help to destroy them, such as that used in penicillin.

Non-micro-organisms

Chemicals

Poisoning from chemicals is rare in the UK, but it does happen occasionally. Some chemicals can get into food accidentally and cause poisoning. Some examples are listed below.

○ Cleaning chemicals can cause poisoning if surfaces and equipment have not been rinsed properly. When the surfaces and equipment are used, the chemical residue can contaminate food.

Figure 5.5 Mould

Did you know?
Some moulds are very useful to us. Particular moulds are produced to ripen cheese, e.g. Danish blue, Roquefort and Camembert.

Figure 5.6 Metal poisoning can be caused by poor storage

○ Pesticides may be present in harvested crops that have recently been sprayed with chemicals. In this case, poisoning can occur if the food is not peeled or washed properly.

○ Metal poisoning can occur if food is stored poorly (e.g. leaving food in unlined tin cans in the fridge), or if food is cooked in unlined copper or aluminium pans, particularly acidic foods such as fruit.

Toxins

Toxins forming in poorly stored oily fish (e.g. tuna, sardines and salmon) can cause severe illness. Shellfish (e.g. mussels) may become poisonous if they have fed on toxic **plankton**. This particular plankton occurs only at certain times of year in specific areas, so fishing is restricted during this season.

Definitions

Plankton – a layer of tiny plants and animals living just below the surface of the sea.
Toxin – a poison produced by bacteria.

Incorrect cooking methods

Some food is poisonous if it is not cooked correctly. Red kidney beans can make people ill if they have not been boiled for at least 10 minutes. (Tinned red kidney beans are safe, as they have been thoroughly cooked as part of the canning process.)

Other food safety risks

Physical contaminants

Any item that is discovered in food when it is not supposed to be there is described as a foreign body. Foreign bodies that may be found in food include:

○ pieces of glass, plastic and metal
○ mouse and rat droppings
○ gemstones and settings of jewellery
○ blue and natural-coloured plasters
○ strands of hair
○ flies, caterpillars and other insects
○ pen tops, drawing pins, paper clips
○ screws, nuts and bolts
○ flaking paint.

Figure 5.7 Foreign bodies that have been found in food

If such an item is found in food, it is extremely unpleasant and upsetting for the consumer, and embarrassing and inconvenient for the business. It is very likely that the presence of the foreign body breaks the law – either the Food Safety Act 1990 or Hazard Analysis and Critical Control Point (HACCP) procedures (see page 41). If this happens, the catering organisation will have to look very carefully into its food safety system to find out where it failed.

Allergies

An allergy is an intolerance that some people have to certain substances, some of which may be types of food. An increasing number of people now suffer from mild allergic reactions to a range of foods, including:

○ wheat products (such as bread and biscuits)
○ dairy products (such as milk and cheese)
○ gluten (the elastic protein found in wheat flour).
○ nuts, especially peanuts
○ fish/shellfish
○ plants/funghi
○ green sprouting potatoes.

Some symptoms of an allergic reaction can be very similar to those of a food-borne illness. It is important that the two are not confused. An allergic reaction will affect only one person, and usually occurs within a very short time of consumption. An incidence of food poisoning can affect a large number of people at the same time.

Symptoms of food allergies include:

○ vomiting
○ difficulty in breathing
○ diarrhoea
○ collapse
○ headache
○ rash.

The most dramatic reactions tend to occur in response to peanuts and shellfish. Some allergic reactions are very severe, come on very quickly, and can be fatal. This is why it is extremely important to inform customers of the precise ingredients in any dish they ask about. It is important to keep all stored ingredients separate, so that one cannot contaminate the other: for example, a dish that has been used for peanuts must be washed thoroughly and dried before it can be used for any other food. If the unwashed dish was then used to serve crisps in a bar, for example, anyone allergic to peanuts could have a reaction from eating any item out of the unwashed bowl.

Prevention of food poisoning

To try to prevent food poisoning:

○ handle food hygienically (pages 139–140)
○ prepare food carefully (page 170)
○ store food in the correct manner (pages 162–167)
○ keep all food preparation areas clean (pages 145–152)
○ avoid cross-contamination (pages 161–162)
○ cook all food thoroughly.

Why is it so important to control these hazards?

If these hazards are not controlled, there is a real danger that you could make yourself ill, or be responsible for making your colleagues and/or customers severely ill. People who are weakened through illness or age are more likely to die from a severe bout of food poisoning. You would not like to be the person responsible for this happening. Particularly vulnerable people are:

○ elderly
○ children
○ ill or recovering from an illness
○ pregnant women.

Fortunately, most outbreaks of food poisoning are not so serious. However, any confirmed outbreak of a food-related illness causes severe problems for a business. Reports in newspapers and on the television and radio will stop many people from visiting a restaurant or take-away outlet. Many catering firms who have had an outbreak of food poisoning have had to close down, so the staff lost their jobs.

Figure 5.8 The symptoms of food poisoning can be very unpleasant

MORE TAKEN ILL IN E. COLI OUTBREAK

CAMPYLOBACTER BUG ON THE RISE

FOOD POISONING SHUTS SCHOOL

Girl, 5, struck down by E. coli

Figure 5.9 Food-borne diseases are widely reported

Did you know?

Shigella bacteria cause **dysentery**. The bacteria are highly infectious, and just a few can cause illness. *Shigella* bacteria do not multiply in food. The bacteria get onto the hands of food handlers from toilet seats, tap handles and nailbrushes in washrooms and toilets. If food handlers do not wash their hands thoroughly, the bacteria are transferred onto any food they touch. If an outbreak of dysentery occurs, all the toilet and washroom areas must be disinfected thoroughly and the nailbrushes sterilised. All staff must receive training in the importance of correct personal hygiene procedures.

Did you know?

Procedures for handling food safely have existed for centuries. Some religious laws mirror basic food hygiene rules.

o Many people from other parts of the world eat with their hands. In these countries, you should only eat with your right hand. This is because when going to the toilet, you should wash your bottom with your left hand.

o Jewish people separate the preparation and consumption of milk and meat products. Sometimes these items are prepared in different kitchens, so that no equipment comes into contact with the wrong food type.

Figure 5.10 Eating with your right hand

Did you know?

Certain types of bacteria are very useful to us. We use some types of bacteria to:

o grow crops
o digest food
o treat sewage
o create medicines
o manufacture cleaning products
o make food (e.g. yoghurt and cheese).

Remember!

Always:

o keep yourself and your workplace clean at all times
o wear suitable, clean, washable protective clothing
o protect food from contamination at all times
o minimise the time that high-risk foods are left at room temperature
o keep hot food really hot, at 63°C or above
o keep cold food in the fridge at below 5°C
o tell your supervisor your symptoms if you are ill
o take responsibility for working safely and hygienically
o follow all instructions and rules at work
o report all potential hazards.

Test yourself!

1 Which of the following is not a pathogenic bacterium?
   a Penicillin
   b Salmonella
   c Staphylococcus aureus
   d Bacillus cereus

2 Which of the following describes the conditions necessary for most bacteria to reproduce?
   a Warmth, oxygen, food, moisture.
   b Cool, oxygen, food, moisture.
   c Warmth, carbon dioxide, food, dryness.
   d Cool, carbon dioxide, food, dryness.

3 Which of the following is not a symptom of food poisoning?
   a Rash
   b Nausea
   c Sneezing
   d Abdominal pain

4 Which Regulation concerns the safe system of food production?
   a COSHH
   b RIDDOR
   c HASAWA
   d HACCP

5 Which of the following statements is true?
   a All pathogens cause illness.
   b All moulds cause illness.
   c All bacteria cause illness.
   d All foreign bodies cause illness.

Personal hygiene

A high standard of personal hygiene is a requirement under the Food Safety (General Food Hygiene) Regulations 1995. Everyone who works in a job that requires them to handle and serve food must:

- be in good health
- have hygienic personal habits
- wear the correct, clean protective clothing
- be aware of the potential danger of poor hygiene practice.

Personal hygiene is very important when working in a catering environment. You need to be pleasant to work with (no body odour!) and feel comfortable in the restaurant. Make sure you wash your hair – if it feels sticky and heavy, it will not be pleasant to work with or look at in a food service area. Clean your teeth regularly – your colleagues and customers will not want to be near you if you have bad breath! Keep your hands and nails clean and in good condition when serving food.

General health

It is important to remember that working in a food service area can involve:

- standing up for long periods
- working in a hot, noisy atmosphere
- having to concentrate and multi-task for long periods
- starting work early in the morning
- finishing work late at night.

Bearing these points in mind, make sure you:

- have sufficient sleep and relaxation during your time off
- eat regular, balanced meals – this is essential as it is too easy to 'pick', which is not good for your digestion in the long term
- drink plenty of water during your shift at work, otherwise your concentration may be affected
- remember that healthy eating applies to staff just as much as to customers.

Clothing

Your uniform should fit correctly and be comfortable to wear. If your shoes are too tight and make your feet hurt, for example, you will not be able to concentrate properly. This could cause an accident if you are using dangerous equipment such as knives or blenders.

It is important to wear the correct clothing in the restaurant, not only for health and safety, but also to create a professional image. Customers, visitors and other members of staff are impressed by restaurant staff who are dressed in a clean, smart uniform (see page 95). Food service areas may have house rules regarding correct dress.

Figure 5.11 General health and good presentation are important

Some food service staff may wear casual, open-necked shirts and trousers. Others may need to be more formally dressed in a bow tie and jacket, for example. Whichever style of clothing you need to wear for work, make sure that you can move easily in it and stretch fully, but do not dress in a uniform that is so loose it can catch easily on table corners and door handles.

You may be issued with a protective coat to wear while preparing a restaurant or serving behind a counter. You must remember to change it when dirty and make sure it is comfortable to wear and that you can reach all the necessary areas on the counter while wearing it. When serving behind a counter, you will also be asked to wear protective headgear to prevent any of your hair falling into the food.

It is important to remember the following aspects of good clothing practice (see Figure 2.9, page 47).

- Clean, comfortable underwear is just as important as a clean uniform.
- Do not work in the restaurant in outdoor clothing – it is contaminated.
- Do not wear your restaurant uniform outdoors, for the same reason.
- Change your uniform as soon as it gets dirty. This is usually every day for aprons and shirts or blouses. Trousers or skirts should be changed once or twice a week. A dirty uniform looks very unprofessional. It is also unhygienic, as it is easy to spread bacteria to other surfaces from the uniform by leaning across tables or touching a range of surfaces with unwashed hands.
- Make sure your uniform is always pressed.

You may need to wear gloves while at work. Types of gloves include:

- thin rubber, latex or vinyl gloves for work with food
- white cotton gloves for food service
- thick protective cotton gloves for cleaning metal (e.g. polishing silver)
- thick rubber gloves for using cleaning chemicals.

The advantages of wearing gloves to work include:

- handling food wearing a fresh pair of gloves is more hygienic than handling food with washed hands
- strong smells cannot be transferred from one food to another
- gloves give the wearer protection from damage caused by constant dampness, extreme cold and heat, and rough surfaces (e.g. when serving on a counter or filling ice buckets)

141

○ it is much more hygienic to cover a cut, burn or other condition (e.g. a boil) with a dressing and also to wear a glove on top – this also gives better protection to the injury

○ wearing gloves when serving food gives customers a more hygienic impression.

However, wearing gloves has some disadvantages, including:

○ it can be difficult to grip certain items (e.g. serving cutlery)

○ failing to use clean gloves can cause cross-contamination

○ it can take longer to complete a task

○ having to keep changing gloves can be fiddly and time-consuming

○ changing gloves frequently is expensive

○ it can be easy to forget to put on a fresh pair of gloves.

Personal habits

Hair

Wash your hair regularly and keep it tidy. Longer hair should be tied back and not allowed to fall over your face. This reduces the danger of flakes of skin or strands of hair falling into food. Beards and moustaches should be short and neatly trimmed. Do not touch your hair while working. When you have your hair cut, make sure you wash it again before you go to work.

Ears

Do not put your fingers in your ears while working in a restaurant. Earwax and bacteria can be transferred to food and work surfaces and equipment this way.

Nose

The pathogenic bacterium *Staphylococcus aureus* (see page 132) is found in many adult noses and mouths. Sneezes and coughs can spread the bacteria over a wide area. This means that work surfaces, food and equipment can be contaminated very easily. A disposable handkerchief should always be used to catch a sneeze or to blow your nose. Always wash your hands thoroughly after using a tissue. Nose-picking is an extremely unhygienic activity, as is wiping your nose on your sleeve, and neither should ever be carried out in a restaurant – or elsewhere!

Figure 5.12 Wash your hand regularly and thoroughly

Mouth

As you are dealing with customers, you must remember to keep your teeth clean and your breath fresh at all times. Do not touch your mouth or pick your teeth when on duty in the restaurant. Spitting is extremely unhygienic – never do this. It is not acceptable to eat sweets or chew gum in the restaurant. Do not lick your finger and then use it to open a bag, pick up small, light items or separate sheets of paper. All these activities can spread bacteria easily.

Neck

Do not wear strong perfume or aftershave, deodorant or cosmetics, as they can taint food and clash with any perfumes and body sprays worn by customers. Do not wear necklaces over your uniform as these could get in the way as you are serving customers. Earrings may not be worn in case they fall into food. Other jewellery for piercings is not appropriate for the same reason, as well as giving a less than professional appearance. Your employer may not let you work with any tattoos you may have on show.

Underarms

Daily bathing or showering removes the bacteria that cause body odour. Perspiration smells can be avoided by using an unperfumed deodorant.

Hands

The most common method of contaminating food is through having dirty hands. It is essential to have clean, well kept hands when working in a food service area. Your hands will be on show to customers all the time. Keep your nails short and clean. Do not use nail varnish. Watches and rings (other than a plain wedding ring) may not be allowed in your workplace, as bacteria can live in food particles caught under them. Gemstones in jewellery may fall out and become foreign bodies in food.

How to wash your hands properly

1 Wet your hands with a non-hand-operated warm-water spray, or fill the wash hand basin with hand-hot water and wet your hands.
2 Use an unperfumed antibacterial liquid soap or gel to provide a good lather over the top and palms of your hands, between your fingers, around your wrists and lower forearms.

Remember!
Do not touch any part of glassware, crockery or cutlery that may make contact with the user's mouth. You would not like to drink out of a cup that someone's fingers had touched around the rim!

Remember!
Always wash your hands:
o when starting work
o after using the toilet or being in any contact with faeces
o between each task
o between handling raw and cooked food
o after touching your face or hair
o after scratching any part of your body
o after coughing, sneezing or blowing your nose into a handkerchief
o after any cleaning activity
o after eating, drinking or smoking during a break
o after dealing with food waste or rubbish.
o when changing a dressing or dealing with an open wound.

143

3 Only use a nailbrush to clean under your fingernails if it is disinfected regularly or is disposable.

4 Rinse your hands thoroughly with clean water.

5 Dry your hands well, preferably with disposable paper towels; hot-air dryers take longer, and roller towels must be clean to be safe.

Wounds, illness and infection

Working in a restaurant with hot items, knives and dangerous equipment means it is likely that you will occasionally suffer a slight injury.

From a hygiene point of view, it is essential that all wounds are covered. This is to:

o ensure blood and bacteria from the injury do not contaminate any food

o prevent bacteria from raw food infecting your wound.

Using a coloured waterproof dressing (blue plaster) keeps the injury clean and protects it. Blue is the best colour for dressings in food areas, as it is easily spotted if it falls off – very few foods are blue.

Spots, blisters and boils are unpleasant skin conditions that can cause problems in food-handling areas because they will be infected with the pathogenic bacterium *Staphylococcus aureus* (see page 132). If you have blemishes on your hands, or if you have an allergic condition such as contact dermititis, work in suitable gloves. If they are on your face, you must be very careful to avoid touching them with your hands while working. In severe cases, your supervisor may give you tasks that do not involve food handling or customer contact until the condition has cleared up.

If you are ill, and suffer any symptoms that could be from a food-borne illness, you must let your supervisor know as soon as possible. The symptoms concerned include:

o diarrhoea

o vomiting

o nausea

o discharge from ear, eye and/or nose

o cold and sore throat

o skin infection (e.g. eczema).

Did you know?

There are three items used in hand washing that can contaminate hands, rather than cleaning them. They are:

o a dirty bar of soap used by many different people

o a non-disposable nailbrush, if not disinfected very regularly

o a roller towel, if not changed very regularly.

Remember!

Always tell your supervisor straight away if you are wearing a waterproof blue plaster dressing and it goes missing in food!

Remember!

Many people pick up 'tummy bugs' while on holiday abroad. If you do so, you need to tell your supervisor before you return to work.

You should not work either in the restaurant or handling food while you display any of these symptoms. It is likely you will have to seek medical help if you suffer severe bouts of these illnesses. You may need clearance from your doctor before you can resume work.

Your supervisor also needs to know about any similar symptoms suffered by the people with whom you live. This is because you may be a carrier of an infection without displaying any symptoms of the illness. If you are a carrier, it means you can transmit the infection to others.

Certain illnesses must be reported to the local health authority as a legal requirement. Many are identified by the symptoms listed above. Your supervisor or doctor should arrange for this to be done if necessary.

Try this!

Produce a presentation that outlines the training requirements of food service staff. Include recommendations for training staff in the following areas:

- *personal hygiene and presentation*
- *good hygiene practice*
- *reportable illnesses*
- *suitable dressings for wounds, with an explanation of the risk of infection.*

Test yourself!

1 How often should you have a bath or shower during a working week?

2 Why should nail varnish not be worn while serving food?

3 What is a 'carrier' of a food-borne disease?

4 Why should you use an unperfumed deodorant?

5 State three types of glove you may need to wear while working in food service.

6 Describe the correct procedure to follow when washing your hands.

Cleaning

Cleaning is an essential process of removing dirt. It is vital to the safe operation of every food business. Cleaning staff are employed in many establishments, but it is the responsibility of all employees to make sure that:

- all equipment and work areas are clean
- the working environment is clean and safe.

Figure 5.13 Washing down the service counter

Regular cleaning is vital in areas where food is handled and served, for the following reasons:

- to reduce the danger of contamination of food from:
  - bacteria (by removing particles of food upon which they can feed)
  - pests
  - foreign bodies
- to create a good impression for:
  - customers
  - other staff and visitors
  - inspectors
- to reduce the risk of:
  - accidents
  - equipment breakdown.

Methods of cleaning

A high standard of cleanliness is essential to keep the risk of food safety hazards low. Cleaning achieves this because it:

- removes food particles on which bacteria can feed
- reduces the risk of contamination of food that is being prepared or stored
- reduces the danger of pests (e.g. insects, rats or mice) coming into the kitchen
- helps prevent accidents by providing a safe work area
- encourages safe working methods
- helps to keep the area pleasant to work in.

Cleaning has to be carried out in all areas of food preparation and service areas. These include:

- surfaces – floors and tabletops
- equipment – manual or electrical machinery
- utensils – hand-held serving tools
- touch points – for example, door handles.

The Control of Substances Hazardous to Health (COSHH) Regulations 2002 (see Chapter 2, page 50) cover cleaning because there are several potential hazards that could occur. These include:

- using dirty cloths to clean, which spreads bacterial contamination
- using the same cleaning equipment for raw food preparation areas as for preparing cooked food, causing cross-contamination (pages 160–162).
- carrying out cleaning poorly or hurriedly, so that contamination remains

Remember!
Remember that COSHH (see page 50) controls all the chemicals used in cleaning.

○ using the same cleaning equipment for both toilet/changing room areas and the restaurant, so that cross-contamination is likely

○ using cleaning chemicals incorrectly, leaving a residue over food service areas that could cause chemical contamination

○ storing chemicals in food containers, which could result in contamination

○ pest infestation (pages 154–156).

Cleaning products

○ **Water** is the most effective cleaning agent. It can be used hot or cold, and also under pressure. When used in the form of steam, it can also disinfect. Water leaves no residue and is very environmentally friendly. It is also used for rinsing.

○ **Soap** is made from fat and caustic soda. Soap can leave a scum on surfaces, so it is not suitable for kitchen cleaning. Disinfectants are sometimes added to soap for hand washing.

○ **Detergents** are chemicals manufactured from petroleum. They break dirt up into fine particles and coat them so they are easy to remove. Detergents can be in the form of a powder, liquid, foam or gel. They usually need mixing with water before use.

○ **Disinfectants** are chemicals that will reduce the number of micro-organisms to a safe level if they are left in contact with the surface for long enough. It is better to apply the chemicals with a spray rather than a cloth. Their efficiency is affected if the surface that is being treated is not clean.

○ **Sanitisers** are mixtures of detergent and disinfectant chemicals. They are often used in sprays for cleaning hard surfaces. They need to be left in contact with the surface to be cleaned for long enough to be effective. Always read the manufacturer's instructions.

○ **Bactericides** are substances formulated to kill bacteria.

○ **Sterilisers** usually use extremely hot water or steam to kill all the micro-organisms on a surface. Alternatively, they may use strong chemical disinfectants or bactericides. It is difficult to sterilise equipment successfully in a normal catering situation.

Area	Equipment	Frequency of disinfection
Surfaces contacted by food	Chopping boards, containers, blenders	Before and after each use
Surfaces contacted by hands	Refrigerator handles, taps, switches	At least once per shift
Contamination hazards	Cloths and mops, waste bins and lids	At least once per shift; cloths and mops after each main use

Figure 5.14 Disinfection frequency table

When using any type of cleaning chemical:

o always follow the manufacturer's instructions correctly
o store chemicals in their original container, away from food and in clean, cool, dry conditions
o never decant a chemical into a different container that is not labelled correctly
o always wear any recommended protective equipment when preparing and using the product
o never mix chemicals
o always dispose of chemicals safely – check the instructions before you pour any chemical down a drain.

Cleaning equipment

To clean effectively, you need suitable equipment. This is likely to include:

o small equipment (e.g. cloths, brushes, mops and buckets)
o large equipment (e.g. dishwashers, jet washers, wet and dry vacuum cleaners).

Small equipment should be colour-coded so that it is used only in the correct areas and for the correct job. For example, red equipment could be used in raw food-preparation areas and yellow equipment in cooked food-preparation areas. A set of blue equipment could be reserved for cleaning changing-room areas, and this should be stored separately.

Cloths frequently spread more bacteria than they clean away. All re-usable cloths should be changed every few hours in a shift, as they will contain constantly increasing numbers of bacteria at room temperature. Re-usable cloths should be washed and disinfected thoroughly before being dried ready to use again. It is more expensive, but much more hygienic, to use disposable cloths. These are available in a range of colours to help with coding and controlling where they are used. Disposable cloths should be thrown away as soon as they are dirty.

Try this!

Some materials will be damaged by the usual cleaning methods and need special attention. Find out how the following materials should be cleaned:

o *cast iron*
o *copper*
o *aluminium.*

Figure 5.15 Small kitchen equipment should be colour-coded according to area

Remember!

Never use a cloth that has been used on a floor or in a toilet area to wipe a work surface.

Energy used in cleaning

Cleaning is an expensive process. As well as specialist chemicals and equipment, it also requires energy – and not just by plugging a machine into an electrical socket! Effective cleaning usually involves two or more of these energy sources:

- physical energy – carried out by people using pressure and movement on surfaces (also known as 'elbow grease')
- kinetic energy – produced by machines using their weight in conjunction with movement (e.g. a floor cleaner)
- agitation – provided by liquids being constantly moved against a surface (e.g. in a washing machine, or when cleaning tubes or pipes)
- thermal energy – using high and low temperatures combined with pressure to remove dirt (e.g. in a steam pressure cleaner, or when freezing a skirt to remove chewing gum)
- chemical – using a chemical reaction between two substances to loosen and remove dirt (e.g. washing powder and water).

Six stages of cleaning

The main stages of thorough cleaning apply to each area. Before starting to clean, switch off and unplug electrical machinery and dismantle any items as required.

1 Pre-cleaning – to remove any loose dirt and heavy soiling (e.g. soak a flambé pan, sweep the floor or wipe down a counter).
2 Main cleaning – wash the item with hot water and detergent, using a suitable cloth or brush to remove grease and dirt.
3 Rinsing – with hot water only, to remove the detergent and any remaining dirt particles.
4 Disinfecting – with extremely hot water (82°C) or steam in a controlled area (e.g. a dishwasher or a second sink). Where this process is not safe or practical, use a chemical disinfectant. Apply it to the appropriate surface and leave it for the length of time stated on the instructions.
5 Final rinsing – to remove all cleaning chemical residue.
6 Drying – air-drying is the most hygienic method, otherwise use paper towels or clean, dry cloths.

When cleaning is finished, put the equipment back together correctly and safely. Put it in the right place ready for use.

Cleaning schedules

A cleaning schedule forms part of the HACCP procedures (see page 171), and may be used together with checklists to ensure a thorough job is done. A cleaning schedule is a written plan that tells everyone in the restaurant:

○ what items and surfaces are to be cleaned
○ where they are to be cleaned
○ who is to carry out these tasks
○ how often the cleaning is to be carried out
○ when the cleaning should be done
○ the method of cleaning that should be used
○ how long it should take to clean correctly
○ what chemicals and equipment are needed to clean it
○ what safety precautions should be taken when cleaning (e.g. wearing goggles and gloves, putting out warning signs).

Frequently used items and work areas may have to be cleaned after each task in preparation for the next. It is the responsibility of all food handlers and waiting staff to carry out this clean-as-you-go system correctly. This is particularly important when you are preparing raw foods. You must disinfect the work area thoroughly once you have cleaned it, to prevent cross-contamination.

Find out!

How frequently are the following cleaning tasks carried out at your workplace?
○ cleaning the coffee machine
○ washing down the service counter
○ cleaning out the refrigerators
○ cleaning the bin area.

Remember!

A cleaning schedule forms part of the HACCP procedures (page 171), and may be used together with checklists to ensure a thorough job is done.

Cleaning schedule and checklist

Area/item of	Frequency	Responsiblity	Cleaning materials	H&S precautions	Method of cleaning	Checked by
Walls of service area	Daily	Kitchen porter/ counter service staff	Detergent and cloth	Use a ladder to reach areas above shoulder height	1) Pre-clean 2) Clean, apply detergent with hand-held spray, leave for 2 minutes 3) Rinse 4) Air-dry	
Floors of service area	Daily	Kitchen porter/ counter service staff	Detergent, mop and bucket	Place hazard notices in entrances to areas being cleaned	1) Pre-clean 2) Clean, apply detergent with mop 3) Rinse 4) Air-dry	
Service stations	Daily	Service staff	Detergent and cloth	None required	1) Pre-clean 2) Clean, apply detergent with hand-held spray, leave for 2 minutes 3) Rinse 4) Air-dry	
Carpeted floor	Daily	Service staff	Vacuum cleaner	None	Remove any large debris physically, then use vacuum cleaner. May need to empty dust collector and clean filter after use	
Carpeted floor	Quarterly	Contractor	Wet-and-dry shampooing machine	None	Use as training requires	
Work surface	Daily	Service staff	Sanitiser and cloth	None required	1) Pre-clean 2) Apply sanitiser with trigger spray, leave for 2 minutes 3) Wipe over 4) Air-dry	
Coffee machine	Daily	Service staff	Manufacturer recommended cleaner	Rubber gloves, overall	1) Ensure machine is turned off and cool 2) Pre-clean 3) Clean, apply cleaning chemical according to manufacturer instruction 4) Rinse 5) Air-dry	
Fridges	Weekly	Service staff	Hot water and detergent	None required	1) Pre-clean 2) Clean, apply detergent with hand-held spray, leave for 2 minutes 3) Rinse 4) Air-dry	
Bin	Weekly	Kitchen porter and second chef	Hot water and detergent	Gloves	1) Pre-clean 2) Clean, apply detergent with hand-held spray, leave for 2 minutes 3) Rinse 4) Air-dry	
Windows	Monthly	Service staff or contract cleaners	Hot water and detergent	Use a ladder to reach areas above shoulder height	1) Pre-clean 2) Rinse 3) Air-dry	

Figure 5.16 Example of a cleaning schedule and checklist

Hygienic work surfaces and equipment

It is very difficult to maintain good standards of work and hygiene in a food service area if the working area and equipment are unsuitable. All equipment and work surfaces should be specifically produced and designed for food service areas.

All surfaces that come into contact with food should be:
○ easy to maintain, clean and disinfect
○ made from a safe, **non-toxic** material that is **inert** and will not react with any food or chemical
○ smooth and **impervious** to water (waterproof)
○ designed to avoid any joins or seams where food particles could lodge
○ resistant to corrosion (e.g. rusting or pitting)
○ strong enough to support heavy weights
○ heat-resistant, so that hot pans can be placed on it.

Stainless steel has all these qualities. It is the most commonly used material in modern counter service areas. For reasons of health and safety, and to follow the HACCP procedures (page 171), it is important to act when you notice any damage to surfaces or equipment in the food service area.

> **Definitions**
> **Non-toxic** – not poisonous or harmful.
> **Inert** – has no reaction with any other substance.
> **Impervious** – does not allow water to pass through it.

Hazardous surfaces and equipment

You should inform your supervisor if you see:
○ broken floor or wall tiles
○ damaged doors or handles of refrigerators, hotplates, cupboards or drawers
○ loose handles on flambé pans
○ failed bulbs inside equipment such as microwaves
○ an electric fly-catcher becoming ineffective
○ gas equipment that becomes difficult to light, or goes off during use
○ blades on machinery that have become blunt or damaged
○ paint flaking from the ceiling and falling on the work surface
○ chopping boards being very scratched or pitted
○ dripping hot or cold water taps that cannot be turned off
○ any blockages (e.g. in preparation sinks or wash hand basins).

There will be many more potential hazards depending upon the size and type of food service area that you work in.

Figure 5.17 This kitchen does not follow HACCP procedures!

Waste management

Every catering establishment wants to manage waste carefully, for several reasons:

- all food thrown away represents lost income for the business
- all businesses have to pay to have their waste removed, and large amounts of waste can increase this cost
- reducing the amount of waste produced helps protect the environment
- waste can attract pests, which can be a food safety hazard.

In every food service area, sufficient waste bins should be provided at suitable points. The bins should:

- have tight-fitting lids
- be lined with a polythene disposable sack (if appropriate)
- not be overfilled
- be emptied regularly
- be cleaned regularly
- not smell
- not be left in the area overnight.

The bagged waste from bins should be transferred to a large, lidded bin in the outside refuse area as soon as necessary. The bags should be tied securely to prevent any spillages. This will help to reduce the hazard of pest infestation. The outside refuse area should be kept clean for the same reason.

Remember!

Some waste can be dangerous – for example:
o broken glass can cause injury
o fat and oil can leak out of containers and make floors slippery.

Figure 5.18 Waste bins should be emptied regularly

Recycling waste

Many establishments are now trying to recycle as much material as possible. Spoiled food may be kept apart from general food waste. Food waste may be kept apart, as it can be collected separately. Spoiled food may be kept apart from general food waste. Individual bins should be provided for paper, cardboard, glass and plastic to allow recycling systems to be used. In large businesses, this type of waste may be crushed by compactor machines to take up less space before binning. Waste oil may be collected separately from the main rubbish collection, as it can be recycled – eventually, this may be used as fuel for cars.

Figure 5.19 A well organised outside bin area

Pest control

Pests are the cause of the majority of food establishment closures by the environmental health officer. Pests may also cause large amounts of food to be wasted due to infestation or contamination. Both staff and customers will become very upset if they find any type of pest on the premises. Under the HACCP procedures (page 171), a catering business is expected to have effective pest control methods in place.

Pests live in or near catering premises because they provide:
○ food in store rooms, waste areas or poorly cleaned production areas
○ moisture from dripping taps, outside drains or **condensation** droplets
○ warmth from heating systems and equipment motors (e.g. refrigerators)
○ shelter in undisturbed areas (e.g. the back of a store cupboard, behind large equipment).

Removing as many of these conditions as possible will help to drive pests away from the food-preparation and storage areas.

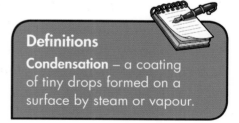

Definitions
Condensation – a coating of tiny drops formed on a surface by steam or vapour.

Signs of infestation

How can you tell if there is a pest infestation in your workplace?
Look for:

○ dead bodies of insects, rodents and birds
○ droppings or smear marks
○ eggs, larvae, pupal cases, feathers, nesting material
○ paw or claw prints
○ unusual smells
○ scratching, pecking or gnawing sounds
○ gnawed pipes, fittings or boxes
○ torn or damaged sacks or packaging
○ food spillages.

Pests may cause hazards in the following ways:

○ bacterial contamination – from pathogenic bacteria found on the surface of the pest's skin or in pest droppings
○ physical contamination – from fur, eggs, droppings, urine, saliva, dead bodies or nesting materials
○ chemical contamination – from using strong chemicals to kill pests, which may then get into food
○ cross-contamination – when a pest transfers pathogenic bacteria from one area to another (e.g. a fly landing on raw meat and then moving onto a cooked chicken).

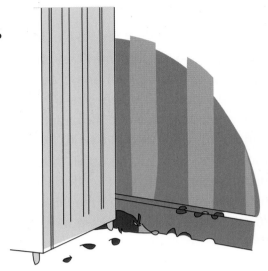

Figure 5.20 Evidence of infestation

Types of pest

Insects

Flies are one of the most common insect pests. They are usually found in places that have not been cleaned thoroughly, and where rubbish is allowed to gather. A female housefly can lay up to 600 eggs in her life. An egg takes about 2 weeks to go through the maggot stage and become a fully grown fly.

Cockroaches are one of the oldest types of insect, said to date from prehistoric times. They do not usually fly, and only come out when it is dark. Their eggs take around 2 months to hatch. They can live for up to a year. Cockroaches can be detected by their droppings or their unpleasant smell.

Weevils are very tiny insects that live in dry goods, e.g. flour, cereals and nuts. They can be seen with the naked eye only if they are moving. It is possible to spot an infestation if there is tunnelling or speckling in the commodity.

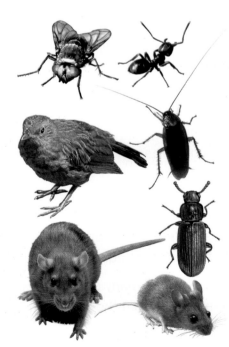

Figure 5.21 Pests that may be found on catering premises

Ants are attracted by sweet items that have not been stored securely. They usually nest outdoors, and follow set paths to food sources.

Rodents

Rats commonly get into buildings through drains or holes, but they can also burrow under walls. Rats are a particular hazard, as they can transmit Weil's disease and a worm-type parasite, as well as food-poisoning bacteria. They also bite. The Norway rat is the most common in the UK. It usually lives outside.

House mice are the main problem in buildings. They can climb very well, and cause considerable damage by gnawing to keep their teeth short. Like rats, their teeth grow throughout their lives and unless they wear them down, their teeth will pierce through their heads! Mice dribble urine nearly all the time and leave droppings at frequent intervals. They breed very quickly – a pair of mice can have 2000 offspring in one year.

Birds

Pigeons, starlings and seagulls can be a problem in outside waste areas if bins are allowed to overflow and are not kept covered. Once in the area, birds may then get into a building through doors and windows, and will often try to nest in roof spaces. As well as contaminating food with feathers and droppings, birds can block gutters with their nests and spread insect infestation.

Domestic pets and wild animals

Domestic pets (e.g. cats and dogs) are classed as pests in this case and should not be allowed to enter catering premises.

Wild cats and foxes can be a problem in outside waste areas if bins are allowed to overflow.

Preventing pest infestation

It is almost impossible to prevent pests from entering a building. It is possible, however, to discourage them from staying. The following lists some ways of preventing pests.

- Regular, thorough cleaning of areas (e.g. changing rooms and food stores), particularly in corners where pests may be able to hide unnoticed.
- Clearing up any spillages thoroughly and promptly.
- Not allowing waste to build up, and keeping bins covered at all times.

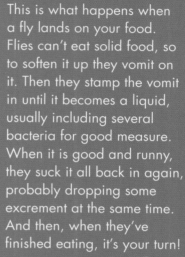

Did you know?
This is what happens when a fly lands on your food. Flies can't eat solid food, so to soften it up they vomit on it. Then they stamp the vomit in until it becomes a liquid, usually including several bacteria for good measure. When it is good and runny, they suck it all back in again, probably dropping some excrement at the same time. And then, when they've finished eating, it's your turn!

- Keeping doors and windows closed, using self-closing doors, or using insect screens across openings.
- Using bristle strips and kick plates on doors that are badly fitting to prevent gnawing damage and rodent access.
- Moving cupboards and equipment as far as possible to clean behind and under them regularly (see safe lifting techniques, page 66).
- Removing any unused equipment and materials from the area.
- Ensuring food storage containers are properly closed when not in use.
- Checking all deliveries – of all items, not just food – for signs of infestation.
- Storing and rotating stock correctly.

Pest control management

Most businesses use a specialist pest control company to monitor and control pest infestations in their premises. They agree a contract that specifies the number of visits per year by the pest control specialist.

The pest control contractor will inspect the premises, looking for evidence of infestation by any type of pest. They will then deal with any pests they discover. Finally, they will complete a report describing what action they have taken. A copy of the report is left on the premises.

A pest control contractor may:
- lay bait and set baited traps
- use sticky boards
- install electric ultraviolet insect-killers
- spray an insecticide chemical over an area.

The contractor will leave instructions regarding the treatments used. It is important not to touch or move any items that have been left to catch pests. Any sprayed areas must be left untouched for the instructed period of time.

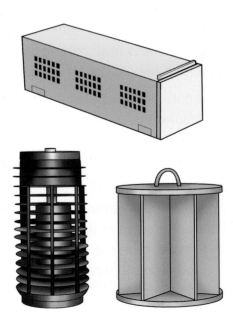

Figure 5.22 Pest control equipment

Storage and stock control

If you were to list all the food and equipment used in your workplace, it could run into hundreds of items! Some food items are stored and used by restaurant staff separately from the ingredients used by the chefs in the kitchen. Some commodities (e.g. salt) can be stored for very long periods. Other food items will remain safe to use for only a short time (e.g. fresh fruit for use in drinks will only last a few days in a refrigerator).

Correct delivery and storage of all foods is required under the HACCP procedures (page 171), and appropriate records should be kept. Efficient stock control and ordering are essential for a well-run catering business, for both food safety and commercial reasons.

Receiving stock

Food items are delivered to a catering business in one of three temperature ranges:

○ ambient/room temperature for fresh, dried or tinned items
○ chilled/refrigerator temperature for high-risk fresh or processed foods
○ frozen/freezer temperature for high-risk items in longer-term storage.

Figure 5.23 Accepting a delivery of food items

157

Checking a food delivery

If you receive a food delivery at your workplace, you need to check the following.

The vehicle delivering the items:
○ is it suitable?
○ is it clean inside?
○ is it refrigerated for the delivery of chilled items?

The temperature of the delivered items:
○ are chilled items below 5°C?
○ is frozen produce kept below −10°C?
○ use a temperature probe to check if necessary.

If the temperature is too high, reject the goods.

The packaging:
○ is it clean and undamaged?
○ is there any sign of mould or other spoilage?
○ are any containers dented, bulging or leaking?
○ are the items labelled with:
  – the name of the company?
  – description of the food?
  – product code?
  – ingredient list?
  – use by date?
  – weight?
○ is the best before or use-by date still several days in the future?
○ do the items delivered match the delivery note provided in terms of:
  – amounts of each item? (e.g. 1 x 25 kg bag)
  – specification of each item? (e.g. unsalted butter)

If you have to reject a delivery, make sure:
○ the delivery person has agreed to return the item to the supplier
○ the item being returned is recorded on either the delivery note or a separate return slip
○ the delivery person signs the delivery note or return slip, as you may need to do if requested
○ you give your copy of the delivery note or return slip to your supervisor as soon as possible – you need to make sure your employer does not pay for goods that have been rejected and returned.

Stock rotation

It is very important to use ingredients in the same order that they have been delivered. This is because:

○ food loses quality the longer it is kept
○ food will have to be wasted if it is not used by the best before date
○ food thrown away is money wasted for the business.

Your employer may have a system for date-coding all items delivered. A date sticker may be attached to items as they are put away. Storage systems must ensure that stock is used in the correct rotation. When putting food away, it is very important that:

○ older stock of the same item is moved to the front so that it is used first
○ new stock is never mixed up with old stock on shelves or in containers.

Did you know?

One way of remembering stock rotation is to think 'FIFO' – **first in, first out** – food that is put into storage first should be used first.

Stock control

Stock control is about maintaining minimum levels of stock to meet requirements for food production. Each commodity should have a minimum stock level set for it. As something is taken out of stores, it should be logged. When a commodity reaches its minimum level, an order should be generated. Sometimes, if there is a large function, for example, additional stock may need to be ordered to meet this need.

Stock checks need to be done at regular intervals to identify ordering requirements and monitor stock shrinkage. A stock-taking sheet should be completed. These days, stock control is often managed using an Electronic Stock Control system. In this case, minimum stock levels are held in the system and an order is automatically generated when stock reaches that level.

Stock ordering process

This begins with the stock-taking sheets or the printout from the Electronic Stock Control system. Once a need for an order is identified, it is important to ensure the correct specification, which means the quantity required and the quality. Quality agreements with suppliers may include agreed delivery dates, e.g. same day, or next day. Many organisations keep a list of preferred suppliers on which this information will be kept. The person drawing up the order may need to get a signature from someone more senior to authorise it. Sometimes a large organisation may have different departments and stock may be requisitioned from one department to another using an internal requisition form.

Once the food has been delivered, an invoice will follow. When received, it should be checked against the order and the delivery note.

Storing stock

A delivery must be put into the appropriate storage as soon as possible (preferably within 15 minutes) after arrival.

Frozen and chilled items must be put away first. Prompt storage is necessary because:

○ frozen items must not be left in warm conditions, where they could start defrosting

○ chilled items must not be allowed to warm to an unsafe temperature at which bacteria could grow – especially important with ready-to-eat items such as salads.

Packaged items should have storage instructions included on the label. These should be followed exactly. This may mean taking off the outside packaging. Any important labels must be kept for reference if necessary.

Fresh items must be put into cool storage to preserve their quality ready for preparation.

Dry goods should be taken to the stores area, where they should be entered on to the stock record to prevent theft.

Handle all items carefully. Do not attempt to lift heavy items on your own (see page 66).

Some items may need to be removed from the original external packaging before storage, for example if a cardboard box is breaking, or there is not enough space to store an item in its full packaging. Care must be taken to transfer any important information (e.g. use-by dates) onto the replacement container. Your workplace should have a system for this.

Some businesses ensure stock rotation of short-life items by marking the item with a coloured sticker to indicate the day of delivery. This encourages the use of food in the correct order.

Figure 5.24 Date-code deliveries

What is cross-contamination?

Bacteria cannot move by themselves, and so are only able to contaminate food by being transferred onto it by something or someone else. This is known as cross-contamination, and is one of the main factors in outbreaks of food poisoning.

Types of cross-contamination

There are three main types of cross-contamination:

- direct – when contaminated food comes into direct contact with another food item and bacteria are transferred from one item to the other
- indirect – when contaminated food comes into contact with a surface that then comes into contact with another food item, which becomes contaminated
- drip – when a contaminated item (usually raw meat or poultry) is stored above other food and the juices from the contaminated item drip down and contaminate the food underneath.

Illness will result if the newly contaminated food item is not cooked thoroughly before service.

The most common type is indirect cross-contamination. The main sources are:

- hands of staff working in food production areas
- cloths and equipment used by staff in these areas
- infestation of pests in the premises
- poor storage of food.

Hands

If hands are not washed thoroughly in between one job and another, cross-contamination can occur very easily. There is a particular risk in the following situations:

- if raw food is prepared, followed by cooked food
- if food preparation is resumed directly after a visit to the toilet or a smoking break.

Cloths and equipment

If cloths are not changed or cleaned regularly, cross-contamination can occur. Cloths can carry large amounts of bacteria, and have been known to spread more bacteria over a surface than were present in the first place!

Marcus says

There is no room for complacency when handling food. In a restaurant the rules should be clearly established and followed by everyone. It doesn't matter what type of restaurant, front or back of house, there is no excuse for sloppiness. Ensure there is adequate space for food preparation carried out by the front of house team, whether it is preparing a cheese trolley, chopping lemons for drinks, or any other task.

Did you know?

Raw food needs some type of preparation before it can be eaten. This usually involves cooking of some sort. Some foods can be eaten in either a raw or cooked state (e.g. tomatoes). Ready-to-eat foods are raw foods that have been prepared in advance and can be served to the customer with no further treatment. Poached salmon, paté and coleslaw salad are examples of this type of food.

It is important to keep raw foods separate from ready-to-eat foods, otherwise cross-contamination can result.

Equipment

This must be cleaned thoroughly after each use, and checked for cleanliness before being used again. Some pieces of equipment may be used only for specific types of food, or in certain areas of the food service area. A sweet trolley will be used only for desserts, and will move between the restaurant and the pastry kitchen.

Pests

Cross-contamination can occur through an insect or animal touching the surface of a raw food product and then one that has been cooked, transferring bacteria from one to the other. Pests can also transfer bacteria by leaving fur or droppings on food (see pages 153–154).

Poor storage of food

If food is not placed in suitably sized containers and covered, spillages may result. This could involve amounts of one item falling into another. Apart from being very messy and wasteful, this can become a food safety hazard, for example if an uncooked chicken defrosting on the top shelf of a refrigerator drips liquid onto an uncovered trifle on the shelf below, it is highly likely that *Salmonella* bacteria will be transferred from the chicken to the trifle.

Methods of preventing cross-contamination

Cross-contamination can be prevented by breaking the chain of raw items coming into direct or indirect contact with other foods. To do this effectively, the workflow and storage systems of a catering business must be looked at carefully to identify where there are weaknesses that may allow cross-contamination.

How cross-contamination can be prevented:
- use colour-coded systems for food types, or store them in separate areas (e.g. a separate refrigerator for raw meat)
- have separate preparation areas for raw and cooked items
- colour-code equipment so that it is used only for either raw or cooked food preparation
- store food at the correct temperature, package it correctly, label it fully and use it in date order
- organise the work area to prevent raw and cooked produce coming into contact with one another – have a linear work flow
- ensure all staff wash their hands thoroughly at the appropriate times (see pages 143–144)

Remember!

Chopping boards may be colour coded to reduce the risk of cross-contamination. The following code is commonly used in the industry:
- red – raw meat
- brown – vegetables
- blue – raw fish
- white – bakery, dairy
- yellow – cooked meat
- green – salad, fruit

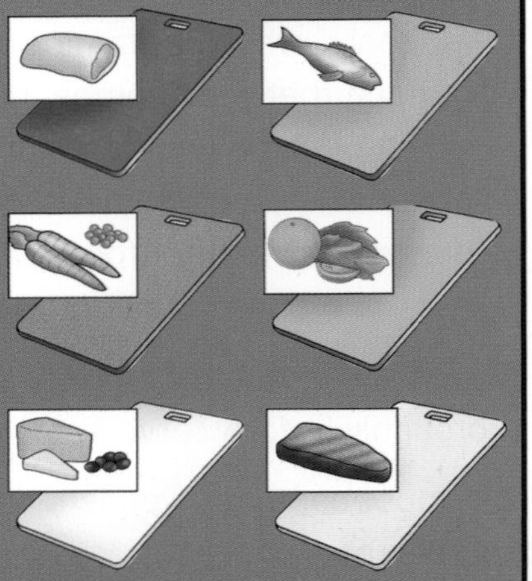

Figure 5.25 Colour-coded chopping boards

Remember!

Even if you are in a hurry, do not add new goods to a container already holding old goods.

- use disposable cloths for one purpose only – it is best if these are colour-coded.

Storing food

All the methods of storing food are intended to keep the food safe from contamination and to reduce the speed at which spoilage occurs. Stored food must be kept covered, cool (refrigerated in most cases) and dry.

There are three main areas where food is stored in the catering businesses:

- dry store
- refrigerator
- freezer.

These may be free-standing or walk-in units.

Follow these general food storage rules:

- always protect food from contamination by keeping it in a suitable container
- store all food items off the floor, on shelves or pallets
- do not overload shelves
- leave space between items for air to circulate
- keep storage areas clean, dry and free from debris at all times
- rotate stock correctly (page 159)
- tell your supervisor about any signs of pest infestation (page 154).

Dry storage

The store should be cool and well ventilated. Loose, dry commodities (e.g. salt) may be stored in wheeled bins to protect them from pests. Bins must be completely emptied and cleaned before new stock is added.

Shelves should not be overfilled, and old stock must always be put in front of new stock. Move items from flimsy bags or unsuitable containers, making sure the description label with the use-by date is transferred.

Cleaning products should not be stored with food – they should be in a separate area.

Figure 5.26 A well organised dry stores area

163

Keep the following items in the dry store:

o dry foods (e.g. pepper, sugar and dried herbs)

o canned and bottled items (unless the label specifies that they need to be refrigerated).

Fruit and vegetable storage:

o fresh fruit and vegetables should be stored in a cool, dry place

o they are often stored in a refrigerator if there is space, in a safe position.

Temperature and conditions for food storage

High-risk foods, and those that will spoil quickly, need to be stored in a refrigerator. This is because most pathogenic and food spoilage bacteria multiply very slowly or not at all between 0 and 5°C – the temperature of a refrigerator.

All industrial refrigerators should defrost automatically. If ice is allowed to build up inside the unit, this will reduce its efficiency.

Refrigerators

If separate refrigerators are not available for raw and high-risk foods, these items have to be positioned carefully in one unit. Raw food should always be stored below other food, so that no blood or juices can drip down and contaminate items on the lower shelf.

Take care with strong-smelling foods (e.g. strong cheese and fish) as they can taint more delicate items (e.g. milk and eggs) and make them taste very strange. All items in a refrigerator should be covered, for example in a container with a fitted lid, or covered with waxed paper, cling film, greaseproof paper or foil. Avoid putting food directly in front of the cooling unit, as this can affect how efficiently the refrigerator operates.

The following foods should be refrigerated:

o raw meat, poultry, fish and seafood

o cooked meat, poultry, fish and seafood

o meat, poultry and fish products (e.g. pies and patés)

o the contents of any opened cans in suitable containers

o milk, cream, cheese and eggs, and any products containing them (e.g. flans)

o prepared salads

o fruit juice

o spreads and sauces

o any other item labelled for refrigeration.

Did you know?

A blown tin has both ends bulging – the contents have spoiled, and gases have been produced in the process. The contents of these tins are not safe to eat and must be discarded. Be careful! The pressure built up inside the tin from the gases may cause the tin to explode.

Remember!

Remember to rotate goods so that the oldest items are used first. Although goods in the dry stores last a long time, they do gradually deteriorate in quality.

Did you know?

Opened cans of food should never be left in a refrigerator. As well as the danger of a cut from the sharp, exposed lid of the tin, if the juices inside the tin are acid (as with tinned fruit), they can react with the lining of the tin once it is exposed to the oxygen in air. This reaction can taint the food and give it a metallic flavour, which is unacceptable. Some tins now have a plastic coating on the inside to stop this. It is still best to transfer tinned items to a different container before storing in the fridge.

Try this!

What problems can you identify with the contents of this refrigerator?

Freezers

Food is frozen to make it last longer without spoiling. It is also kept safely, as pathogenic bacteria cannot multiply in temperatures below –18°C. However, as soon as the temperature rises, bacteria may start reproducing. Food that has been allowed to thaw should not be refrozen. This is in case the number of bacteria present have been able to reach a dangerous level and cause food poisoning. If a thawed item has been cooked, it may be refrozen. This is because the cooking process will have killed any pathogenic bacteria present.

Storing foods inside a freezer

When loading a freezer with frozen food, remember to:
o make sure all items are well wrapped
o label items clearly and include the date
o stack items close together to maintain the temperature
o place raw food below high-risk foods
o put stock with the shortest shelf life at the front.

Food storage and temperature control documentation

Under the HACCP procedures (page 171) it is important to record readings and actions taken while preparing food. These procedures provide protection for the catering business and its employees in the event of a food safety issue.

The environmental health officer visits all catering businesses regularly to check that food is being prepared according to the

Regulations. The Officer will expect to see evidence of how food safety is being maintained. They will expect to see records of a variety of monitoring procedures, including:

○ temperature records of all refrigerators and freezers
○ pest control reports
○ probe temperature records of reheated foods and those held at hot temperatures
○ cleaning checklists and schedules
○ delivery monitoring forms recording the temperature of foods at time of delivery.

If there was an outbreak of food poisoning in a restaurant, the manager should be able to prove that all the food safety procedures have been carried out correctly. This process is known as showing **due diligence**. The environmental health officer may decide that the blame for the outbreak is not with the restaurant, and may investigate other possible causes (e.g. the food suppliers).

Did you know?
Some tinned foods have been opened after hundreds of years and the contents have still been edible – although not very nice to eat!

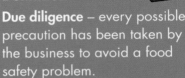

Definition
Due diligence – every possible precaution has been taken by the business to avoid a food safety problem.

Try this!
Produce a flow diagram of the key stages of food receipt and storage, to include:
○ *key checks that need to be made on receipt of goods*
○ *stock-rotation systems*
○ *food types and storage conditions*
○ *temperature for food storage.*

Try this!
Imagine you have been asked to put away a delivery of the following items:
○ *a half-gallon container of fresh cream*
○ *a 500 g container of chicken liver pate*
○ *12 fresh lemons*
○ *one case of fresh eggs*
○ *a box of bananas.*
Describe exactly what you would do with each item and give the reasons why.

Did you know?
Some ingredients in dishes do not freeze well. A sauce that is to be frozen should not be made with wheat flour because, once defrosted, it will separate if not used within a few weeks. Sauce recipes should be adapted to use modified starch instead.

Holding hot and cold food for service

Hot food

Hot cupboards and counter service equipment are designed to store food for a few hours at a safe hot temperature. The heating elements in this equipment are not sufficiently powerful to raise the temperature of the food quickly. This could mean that pathogenic bacteria could survive and reproduce to a dangerous level during the slow heating process.

The following rules apply when using hot holding equipment:

- always preheat the equipment before use
- do not use the equipment to reheat food
- check the equipment regularly if hot water is used – if it needs topping up, use hot water (not cold)
- if heated lights are used, keep the food fully in the lit areas.

When hot food is out on display and cannot be kept above 63°C, it can be put out for only one continuous period of up to 2 hours. After this period, the food must be thrown away. This is because it will have been at a temperature at which bacteria can multiply rapidly for too long, and may no longer be safe to eat.

Figure 5.27 A bain-marie, one type of hot holding equipment

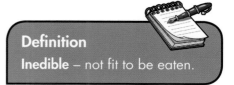

Definition
Inedible – not fit to be eaten.

Cold food

Food that is to be held for service at room temperature has to be treated very carefully. This is because the temperature at which it has to be kept is ideal for bacteria to multiply rapidly. But if the food was held at a lower temperature, it could be unpleasant to eat – imagine eating a sandwich that has been taken straight out of a refrigerator.

Cold food in a display cabinet or vending machine must be kept below 8°C, and ideally below 5°C. Where this is not possible, cold food can be put out on display at room temperature for only one continuous period of up to 4 hours. After this time, it must be thrown away. The length of time the food is left out must be recorded so that it is never left out for too long. Different establishments use different systems to record this information. It is very convenient when the meal service time lasts 4 hours, as the food put out at the beginning and left unsold can be thrown away when service finishes.

Figure 5.28 Is your Christmas turkey safe?

How to use a temperature probe

Some food may reach the required temperature on the outside, but still be a very different temperature in the middle. A temperature probe is needed to check that the internal temperature has reached the necessary level.

A temperature probe is a type of thermometer on a long stick that is used to take the core temperature from the middle of food. It is particularly useful when:

○ reheating a tray of cottage pies ready to serve on a counter
○ testing to see if the inside of a whole chicken is cooked.

Temperature probes are usually digital, and can be battery-operated. It is important to keep them very clean. They should always be sterilised before and after each use, otherwise they could transfer dangerous bacteria from one food to another.

> **Remember!**
> All food must be heated to at least 75°C, and that temperature must be held for at least 2 minutes to make it safe. In Scotland, food must be heated to at least 82°C for at least 2 minutes. No food should be reheated more than once.

Figure 5.29 Using a temperature probe

> **Remember!**
> Hot food should be held at 63°C prior to and during service. Cold food should be held below 8°C.

Temperature probes need to be checked regularly to make sure they are working correctly. If they are not accurate, they should not be used until they have been repaired or replaced.

Figure 5.30 A blast chiller

Figure 5.31 A shallow, flat container allows faster cooling

> **Remember!**
> Frequent opening and closing of the refrigerator door will cause the temperature inside to keep rising and falling.

Test yourself!

Complete the following statements:

1 The transfer of bacteria from raw to cooked food is called
_____.

2 The person authorised to enter food premises to inspect them for food safety is called _____.

3 The main law controlling the hygienic supply, preparation and service of food is called the _____.

4 To make it safe, all raw food should be heated to _____°C in England and Wales and _____°C in Scotland for _____ minutes.

5 To find out if food being heated is the correct temperature all the way through, a _____ needs to be used.

6 The _____ of bacteria may survive high temperatures.

Food safety procedures

To ensure that all food served to the public is safe, there are a range of laws and regulations that must be followed by all catering businesses. Each catering organisation has to produce a policy document giving details of the standards it is setting and the training it undertakes to give all the catering staff. A detailed set of records has to be kept on a day-to-day basis in a catering kitchen to prove that the correct procedures are being followed. In this way, customers should be confident they will not be made ill by eating food produced by the establishment. Environmental health officers regularly inspect all the hygiene, health and safety aspects of businesses to make sure the standards are met.

> **Did you know?**
> The **basic food hygiene test** makes sure food handlers know the main principles of food safety. Some food handlers take the **intermediate food hygiene** examination. Supervisors may take the **advanced food hygiene** qualification.

Key requirements of food safety legislation

Food safety laws require all catering businesses to ensure:

- all their food production and service staff practise a high standard of personal hygiene (pages 139–144)
- all their staff have regular training in all hygiene, health and safety matters relating to their workplace (page 40)
- all their staff comply with the rules and regulations of their organisation, particularly regarding the preparation and service of food
- all their staff obey the requirements of the food safety legislation that relates to them – this should be explained clearly to staff by their employer, and training records should be kept.

It is very important that all records required (e.g. temperature records) are kept accurately. They may be needed as evidence if there is a food safety incident. If an organisation is investigated, but can show that it has kept all the records correctly and has high food safety standards, it may be given a lower penalty if it is prosecuted, or may not be prosecuted at all. This defence is called 'due diligence' (see page 166).

Figure 5.32 Completing a checklist

HACCP practices and procedures

In every business that produces, serves or sells food, it is vital that there is an organised system to reduce all risk of food safety hazards.

The HACCP procedures require there to be a **documented** system highlighting all areas where special attention should be paid to food safety. The system should cover all food used on the premises, and should follow the route from delivery of the raw materials through to consumption, service or sale of the items.

Definition

Documented – when a detailed record of information is made.

Step	Hazard	Action
1 Purchase	High-risk (ready-to-eat) foods contaminated by food-poisoning bacteria or toxins	Buy from reputable supplier only. Specify maximum temperature at delivery
2 Receipt of food	High-risk (ready-to-eat) foods contaminated by food-poisoning bacteria or toxins	Check that food looks, smells and feels right. Check the temperature is right
3 Storage	Growth of food-poisoning bacteria, toxins on high-risk (ready-to-eat) foods. Further contamination	High-risk foods stored at safe temperature. Store them wrapped. Label high-risk food with the correct use-by date. Rotate stock and use by recommended date
4 Preparation	Contamination of high-risk (ready-to-eat) foods. Growth of food-poisoning bacteria	Wash hands before handling food. Limit any exposure to room temperatures during preparation. Prepare with clean equipment and use this for high-risk (ready-to-eat) food only. Separate cooked foods from raw foods
5 Cooking	Survival of food-poisoning bacteria	Cook rolled joints, chicken and re-formed meats (e.g. burgers) so that the thickest part reaches at least 75°C. Sear the outside of other, solid meat cuts (e.g. joints of beef, steaks) before cooking
6 Cooling	Growth of food-poisoning bacteria. Production of poisons by bacteria. Contamination with food-poisoning bacteria	Cool foods down as quickly as possible. Don't leave out at room temperatures to cool unless the cooling period is short (e.g. place stews or rice in shallow trays and cool to chill temperatures quickly)
7 Hot-holding	Growth of food-poisoning bacteria. Production of poisons by bacteria	Keep food hot, above 63°C
8 Reheating	Survival of food-poisoning bacteria	Reheat to above 75°C
9 Chilled storage	Growth of food-poisoning bacteria	Keep temperatures at right level. Label high-risk ready-to-eat foods with correct date code
10 Serving	Growth of disease-causing bacteria. Production of poisons by bacteria. Contamination	Cold service foods – serve high-risk foods as soon as possible after removing from refrigerated storage to avoid them getting warm. Hot foods – serve high-risk foods quickly to avoid them cooling down

Figure 5.33 Critical control points – Department of Health

Action to take when monitoring reveals a problem

The purpose of monitoring and checking is to spot a potential problem or risk before it becomes a serious hazard. If checking is carried out regularly, any difference in results should show up very quickly.

The action taken depends on the type of problem. Urgent action is necessary if the problem concerns a possible food safety hazard. Figure 5.35 shows the type of action that may be necessary to prevent food from becoming a hazard.

Figure 5.34 *What to do when plated food items do not look like the prepared photograph?*

Problem	Possible action to be taken
Poor standard of work produced by food service staff	Retraining and closer supervision by restaurant manager
Refrigerator temperature rises significantly	Check that the refrigerator is not defrosting automatically. If this is not the case: ○ move items to another fridge at the correct temperature ○ unplug the fridge if possible ○ put an 'out of order' notice on it ○ tell your supervisor as soon as possible.
A mouse is spotted in the corner of the restaurant	○ Tell your supervisor as soon as possible. ○ The pest control contractor will be called out immediately. ○ Kitchen staff will need to look out for evidence of mouse infestation. ○ Make sure no food crumbs are left around, or any food left uncovered, in kitchen and stores areas.

Microwave does not heat the food properly	o Check that the portion of food is the correct size for the time allowed. o Test the microwave by heating a cup of water. o If it does not perform as it should, unplug the equipment so it cannot be used. o Put an 'out of order' sign on the machine. o Tell your supervisor. o An engineer should attend to rectify the problem.
Chilled produce is delivered in a van that is not refrigerated	o Check the temperature of the items delivered. If over the safe limit of 8°C, refuse to accept the delivery. o Tell your supervisor, as this may have been a problem before and the supplier may be charged.
Out-of-date salad items are found at the back of the refrigerator during a stock take	o Throw the out-of-date items away. o Tell your supervisor, as stock figures will be affected.
A large amount of sliced bar fruit waste is found in the bin	Restaurant manager to retrain staff in efficient preparation methods.
A large amount of cooked waste is found in the bin	Restaurant manager to investigate and liaise with the head chef to take action. Possible reasons: o portions served too large o quality of food poor.
Plated food items do not look like the prepared photographs	Head chef will investigate and take action. Possible reasons: o poor quality food used o staff not trained correctly.

Figure 5.35 Action to take when monitoring reveals a problem

Try this!
Which monitoring processes would you use for the following situations?
o *Keeping the results of refrigerator temperature checks.*
o *Making sure all areas of the staff changing room have been cleaned thoroughly.*
o *Checking that a meat delivery is correct.*
o *Finding out if there is any evidence of mice in the dry stores area.*

Definition
Monitoring – regularly checking condition and progress.

173

The relative importance of different hazards

It is important to be able to identify which situations require urgent action and which problems can be solved a little later.

All circumstances that put any person in danger should be dealt with immediately. These include:

- fire or security alert
- accident to any person in the area
- foreign body found in food
- equipment found in a dangerous condition
- floor surface found in a dangerous condition
- food left in an unsafe condition
- food stored in an unsafe condition.

Identifying types of food safety hazard

Food safety hazards can come from the most unlikely sources – some of them quite unexpected. When trying to identify possible food safety hazards, you need to be very open-minded. Figure 5.36 shows the questions you need to ask when trying to identify food safety hazards.

Question	Possible answers
Where could harmful bacteria be found in the workplace?	<ul><li>Poor cleaning of equipment.</li><li>Insect or rodent infestation.</li><li>Poor hygiene practices of staff – not washing hands sufficiently, staff being ill and still coming to work.</li></ul>
How is cross-contamination caused?	<ul><li>By using the same chopping boards for raw and cooked foods.</li><li>By storing raw food above cooked food in the refrigerator.</li><li>By food handlers not washing their hands thoroughly in between dealing with raw and cooked foods.</li></ul>
What other possible ways are there for food to be contaminated in the workplace?	<ul><li>Cleaning chemicals getting into food due to poor storage or not rinsing properly.</li><li>Foreign bodies getting into food due to breakages not being cleared away carefully.</li></ul>
Which high-risk foods come into the catering premises in an uncooked state?	The following are high-risk due to the food poisoning bacteria or toxins that may be found in them in their raw state:<ul><li>chicken</li><li>eggs</li><li>meat</li><li>vegetables.</li></ul>

Is it possible for harmful bacteria to be able to multiply to a dangerous level?	o Is any food cooked and then left out at room temperature for a long time before being put in the refrigerator? Is there a better procedure that can be used? o Is any high-risk raw food left out for a long time at room temperature? Can this be avoided? o Is there ever a significant delay between cooking food, keeping it hot and it being served? Is there an alternative to this practice?
Is a probe used correctly to ensure thorough cooking and reheating of food?	If no, what happens instead?
Is food ever served before it has been reheated properly?	If yes, why and how can this be avoided next time?
Is frozen food sometimes not defrosted in time?	If yes, what happens?
Does the correct equipment exist on the premises for certain processes? Is it used when it should be (e.g. a blast chiller used to chill food quickly)?	If the equipment is not available, what happens?
What happens when demand is unpredictable? How is extra food provided at short notice?	Is there a stock of stand-by items kept in a freezer? How long does it take to get this ready for service?
What happens when food has to travel some distance between preparation and service? Does this happen when the food is hot or cold?	Is specialist equipment provided? If not, how is the food kept free from contamination and at the correct temperature?

Figure 5.36 Identifying food safety hazards

Try this!

Look at Figure 5.36. Now think about your workplace. Make a similar list identifying risk areas that exist with present work practices. This is the first stage of the HACCP procedures for creating a food safety management system.

It is very important to report all possible hazards to your supervisor. The situation may result in:

○ a serious safety hazard (food or health and safety)

○ a high level of wastage, leading to shortages and inaccurate stock records

○ a repair or service call-out to fix or maintain a piece of equipment or to maintain the hygiene of the premises

○ identification of a need for staff training.

Try this!

Arrange the following incidents in the order you would deal with them if they all happened together. Then state the action you would take in respect of each hazard.

○ *A carton of cream is past its use-by date in the refrigerator.*

○ *There is a pool of water around the door of an upright freezer, and the contents are thawing.*

○ *A waiter cuts their finger and needs a plaster.*

○ *A fly falls in a jug of milk on a customer's table.*

○ *A fire is discovered in a store cupboard.*

Figure 5.37 Hazards may need to be prioritised

Key elements of a food safety policy

Current food safety legislation recommends that all catering organisations have a food safety policy. The food safety policy describes how the business provides training and maintains standards to keep within the food safety laws. A policy will include:

- standards of personal hygiene required by all food handlers (pages 139–144)
- procedures for reporting sickness and accidents within the workplace (pages 46–47)
- requirements for pest control measures within the building (page 153)
- minimum acceptable standards of cleaning and disinfection in food production areas (page 150)
- requirement for all visitors to the production areas to wear suitable protective clothing – usually a white coat and hat, and sometimes gloves, hairnets and special footwear are also provided.

Records and reporting procedures

Under the HACCP legislation (page 171), there is a requirement to keep records relating to the hazard analysis and monitoring process. The type and number of records kept will depend on the size and type of catering operation. The most common types of records and reporting systems are:

- training records for the use of dangerous machines, cleaning procedures, hygiene requirements, etc.
- pest control records
- temperature records for freezers, refrigerators, hot and cold holding equipment, cooling food, etc.
- accident report forms (page 56)
- sickness records of any notifiable illnesses
- customer complaints regarding possible food safety issues
- maintenance record of equipment that could affect food safety.

Fridge temperatures

Week commencing: _____

	Time	Signed	Time	Signed	Time	Signed
MON	Temp		Temp		Temp	
TUE	Time	Signed	Time	Signed	Time	Signed
	Temp		Temp		Temp	
WED	Time	Signed	Time	Signed	Time	Signed
	Temp		Temp		Temp	
THURS	Time	Signed	Time	Signed	Time	Signed
	Temp		Temp		Temp	
FRI	Time	Signed	Time	Signed	Time	Signed
	Temp		Temp		Temp	
SAT	Time	Signed	Time	Signed	Time	Signed
	Temp		Temp		Temp	
SUN	Time	Signed	Time	Signed	Time	Signed
	Temp		Temp		Temp	

Comments

_____

_____

_____

Figure 5.38 Temperature control record sheet

Test yourself!

1 Which of the following is an example of monitoring food safety?
   a Taking fridge temperatures.
   b Writing weekly menus.
   c Washing the service area floor.
   d Counting the takings in the till.

2 What is the process of collecting information to prove food safety called?
   a Assessing hygiene methods.
   b Monitoring bad practice.
   c Copying clear records.
   d Demonstrating due diligence.

3 Which of the following is not an example of a HACCP record?
   a Staff rota
   b Temperature chart
   c Cleaning schedule
   d Equipment checklist.

4 Complete the table below, indicating the conditions and location where you would store the following items, and which you would put away first:

Item	Order of storage	Location	Conditions (e.g. temperature)
Fresh fish			
Tinned tomatoes			
Dried basil			
Fresh garlic			
Chilled potato salad			
Frozen peas			

6

Dealing with payments

In this chapter you will cover skills and knowledge in the following units:

- 7132 – Unit 205 (2Gen9): Maintain and deal with payments
- 7091 – Unit 260: Dealing with payments
- 7103 – Unit 107: Dealing with payments and bookings; and part of Unit 104: Legislation in food and beverage service
- 7103 – Unit 207: Handling payments and maintaining the payment point; and part of Unit 204: Legislation in food and beverage service

Working through this chapter could also provide evidence for the following Functional Skills at Level 1:

Functional Mathematics – Analysing Level 1 – solve problems requiring calculation, with common measures, including money

Functional ICT – Developing and presenting communication information Level 1

In this chapter you will learn how to:

- work with food and drink control systems
- maintain a payment point
- deal with payment transactions
- deal with errors and problems when handling payments

Food and drink control systems

Handling cash or cash equivalents is a very responsible job. It is important to follow the cash-handling procedure of your own establishment. This will reduce the risk of errors, and maintain the security of customers and staff.

In some establishments, dealing with payments may be the role of a cashier, who will create the customer's bills and deal with all transactions. In others, it may be one of the many tasks of a waiter.

The customer's bill can be produced electronically or manually – the method and the end outcome involve the same basic process.

Staff training for cash handling is really important. The set procedures must be followed by all staff. If you do not understand the process, you must ask.

All food and drink control systems operate using documentation. For every sale, an order must be taken from the customer. This will result in a bill that is presented to the customer for payment.

There are two main types of food control system:

○ manual
○ electronic.

Whichever system is used, the customer's order will include a table number, number of covers, date and the waiter's signature, as well as the food order clearly written. With electronic systems, the date is generally registered electronically, and the 'signature' is applied through a signing-in process.

Manual control systems

The waiter will write down the customer's order, usually on a **carbonised triplicate order pad**. Using a triplicate order pad provides three copies of the order. The order includes the table number, number of covers, date and the waiter's signature, together with the order.

Definitions

Carbonised paper is treated so that if you write on the top copy, the writing also appears on the following sheets as well. This saves writing out multiple copies of the order.

Triplicate order pad – every third sheet is a top sheet, the other two are carbonised so they will show a copy of what is written on the top sheet. Different colours may be used for the three sheets. You need to make sure that all three sheets are above the card, to make sure that three (but no more than three) sheets record what you write.

The top copy of the order goes to the department that will issue the food or drinks ordered. For example, if food is to be issued from a kitchen, the chef would be handed the top copy. The second copy is generally for the cashier, and the third copy for the server's own information.

Every time a customer makes an order, a new order is written and the copies issued as above.

The cashier will produce a handwritten bill using the **dockets** for that customer's table. On request, the bill will be totalled and presented to the customer. The transactions are often entered into a standard cash till that registers all sales. These cash tills offer limited sales analysis, but do provide total sales figures.

Manual systems are still found in many quality, well established restaurants.

Electronic control systems

Electronic control systems (also known as 'electronic point of sale' or EPOS) perform all the same tasks as manual systems, but automatically. This can save time and reduce the likelihood of errors. Some of the more advanced electronic systems can also do many other things, for example:

○ providing detailed sales analysis to help the business with menu planning and pricing
○ linking to stock control and ordering systems.

These range from simple pre-set or pre-priced systems to sophisticated computerised food and drink management systems controlling all aspects of food control, even stock control.

Electronic till

The simple electronic till is used to place orders. It provides duplicate print-outs of orders, and stores a record of each transaction. Most will have all the items pre-set and pre-priced, so that the person placing the order needs to hit only one button for each item.

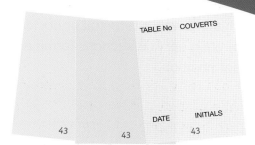

Figure 6.1 A triplicate order pad produces separate copies for different people

Definition

A **check** or **docket** is a copy of a customer's food or drink order. It is used to communicate information to restaurant staff, for example in the kitchen or bar, or to the waiter or cashier. It is also used to control food and drink stocks issued.

Remember!

No order – no food or drink!

Remember!

You must make sure the information on an order you write is readable (legible).

TABLE No	COUVERTS
1	4

2 x SOUP
2 x PATE
-
2 x SALMON
2 x CHICKEN
4 x POTATOES
4 x VEGETABLES

DATE	INITIALS
30/11/07	J. NIXON
	16

Figure 6.2 The order must contain certain basic details – and must be readable

Point-of-sale system

This involves a terminal or docking station for hand-held terminals at each service section. Terminals are electronic keypads fixed in a set position.

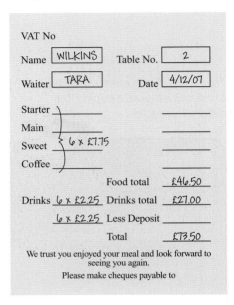

```
VAT No
Name  WILKINS       Table No.    2
Waiter  TARA        Date  4/12/07

Starter  ⌉
Main     │
Sweet    ⎬ 6 x £7.75
Coffee   ⌋
                Food total      £46.50
Drinks 6 x £2.25  Drinks total   £27.00
       6 x £2.25  Less Deposit
                Total            £73.50
We trust you enjoyed your meal and look forward to
            seeing you again.
      Please make cheques payable to
```

```
        Your Receipt
         Thank you

          The Boat
          Banbury
        VAT: 123 456 78

*****************************
OTHER HOT DRINK           1.60
OTHER HOT DRINK           1.60
COFFEE                    1.40
COFFEE                    1.40
COFFEE                    1.40
COFFEE                    1.40
COFFEE                    1.40
COFFEE                    1.40
COFFEE                    1.40
COFFEE                    1.40
ITEM CT              10
CASH                    14.40
03-03-2008                11:12
                          009790
```

Figure 6.3 A handwritten bill and one from an electronic till

Hand-helds are mobile terminals used by staff. These terminals may be linked to a remote printer, and the orders sent to the appropriate section. For example, a drinks order would be transmitted to the bar, and the contents of the sale would be stored.

For bill presentation, the customer's total sales can be retrieved and printed on request by the cashier or waiter.

> **Remember!**
> The more sophisticated the system, the more sales performance analysis is available.

Test yourself!

1 What five main items should the waiter record on the customer's order?

2 How many copies of the order are normally kept by the cashier?

3 Why do you need to write the order very clearly?

4 Give three advantages of electronic control systems.

Maintaining a payment point

To operate any system (manual or automatic), setting up and organising a payment point (or points) is critical for smooth customer service. The payment point is opened at the start of the day's trading.

Taking a Z-reading

Before undertaking any tasks, a **Z-reading** should be taken to check that it gives a zero balance. If the Z-reading is not zero, you should report this to your supervisor. He or she must complete this task before the day's trading begins.

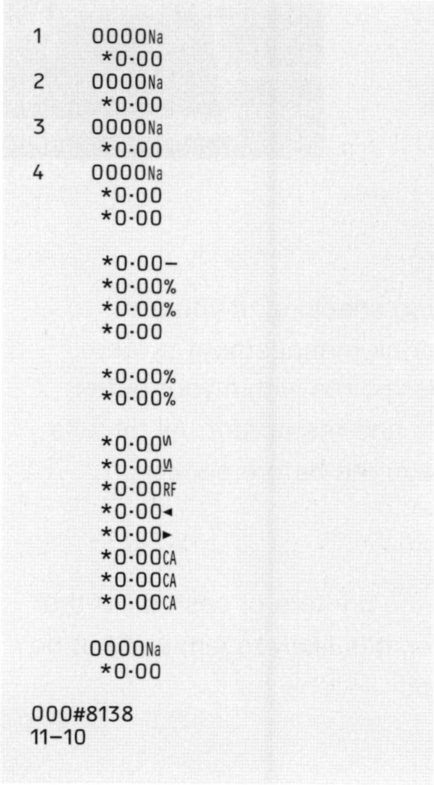
1 0000Na
*0·00
2 0000Na
*0·00
3 0000Na
*0·00
4 0000Na
*0·00
*0·00

*0·00–
*0·00%
*0·00%
*0·00

*0·00%
*0·00%

*0·00
*0·00
*0·00RF
*0·00◂
*0·00▸
*0·00CA
*0·00CA
*0·00CA

0000Na
*0·00

000#8138
11–10

Figure 6.4 The Z-reading must be zero at the start of trading

> **Definition**
> A **Z-reading** provides a read-out of all sales and transactions. At the start of the day, this should be zero. If the till read-out is not zero, this indicates that the previous trading session has not been completed.

Collecting the float

The **float** should be collected from an authorised person. It must be counted in the presence of that authorised person, and signed for by both the issuer (the authorised person) and the receiver of the float.

If the float is not the correct amount, it needs to be adjusted in the presence of an authorised person and then both issuer and receiver should sign.

> **Definition**
> **Float:** a small amount of cash, including coins of all values. The float is put in the till at the start of the day's trading so that cash customers who do not have the correct money can be given change.

The purpose of the float is to allow you to give change to customers. It should cover the full range of coins and notes. Regardless of the customer's total bill, you should be able to provide change.

The float, once received, should be placed in the till. The coins must be properly organised in separate compartments and the notes segregated. The till should now be locked or otherwise kept secure until trading begins.

Figure 6.5 The float must be carefully organised in the till

Checking till rolls

Before service, the till roll or rolls need checking. If you are operating a computerised food and drink management system, there may be several stations or order points within your outlet. These may include bar, kitchen, cellar and restaurant. All till rolls should be checked and replaced if required before service.

Replacing till rolls

The correct till roll must be placed in the printers or cash till. If the incorrect till roll is placed in any printer, it is likely to jam and not be able to print. In the worst case, it could block the whole system.

Till rolls vary in width size and type: they may be paper rolls or thermal rolls.

Paper till rolls

In older cash registers, the till roll is likely to be made from pulped paper. Often the machine requires two till rolls: one for the customer receipt and the other for auditing purposes. A paper till roll that is about to run out usually shows a warning stripe. If this appears, the roll should be replaced immediately so that service is not disrupted.

Figure 6.6 Replacing a till roll

Thermal till rolls

Computerised systems may have thermal rolls, which rely on heat rather than a ribbon to print. These are silent when printing, so they are often used in restaurants and guest areas to avoid noise. But as they are thermal, they cannot be used in hot areas such as a kitchen.

Paper printer rolls

Paper printer rolls (sometimes called 'non-thermal' rolls) are used for back-of-house areas such as kitchens, so the order can be heard printing.

Checking the card authorisation machine

In many outlets, card transactions are the preferred payment method for most customers. Before trading, you should check that the card authorisation machine is working.

Stationery requirements

To operate an efficient payment point, various stationery items need to be readily available. Sufficient stock of all stationery is the key to a smooth cashiering operation.

Stationery goods should be ordered using a requisition book listing items and quantities. The order will be issued by an authorised person, and you sign on receipt of the goods.

Stationery items required by a cashier should include the following:

○ Spare till rolls – all types should be readily available for replacement during service.
○ Waiter's order pads – these are numbered and checked for control purposes. Waiters are issued order pads individually and the numbers are recorded.
○ Reservations list – provides information already known about customers who have pre-booked, for example their expected time of arrival and any special requests. By looking at the reservations list, the cashier will know the total number of expected guests and the number of guests per booking, as well as any special prices for certain bookings (such as for large

parties). In addition to those on the reservations list, there will usually be some chance customers (or 'walk-ins') who are unexpected but very welcome. Stationery orders need to allow for this factor.

○ Menus – sufficient numbers for the session's business. The complete range of menus appropriate for the session should be readily available in case of queries over a customer's bill.

○ Drinks list – as above, sufficient numbers for the session's business, and the complete range available.

○ Promotional information – current and future promotions should be on display and or handed to customers at the appropriate time. Promotions should be checked as being current for pricing of bills. Future offers can be presented with the bill or printed as a message on bills, for customer information.

○ Guests' bills – these might be settled immediately on receipt of food and drink, or at the end of a meal, or at the end of a stay in a hotel. The bill may be printed or handwritten. Guests' bills are usually personalised for the business with the company logo and company information. A copy of the guest's bill, once settled, becomes their receipt.

○ Bill holders – these are used to present the bill to the customer. They usually take the form of a folder, so that the bill is hidden within the folder when it is given to the customer. This allows the customer, who may be paying for his or her guests, to check the contents are correct and discreetly settle the account. Alternatively, a plate or small bill tray can be used.

○ Business cards – these are useful to hand to visitors so that they have something to take away for future reference. A business card may be placed in the bill holder when presenting the bill.

○ Pens – these may be branded with the company name in order to promote the establishment. They are often offered as a souvenir. Corporate pens should be issued to all service staff to set standards and for promotional use. A pen should be offered together with the bill holder for customers to use if signing, and for completing customer comment cards.

○ Comment cards – these are sometimes presented to the customer with their bill. Comment cards are useful as feedback to any business. They also provide the customer with the opportunity to compliment or complain politely. Completed

> **Remember!**
> Check that menus are for the right date and session, and for the right outlet – make sure a dinner menu is not presented for a lunch session.

Figure 6.7 The bill holder both promotes the restaurant brand, and is useful for concealing the bill

comment cards should always be collected and read, and comments passed to the management so that they can be discussed in meetings, and if relevant, changes made to service procedures. It is a legal requirement under the Data Protection Act 1998 for completed comment cards to be stored securely in order to protect customers' personal details.

YOUR FEEDBACK WOULD BE APPRECIATED

Table No .... Number of Guests ....

Personal Comments

Please tick the relevent box

	Excellent	Good	Average	Poor
Was the service friendly?	☐	☐	☐	☐
Did you enjoy your meal?	☐	☐	☐	☐
Was it value for money?	☐	☐	☐	☐
Menu choice & dish availability?	☐	☐	☐	☐
Drinks service prompt and correct?	☐	☐	☐	☐

What made your visit memorable?

Waiter/ess Name .... Date .... Lunch/Dinner
Would you like to make a future reservation? Yes/No
When? ....

How often do you visit Blades Restaurant?
First visit ☐
Once a week ☐
Once a month ☐
2 to 3 times a month ☐
Other ☐

Your contact details:
Name ....
Contact Tel. No ....
Best time to call ....

Please hand to your Waiter/ess or Head Waiter.

Figure 6.8 Comment cards provide customers with the opportunity to compliment – or to complain!

○ Cash summary sheets – these are required if you are operating a manual cashiering system. A cash summary sheet is completed by the cashier each trading session, using information obtained from customers' bills (see pages 193–195). A simple cash summary sheet is used to record the revenue per sale of food and drinks, and the total takings for food and drinks for each trading session. Computerised cashiering systems can provide all this information automatically.

○ Error slips – these are used to record any errors made on a till, such as over-rings or under-rings (see page 205). They are signed by the cashier and used to adjust the till totals at the end of trading.

○ Miscellaneous items – to operate the payment point successfully, the cashier may also need items such as paper clips, stapler, hole punch, sticky tape, extra money bags, money box and calculator. All cashier stationery should be stored in an organised manner to keep the stationery flat and presentable – but should also be easily accessible during service.

Definition

The Data Protection Act (1998) lays out rules governing the collection and storage of personal information about people.

Legal requirements for operating a payment point

The Trades Description Act 1968

This Act governs the sale of any products. In a catering establishment, the food and drink served and sold must be advertised correctly. Any description of the product must be accurate. The price charged to customers must be as displayed on menus, drinks lists and promotions. For example, a branded gin must be used if advertised; cuts of meat must be correct as described (e.g. fillet not rump) and there must not be any substitutions unless stated – see page 116.

Price Marking Order 2004

(An Order is a subset of an Act – the Price Marking Order 2004 is an updating of the Prices Act 1974.) The purpose of this Order is to make sure customers are fully aware of the charges for food and drink before entering premises such as a restaurant. The menu and drinks list must be displayed in a prominent position outside the premises. If the drinks list and menu are extensive, only a sample list needs to be on display. The sample must represent fairly what is on offer. It usually covers a selection from each menu section, with prices. A sample drinks lists would provide a selection from each section – for example, wines, spirits, liqueurs, vermouths, fortified wine, alco-pops, cider, beers, minerals, juices – all with prices.

Establishments offering food and drink from a self-service counter must also display the priced menu and drinks list at a point where the customer can read it before they select their purchase. All prices listed must include VAT. This rule does not apply to members' outlets such as clubs, schools, colleges or offices.

Any **service charges** or **cover charges** must be shown as prominently as the prices of the food and drink prior to ordering.

Figure 6.9 Prices must be displayed clearly outside the restaurant

Weights and Measures Act 1985 and the Weights and Measures (Intoxicating Liquor) Order 1988

As cashier, remember to check and charge for the quantity sold, for example, measures of drinks (see page 116).

Data Protection Act 1998

The aim of this Act is to protect customers from the misuse of their personal information, obtained through being a customer.

Today, with the widespread use of computerised systems, customers' personal information (such as name, address, date of birth) is often collected and held on a computer. This is permissible providing the personal information is processed and obtained legally and fairly. There must be security measures in place so that unauthorised access to this information is not possible. Security measures must safeguard against the disclosure, alteration, destruction or loss of this personal data.

Remember!

Overcharging is disastrous for customer satisfaction; undercharging is disastrous for the business.

Definitions

Service charge: an extra charge placed on a customer's bill to cover the cost of the waiting staff. The charge may be a fixed amount, or a percentage of the total bill.

Cover charge: a minimum charge placed on a customer's order. It is used to avoid tables being blocked with diners ordering very little but staying a long time.

Security procedures for dealing with cash and other payments

A successful business can handle significant amounts of cash in the course of a session, as well as having a lot of valuable stock and dangerous equipment. Security on the premises needs to be robust to prevent theft, attack and opportunist crime. All employees have a duty to protect the property of their employer and the safety of customers.

Position of cash desk

The cashier's area needs to be secure and well situated. The cashier will often be behind a counter.

The cashier's area is often situated near the entrance or exit of an establishment. Cashiers can contribute to the security of the premises by keeping a close eye on customers coming in and out.

Figure 6.10 The cashier is in a good position to see people coming in – and out

Keys

Only nominated people should be given keys, which then become the responsibility of that individual. Keys that are used by other staff should always be returned to an authorised person or stored in an agreed secure place.

If a key goes missing, it should be reported to the management. If the keys are not found after active searching, it will be necessary to replace all the locks that are affected.

Petty cash

If cash is taken from the petty cash box, then a receipt for the items purchased and any change must be brought back to the cashier. The cashier should keep a record of the amount of cash in the box, and any amounts taken out, and by whom.

Money box

During business hours, cash builds up in the till. It is more secure to remove some of the cash from the till at intervals and transfer it, via a money box, to the safe for security.

Safe

A safe is a secure location to store cash taken during and after trading and before banking. It is often made of thick, fireproof metal, with a key or a combination lock. The manager will hold the key or combination for the safe.

> **Try this!**
> **Make sure you know the security procedures for handling cash at your place of work. How often is cash collected from the till? Who collects it? Where is it taken?**

> **Definition**
> **Petty cash:** a small amount of cash that is stored in a cash box for incidental small expenses.

Figure 6.11 The manager should know the combination for the safe

Suspicious items

All staff should keep an eye out for any suspicious items, for example a bag left behind under a table after the guest has left. It may be a simple mistake – but in the worst case, it could be a bomb.

You should report any suspicious item to management or security personnel. Do not touch it – it could be dangerous, and evidence could be spoiled, for example if fingerprints are damaged. (See page 68.)

Lost property

All lost property found in the establishment should be reported and the details entered in the lost property book (see page 68). The details should be noted, including day, date, time, location, description of goods and contents, and name of finder. A reference number may be allocated. If you need to check the contents of a wallet or handbag that has been found, you should always do so in front of a witness.

A label should be attached to the item, showing the date it was found. The item should then be kept in a designated place. Valuable items such as wallets or handbags should be kept in a safe; other items such as clothes or umbrellas may be kept in a box or other safe storage area.

When someone comes to claim an item of lost property, you should check the details they give against the item details. For example, you could ask them about the colour, shape or size of the item they have lost. Always take the person's name and address. If your establishment requires it, refer the matter to the manager.

Visitors

In large organisations (for example a hotel), visitors other than customers may be required to sign in and provide information outlining the company they represent. They may be issued with a visitor's pass so that staff are aware of their identity. In these circumstances, any visitor without a valid pass should be regarded as suspicious.

Whether or not your establishment issues visitor's passes, if you have any doubts about someone, you should call your manager or supervisor (see page 68).

Test yourself!

1 Why should two people count the float together?

2 What would the takings be if the float was £50 and the till reading was £2,575?

3 What is the purpose of a Z-reading?

4 What is the difference between a float and petty cash?

5 What is the difference between a service charge and a cover charge?

6 Which Act dictates how you deal with customers' details?

7 Which Act relates to how you describe the items you are selling, and which Act relates to the amounts that you sell?

8 Name three paper items needed to operate a payment point.

Dealing with payments

In order to maintain the payment point, the cashier must:
- maintain the cash float
- prepare customers' bills
- count the money received from customers
- always count out change to customers
- never leave the payment point unattended
- store tips away from the payment point
- not allow any unauthorised person at the payment point
- keep any key for cashier's use only
- be alert to security issues.

Remember!
Waiters should not count the money left by customers at the table, but should give it directly to the cashier.

Figure 6.12 This is not the way to run a secure payment point

Preparation of customers' bills

Customers may be requested to settle their bill at various stages of the meal, according to company policy. The bill may be paid:
- before service, at the point of ordering at a bar or take-away, then the food and drink is prepared and cooked to order
- at the end of the meal or following after-dinner drinks, as in a restaurant
- as soon as food or drinks are brought to the customer's table, as in a café or in some bars
- at a self-service counter or bar, when food or drink have been given directly to the customer.

All customers' bills are prepared in a similar manner, whether they are created manually or electronically. The sequence for producing customers' bills does not vary, but some of the processes have been replaced by machines for accuracy and speed. Even a calculator reduces errors.

Preparing a bill requires the cashier to:
○ identify the items sold
○ price each item sold
○ add the prices together to give a total, including any additional charges (such as a set service charge, see page 189)
○ store the prices for individual items and the total charged
○ present the bill.

Identifying the items sold

When taking payment, it may be possible to identify the items the customer is purchasing because they are on display on a tray, or on a bar counter. In this situation, all that is required is to check quantities (e.g. a 125 or 175 ml glass of wine).

If a waiter took the customer's order, then the items will be listed on the cashier's copy of the order and can be checked by the cashier. It is very important that the orders provide table numbers, number of covers, date and signature of server (see pages 297–299). This information is needed to open up a bill. The cashier will transfer this information onto a new customer bill.

If orders are produced electronically, the information will be stored in the cashier's terminal and can be retrieved by table number. Access to the cashier's terminal should be limited to the cashier and the management.

Pricing each item sold

When pricing items manually, it is important to refer to menus, price lists and any promotions. The items and prices may be handwritten on the bill, together with the quantity of each item sold.

If pricing is done using an electronic system, it is usually automatic. It is very important that the correct code is entered for the right table.

Drinks and food sales are usually listed in separate sections on the bill.

Marcus says

The bill is the last thing the guest remembers as they leave, so ensure every bill is accurate and detailed. There is nothing worse than a guest being charged for something that they didn't consume. Not only does it look unprofessional but the business loses out as no one gets charged for the item!

Calculating prices and totals

All bills should be ready to be totalled at any time, so the customer is not kept waiting to settle up. To total the bill, you need to total all sales for that table number. If a waiter is to present the bill, ensure that they check that all sales items on the bill are entered correctly against the right table. The cashier may need to adjust the bill if necessary.

If a bill is being prepared manually, it should be totalled using a calculator and double-checked for accuracy. Here is the process you need to go through:

1   Multiply the quantity of each item sold by the price of the item:

Roast beef   4 portions @ £10.95   = 4 × £10.95   = £43.80
Cod and chips   2 portions @ £7.50   = 2 × £7.50   = £15.00

2   Add together all the totals for each food item sold:

Total food cost = £43.80 + £15.00 = £58.80

3   If there is any service charge or cover charge (see page 49), you should add this at the end. It may be calculated as a percentage of the total food bill:

Total food bill   = £58.80
Service charge (10%)   £58.80 × 10/100   = £5.88

4   Add the total food bill and the service charge together to obtain the grand total:

Grand total = £58.80 + £5.88 = £64.68

If the bill is being prepared electronically, all these calculations will be done automatically. This saves time and reduces the likelihood of errors occurring.

Storing the charges

Electronically, the sales are stored by table and the cashier can retrieve the bill by entering the table number.

Figure 6.13 *If you are totalling the bill manually, it is important to follow a system*

Remember!
10% means 10 parts out of 100. To do this calculation, you write 10/100.
To calculate a service charge of 10% on a bill of £58.80, you should write:
£58.80 × 10/100 = £5.88

Remember!
Any food items that were served but not featured on the bill will have been given away free!

Presenting the bill

How this is done will vary according to company policy. The following list summarises the main points to be addressed.

○ The bill should be presented so that the contents are not on view to all – either folded or within a bill holder – to allow the host to view it discreetly.

○ The timing of presenting the bill will vary depending on the establishment. Try to judge your customers' mood – are they in a hurry and expecting the transaction to be handled instantly, or do they have plenty of time?

○ Keep your customers informed if there is to be a delay.

Remember!
Always double-check that the correct bill is being presented to the correct table. This is an easy mistake to make in a busy restaurant, but it can be very embarrassing for everyone concerned.

Figure 6.14 It is very important to make sure the right bill goes to the right table

Dealing with payment transactions

The payment transaction is the most vulnerable control procedure in any operation. It is open to error, theft and fraud. It is very important that these transactions are always carried out in line with company procedures, after training. These procedures have been set up to safeguard against theft and fraud and to reduce errors.

The till

To ensure security in payment transactions, a till must be provided to store the float and money taken securely. The till should:

○ display cash sales to the cashier, supervisor and customer

○ be set to prevent unauthorised access

○ store all transactions made

○ record the money offered and the change given

○ record sales by all the following methods: cash, cards, vouchers, cheques, complimentary, ledger

○ record 'no sales' – any time the till is open but no transaction is made.

Process for accepting payment

The customer is given a copy of the bill as a receipt on completion of their transaction. The customer also receives any associated paperwork in connection with the payment, for example a copy of their credit card transaction. Customers' bank or credit cards should be returned with the receipts.

All other non-cash payments (cash equivalents) require the cashier to retain documentation for the transaction. These might include vouchers for a company with a special arrangement, promotional discount vouchers or luncheon vouchers. These are stored securely in the till.

Methods of payment

Customers have several options to settle their bill:

- cash
- cheques
- traveller's cheques
- foreign currency
- credit card/debit card
- vouchers
- ledger payment
- complimentary.

We will look at how to deal with each of these in turn.

Figure 6.15 All notes should be checked – especially £50 notes

Cash

First, check that the notes are genuine – look for a watermark and a small line of silver foil running through the note. Some organisations have an infrared light machine to check that notes are genuine. Many organisations have a policy of not accepting £50 notes, or may have a special method for checking these. Check that the cash received covers the amount on the bill.

Key all the sales figures into the till and – depending on the particular till – press 'subtotal'. Key in the money given and press 'total'. The till will show you how much change to give. Keep the banknotes visible until change has been given and the customer agrees that the change is correct.

Remember!

Always key in the amount of money given and use the change-giver on the till to work out the money required for change. This reduces the risk of error.

Remember!

Do not short-cut cashier systems. That is how errors occur.

Personal cheque

When you are given a personal cheque, you should look for the following:

o does it show today's date?

o is the amount written in words and numbers correct?

o is it payable to the correctly named establishment?

o is it signed?

All cheques should be backed up by a cheque-guarantee card. You should check the following:

o does the card show signs of tampering?

o does the card cover the value of the cheque?

o does the signature on the card match the signature on the cheque?

o are the account number and name on the cheque the same as the account number and name on the card?

o is the expiry date on the card for some time in the future?

If there are no problems arising from all the above checks, then enter the sale into the till – different tills will have different methods of recording cheque sales. Depending on the system in your establishment, you may have to write details on the back of the cheque.

Traveller's cheques

Not all establishments accept traveller's cheques – but some do. Traveller's cheques are most often used by people travelling abroad. They are sold in different values, for example £5, £10 or £20. They are pre-signed when they are purchased, and they must be signed a second time in front of the cashier when paying for goods. A valid passport must be shown to support the sale. Different tills will have different methods of recording traveller's cheques, if your establishment accepts them.

No change is given with traveller's cheques. This means that the sale is often part-cash, part-traveller's cheques to the value of the bill. For example, if the bill was £58.80, the customer might give traveller's cheques to the value of £55 and then make up the £3.80 difference in cash. Different tills will have different methods of dealing with this.

Figure 6.16 Make sure you check and record all the details needed when accepting a cheque

Figure 6.17 Check to see if your place of work accepts traveller's cheques

Foreign currency

Some outlets accept foreign currency – check with your manager. They will usually have a till that can automatically convert the sale into different currencies. The amount charged depends on the daily exchange rate. Rates can also vary according to the individual outlet. Some outlets, especially in tourist areas, will accept Euros, but may prefer not to accept larger Euro notes for fraud reasons.

Payments made in foreign currency are entered into the till as cash and the till is set to convert the amount to whatever currency is required.

You should also know what different types of currency are legal tender, for example Scottish notes look different from English ones but should be accepted.

Figure 6.18 Scottish currency looks different – but it is legal tender throughout the UK

Find out!

What types of currency are legal tender in England? Is an establishment obliged to accept: Scottish currency, Northern Irish currency, Isle of Man currency, Channel Islands currency?

Try this!

A large party of visitors to your restaurant, who plan on spending a large amount of money, ask if you can accept Euros – what will you do?

Figure 6.19 How will you deal with this French party?

Credit card or debit card

Credit and debit card payments are processed using a card machine. The machine prompts the cashier through the process. The card is swiped through the card machine. Customers are required to enter their PIN to authorise the sale. On completion, the card and a paper record of the transaction are returned to the customer. The sale is then entered in the till – different tills will have different methods of recording card sales. A copy of the paper transaction record is stored in the till.

Figure 6.20 Chip and PIN is now accepted in most restaurants

Definitions

Credit card: a card that allows the customer to pay for goods on credit, and settle the bill with the credit card company at a later date. Interest will be charged by the credit card company if the bill is not settled in full each month. Examples of credit cards are Barclaycard and American Express.

Debit card: a card that allows the customer to pay for goods without using cash, provided they have sufficient funds in their bank account. If the customer does not have the money in their account, the payment will not be authorised.

PIN: Personal Identification Number. The secret number that the customer types into the card machine to validate the payment.

Try this!
What methods of payment does your place of work accept?
Make a list. Which method is the most popular?

Vouchers

Vouchers are pre-paid expenses for food or drinks consumed within named outlets. Large companies sometimes give their employees vouchers as part of their payment package; or vouchers may be issued as part of a promotion. Vouchers may be presented by the customer in place of payment, or as part-payment.

Once vouchers have been accepted, the cashier must cancel the voucher and store it in the till. The sale is usually entered into the till as cash, as the voucher is a cash equivalent.

Ledger payment

This is an internal transfer of funds within an organisation. The customer agrees that the bill is correct by signing it, but they do not give any payment. Money is then internally transferred into the outlet's account or invoiced to an external customer. The sale is entered into the till as a ledger sale.

Complimentary

All complimentary bills should be put through the till as a sale. This is so that stock is controlled. The bill is not charged to the customer. Any complimentary bill requires a signature for authorisation. The signature and the bill would normally be settled by the appropriate department head. This signed bill is a cash equivalent, and is included in the sales figures.

> **Definition**
> **Complimentary:** something that is given as a free gift.

Power failure

In the event of a power cut, the till will not function. There is a release catch underneath the till. This will allow the till drawer to open to give change. Once the power is resumed, all transactions can be entered into the till using the copies of the bills.

Balancing payments received with sales

After trading, the cashier must be able to:
○ balance payments received with sales
○ produce a signed banking receipt.

At the end of each trading session, the cashier checks that the amount of money in the till is equal to the value of sales processed through the till. This is called balancing the till.

Figure 6.21 Balancing the till

The process for doing this is as follows:

o a record of the total payments made through the till is printed out

o a cash summary sheet is completed to show the total amount of money taken by all the different payment methods

o the totals from these two documents are compared – they should be equal.

```
                28-11·07         ----------------------------
                  *2·25          AMEX
                  *2·25          NO BUSINESS
                  *4·50          ----------------------------

                  *0·00          BARCLAYCARD BUSINESS
                                 FOR RECEIPTS 0053-0053
                                        1        573.50DR
                                                   0.00CR
                28-11·07         TOTAL   1        573.50DR

                 2943Na          MASTERCARD
               *000037                  1        573.50DR
               0028·89                             0.00CR
                                 TOTAL   1        573.50DR
   1         0035Na              ----------------------------
             *94·40             GRAND TOTAL
   2         0003Na                     1        573.50DR
             *603·75                               0.00CR
   3         0000Na              TOTAL   1        573.50DR
             *0·00               ----------------------------
   4         0000Na
             *0·00               TOTALS RESET
             *701·14
                                 14:20 27/11/07
             *0·00-
             *0·00%
             *0·00%
             *701·15
```

Figure 6.22 Z-readings from the till and from the card machine

Recording total payments

All bill payments are stored in the till or computer. A Z-reading from the till (see page 183) or a print-out from the computer will give a total sales figure. The total money taken will be divided up to show how much was taken by each of the different payment methods (cash, card, cheque, other).

Completing the cash summary sheet

A cash summary sheet is used to produce the summary of total payments manually. It lists all completed transactions. This information is on the cashier's copy of all the paid bills. The cash summary adds the total column from all the bills – (Figure 6.23). This should equal the Z-reading from the till.

Figure 6.23 A completed cash summary sheet

RESTAURANT CASHIERS SUMMARY SHEET

Date ___6/5/2008___

Bill	Table	Covers	Food	Drinks	Total		Reconcilliation		
HALL	8	2	15.50	2.25	17	75	Total Cheque	15	50
BROWN	4	2	15.50	—	15	50	Total Credit	287	00
COMPTON	9	2	15.50	2.00	17	50	Notes £50	—	—
KNIGHT	7	2	15.50	—	15	50	£20	100	—
PAYNE	6	2	15.50	6.75	22	25	£10	70	—
SHAW	1	4	31.00	—	31	00	£5	10	—
LAW	11	4	31.00	6.75	37	75	Coins £2	2	—
GOODY	20	10	77.50	2.25	79	75	£1		
GILL XMAS PREPAYMENT		2	31.00		31	00	50p		50
CLARKE XMAS PREPAYMENT		14	217.00		217	00	20p		
							10p		
							5p		
Bar Sales							2p, 1p		
		Totals	465.00	20.00	485	—			
Details of less paid out credit									
			Final Total				Final Total	485	00

Cashier:	Admin:
J. Mikou	A Brown

'Z' READING
£660 —
less   £175
O/RING   £485 · 00

Now the cashier has to check that the money in the till equals the till reading. The process for doing this is as follows:

- remove the float value from the till (see Figure 6.24)
- obtain a Z-reading from the card machine for total sales and enter this figure in the credit/debit card column
- add up the totals from all cheques and enter this figure in the cheque column
- count all cash taken and place total figures in the correct cash column (e.g. 6 × £10 = £60, etc.)
- add all the amounts in all the columns to give the total amount of money taken
- add the total of ledger or signed bills and place it in the correct column.

Balancing the till

The total figure for the amount of money in the till should equal the till Z-reading. If it does, then the till is balanced. The cashier signs and dates the cash summary sheet. The money and dockets taken are bagged up with the cash summary sheet and stored in the cash box. The float is bagged up separately, ready for the next service.

OUTLET: _____

DATE: _____

TIME: _____

FLOAT ANALYSIS SHEET

CURRENCY	AMOUNT	
Notes	£	p
£20		
£10		
£5	15	00
Coins		
£2	8	00
£1	10	00
50p	10	50
20p	2	00
10p	2	50
5p	1	00
Coppers	1	00
TOTAL	£50	00

ISSUER:

SIGNATURE _____

CASHIER:

SIGNATURE _____

Figure 6.24 A completed float analysis sheet

Preparing money for banking

The money is now ready for banking. The cash summary sheet provides the information needed to check notes, coins and credit card Z-readings, cheque totals, cash equivalents, and Z-reading of the till, to confirm the accuracy of the amount to be banked. The finance department will check and issue a receipt for the total money received for banking. The receipt confirms the amount of money taken for a given session.

```
            29NOV/2007
RESTAURANT          698.90
SUBTL               698.90
DUE AMOUNT      698.90
CHEQUE               31.00S
VISA                573.50S
CASH                 94.40
#001-4455           11:08R
```

Figure 6.25 The banking receipt confirms the amount of money taken during a session

Problems when operating a payment point

Over-rings

Any over-rings should be cleared as though the amount has been received. This transaction should be marked with a pen on the till roll. The transaction should now be entered correctly in the till. When balancing the till, any over-rings must be deducted from the till Z-reading to make it balance with the total cash.

> **Definition**
>
> **Over-ring:** the wrong figure is keyed into the till. For example, someone may accidentally forget the decimal point and key in £100 instead of £1.00.

Error slips

Everyone makes mistakes from time to time, especially if they are very busy. You should always take care when using the till, but if you do accidentally key in an over-ring, you should fill in an error slip. This slip is signed by you and dated, and gives the amount of the over-ring and the reason for it. Error slips should be used to report all errors, so that if the till does not balance, it is easy to spot the reason and correct it. This will save a lot of time and unnecessary checking and recounting.

Till Error Report

Cashiers Name ___E. SHARMAN___

Till Number _____

Amount of Over-ring £ ___£175___

Department ___BLADES___

Reason ___PRESSED WRONG TILL NUMBERS___

_____

_____

Cashier's Signature ___E Sharman___

Date ___11/10/07___

Figure 6.26 Always fill in an error slip – however busy you are!

Short of small change

Never use your own money to supply change to guests. If it is not possible to provide the correct change, ask the customer if they could offer the right amount. As soon as possible, obtain more change from an authorised person.

Request to provide change for a 'no sale'

Sometimes a customer may ask you to change a large note for smaller change. This means opening the till when no sale is being transacted. You should politely refuse to do this – there is a risk that you may be accepting forged notes in exchange for legitimate money.

> **Definition**
>
> A **'no sale'** is when the till is opened without a transaction taking place – no goods are bought and no money is paid.

Refunds

Authorisation is normally needed from a supervisor or manager before a cashier can give a refund.

Cash refunds may be written in a duplicate book, and the customer signs and dates the top copy and keeps this. The cashier keeps the bottom copy, which is placed in the till. This amount will be deducted from the cash totals, as it has been taken from the till.

Credit/debit card refunds are processed in the same way as a sale, but will be recorded differently depending on the till and the system used. The process is generally as follows:

- swipe the customer's card
- swipe your supervisor's card
- enter the amount to be refunded and press enter
- follow your terminal prompts.

The amount to be refunded will be deducted from the customer's next credit card balance.

Some refunds are settled by offering vouchers to the value of the agreed refund. This ensures the customer will return, and indicates some customer satisfaction with the handling of the refund issue.

Omitting to enter card sales through the till

If you forget to enter a credit/debit card sale through the till, the total amount of money taken will exceed the till Z-reading. This will mean that a recount is needed. The missing sale will have to be entered and a second till Z-reading taken.

A customer queries their change

Think about this example: you have been given a £10 note for a £3.50 sale. You give £6.50 change. The customer states that she handed you a £20 note. If you have observed the cash sale rule, the customer's £10 note will still be outside the till. You can produce the note and prove that the change given was correct. You may need to consult with your supervisor if you are unsure. If you had already put the note in the till, you would not have been able to prove who was correct. In that case, you would need to take the customer's details, and if the cash balance was over at the end of the session, a refund could be issued.

Credit/debit card authorisation refused

If a customer's credit/debit card is declined, you should politely and discreetly inform the customer and request another means of payment.

If the card is declined and the terminal reads 'hot card', this means that the card is stolen or fake. At this point your response will depend on the policy at your place of work, and you should consult your supervisor. You will need to ask for an alternative means of payment. Your establishment may keep the card, which should be removed from circulation. The establishment is sometimes rewarded by the card provider if this happens.

The customer forgets their PIN

If this happens, you should return the card to the customer and ask politely for an alternative means of payment.

Skippers

These are customers who walk out without paying. As a cashier, beware, it does happen. It is important for the cashier to be as observant as possible of the movement of customers in and out of entrances and exits. The problem is highlighted particularly in hotel restaurants and bars, or anywhere the cashier is sited away from the access points of the outlet. To prevent customers becoming skippers:
○ there should be no delay in presenting the bill to the customer
○ settlement of presented bills should be monitored by the waiter and cashier.

Try this!
A customer's bill totals £24.75. The waiter is given a £20 note and a £10 note. Which notes and coins in Figure 6.27 would you give as change?

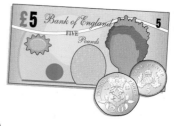

Figure 6.27 Which is the correct change?

Test yourself!

1 How would you correct a mistake on the till?

2 What would you do if you had to leave the payment point during service?

3 State two examples of security measures that apply when cashiering.

4 Would you accept a Scottish £10 note?

5 The cash and the Z-reading do not balance. State why this might be.

6 How might you manage the payment point in the event of power failure?

7

Menu knowledge and design

In this chapter you will cover skills and knowledge in the following units:

- 7103 – Unit 105: Understand menus
- 7103 – Unit 205: Menu knowledge and design

Working through this chapter could also provide evidence for the following Functional Skills at Level 2:

Functional Maths – Representing – carry out calculations with numbers of any size in practical contexts, to a given number of decimal places; understand and use equivalences between fractions, decimals and percentages

In this chapter you will learn about:

- the purpose of a menu
- different types of menu
- factors to consider in menu planning
- creating menus for customers with special diets

Why have a menu?

The content of a **menu** creates an image, which reflects the overall style of the catering establishment. Creating a menu is one the most important processes that any establishment goes through because it sets out the type and style of business that they are. A good waiter should have an in-depth knowledge of the menus offered by the organisation and be able to explain and sell them to the customer. He or she must understand the ingredients used, the seasonality, the different tastes and textures of the food, and any possible health or cultural issues related to dishes on the menu.

Communication with customers

In the past, eating out in the UK was sometimes intimidating, as menus were complicated and used unfamiliar words or a foreign language. Fortunately, even a formal dining restaurant now tries to put customers at ease. A good starting point is to provide a menu that customers can understand.

A menu is a way of communicating and is the main means of selling food to customers. A menu needs to attract people to eat at the catering establishment and encourage customers to order as much as possible and/or order particular items, e.g. a daily special. The information on a menu needs to be stated clearly and certain information is required by law, e.g. service charges. Menus are usually set out in courses so they are easy to understand.

A good menu will inform customers about:
○ the price and any extras that have to be paid for
○ the quality of the dish, e.g. fresh green beans, locally sourced best beef, prime rib of beef, freshly cooked
○ an indication of the size of the dish, e.g. 10-inch pizza, 100-gram rump steak
○ how the dish is prepared, e.g. grilled, pan-fried, roast
○ which ingredients are used
○ an explanation of any foreign or unusual terms
○ what the dish is served with, e.g. a side salad or a baked potato
○ whether it is suitable for people on special diets, e.g. vegetarian or vegan.

Definition
Menu: a list of dishes that may be ordered for a meal, e.g. in a restaurant, or to be served, e.g. at a wedding.

Figure 7.1 Rick Stein's fish restaurant, Padstow. What information do you think these visitors are looking for?

Remember!
It is good practice to identify ingredients to which people may be allergic, e.g. eggs, fish, shellfish and nuts. Many menus include a **disclaimer** which states that it is not possible to guarantee dishes are completely free of such ingredients.

Definition
Disclaimer: a statement that denies responsibility for something.

Style

The trend today is to present a simple, clear menu that helps the customer to make informed choices. The style of the menu will depend on the establishment:

- in a bistro the menu may be written on a blackboard
- in a pub the menu may stand on the counter
- in a pub restaurant there may be a menu on each table plus daily specials on a board
- in a first class restaurant the menu would be presented to the customers once seated.

Using a menu as a planning tool

A menu is an important planning tool. A menu tells:

- the Head Chef what to order
- the kitchen brigade what to prepare and finish for service
- the waiting staff what is available.

The menu plays a major part in:

- working out the cost of the dishes
- deciding on the price to be charged
- working out what staff and other resources will be needed
- deciding on the type of service required.

Some of the most successful menus contain a balance of traditional and modern dishes. A well-planned menu will:

- balance the choice of dishes within courses, e.g. a five-course menu is likely to include lighter, smaller dishes than a three-course menu
- balance the choice of dishes across courses, e.g. a main course dish will be more substantial than a starter
- be well-balanced from a nutritional point of view and include some healthy eating options
- have sufficient choices for the customer
- use a variety of ingredients, flavours, textures, seasonings and colours
- balance expensive ingredients, e.g. **foie gras** and **truffles**, with cheaper ingredients, e.g. potatoes
- use a mix of cooking techniques
- offer fewer good-quality dishes rather than lots of lower-quality dishes.

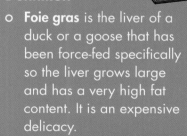

Definition

- **Foie gras** is the liver of a duck or a goose that has been force-fed specifically so the liver grows large and has a very high fat content. It is an expensive delicacy.
- **Truffles** are funghi that grow deep beneath the ground. Traditionally, pigs were used to sniff out the truffles. They vary in quality and price and are used to flavour and to garnish dishes.

Legal requirements

The following legal points apply to menus:

○ The descriptions of ingredients and cooking terms must be true and accurate. Particular care must be taken when using words such as: *British, home-made, fresh* and *organic*.

○ The prices must be accurate.

○ Any additional charge, e.g. a service charge, should be included in the menu prices or clearly stated on the menu.

○ Dishes containing genetically modified (GM) soya or maize must be clearly labelled.

Different types of menu

The origins of menus

Originally the menu or bill of fare was not given to diners at the table. Banquets used to be made up of lots of dishes served in two courses. The first course would be put on the table before the diners entered. This is where the term *entrée* comes from. Once eaten, these dishes would be removed and replaced by the second course, which is where the words *removes* and *relevés* come from.

Later, a very large menu or bill of fare was put at the end of the table for everyone to read. In time, menus became smaller and several copies were made so that diners could have their own.

Modern menus first appeared during the early nineteenth century in a restaurant in Paris.

Types of menu

There are several types of menu. The main ones are *à la carte*, *table d'hôte* and *function*.

À la carte menu

This is a menu with each dish priced individually. Customers choose from a range of dishes. The menu is usually divided into courses, e.g. starters, main course and dessert. They may also be divided in other ways, e.g. meat, fish, pasta. The variety of dishes offered is changed to suit the seasons. Today you will find à la carte style menus in a wide range of catering establishments from fine dining restaurants to quick service restaurants.

Did you know?
The word 'menu' comes from the French *menu de repas* which means 'list of items for a meal'. 'Menu' has been used since the eighteenth century. The first recorded use in English was in 1837.

Did you know?
'Bill of fare' is an old-fashioned English term that means 'list of dishes'.

Did you know?
Other terms sometimes used for a menu are 'bill', 'card', 'carte du jour' and 'carte' but 'menu' is the most common.

Please enjoy a complimentary selection of bread, oils and balsamic vinegar as a small appetiser while you select your meal

Bruschette

Our Bruschette are freshly prepared in the traditional Italian way using toasted rustic bread, garlic and olive oil.

Formaggio di capra
Creamy goats' cheese baked on bruschetta bread, topped with green pesto & served with a sweet tomato chutney £4.25

Funghi e pancetta affumicata
An exquisite selection of wild & button mushrooms, bacon & mozzarella cheese, baked & served on bruschetta bread £4.25

Antipasti

Risotto ai funghi e asparagi
A creamy mixture of Arborio rice, mushrooms & Parmesan cheese, topped with delicately flavoured asparagus spears £4.45

Selezione di formaggi e salumi
A selection of Italian cured meats, hard & soft cheeses, sun-blushed tomatoes, olives, rustic bread & dipping oil - ideal for sharing £6.75

Zuppa rustica
A traditional Italian vegetable broth served with a chunk of rustic bread £3.40

Gnocchi con pesto
Traditional potato dumplings filled with green pesto, served with a rustic tomato & pesto sauce £4.25

Stuzzicherie

Pizza all'aglio
Freshly baked pizza dough brushed with our garlic & parsley butter £2.85

Pizza all'aglio con formaggio
Freshly baked pizza dough, brushed with our garlic & parsley butter and topped with mozzarella cheese £3.00

Insalata mista
A small side salad of rocket leaves, ripe cherry tomatoes, fresh cucumber & spring onions £2.65

Pasta al forno

Lasagne con carne
A traditional Italian dish - sauces of Bolognese & béchamel layered between sheets of pasta, baked with tomatoes & mozzarella £7.45

Lasagne con funghi e porri
Field mushrooms and leeks bound in a béchamel sauce, layered between sheets of pasta and topped with mozzarella cheese £7.45

Specialità di Pasta Ripiena
Choose from green pesto, chilli oil or a rich pomodoro sauce to complement. All are served with Parmesan cheese & cracked black pepper on request

Tortellini spinaci e ricotta
Pasta filled with spinach & ricotta £7.95

Tortellini funghi porcini
Pasta filled with rich porcini mushrooms £7.95

Pizze

As all of our pizze are made freshly to order we are able to offer pizza bases of tomato sauce, bechamel sauce or green pesto. The chef has made the following recommendations; however, please feel free to ask for an alternative

Margherita
Tomato sauce, sliced tomatoes & mozzarella £5.95

Carnivora
Tomato sauce, chorizo, pepperoni, salami, red onion & mozzarella £7.75

Ai quattro formaggi
Green pesto, mozzarella, Parmesan, gorgonzola & goats' cheese £7.95

Pizza con pollo alla Vivaldi
Tomato sauce, sliced breast of chicken, Parma ham & mozzarella cheese £8.45

Verdura al forno e formaggi
Tomato sauce, aubergines, courgettes, mixed peppers, red onions, cherry tomatoes, gorgonzola, ricotta, mozzarella & olives £7.95

Pizza ai gamberoni
Béchamel sauce, topped with marinated anchovies, crayfish tails,and black & green olives, finished with dressed rocket £8.75

Specialità di Pasta

As all of our pasta dishes are made freshly to order. We are able to offer you a choice of penne, spaghetti, fettuccine, coralli or rice and millet pastas. The chef has made the following recommendations; however, please feel free to ask for an alternative.

Fettuccine con carne di manzo
Beef strips sautéed with garlic, basil, red onion & red peppers in a chunky tomato sauce combined with fettuccine pasta £8.45

Napolina
Coralli pasta with a simple tomato sauce, flavoured with basil, Peperonata & finished with mozzarella £7.25

Pasta alla marinara
Coralli pasta bound with a tomato & garlic sauce, mixed fish & shellfish £8.45

Spaghetti con ragù alla Bolognese
The classic Italian sauce served on well seasoned spaghetti £7.25

Giardinara
Rice & millet pasta and Mediterranean vegetables bound in olive oil with fresh herbs £7.95

Specialità

Italian speciality dishes served with rissole potatoes & roasted Mediterranean vegetables

Branzino fritto in casseruola
A succulent pan-fried fillet of seabass served with a luxurious, creamy lobster sauce £11.45

Coscio di anatra
Slow cooked leg of duck, balsamic marinated onions, wild mushrooms & cherry tomatoes £12.45

Peperoni rossi e formaggio di capra
Roasted red peppers and goat's cheese with black olives and sun blushed tomatoes, finished with pesto & a balsamic vinegar reduction £7.95

Insalata della Casa

Insalata nizzarda
A classical salad combining flaked tuna, boiled egg, green beans, potatoes & tomatoes with olives, marinated anchovies & capers £8.25

Insalata di pollo
Fresh salad of chicken breast, goats' cheese, red peppers & black olives served upon rocket & little gem leaves, flavoured with our own Parmesan dressing £8.25

For our tempting selection of desserts & ice creams please ask for a dessert menu

Figure 7.2 Part of an à la carte menu from Luciano's, Center Parcs

A full à la carte menu can consist of as many as 17 courses (including coffee) although nowadays you would expect 5–6. The number of courses offered on an à la carte menu depends on the size and status of the restaurant. Customers can choose as many courses as they wish. Every dish is individually priced. À la carte dishes are cooked to order, so there can be a waiting time for customers.

Table d'hôte menu

This is a set price menu offering a complete meal of two or more courses at a single price. There may be a choice in one or more courses. Sometimes there is a supplement for more expensive dishes. Table d'hôte menus usually represent good value for money and work out slightly cheaper than ordering the same dishes from the à la carte menu because a set menu is often more efficient. The chef can influence and anticipate demand more easily. It reduces the range of what must be bought in and the chef can order larger quantities, which reduces the cost of food items. With a limited menu, much of the preparation can be done in advance, which reduces the time taken to cook the dishes, and helps to speed up the turnover of customers. The food items on a table d'hôte menu are ready to serve, so this service is generally available at set times. The **cover** prepared is the table d'hôte cover.

> **Did you know?**
> *Table d'hôte* is a French phrase meaning 'host's table', and originally meant a common table for guests at a hotel or eating-house. It is now used in restaurants for a menu where meals of several courses with limited choices are charged at a fixed price. Such a menu may also be called *prix fixe* ('fixed price').

> **Definition**
> **Cover** – a place setting at the table. There are different types of cover for different menus.

Cream of asparagus soup with croutons

Chicken risotto with baby leaf spinach salad

Figure 7.3 A two-course, no choice, table d'hôte menu by an industrial caterer

Starter/Soup	Main course	Dessert
Fish	Fish	Hot pudding
Meat/Poultry	Meat	Cold dessert
Vegetarian	Poultry	Cheese
	Vegetarian	
	Special	
	Side orders	

Figure 7.4 A simple menu grid which can help with basic menu planning

Try this!

Choose a type of small catering operation, e.g. a café or bistro and a location. Use Figure 7.4 to help you put together a lunchtime table d'hôte menu. Make sure that the menu is well-balanced and in line with the style of the catering establishment, customer types and requirements, location, opening hours and price range. It should also meet all legal requirements.

Did you know?

Do you know the meaning of these terms from a classic menu sequence? The full menu consists of 14 courses.

Hors d'oeuvres: a French term for a cold dish served at the beginning of a meal, consisting of items such as pâté, hard-boiled eggs with mayonnaise, salad or several items brought together as mixed hors-d'oeuvres.

Potage: the French word for soup. Served after the hors d'oeuvres. Now often included as one of the starters on simpler menus.

Farinaceous dishes: starchy dishes including all pasta and rice dishes.

Entrée: if served as part of a classic menu, these are small, garnished dishes served without vegetables, e.g. tournedos, filled vol-au-vents. If served as a main course, the dishes may be meat, fish, poultry or other, and will be served with vegetables.

Relevé: Roasted items are served with a green salad.

Fromage: the French word for cheese. Served towards the end of a meal, normally includes a selection of cheeses with accompaniments such as biscuits or grapes.

Function menu

The function menu is a pre-selected set menu. The menu and price have been agreed before the function date. All guests are served the same food, and are not offered the option of choosing their food at the point of service. Any special requirements and requests will have been pre-ordered by the function organiser. The food is served to every guest at the same time. Clearing takes place when every guest has finished eating. The function menu allows the waiter to know exactly what is to be served and the number of guests to be served.

The cover to be set is as the function menu.

Different meal occasions

Different meal occasions require different approaches to the menu. Here are four of the main UK meal occasions.

Breakfast

Breakfast menus in the UK tend to be either Continental or Full English Breakfast (or equivalents in Scotland, Wales and Northern Ireland). There may be an à la carte menu to choose from or a table d'hôte menu. Service ranges from counter (e.g. in a small café), self-service counter (e.g. in an industrial restaurant), selection from a chilled and/or hot buffet (e.g. conference hotel) and full table service (e.g. in a good-quality hotel). Fish dishes may be included on an English breakfast menu. The most common dish is kippers, or haddock and poached eggs, while smoked salmon and scrambled eggs is a popular modern choice.

Did you know?
Kedgeree is a fish dish traditionally made using smoked haddock mixed with rice and eggs. It is either flavoured with curry sauce or served with a curry sauce. It originated in India and was developed by British colonials living in India during the 19th century, who brought it back to Victorian England where it became popular as a breakfast dish.

Try this!
Find a breakfast menu for an establishment of your choice. What do you think is good or bad about this breakfast menu? Are there enough courses? Is the choice wide enough? Is it suitable for the establishment?

Lunch and dinner menus

Lunch menus in the UK tend to be shorter and lighter than dinner menus, as most diners have more time in the evening. The exception is Sunday lunch, for which most catering establishments will have a special menu. Menus for both lunch and dinner may be à la carte or a set price table d'hôte menu of one or more courses, with or without a choice of dishes.

Afternoon tea

Afternoon tea is a particularly British occasion. It may be a no-choice item on a larger menu (see Figure 7.5). An establishment that specialises in afternoon tea may offer a wide choice from an à la carte menu, e.g. sandwiches, cakes, hot buttered tea cakes, pancakes, pastries, gateaux and ice creams. There may also be a range of different types of tea.

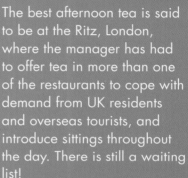

Afternoon Tea: £4.50

Two scones with strawberry jam and cream

Pot of tea for one

Figure 7.5 An afternoon tea menu item

Different types of organisation

The type of catering operation and the types of customer that use it help to decide what goes onto the menu and the prices charged. The location of a restaurant will also affect the menu. A city centre location may require a menu that can be served quickly. In the middle of the countryside, heartier, more leisurely food may be preferred. If there is a regional speciality, e.g. Lancashire hot pot, customers are likely to look for it on the menu. When designing a menu, it is important to look at what nearby establishments are offering in terms of style, price and quality. A similar menu will be in direct competition, so something a little different might be better.

Hotels

Hotels provide breakfast menus for guests booking bed and breakfast, dinner menus for half-board guests and lunch menus for full-board guests. Many hotels also provide a room service menu and a breakfast menu for guests wanting to eat breakfast in their room. There may also be a snack bar in the leisure complex.

Restaurants

Each restaurant will develop a menu that suits the:

○ style of the establishment
○ customers
○ location
○ facilities and the staffing.

Restaurants serving ethnic cuisine, e.g. Chinese, Indian or Greek food, normally offer more than one type of menu. There may be an à la carte style menu, see Figure 7.6, and a range of set price menus with inclusive prices based on the number of people the meal is for, see Figure 7.7. Some restaurants also offer a takeaway at a slightly lower cost. A popular trend is to offer a set price hot and/or cold buffet, where customers serve themselves from a selection of dishes.

À la carte menu selections

Starters

2. Crispy Seaweed   £2.00

Mains

14. Chicken Chow Mein   £4.15
56. Beef Chop Suey   £4.50

Accompaniments

72. Special Fried Rice   £2.50
99. Prawn Crackers   £1.00

Desserts

110. Lychees   £1.50

Menu for 2 persons
£14.75 per person

Prawn Crackers
Crispy Seaweed
Chicken Chow Mein
Beef Chop Suey
Special Fried Rice
Lychees

Figure 7.6 Part of an à la carte menu from a Chinese restaurant. Note the use of numbers for each dish

Figure 7.7 Part of a set menu from a Chinese restaurant

Hospitals

Hospitals have different types of catering operations and menus:

○ NHS patients will often be given a card with a set menu without any prices giving the choices for breakfast, lunch and dinner. The menu card is often given to them the day before and they mark their choices on it. Patients with particular dietary requirements will normally be catered for.

○ Private hospital patients will be given an à la carte or a table d'hôte menu for each meal occasion. It will usually show the prices, as the patient will be charged.

○ Visitors and staff are likely to go to a self-service counter restaurant. The limited menu of hot and cold food is suitable for people in a hurry.

Industrial catering

Menus for people at work will vary. The lunchtime menu is the most important as it needs to be served to a large number of people in a short period of time. Some industrial caterers also provide breakfast menus, limited evening service and snacks. There may also be a fine dining room for directors and business visitors, offering a set or an à la carte call order menu. For example, Aramark UK at their Slough estates restaurant offer a daily counter service, plus fine dining for directors' meetings and buffets for special evening events.

Case study – Baxter and Platts

Read about industrial contract caterer Baxter and Platts' fine dining restaurant in an article on the Caterer and Hotelkeeper website. A link has been made available at www.heinemann.co.uk/hotlinks. Just follow the links and enter the express code 7193P.

School meals

There are now government guidelines on healthy eating for school children in different age groups. Usually there is a counter service offering a limited choice of main courses and desserts which often include salad and fruit. The menu will normally have to cater for different ethnic and religious groups and for special dietary needs, e.g. vegetarians and children with food allergies.

In situ catering

In situ means to be served where you are by a trolley or tray. Examples include service on a train, a plane or in a hotel room, or a delivery to your home. Menus in these situations may be quite limited, or set.

Other factors to consider

Type of customer

It is important to find out what customers like and want. What people want to eat and the surroundings they want to eat in will change according to:

o the time of day or meal occasion, e.g. breakfast, lunch, dinner, coffee break, brunch, afternoon tea, supper, late night snack
o how hungry they are
o how much time they have, e.g. enough time to eat a three-course set lunch or just a sandwich
o how much money they have to spend on a meal
o the purpose of the meal, e.g. a business lunch, a quick bite before an evening out or lunch during a visit to a museum
o their style, taste and how influenced they are by fashion
o where they come from, e.g. the local area or region, or international visitors
o whether they have special dietary needs because of age, health, allergies, religion, etc.

Remember!

If a dish is not selling, a restaurant must find out why it is unpopular, e.g. too strong a flavour or too expensive, and make the necessary changes, or take it off the menu.

Remember!

A catering establishment may need to vary the content of a menu and how it is presented, in order to encourage repeat custom or to try and attract new customers.

Try this!

What types of customers are likely to be attracted by:

○ *a children's menu in a fast-food establishment, e.g. McDonald's, in a shopping centre*

○ *a carvery 'Early bird' menu such as that offered in Harvester restaurants*

○ *an à la carte menu in a smart restaurant in a town centre?*

Investigate!

Imagine you work in a restaurant that always offers a main course vegetarian dish and a healthy option dish. You have been asked to add a gluten-free dish but do not want to increase the number of dishes on the menu. Find a dish that is vegetarian, gluten-free and a healthy option.

Definition

Gluten-free: made without using any wheat, barley, oats, rye. For advice on gluten-free ingredients visit the Coeliac Society UK website: www.coeliac.co.uk

Price being charged

The prices catering establishments charge for food are to some extent based on the cost of the food. The prices to be charged need to represent value for money for the customer. It is important to be able to predict what a customer is likely to buy and how much they are likely to spend. This is called 'customer spend per head'. For example, a customer eating lunch in a fast-food restaurant may be prepared to spend £3.50 on a meal, while a customer eating lunch in a smart restaurant is likely to be prepared to spend £10 or more on a two-course set lunch.

Try this!

Look at Figure 7.8.

1 *Add up the cost of each dish. This gives you the total food cost. What is it?*
2 *Divide the total food cost by the number of dishes. This is the average food cost. What is it?*

Menu items	Cost per dish
Cream of asparagus soup with croutons	£1.20
Onion tart served on a bed of green salad	£0.80
Mozzarella and tomato salad with basil	£1.40
Chicken risotto with baby leaf spinach salad	£2.75
Lancashire hot pot with boiled potatoes, fresh carrots and green beans	£2.50
Chilli fried prawns with angel hair pasta	£2.90

Figure 7.8 A table d'hote menu developed by a contract caterer for a business lunch in the directors' meeting room at an industrial site

Availability of food commodities

Catering establishments can now source almost any food product from around the world, at most times of the year. Seasonal ingredients are usually easy to get hold of and reasonable in price. Out-of-season ingredients, however, are likely to be more expensive, more difficult to source and may not be as fresh or of the required quality.

Seasons affect customers' expectations and they will prefer comfort food in the winter and lighter dishes in the summer, e.g. a chilled soup or a salad will be welcome in the summer but not in the winter.

Try this!

Look at the menu above and identify a suitable two course meal for a vegetarian.

Investigate!

Choose a month of the year. Find out what food products are in season in the UK in that month. Create a table d'hôte lunch menu (or adjust the one you created earlier) so that it uses mainly fresh food that is in season during that month. Include at least one healthy option dish. Use Figure 7.4 to help you.

Availability of equipment and space

A menu should only include dishes that the kitchen is capable of producing. This applies whether the kitchen cooks everything from scratch or uses prepared or partly prepared food products.

If the menu cannot be produced because of lack of equipment or space, then either the menu must be changed or the kitchen redesigned and the correct equipment bought.

Availability of staff

The menu needs to take into account the number, availability and skills of the kitchen brigade and service staff. There is no point including complicated dishes that take ages to prepare and cook if there are not enough staff in the kitchen brigade or they lack ability or experience.

Special diets

Increasing numbers of people are adopting diets that cut out certain types of food, or allow only food of a particular origin. People may follow these diets for religious, medical or ethical reasons. Establishments serving food must respect such diets, and give customers enough information about the food to make sure they order appropriate items.

Vegetarian and vegan diets

A vegetarian diet is one of the most common special diets. A vegetarian will not eat any item made from meat or fish. To help customers to make their food choices, menus often depict the vegetarian or healthy diet sign alongside the appropriate dish.

If dishes are marked vegetarian on the menu, they should not include stocks, flavourings or setting agents of animal origin.

A vegan will not eat any food of animal origin, including dairy products, honey and eggs. Pasta made without eggs, soya products and pulses are suitable to accompany the vegetables, fruits and grains that make up the vegan diet.

> **Remember!**
> Check daily for menu changes to make sure you are always up to date with what is on the menu. If you are unsure of anything, then ask your supervisor or the chef.

www.vegsoc.org

Figure 7.9 Vegetarian items may be indicated in different ways on the menu

223

Diets for religious reasons

Muslim and Jewish people will not eat pork. They prefer meat to be slaughtered in a particular way, which is indicated by the description halal (Muslim) or kosher (Jewish). Jewish people eat meat dishes separately from milk or dairy items. Hindu people will not eat beef. Some religions do not allow alcohol to be consumed, and this means people should be made aware if there is any alcohol in food or sauces.

Diets for medical reasons

Medical diets are required by people who are unable to eat certain foods or seasonings that may aggravate their condition and make them ill. A medical diet may mean that ingredients and cooking methods must be as low as possible in fat, salt or sugar, or high in fibre.

Food intolerance

Many customers have allergies to certain foods. If, at the point of ordering, one of your customers claims to have a life-threatening food allergy, take the customer very seriously. If there is a doubt whether a dish on the menu is free of a certain ingredient, such as nuts, admit to the customer that you are unsure and obtain exact information from the chef.

The waiter should study the menu prior to service so that dishes may be recommended for certain diets. The most common dietary requests are gluten-free, fat-free, dairy-free, diabetic and low-sodium.

A person who has coeliac disease, for example, is allergic to the gluten found in flour. This means they cannot eat wheat, rye, barley or oat products (or products such as malted drinks, ready-made sauces and some brands of mustard, as these all use grains in their production). If a person with coeliac disease eats a grain-based item, they will have an upset stomach. Rice, potato and sago are useful alternatives to grain.

Find out!
What food items can a diabetic not eat?

Lactose intolerance means that a person cannot digest milk and dairy items properly. They will have an upset digestive system if care is not taken to avoid serving them with milk, cream, cheese or any other dairy-based product.

Try this!

Name a dish on your menu to suit these common dietary requests:

- *gluten-free*
- *fat-free*
- *dairy-free*
- *low-sodium*
- *vegan.*

Test yourself!

1 List five things that are important when planning a menu.

2 What are the advantages of planning a menu that offers seasonal foods?

3 Write down two features of an à la carte menu.

4 Define a table d'hôte menu.

5 What are the differences between a lunch menu and a dinner menu? Why?

6 A good menu will inform customers about many things. Give four of them.

Assignment Practice

1 Research the dietary requirements for the following religions:
Jewish
Muslim
Hindu

2 Explain why the religious belief restricts the diet.

8 Preparing and clearing food service areas

In this chapter you will cover skills and knowledge in the following units:

- 7132 – Unit 105 (1Gen5): Clean and store crockery and cutlery; Unit 107 (1FS1): Prepare and clear areas for table and tray service; and part of Unit 109 (1FS3): Prepare and clear areas for counter and takeaway service

- 7132 – Unit 206 (2FS1): Prepare and clear areas for table service

- 7132 – Part of Unit 109(1FS3): Prepare and clear areas for counter and takeaway service

- 7091 – Unit 257: Preparation and clearing of service areas

- 7103 – Part of Unit 108: Food and beverage service skills

- 7103 – Part of Unit 209: Food and beverage service skills

Working through this chapter could also provide evidence for the following Functional Skills:

Functional Maths – Interpreting – using data to assess the likelihood of an outcome

Functional ICT – Using ICT Level 1 select and use software applications to meet needs and solve straightforward problems

In this chapter you will learn:

- the information needed before preparing for a service session
- how to prepare a service area and equipment for service
- how to prepare the customer and dining areas for service
- how to clear the dining and service areas after service
- how to close down the service area

Importance of good preparation

Preparation is the key to a smooth and successful service for all your customers. Whether you are working in a table service restaurant or providing a counter/take-away service, the same principles apply. The better the preparation, the better the service that the staff can provide for their customers.

This chapter tells you how to prepare for full table service. A counter/take-away service will have some, but probably not all, of the equipment and facilities discussed here. However, much of the basic underpinning knowledge about equipment, cleaning and preparation are the same in all types of service setting. More specific information about providing a counter/take-away service can be found in Chapter 9.

All service staff should be suitably dressed for the preparation of the dining room and service area. Anyone working in this area should be trained in food hygiene and, ideally, should hold a current food hygiene certificate.

The preparation tasks are normally carried out at the start of a trading session and then maintained during service and in quieter periods. Breakfast service is the one exception to this rule. Breakfast service is usually prepared after dinner service, due to the early start. For all types of service, basic preparation tasks have to be completed before the customers arrive.

Information needed before preparing for a service session

In order to prepare for service, waiting staff need to have the following information:

○ the number of customers booked in (or the expected number if bookings are not taken)
○ the menu(s) being offered.

Number of customers

If an establishment takes bookings, the **reservations list** will contain the information about how many customers are booked in. If the establishment does not take bookings, they will need to estimate the likely number of customers. They can base their estimate on customer numbers in previous weeks. They should also take into account any special local events – for example, a festival or a market day is likely to increase the number of customers.

Menu(s)

The menu is central to any preparation task undertaken by the waiters. It gives information about the food and drinks being served. This information helps the waiters to identify what they need to set out the dining room and the types of equipment that will be required.

Types of menu

The menu(s) to be served could be:

○ table d'hôte menu
○ à la carte menu
○ function/banqueting menu.

Table d'hôte menu

A table d'hôte menu is a set menu of two or more courses, offering choices for each course. It is available at a set time and at a set price for the courses offered. For example, a three-course lunch available between 12 and 2 p.m. for £19.50.

> **Definition**
>
> **Reservations list** – a list of all the bookings for a particular service session. In table service settings, the reservations list provides the waiters with the name of the customer, the number of covers, the time of arrival and any special requirements.

À la carte menu

An à la carte menu offers an extensive range of dishes. These dishes are grouped under course headings, such as Starters, Main courses and Desserts. The dishes are individually priced. Customers choose what they would like from the menu and the dishes are cooked to order.

> **Remember!**
> As a waiter you could be serving several different menus during a service session.

Function/banqueting menu

A function menu is a set menu served to a large number of customers – for example, at a wedding or conference. The menu is selected in advance by the organisers of the event. All customers are served at the same time. With this type of menu, waiters know in advance how many customers there are and what they are going to eat.

Starter Menu

Pumpkin and sweet potato veloute with parmesan, truffle oil and wild mushroom £5.95

Terrine of foie gras, confit duck, baby leeks and artichoke en presse salad croustillant, Riesling and peppercorn jelly £8.95

Home smoked salmon with a tian of Cornish crab, cured tuna and confit tomatoes with a tarragon & caviar dressing £12.95

Spiced rabbit & truffle sausage with Soya braised pakchoi red onion chutney £9.50

Salad of baby lobster, celeriac and marinated scallops dressed with a roasted vegetable and lime oil jus £13.95

Main Course Menu

Valentine of lamb with braised shank, mint hollandaise served on a smoked potato gratin with haricot beans, roasted garlic and puy lentil jus £21.95

Fillets of seabass with crisp prosciutto, baby spinach and Cornish crab drizzled with a rosemary beurre blanc £23.75

Seared saddle of venison with roasted foie gras, baby leeks and girolle mushrooms, spiked with sunblushed tomatoes £23.50

Millefeuille of monkfish and aubergine set on a smoked haddock and saffron risotto dressed with and orange and star anis essence £22.50

Fillet of Angus beef with savoy cabbage, caramelised endive, truffled parsnip puree and port wine £23.95

Dessert Menu

Classic pineapple tarte tatin with a coconut and rum ice-cream complemented with a pineapple & ginger salad £8.25

Assiette of chocolate with an orange blossom sorbet £7.50

Liquorice and caramel bavarois, with roasted figs cooked in a vanilla and pistachio syrup £6.95

Classic lemon tart £5.95

Selection of British and French farmhouse cheeses £7.95

Coffee & homemade petit fours £3.25

Figure 8.1 Examples of the three types of menu. Can you work out which is which?

Forbes Restaurant

Lunch Menu

Starters
Rich Mushroom and Herb broth with crème fraîche
Tuna Niçoise style salad with a lemon vinaigrette
Vegetable spring rolls with a sweet chili sauce

Mains
Vienna steak on tomato bruschetta
Chicken Fillets in herb crumb with a garlic mayonnaise dip
Grilled and marinated delice of Mackerel with a Moroccan couscous and red pepper dressing
Baked leek and gruyere cheese tart with baked cherry tomatoes

Accompaniments
Ratatouille of vegetables
Sauteed potatoes

Desserts
Sticky toffee pudding with vanilla ice cream
Chocolate panna cotta with a sweet basil mascarpone
Baked apple and rhubarb crumble with a hint of ginger

Tea/Coffee

3 courses@ £7.75 per person
Dishes may contain traces of nuts

For reservations, please ask your waiter

Wedding of Mark Darby and Mary McLaughlin

Wednesday 3rd March 2008

MENU

Seafood Salad with Smoked Salmon, Crab, Prawns and Peppers

...

Noisettes of Lamb with a Wild Mushroom Sauce
Fresh Vegetables and Potatoes

...

Summer Pudding with Raspberry Coulis and Fresh Cream

...

Coffee and Mints

Try this!
Use each menu to list the equipment needed for every item on
the menu. Then use this as a checklist.

Promotional materials

Promotional materials are used to promote and sell products by
gaining the attention and interest of the customer. Successful
promotions encourage sales by helping the customers to make a
choice before being served – for example, while queuing for counter
service.

Promotional materials on display should be appropriate for the
time of the day. For example, lunch special offers are no use to
customers once lunch service has finished. Keep any promotional
material clean and attractive. To avoid disappointing customers,
remove any out-of-date promotional material immediately.

Promotional materials used may include:
- menus
- posters
- blackboards/whiteboards
- illustrated menu boards
- additional promotional ideas.

Menus

Menus that are visually appealing help to promote products and
the establishment. The menu must be clearly laid out, with correct
spelling and pricing, easy to read and correct for the time of the
day. Menus must be clean and presentable. Before service inspect
all laminated menus and clean them as necessary. If you use paper
menus, discard and replace any that are out of date or dirty. Ensure
there will be enough menus for the whole of the service period.

Descriptions of dishes can encourage sales – either next to the
dish on the menu or described to customers by the service staff.
Display offers such as dish of the day, chef's specials and meal
deals separately from the menu to add extra impact and interest for
the customer.

On the table, menus can be displayed as tent cards, in a menu holder or as placemats. For counter service, display the menu before the counter and at the start of the counter, so customers can decide before they reach the service point. For take-away service, menus should be available on the counter. Menus must cater for all customers. To promote sales have to hand all menus available – for example: children's menu, light diet menu with calorie counts, healthy menus, etc.

Menus that are well displayed promote sales. If a customer has to ask for a menu the sale can be lost. The menu, however attractive it is, will only promote sales if displayed at critical points from the customer's viewpoint.

Figure 8.2 How a menu is displayed can have a big effect on attracting customers

Try this!

The next time you eat out as a customer, check where the menus are displayed. Could it be improved? What suggestions would you make to the establishment?

Posters

The purpose of posters is to shout about the products or promotions being offered. Otherwise the customers will not know about what is on offer. A poster could be an enlarged version of the menu or special offer on display outside the establishment, at the entrance or at the start of the counter. This allows customers to see exactly what is on offer.

Posters should be colourful, readable from a distance and at the right eye level. Getting all these right will help attract attention and entice the customer into the premises.

Promotional posters can be linked with sponsors of products.

Blackboards/whiteboards

Blackboards or whiteboards are used outside the premises to promote current or future events or to announce special offers.

Boards may also be used inside the restaurant to list and promote the menu and specials. Before updating the boards they should be thoroughly cleaned. The writing on the boards must be interesting for the potential customers – the use of colours and illustrations can help with this. It is useful to list the information under headings, such as Starters, Mains and Desserts.

The writing must be clear to read and the spelling and the pricing must be correct. It is important to check that the written information is correct and that all the items available are listed. An advantage of using boards is that food items can be added or removed continually during service.

Illustrated menu boards

Illustrated menu boards include photographs or drawings of all the food dishes and meal deals on offer. When potential customers are queuing at the counter to order food, these menu boards are visually selling the dishes and helping the customer to choose.

These menu boards promote the products prior to service. At the point of service, the staff can then promote by suggesting daily specials, offering additional items or **upselling** to customers.

Illustrated menu boards can be understood by speakers of any language. They therefore overcome any language barriers, which helps both the customer and the promotion process.

Vouchers and loyalty cards

The aim of any establishment is to make sure that customers come back again and again. To encourage this, vouchers may be given out to customers who spend over a certain amount. The vouchers can offer a reduction on the next sale or offer one item free.

Loyalty cards reward customers for repeat visits to the outlet. A loyalty card can be stamped each time the customer spends a certain amount (for example £10 or over). When the card is completed, the next purchase is free of charge.

Remember!
- Check that all items for sale are listed on the board, or they will not sell!
- Check that the board information is accurate.
- Check that the board is readable from a distance.

Remember!
Check that the completed board complies with the Trade Descriptions Act and the Price Marking Order.

Definition
Upsell – to suggest higher priced products or additional products, such as side orders to a customer in order to increase revenue.

Figure 8.3 Illustrated menu boards can be used to visually sell your dishes

Gifts

Gifts such as hats, toys, crayons, colouring books and prizes are provided free to children in certain restaurants to encourage the family to return and to create customer loyalty.

Additional promotional ideas

Using additional promotional ideas helps to actively sell stock items and encourages repeat business from customers.

Additional promotional ideas might include the attractive aromas of your products – for example, freshly baked bread or coffee brewing. Try displaying food items to create the most impact – for example, exotic fruit in large wicker baskets and fully stocked cabinets. Position food products so that labels and descriptions can be read by the customer.

For counter service, ensure the products are easily accessible, especially the most profitable ones. Group together products in a way that benefits both the customer and the organisation. For example, position the Danish pastries near the coffee service. Have promotion notices perfectly sited to lead to the offer. Make displays of products to encourage impulse sales.

Remember!
Empty spaces don't sell, so make sure they are filled.

Test yourself!

1 Why is it useful to keep a list of reservations for a service session?

2 Name three types of menu.

3 Give three examples of promotional materials that could be used to attract customers.

4 What should be included on the food menu?

Preparing the service area and equipment for service

Job rota

Many establishments draw up a job rota. This lists all the tasks to be covered in each service session. Jobs are sometimes rotated so that members of staff do different jobs at different times. This will be organised in a way that suits the establishment and makes sure that staff days off are covered.

The tasks to be covered are usually:
○ cleaning crockery, cutlery and service equipment
○ cleaning and stocking the hotplate
○ cleaning and preparing the still room (not in all establishments)
○ cleaning the dining room
○ laying out the dining room
○ preparing cutlery, crockery and flatware, if applicable
○ preparing sideboards
○ laying out linen
○ laying tables
○ cleaning and polishing glassware
○ preparing condiments and accompaniments.

Service equipment

Crockery

The crockery used plays an important part in the presentation of the food. It needs to be carefully chosen, taking into account the following factors:
○ design – nowadays this is increasingly important; the design reflects the style of the restaurant
○ weight – it must not be too heavy for carrying
○ shape – it must be suitable for waiters to clear and carry easily
○ durability – the lifespan of the crockery will affect costs.

Listed below are the main types and sizes of crockery. They are guidelines only – not all of these are used in all establishments.

- ○ soup plate (8 in/20 cm): for soups, curries, stews/casseroles
- ○ fish plate (8 in/20 cm): for starters, fish course
- ○ joint plate (10 in/25 cm): for main course service
- ○ sweet plate (7 in/18 cm): for sweets and puddings
- ○ sweet bowl (5 in/13 cm): for milk puddings, cereals
- ○ side plate (6 in/15 cm): for bread and rolls, cheese service
- ○ salad crescent: for salad service.

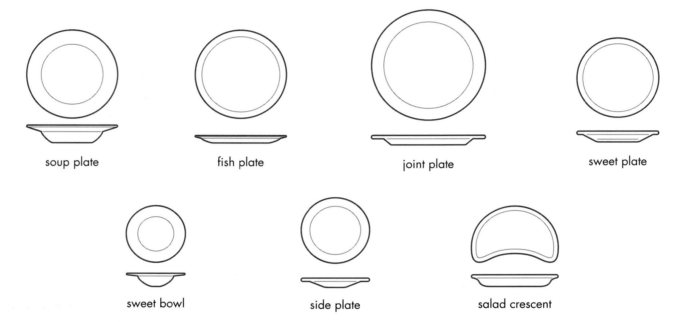

Figure 8.4 The crockery items used in food service

Underplates

Underplates are cold plates which are used underneath hot plates. These allow the service staff to carry hot, ready-plated food easily to the table. Examples of this might be:

- ○ for soup service, the hot soup plate could be placed on a cold joint plate
- ○ for vegetables, the vegetable dish could be placed on a cold fish plate.

Cups

A range of cups are needed, including:

- consommé cup and saucer
- breakfast cup and saucer – $\frac{1}{2}$ pint / 275 ml cup
- tea cup and saucer – $\frac{1}{3}$ pint / 200 ml cup
- coffee cup and saucer – $\frac{1}{3}$ pint / 200 ml cup
- demi-tasse cup and saucer – $\frac{1}{6}$ pint / 100 ml cup.

Remember!

Demi-tasse cup and saucer is used for coffee after lunch and dinner

consommé cup
and saucer

tea cup
and saucer

coffee cup
and saucer

breakfast cup
and saucer

demi-tasse

Figure 8.5 The crockery items used to serve beverages

The menu dictates what crockery has to be cleaned ready for service. Before cleaning, all crockery for the food service must be checked for chips or cracks.

Cutlery and flatware

Cutlery and flatware can be made of stainless steel or silverware.
The main items of cutlery and flatware include:

- soup spoons for soup service
- fish knives and forks for fish dishes
- joint knives and forks for meat dishes
- dessert spoons and forks for sweets
- side knives for side plates and cheese
- teaspoons for tea and fruit starters
- ice-cream spoons for ice-cream
- coffee spoons used for coffee service when using demi-tasse cups and saucers
- service spoons and forks for service of all food items
- sauce ladles for the service of sauce
- specialist items for menu dishes.

Did you know?

Cutlery refers to knives or cutting utensils.
Flatware refers to spoons and forks.

| soup spoon | fish knife and fork | joint knife and fork | dessert spoon and fork | side knife |

| teaspoon | ice-cream spoon | coffee spoon | service spoon | service fork | sauce ladle |

Figure 8.6 The cutlery and flatware items used in service

Other food service equipment

The following service equipment may also be used for
serving food.

○ Oval flats of various sizes are used for presenting food,
silver service of sliced meats and as under liners for
vegetable and entrée dishes and sauce boats. When used
as under liners they should fit the dish tightly to avoid
slippage and accidents.

○ Cloches are dome-shaped plate covers used to keep food
hot.

○ Plate covers have the same purpose as cloches, to
keep food hot for service. Plate covers can be plastic or
aluminium and are useful when carrying several plates
of ready-plated food. These covers are removed at the
sideboard.

○ Plate rings allow several plates of ready-plated food to
be stacked. The top plate should have a plate cover for
hygiene and temperature reasons. Usually plastic and
easy to clean to meet hygiene regulations.

○ Vegetable dishes are round or oval and can have two or
three divisions for different vegetables.

○ Sauce boats and ladles are used to present and serve
gravies and sauces. Place sauce boats on an under liner
of a suitable size, together with a ladle. Present more
than one sauce on a large under liner with one ladle per
sauce.

○ Soup tureens and ladles can be used to serve soup at
the sideboard or table. They help to ensure that the soup
is served hot. Use a ladle of the correct portion size.
Individual soup tureens served at the table do not need a
ladle.

○ Entrée dishes and lids are used to serve food dishes in a
sauce, for example chicken chasseur. They are oval and
similar to vegetable dishes, but deeper.

○ Milk jugs are used to serve hot and cold milk for tea and
coffee. Jugs for hot milk should have a hinged lid to keep
the milk hot.

○ Sugar bowls and tongs are used to present sugar for
service. White and brown cubes should be available and
are often presented in the same bowl.

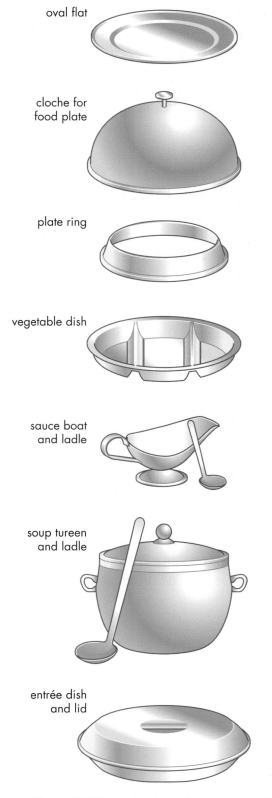

oval flat

cloche for
food plate

plate ring

vegetable dish

sauce boat
and ladle

soup tureen
and ladle

entrée dish
and lid

Figure 8.7 Other food service equipment

- Teapots and coffee pots come in a range of sizes. Coffee pots are also used for hot water for tea service.
- Butter dishes and butter knives are used to present butter portions at table. The butter is prepared and stored in a refrigerator until just before service. The butter dish is then placed on an under plate together with the butter knife at table. The butter knife is used by the customer to transfer butter from the dish to their side plate.
- Salvers are round trays used for carrying equipment, drinks and food to and from the table. Sizes range from 12 in (30 cm) to 16 in (40 cm). They are made of stainless steel, silver or tough plastic. The non-slip tough plastic salvers are ideal for carrying glassware.
- Trays are usually rectangular and are used for carrying food and equipment to and from the service area to the restaurant. Used to store dirty clearance items at sideboard. They are used at table until customers have gone. Made of plastic or resin and fibreglass and easy to clean.
- Room service trays are rectangular and have raised sides and handles for easy carrying. Wood finish to high standard for presentation.
- Cutlery and flatware for serving food include large tablespoon and joint fork for silver service. Dependent on menu items, might also include fish knives for service of flat omelette, gateau, battered fish, dessert spoons for family service of vegetables.
- Table numbers let staff know the number of the table to be used in all ordering and control systems.

teapot, coffee pot

milk jug, sugar bowl and tongs

butter dish and knife

salver and tray

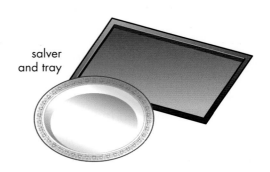

table numbers

Figure 8.8 Additional items that may be used in food service

240

The service area

The service area provides access to small items of equipment, as well as crockery and cutlery. In this area there are often places to store food items such as condiments and facilities for clearing down the food service – for example, bins and sinks.

The service area may include:

○ wash up
○ hotplate
○ silver or plate room (only in very exclusive establishments)
○ still room (may not be a separate room in many establishments)
○ linen store (if table linen is used).

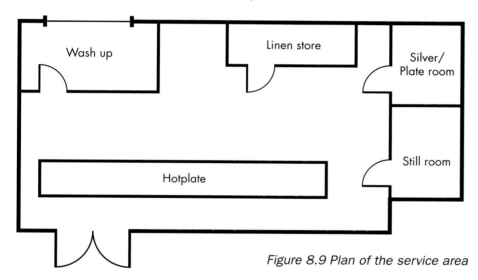

Figure 8.9 Plan of the service area

The wash up

The wash up is the area where all the table equipment used in the restaurant is cleaned, including crockery, cutlery, flatware and serving dishes.

All the service equipment required by the waiters is thoroughly cleaned in the wash up and then stored in the correct section of the service area. The restaurant staff collect the required number of cleaned and checked crockery, cutlery and flatware for the service session.

Stainless steel equipment is washed in detergent and hot water, rinsed and sterilised and air dried. It is then stored ready for use.

The wash up section does not clean glassware. Glassware is usually cleaned at the restaurant bar.

Remember!

Before cleaning the service equipment, it is useful to know the number of covers booked, the mix of tables and the menus to be served. The menus will dictate the crockery, cutlery and flatware.

Operation of the wash up

The wash up area is usually sited so that customers cannot hear any operational noise from the dining area. It also needs to be in a suitable position so that food service staff can offload clearance from tables as efficiently as possible. The wash up area must have refuse and waste food containers clean and ready for service.

During service the waiters stack the dirty plates at the sideboard, together with the dirty cutlery onto a tray. They then carry it to the wash up for cleaning.

Once in the wash up, the waiters arrange table items ready for cleaning. They scrape uneaten food from plates into the refuse bin. They stack the scraped plates in order of size ready for washing up.

Cutlery can be placed in containers with hot soapy water to soak off any food before the washing process. The containers should be labelled Knives, Forks, Spoons and the waiters should separate the cutlery into the correct containers. This reduces time and makes the process more efficient.

Cleaning of crockery and cutlery

Crockery and cutlery can be cleaned by either hand or machine washing. Whichever method is used, the process has the same four basic steps, as follows:

1. Pre-clean by removing loose material and any dried sauce etc. sticking to the surfaces.
2. Wash with detergent and hot water.
3. Rinse and disinfect by immersing in very hot water that is at least 82°C OR rinse and then submerge in a chemical disinfectant solution to kill any bacteria present on the surfaces of the equipment.
4. Allow to air dry.

Process 4 ensures the items will be free from smears and not contaminated by bacteria which may be on the cloths used for drying.

Note that Protective Personal Equipment should be worn – particularly with the very hot water for rinsing and disinfecting.

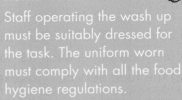

Remember!
Staff operating the wash up must be suitably dressed for the task. The uniform worn must comply with all the food hygiene regulations.

Double sink washing up of crockery

○ Pre-clean crockery to remove any loose material sticking to the
surfaces.
○ Wash the crockery by hand using detergent and hot water and
place it in plastic-coated wire racks.
○ When the racks are full, lift them by the handles and place them
in the adjoining sink containing either water heated to 82°C or a
chemical disinfectant solution.
○ Remove the rack and allow the crockery to air dry.
○ When dry, remove the crockery from the racks and stack onto a
trolley, ready to move back to the store area.
○ Then store the cleaned crockery in size order on the shelves.

Remember!
Wash all items of the same
size together. This makes
offloading from the racks to
storage so much quicker.

Double sink washing up of cutlery

○ Pre-clean cutlery to remove any loose material sticking to the
surfaces.
○ Wash the cutlery by hand using detergent and hot water and
place it in flat wire trays or a cutlery basket.
○ When the trays or baskets are full, lift them and place them in
the adjoining sink containing either water heated to 82°C or a
chemical disinfectant solution.
○ Then remove the tray or basket and allow the cutlery to air dry.
○ When dry, remove the cutlery from the trays or basket and store
it appropriately.

Remember!
If using flat wire trays, have
a separate tray for each type
of cutlery item. This makes the
storage process quicker.

Machine washing crockery

○ Place the dirty plates upright in a plastic rack.
○ Place the rack over the sink and use the water spray gun to
remove any food debris.
○ When the rack is full, place it into the machine. Wait for the
wash, rinse and sterilising cycle to finish.
○ Remove the rack from the machine and allow to air dry for two
minutes.
○ Remove the plates and stack and store in size order onto shelves.

Remember!
If using flat wire trays, place
the spoons bowl side down
on the tray. This helps when
removing from the sterilising
sink or dish washer. You will
not have spoon bowls full of
water!

The process for machine washing cutlery is the same as for
crockery, but the cutlery can be placed in flat wire racks or baskets.

Once cleaned, the cold plates required for service can be issued to
the correct kitchen section and the waiters help themselves to the
crockery as required. Crockery is stacked in an orderly fashion on
shelves for easy access by the waiting staff.

Washing service dishes

Service dishes and lids are washed in the wash up area, then air dried and polished if necessary. All service dishes are then stacked in size order and stored until needed for service

The hotplate

The hotplate is the dividing point between the waiting staff and the kitchen staff. The waiters stay on the service side of the hotplate and the kitchen staff stay on the kitchen side. It is the communication point between the service and kitchen staff. The food for service is placed on the hotplate, checked by the aboyeur (see page 241) and taken by the waiters into the restaurant.

The hotplate has a hot cupboard underneath. The hot cupboard has sliding doors on both sides of the hotplate so that it can be accessed from the restaurant or kitchen side. The hotplate is used to heat crockery and service dishes ready for service.

Organisation of the hotplate

The hotplate is stocked with all the crockery required for the hot dishes on the menu(s). Before service, the plates are checked for cleanliness and counted. The plates are stacked neatly and placed in a logical order in the hotplate – for example: starter plates and soup bowls on the right-hand side of the kitchen side of the hotplate, then fish plates, joint plates and dessert plates in separate sections. Coffee cups and tea cups should also be placed in the hot cupboard, as well as the hot service dishes required for the service of food.

Plate warmers

An electric plate warmer is sometimes used to store and warm plates ready for service. Plate warmers are situated at waist height to allow easy access to heated plates.

For table service the plate warmer can be sited next to the food issue point within the kitchen, especially if the hotplate is not used for heating plates. For hot buffets, carvery and counter service the plate warmer can be sited at the most suitable position for service.

The plates are checked for cleanliness and damage and then loaded from the top into the plate storage section. The machine

Remember!
Turn the hotplate on or light it in plenty of time to heat the plates for the service.

Remember!
Plates should not be overheated as they will become too hot to handle and a possible danger to customers. The presentation of food on overheated plates is poor as the food tends to dry out.

Marcus says
When a plate leaves the hotplate it should have been wiped clean of finger marks and finally any splash marks. Equally important: when the plate is cleared from the table it should not leave a black mark on the tablecloth! Remember to clean the underside of the plate before it is dressed!

If you are using linen tablecloths, try to remove the creases from the top and the drop – try a cordless iron.

is then switched on and heats the plates. The plates are removed
from the open top as required. As the plates are removed from the
top of the plate warmer, a high-tensioned spring lifts the remaining
plates to the top.

Plates for cold food items are stored in chiller units ready for service.

Service dishes

The correct number and size of dishes and service flats should
be placed in the hotplate to reach the right temperature in time
for service. Lids and cloches are placed adjacent to the hotplate.
These are used to cover the heated service dishes just before the
food leaves the kitchen.

The still room

In a traditional establishment, the still room provides all the food and
equipment that the kitchen does not supply to the service staff.

It is used for the preparation and storage of:
- beverages: teas, coffee, hot chocolate
- assorted fruit juices
- milk, cream
- sugars
- butter and butter alternatives
- prepared bread items
- assorted toasts
- biscuits for cheese
- teacakes and scones
- sandwiches
- preserves
- cereals
- condiments, such as mustards,
  sauces and salad dressings
- dry seasonings and flavourings
- accompaniments.

Modern restaurants may have a
separate area for the preparation
of hot and cold drinks.

Figure 8.10 The still room is an important food preparation area for the
service staff

245

Dry seasonings and flavourings

All dry seasonings should be stored in separate dry, clean and covered airtight containers. They should be in a well-ventilated still room away from excess moisture, such as the still-set machine.

Dry seasonings and flavourings include: salt and pepper, cayenne pepper, whole pepper for peppermills, ground ginger, a range of sugars and sweeteners, a range of teas, including herbal teas, coffee, malted drinks, hot chocolate and Parmesan cheese.

All service containers – for example, salt and pepper pots – must be thoroughly dry before filling and the holes must be clear. Once you have filled a salt pot, place a few grains of uncooked rice in the pot before replacing the stopper. The rice absorbs any moisture and allows the salt to flow freely. Replace the storage container lid as soon as you have finished restocking.

Mustards, sauces and salad dressings

Mustards can be made from mustard powder or you can use pre-prepared mustard from a jar.

Pre-prepared mustard is often served from the pot and then finished as for fresh mustard.

Salad dressings can be produced by the kitchen and issued to the still room or purchased ready-prepared. They are presented and issued by the still room in salad dressing bottles on a stand or in sauceboats. Sauces issued in sauceboats should have an under liner and sauce ladle.

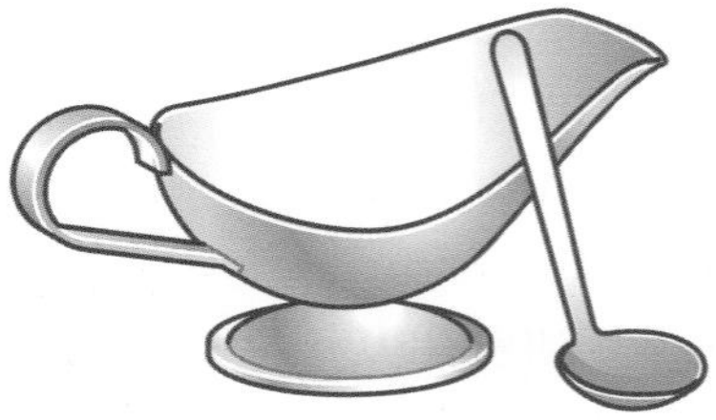

Figure 8.11 Sauceboat and ladle

Prepared bread items

Bread and butter: Prepare by spreading butter evenly on one side of the sliced bread. Remove the crusts and cut into four diagonally. Serve individual portions on small plates.

Melba toast: Toast sliced bread on both sides. Whilst hot remove the crusts and split through the toasted bread to make two thin slices of bread toasted on one side. Place the uncooked side uppermost on a tray and place under the grill. Wait at the grill and remove the toast when golden brown – a very quick process. The curled, thin toast is then served piled up on a side plate.

Breakfast toast: Toast thick sliced bread. Remove crusts and cut diagonally in two. Can be presented in a toast rack or served in a napkin to keep warm on a plate.

Rolls, brioches and croissants: These are all issued from the still room. They are often served warm and presented in a basket, or on plates.

Bread sticks: Can be served in a glass tumbler and left for the customers to serve themselves. Individually wrapped bread sticks are better for stock control, storage and hygiene.

Sandwiches: Can be prepared by the still room or by the kitchen and then issued by the still room. They should be served according to company policy – with or without crusts, cut into two or four, presented on a plate.

Still room equipment

To store, supply and prepare the above food items, the still room needs to be equipped with the following items.

A still-set machine

The still-set machine (often called simply "the still") is the reason for the name of the still room. Most still rooms have still-set machines, which are essential for making tea and coffee. These machines need heating to a certain temperature and then provide constant boiling water at the flick of the tap. Milk is heated by means of a steam jet.

The still-set machine can be used to make large quantities of coffee. This prepared coffee is then stored in urns within the still-set machine. The coffee can be held at the correct temperature ready for service. It can be instantly issued on demand.

Many still rooms now also have an espresso coffee machine.

Tea bags and tisanes

The stock of all tea bags needs checking and restocking for service. Rotation of stock is important to ensure that the tea is fresh. The tea bags should be stored in a suitable position next to the teapots for speed of production.

Definition

Tisane: Another name for herbal tea.

Teabags are used instead of leaf tea in many establishments because stock control is easier and the product is less messy than using tea leaves. The number of teabags needed per teapot size should be listed. This ensures quality control of tea making.

A large range of herbal teas are available, usually in individually wrapped teabags. This maintains the quality of the product during storage prior to service. It means that a wide range can be offered for the customers with less stock investment.

Coffee grinding machines

Coffee grinding machines are used to freshly grind specialist coffees on request. In a busy still room there may be several grinding machines, each machine filled with a particular type of ready roasted coffee bean. The freshly ground coffee can then be made by a range of different methods. For more information see Chapter 18.

Coffee making machines

Coffee making machines are portable and can be used within the dining room or at a bar. They are electrical machines. To prepare them, they need refilling with coffee, filter papers and water. Coffee jugs and containers also need checking for cleanliness before the service.

Cupboards

The still room will contain cupboards and open shelves for storing:
- dry food goods
- incidentals such as dish papers, serviettes, filter papers
- crockery
- small service equipment, such as milk jugs, coffee pots and teapots.

Refrigerator

A refrigerator is needed to store all perishable items, including dairy products such as milk, cream, butter and yoghurts, margarine, eggs, fruit juices and pre-prepared sandwiches.

Figure 8.12 Coffee grinding machines are used to grind specialist coffees on request

Butter pat machine

In some establishments a butter pat machine is used to provide controlled portions of butter for table service. Once prepared, the butter pats can be placed in a container with iced water and stored in the refrigerator until required.

Other ways of preparing butter pats include:

○ using a butter curler to create butter portions which are placed in iced water
○ cutting the butter into slices and placing directly onto a butter dish
○ individual pre-wrapped butter portions.

Butter is always stored in the refrigerator until service.

Remember!
Clean all preparation equipment as soon as you have completed a task.

Other still room equipment

Hot cupboard: for storing heated crockery, cups, plates.

Work surface and chopping board: for preparing food items such as bread and butter accompaniments, breakfast toast, toast fingers and sandwiches.

Bread slicing machine: this machine ensures that bread is cut to the thickness required. It also allows for bread to be cut lengthways for sandwich production.

Toaster: a commercial toaster, which can produce large quantities of toast, is ideal for breakfast service when fast production of toast is required. It is also used for pre-toasting bread for melba toast, which is then completed under the salamander.

Salamander: a salamander can be used to make toast if the toaster is out of action. It is also used for toasting scones and teacakes for afternoon tea service and for heating up extra plates quickly.

Cooking hob: some still rooms have a hob, which is used for boiling eggs, making porridge and for emergency use to boil water.

Cooking equipment: a range of saucepans is needed for cooking on the hob.

Double sink: the still room usually has at least one double sink and draining boards for washing up equipment used in the preparation of food items.

Dishwasher: subject to space, there may also be a dishwasher.

Operation of the still room

The still room is an extension of the main kitchen, providing a diverse range of food and drink items. The still room staff must meet all the food hygiene regulations. The food issued must meet the standards set by the establishment.

Before service

The first task when opening up the still room is to light or turn on the still-set machine. Switch on any other beverage-making machines at the same time. This will ensure that the equipment is at the correct temperature for service. It also provides a check that the machines are working. If there is a problem, maintenance can be called to inspect the machine.

The stock held in the still room needs ordering from the main stores. The stock control system should ensure that all the necessary food stock is available at all times. This is especially important for early morning starts. Condiments and accompaniments and all food service items must be readily available throughout all the service periods.

Stock of the following items should be checked and restocked in sufficient quantities:
○ all items on the drinks list: coffee, tea, specialist teas, hot chocolate, filter papers, etc.
○ all dairy products: milk, cream, yoghurts, butter, cheese, eggs
○ all types of bread, fruit juices, cereals, porridge, jams, preserves and table accompaniments
○ all sugars, sweeteners and condiments.

On receiving new stock, expiry dates should always be checked to ensure that the items are fresh and safe to use. New stock must be stored at the right temperature and in the right location. Surplus dry goods need to be stored in the still room cupboards to provide cool, clean and dry conditions. Remember to rotate stock so that the oldest is used first.

Remember!
First in, first out!

Coffee can be produced in readiness for service but not too soon or it will spoil. Coffee pots, teapots, hot water jugs, milk jugs, cream jugs should be steam-polished.

During service

The still room is used to prepare the orders as they are received and issue them to waiters.

Depending on the type of establishment, the still room is usually open from start of trading (usually 6 a.m.) to closing time (usually 11 p.m.). Still room staff normally work either the early or the late duty shift. The early shift covers breakfast, morning coffee and lunch. The late shift covers afternoon tea, high tea, dinner, late night drinks service and possibly room service.

The linen store

The linen store is located close to the service area. It stores the full range of clean linen and is kept locked. During service, the head waiter should have the key in case of emergencies. The linen is stored on slatted shelves, labelled by size. This makes it easier to carry out stock control and issue the linen as needed. Note that it is increasingly common for establishments to use disposable items in place of linen, or no tablecloths at all.

Issuing linen

Controlling the issue of linen is important, as linen is an expensive item. Linen is issued on a one-for-one basis. This means that for each dirty cloth a clean one of the same size will be issued.

Remember!

All working surfaces and equipment should be kept thoroughly clean during the service. Any spillages should be cleaned or mopped up as soon as they occur. If necessary you should use hazard signs to warn other staff.

Remember!

The still room is a food preparation and production area. It is important that the area is kept clean and hygienic, in order to:
○ meet the food hygiene regulations
○ prevent the risk of cross-contamination
○ avoid pest infestation and bad smells.

Test yourself!

1 Why is it important to turn on service equipment as soon as possible?

2 Explain the function of the still room.

3 Why is it important to have a constant stock of food service items during service?

Preparing the customer and dining areas for service

The dining area must meet all the hygiene regulations as well as offering a warm welcome to customers.

Cleaning the dining area

The dining area needs cleaning both before and after service.

Firstly the dining area should be aired by opening windows or increasing the air conditioning. The daily cleaning process should be to sweep first, then dust, then vacuum. All furniture needs dusting, including tables, chairs and sideboards. The heavy cleaning often takes place out of hours by contractors.

Mirrors and glass panels need polishing and smear marks need removing. Door panels should be cleaned to remove any food debris or finger marks. Brass should be polished. Any machinery on display such as coffee machines should be checked to ensure that it is in working order and cleaned.

Room layout

The reservations book should be checked. Depending on the bookings, tables may need to be repositioned to suit the number booked in or any special customer requirements. Tables may need arranging for function bookings with a pre-selected menu for a requested number of covers. As well as any function or party bookings, other tables should be arranged for normal restaurant table service offering the table d'hôte or à la carte menus.

Figure 8.13 The final room layout should be welcoming and have impact

When planning the room layout to fit in with the bookings, you will need to consider several factors:

○ fire exits – these should be clear and allow access to customers from all tables

- customer requirements – such as wheelchairs, disabled customers, young children
- customer requests – such as a window seat
- customer privacy – enough space between tables
- kitchen service doors – allow space for waiters to go in and out and to distance customers from operational noise
- traffic flows – the movement of waiters to and from the kitchen/ service area
- space allowance between guests – allow the service at table to be comfortable for all guests
- chair widths – the space allowance from table to chair back once the guest is seated
- customer entry points – space allowed for entry to and from the dining area
- access to toilets – space allowed to access the toilets and to distance guests from the location of the toilets
- visual impact – the final room layout should be welcoming and have impact
- maximising capacity – within the space available increase the number of covers to allow sales from 'chance' customers.

Moving tables and chairs should be carried out with great care. Use the correct manual handling procedures. Use furniture trolleys where possible and seek assistance if necessary. It is a good idea to plan the room layout before moving any furniture to avoid excessive movement of furniture.

Checking and cleaning furniture

Once the tables and chairs have been repositioned, they should be checked and cleaned.

Chairs

Check chairs for cleanliness and safety. Chairs should be brushed or vacuum cleaned. Remove and report any damaged chairs straightaway. This will avoid accidents or injury to customers. Check that the right number of chairs are at each table and in the desired position in line with the reservations. Chairs should be placed between the table legs. This is easy to do with rectangular tables but not always so easy with round tables. The waiter will lay place settings where the chairs are sited.

Tables

The dining tables should be checked for stability. Reduce wobbles by levelling any uneven table legs with a wedge. Lean on all trestle-type tables to check that they are assembled correctly. Correct immediately if necessary.

Check that each table is the right size for the number of guests and for the style of service. **Family service** may require a larger table for the number of customers because the food is placed in the centre of the table.

Preparation of cutlery and flatware

The type of cover to be set will help you decide what cutlery to lay out. The cover is named after the menu type – it could be function, table d'hôte or à la carte. Polish all cutlery before laying it out.

Definition

Family service – in this style of service, the food is placed in the centre of the table for people to serve themselves.

Remember!

Everyone is responsible for the safety of customers.

Remember!

For the comfort of certain guests you may need to increase the space allowed – for example, if there is a reservation for a wheelchair user.

Cover for a function menu

Lay out the cutlery and flatware that is needed for the set menu of the function. The cutlery for the whole meal should be on the table before the customers arrive.

Wedding of Mark Darby and Mary McLaughlin
Wednesday 3rd March 2008

MENU

Seafood Salad with Smoked Salmon, Crab, Prawns and Peppers

...

Noisettes of Lamb with a Wild Mushroom Sauce
Fresh Vegetables and Potatoes

...

Summer Pudding with Raspberry Coulis and Fresh Cream

...

Coffee and Mints

Figure 8.14 A function menu

Cover for a table d'hôte menu

If a table d'hôte menu is offered, all
the equipment for that menu should be
cleaned and polished and on the table
before the customer arrives.

Forbes Restaurant
Lunch Menu

Starters
Rich Mushroom and Herb broth with crème fraîche
Tuna Niçoise style salad with a lemon vinaigrette
Vegetable spring rolls with a sweet chili sauce

Mains
Vienna steak on tomato bruschetta
Chicken Fillets in herb crumb with a garlic mayonnaise dip
Grilled and marinated delice of Mackerel with a Moroccan couscous and
red pepper dressing
Baked leek and gruyere cheese tart with baked cherry tomatoes

Accompaniments
Ratatouille of vegetables
Sauteed potatoes

Desserts
Sticky toffee pudding with vanilla ice cream
Chocolate panna cotta with a sweet basil mascarpone
Baked apple and rhubarb crumble with a hint of ginger

Tea/Coffee

3 courses@ £7.75 per person
Dishes may contain traces of nuts

For reservations, please ask your waiter

Figure 8.15 A table d'hôte menu

Cover for an à la carte menu

An à la carte menu is extensive and has
many courses. To try to lay all the cutlery
required for the whole meal would take up
too much space. The equipment is cleaned
as for a table d'hôte cover but only some
of the prepared equipment will be placed
on the table before the customer arrives.
The remainder of the cleaned cutlery will
be stored in the sideboard for use during
service.

Starter Menu
Pumpkin and sweet potato veloute with parmesan, truffle oil and wild mushroom £5.95

Terrine of foie gras, confit duck, baby leeks and artichoke en presse salad
croustillant, Riesling and peppercorn jelly £8.95

Home smoked salmon with a tian of Cornish crab, cured tuna and confit tomatoes
with a tarragon & caviar dressing £12.95

Spiced rabbit & truffle sausage with Soya braised pakchoi red onion chutney £9.50

Salad of baby lobster, celeriac and marinated scallops dressed with a roasted
vegetable and lime oil jus £13.95

Main Course Menu
Valentine of lamb with braised shank, mint hollandaise served on a smoked potato
gratin with haricot beans, roasted garlic and puy lentil jus £21.95

Fillets of seabass with crisp prosciutto, baby spinach and Cornish crab drizzled
with a rosemary beurre blanc £23.75

Seared saddle of venison with roasted foie gras, baby leeks and girolle
mushrooms, spiked with sunblushed tomatoes £23.50

Millefeuille of monkfish and aubergine set on a smoked haddock and saffron
risotto dressed with and orange and star anis essence £22.50

Fillet of Angus beef with savoy cabbage, caramelised endive, truffled parsnip
puree and port wine £23.95

Dessert Menu
Classic pineapple tarte tatin with a coconut and rum ice-cream complemented
with a pineapple & ginger salad £8.25

Assiette of chocolate with an orange blossom sorbet £7.50

Liquorice and caramel bavarois, with roasted figs cooked in a vanilla and pistachio
syrup £6.95

Classic lemon tart £5.95

Selection of British and French farmhouse cheeses £7.95

Coffee & homemade petit fours £3.25

Did you know?
Cover means a place setting.

Figure 8.16 An à la carte menu

Polishing cutlery

Before laying the table, all cutlery should be polished. Cutlery can be made of stainless steel or silverware.

Polishing stainless steel cutlery

Stainless steel cutlery is inexpensive and hardwearing. It is available in several finishes: high polish, dull polish or matt finish. Stainless steel resists damage and scratching better than other metals and is considered to be more hygienic. It needs polishing by first dipping in hot water and then drying with a dry linen cloth to remove water marks. The polished cutlery should be stored on a salver or tray ready for laying the table.

Cutlery items

Service equipment to be polished should include the cover and any change of covers. The main items to be polished might include:

- soup spoons
- fish knives and forks
- joint knives and forks
- dessert spoons and forks
- side knives
- teaspoons
- ice-cream spoons
- coffee spoons
- service spoons and forks
- sauce ladles
- specialist items for menu dishes.

Certain menu items require equipment that are not on the cover. Once polished, all specialist equipment and **change of cover** and spare covers should be stored in your sideboard.

Definition

Change of cover – the additional cutlery or flatware required by the customer to eat a menu item.

Other cutlery and flatware items

Service spoons and forks: these include the large joint spoon and
joint fork used together to serve bread rolls to guests. Serving
spoons are placed in vegetables dishes for the guest to serve
themselves for family service.

Sauce ladles: used to serve accompanying sauces to the guest, for
example, tartare sauce with fish. Sauce ladles should be cleaned
and stored in the sideboard.

Teaspoons and coffee spoons: these need cleaning before service
and should be placed in the sideboard ready for use.

Salvers and trays: these should be cleaned and prepared for use
by lining with a napkin or serviette. This provides a hygienic surface.
The salver has many different uses during service, including:

○ carrying cutlery and flatware to and from the table
○ carrying glassware to and from the table
○ removing unwanted items from the table at the end of the main
  course – for example, the cruet set and butter
○ collecting crumbs from the table (known as crumbing down)
○ presenting and holding dishes during silver service of vegetables
  and sauces.

Sideboards

A **sideboard** or station covers a set of tables with approximately
20 covers. It may be shared by several waiters. The sideboard
needs to be of an appropriate size. It must be large enough
for purpose but it must not reduce the seating capacity of the
restaurant. Sideboards should be movable, to allow for different
room layouts.

Sideboards can sometimes be replaced by a side table covered
with a cloth for hygiene and presentation. A side table stores items
on the open table top. It is on view to all, so it is essential to keep
it well organised, clean and tidy at all times.

Sideboards are a base for the waiter within the restaurant and a
halfway house from kitchen to table. Every sideboard in the dining
room should have the same layout. The staff can then work at any
station and know where everything is.

Definition
Sideboard – the waiter's
work station. It holds all the
equipment needed to provide
an efficient food service to
customers. It is sometimes
called a station.

A sideboard consists of a work top with a shelf above for the storage of accompaniments. Accompaniments for all the dishes to be served are obtained from the still room and placed on the sideboard ready for service. Supplies are replenished during service by ordering from the still room. At the end of service all accompaniments are returned to the still room.

The work top stores a salver, order pad or hand-held, pen, menus, bread basket and corkscrew. During service, the work top is used to place trays from the kitchen with food or cleared plates from the table. For this reason during the service the sideboard must be cleaned and cleared continuously.

Below the work top is a set of drawers to hold cutlery and flatware. Before filling with equipment the drawers should be vacuum cleaned. The drawers are filled with cleaned cutlery in a set order for ease of use. The logical and easy to remember order for a six-drawer sideboard is from left to right:

○ side knife
○ dessert cutlery
○ meat cutlery
○ fish cutlery
○ soup spoons
○ service cutlery.

The cutlery placed as above will allow you to work from right to left in the same order as for a meal of:

○ dessert, meat, fish, soup.

Below the cutlery drawers there is a shelf and a cupboard. The shelf is for storing cold crockery and clearing trays and spare salvers. The cupboard stores clean spare linen.

After service all equipment and tableware is returned to its original storage area. If the sideboard is lockable, it could be restocked with tableware for the next session and then locked for security. All rubbish should be cleared from the sideboard and disposed of correctly. The sideboard should be cleaned and left tidy.

Linen

Linen tablecloths and napkins may not be used in your establishment. Many restaurants use paper or plastic tablecloths and paper napkins instead.

If used, linen tablecloths and napkins will need to be collected and signed for. At the end of a session the dirty linen should be counted and bundled.

Tablecloth sizes

Square tablecloths

- 54 × 54 in / 137 × 137 cm
- 72 × 72 in / 183 × 183 cm
- 90 × 90 in / 285 × 285 cm

Rectangular tablecloths

- 54 × 72 in / 137 × 183 cm
- 54 × 108 in / 137 × 244 cm
- 72 × 96 in / 183 × 244 cm

The size of the tablecloth selected should cover the table top and allow an equal overhang on all sides of the table to hide some of the table leg.

Buffet cloths

- 6 ft × 12 ft / 2 m × 3 m

Buffet cloths are used to cover the top, front and sides of the buffet table.

Slip cloths

- 3 ft × 3 ft / 1 m × 1 m

Slip cloths are used to cover an existing tablecloth. The slip cloth is laid on top of the existing tablecloth and so extends its life. Slip cloths can be the same colour as the existing tablecloth or a different colour. For a large table, several slip cloths are used. Slip cloths are also used as trolley cloths.

Napkins

○ 18 in × 18 in / 46 cm × 46 cm

Napkins can be ordered in white and various other colours. As well as being used as napkins, they are also used to line bread baskets, salvers and as tray cloths.

Other linen items

Waiter's cloth or service cloth

This is used for carrying hot food and plates and is regarded as part of the waiter's uniform. It must be clean in order to meet the hygiene regulations.

Glass cloths

Glass cloths are made of linen. They are used only for glassware polishing.

Laying the table

Check that there are enough cloths for the complete lay up of all tables. Check that the cloths are clean and damage free. Re-order replacement cloths or order slip cloths ready for table lay up.

Laying the cloth

1 Check that the cloth is clean and undamaged.
2 Check it is the correct size – do this by placing the folded cloth lengthwise across the top of the table.
3 The tablecloth consists of one double fold and two single folds. Standing in the centre of the length of the table, place the cloth on the table with the double fold uppermost.
4 Using both hands stretched apart, hold the top single fold and double fold of the tablecloth with the thumb and index finger of each hand. Raise the cloth, then release and place the bottom fold over the far side of the table. Use the creases to line up the cloth.
5 With the remaining double fold on top and one single fold underneath, grip the single fold with your thumb and index finger. Raise the single fold and draw the opened cloth towards you.
6 Adjust the cloth so that the overhang is even on both sides. Straighten the cloth.

Setting the table

Figure 8.17 Carry the polished cutlery and flatware to the
table on a salver that is lined with a napkin

Figure 8.18 Use the side plate as a guide for laying the
cutlery and flatware

Figure 8.19 When the equipment is in place, move the
side plate to the left

1 With the tablecloth in place, collect your polished cutlery. Carry
   all cleaned and polished cutlery and flatware on a lined salver.
2 Start the laying up process by placing a clean side plate in the
   centre of each cover. If the crockery is badged, place the plate
   so that the badge is at the top centre of the cover.
3 Line up the side plates so that place settings opposite each
   other are in line. Use the side plate as a guide to space the
   covers equally.
4 The cutlery is added on either side of the side plate when laying
   the cover. Place the cutlery ½ inch (1 cm) from the table edge.
5 Lay the cover from the inside to the outside. When all the
   equipment is in place, move the side plate to the left of the cover.

6 Carry cleaned glassware to the table on a salver or tray. Place the glassware at the top right of the cover, just above the knives. The glassware should be turned down for hygiene reasons.

7 Add the napkin to the cover.

8 Always give your prepared place settings a final inspection.

Figure 8.21 The finished place setting for a table d'hôte cover. Sometimes this also includes a butter knife

Figure 8.20 Place the glassware turned down at the top right of the cover

Laying a table d'hôte cover

The table d'hôte cover is listed in the order of laying the cover from the inside to the outside of the cover and consists of:

1 joint knife and fork
2 fish knife and fork
3 soup spoon
4 dessert spoon and fork
5 side plate (already in place) and side knife
6 napkin
7 glass – top right of cover.

(See Figure 8.21.)

Laying an à la carte cover

An à la carte cover is a simple place setting
consisting of:

1 cover plate or fish plate
2 fish knife and fork
3 side plate to the left of the cover and side knife
4 napkin on cover plate
5 glass – top right of cover.

Figure 8.22 An à la carte cover
contains only basic cutlery

Use the side plate as a centre plate to line up the
covers and as a guide to lay the equipment at each side
of it. Place the fish knife and fork either side of the side
plate. Place the side knife on the side plate. Then move
the side plate and knife to the left of the cover. Place the glass at the
top right of the cover. Place the cover plate or fish plate in the centre
of the cover. Finally, place the napkin on the cover plate.

Extra table equipment should be stored in the sideboard, including:
soup spoon, joint knife and fork, dessert spoon and fork, small
knife and fork for starters, side knives for cheese service and any
other items to suit the dishes on the menu.

Laying a function cover

The function menu will be pre-selected, so the waiter will know in
advance what the customers are eating. The number of customers is
also known in advance. Set the cover according to the menu, with the
addition of a side plate and side knife if bread rolls will be offered.

Use the side plate as a centre plate for lay up. Check that the centre
plates line up with any covers on the opposite side of the table. If not,
correct this now, in order to avoid having to realign the covers later.

According to the set menu, start laying up from the inside to the
outside. For example, if the menu includes soup and a chicken dish
for the main course, the first cutlery to lay will be the joint knife and
fork, and then the soup spoon on the outside of the joint knife. Add
the rest of the cutlery to suit the menu. When complete, remove the
centre side plate to the left and check the side knife on the plate.

Add the correct number of glasses – the first glass goes on the
outside right and the last glass on the inside right. Add the napkin,
the menu and place cards. Make sure that the room plan is clearly
on display.

Napkins

Napkins can be folded quite simply or very elaborately. They should be placed in the centre of the completed cover.

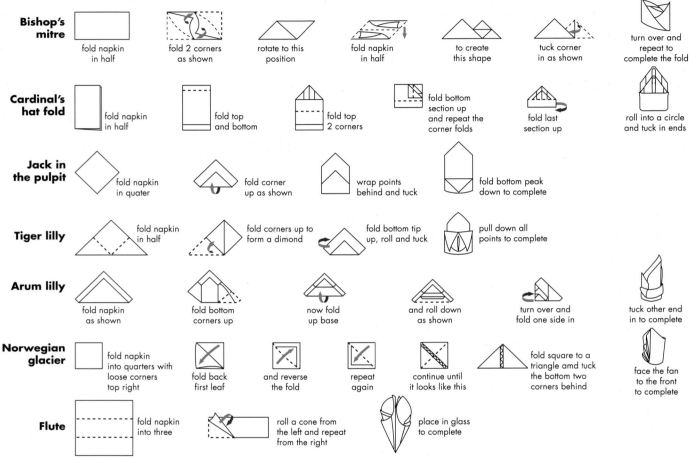

Figure 8.23 An elegantly folded napkin creates a good impression with customers arriving at the table

Glassware

Glasses should first be washed in a glass washer or by hand (see page 409). Then they should be polished as follows:

○ Hold the glass by the stem and place it over a container of boiling water. Polish the steamed glass using a clean, dry linen glass cloth.
○ Polish the base in the same way.
○ Hold the polished glass up to the light to check for smears and cleanliness.
○ Hold the glass by the stem and place on a lined salver to carry to table.
○ Place the glass turned down onto the table at the top right of the cover.

Remember!
Replace boiling water regularly when cleaning glassware. Always carry glasses on a salver for safety reasons.

Clearing broken glassware

Broken glassware should be cleared immediately. Get help if you are serving food or drink to customers. Large pieces of glass may be picked up by hand only if using heavy duty protective gloves. Small broken glass will need brushing into a dustpan and placing in a cardboard box. The dustpan and brush should be checked for any glass fragments – place these in the box. Now wash your hands.

If you accidentally break a glass while the customers are at the table, do the following.

If a spare table is available:
1. apologise and transfer customers to the spare table to continue their meal
2. reorder the customers' food and drink
3. serve any wine that the customers were drinking
4. serve the new order of customers' food
5. apologise for the inconvenience.

If a spare table is not available:
1. apologise and transfer customers to bar area
2. remove the customers' plates and reorder the customers' food
3. check the food plates for any glass fragments before placing at wash up
4. clear the table of table equipment completely
5. clear the broken glass and sweep into dustpan
6. place broken glass into a cardboard box
7. turn the corners of the tablecloth into the centre, then repeat this twice
8. place a clear plastic sack on the table and transfer the folded cloth carefully into the sack
9. tie a knot in the top of the sack
10. remove the clear plastic sack to the waste section of the service area to be dealt with after the customers are served
11. check the table top is clear of glass fragments
12. replace the tablecloth and reset the table
13. invite the customers back to the table
14. serve the new order of customers' food
15. apologise for the inconvenience.

Did you know?
Some people say that napkins should not be over handled at the folding stage, for hygiene reasons.

Disposing of broken glassware

Dispose of the broken glass at the end of session, so that any further breakages during service can be stored in the same cardboard box ready for disposal.

The cardboard box should be sealed with sticky tape and disposed of into the correct outside waste container. Now wash your hands.

When the area is empty, if necessary, use the vacuum cleaner to remove any fine particles of glass.

Table accompaniments

Table accompaniments are added to the table after the place settings are complete. They consist of the following items.

- **Condiments:** salt, pepper, olive oil, balsamic vinegar, etc.
- **Butter dish** and butter knife – allow one per four covers. The butter is added later.
- **Table number** – if used.
- **Table decorations** – for example, candles and flowers.

Menus

Displaying the menu

It is a legal requirement under the Price Marking Order 2003 that the menu must be displayed in a prominent position which can be seen by customers entering the restaurant. If the menu is extensive, a sample of the menu dishes can be displayed. The menu must also list the prices inclusive of VAT. Any service charges or cover charge must also be included.

Use of the menu in service

Menus are very important when preparing for service and when serving restaurant food. The menu is the link between the kitchen, the restaurant and the customers. The menu's contents and presentation will be seen by customers to reflect the skills and standards of the outlet.

Often there may be several types of menu on offer at any session, as well as special offers and promotions. The waiters need to study the menus in order to decide on the preparation tasks needed.

Remember!
The menu must comply with:
- Trades Description Act
- Price Marking Order

Remember!
Some customers have allergies or other dietary requirements. The information you give them needs to be correct.

Remember that the menu is to be used to sell and promote your products to your customers. As the waiter you should check that:

○ the menu is for today and for this session – not last night's dinner menu when you are serving lunch
○ the menus are clean and presentable
○ enough menus are available
○ you have read the descriptions of the dishes on offer
○ all the dishes are available
○ you know the prices of the dishes and are aware of any special offers and promotions.

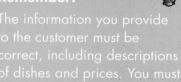

Remember!
The information you provide to the customer must be correct, including descriptions of dishes and prices. You must not mislead your customers.

You should study the menu so that you are familiar with all the dishes, including the ingredients, the cooking method and the description. You should also know:

○ the accompaniments to offer your guests if they order certain dishes
○ the change of cover required for every dish and how to serve it
○ the price of the dishes or menu that you are serving.

If in doubt, ask now, so you will be ready for service.

If the chef provides a briefing on the menu, listen and make notes. Keep the notes as reference.

Setting the scene

Before the customers arrive, check that all appliances are in working order and set to suit the environmental conditions. Put in place the final touches to create a welcoming atmosphere and make the dining room comfortable for customers.

○ Heating – adjust to suit the weather and the type of guests expected.
○ Ventilation – the room should be aired by turning up the ventilation fans or opening a window. Just before customers start arriving, set the controls to suit the number of expected guests.
○ Lighting – adjust to suit the time of day/night.
○ Exit and entry points – check that these are well lit.
○ Light bulbs – check and replace as necessary.
○ Music – select to suit the clientele. Set the volume and set to play before customers arrive.
○ Staff – should all be dressed according to the dress code of the establishment. They should be ready and waiting to greet customers on arrival.

Service preparation checklist

Tables

1	Clean cloth	
2	Correct number and placement of chairs	
3	Correct cover lay up	
4	Glasses	
5	Napkins	
6	Condiments	
7	Butter dish and knife	
8	Melba toast – if offered	
9	Table number	
10	Table decorations	

Sideboard

1	Working area clean and tidy	
2	Correct cutlery for service	
3	Service gear	
4	Trays and salver	
5	Bread basket – if applicable	
6	Order pad or hand-held	
7	Menus	
8	Hotplate clean and switched on	

Restaurant – general

1	Area clean and tidy	
2	Chairs brushed	
3	Floor clean	
4	Specialist equipment	
5	Cash desk presentable	
6	Waiters briefed on menu(s), ingredients, accompaniments	
7	Reservation list complete with table numbers, number of guests and service waiter	

Reception/Entrance

1	All areas clean	
2	Welcome board complete	
3	Correct menu in display case	
4	Lights on in toilets	

Hotplate

1	Power on	
2	Stocked with clean, correct crockery for the menu(s)	
3	Stocked with correct quantity of crockery	
4	Service dishes in hotplate	

Still room

1	Working area clean and tidy	
2	Accompaniments ready	
3	Butter prepared	
4	Beverage equipment clean	
5	Correct crockery in hot cupboard	
6	Hot cupboard switched on	
7	Fridge and storage areas clean and tidy	

Wash up

1	Working area clean and tidy	
2	Containers filled with soapy water for cutlery	
3	Food waste bin in place	
4	Spare rubbish sacks	
5	Clean tea cloths	
6	Disposable cloths	
7	Enough dishwasher cleaning supplies for the session	
8	Plate racks clean and ready to fill	

Linen

1	Spare linen for emergency	

Figure 8.24 Adapt this checklist to suit your own workplace and use it to check you are ready for service

Try this!
Draw a table d'hôte
cover.

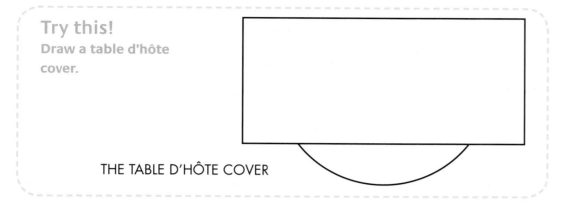

THE TABLE D'HÔTE COVER

Try this!
Draw the cover for an
à la carte menu.

THE À LA CARTE COVER

Test yourself!

1 What do you understand by the term cover?

2 List all the items that should be included in an à la carte cover.

3 What problems can occur if a waiter does not check the
menus before service?

4 How would you clean and polish glassware?

5 List in order the tasks involved in preparing the dining room
for service.

6 List the items stocked in a sideboard ready for service.

Clearing dining and service areas after service

Clearing tables should be a continuous activity throughout the service. This means that cleaning can also be an ongoing process throughout the session, so the final clear down does not take too long.

Clearing is a legal requirement within the catering industry. It is part of the food hygiene regulations and is for the safety of all – staff and customers.

Clearing the customer dining area
Clearing tables

When the table service to all guests is complete, the tables need to be cleared of all equipment and food waste. If there are no customers in the restaurant, it is quicker to clear onto a trolley.

Using a trolley

Wheel the trolley alongside the table being cleared. Place any rubbish directly into a rubbish sack. Scrape the plates, putting the food waste onto one plate. Stack the crockery into sizes. Place the cutlery directly into cutlery baskets obtained from wash up. Stack any service dishes onto the trolley. Check there is no rubbish on the floor. Check for lost property by the table. Move the trolley to the next table and repeat the process. When the trolley is full, wheel it to the wash up and offload the contents of the trolley.

Using trays

Place a clearing tray on the sideboard. If customers are in the restaurant, remove any items no longer needed directly onto a salver. When the salver is full, transfer the cleared items to the tray on the sideboard. Continue the process until the clearing tray is full and then carry to the wash up and offload correctly. If the restaurant is free of customers, you can fill the clearance tray directly at the table.

Clearing cutlery and silverware

If the cleared cutlery has not already been placed in the cutlery baskets, you will need to sort it and place it in the cutlery baskets at wash up. Once cleaned, washed and dried, the cutlery can be:

○ stored in sideboards if lockable
○ or used to set the tables for the next session
○ or placed in the store room.

Silverware dishes should be scraped and any food debris placed in the rubbish food bin. Place the scraped dishes at the wash up for cleaning. After washing and drying, store the silverware dishes in the plate room if there is one.

Clearing glassware

All glassware should be removed from the table using a salver or clearing tray. The tray should be filled with glassware only. This is because the glassware is cleaned at the bar. It helps if the same types of dirty glass are cleared onto one tray. A full tray of dirty glasses should be left on the bar and an empty tray taken for further dirty glasses. In the case of a large function, once the guests have left, you could use a trolley to clear the glassware.

At the end of the session, all trays should be cleaned at wash up. Trolleys should be cleaned down thoroughly after use.

Remember!
Leave the full tray of dirty glasses – do not offload the glasses from the tray as this would make more work for the bar staff.

Menus

Menus should be collected after service. If the menus are presented in menu holders, the holders will need to be wiped down. Divide the menu holders into those containing à la carte, table d'hôte, special offers, or promotions menus and stack them accordingly. Remove any menus not needed for the next session from the holders.

Remember!
Keep the menus and your copies of the food orders as evidence. On the menus mark the dishes that you served and make comments.

Table decorations

Collect table decorations from the tables, check them for damage and store those that can be reused. Extinguish candles and allow them to cool before storing them according to company policy.

Condiments and accompaniments

Return condiments to the storage trays in the still room. Return any accompaniments, used and unused, to the still room.

Napkins and tablecloths

Count used linen napkins and collect them in bundles of ten. Return the used napkins to the laundry or linen store. Remove paper napkins and dispose of them in the wastepaper bin or the recycle bin.

Remove tablecloths from the tables and refold them as received. Retain any tablecloths that can be reused, possibly by the addition of slip cloths. Place dirty cloths in size order and return them to the laundry or linen store.

Figure 8.25 Return condiments to the storage trays in the still room

Sideboards

Subject to the policy of the organisation, sideboards can be cleared completely or restocked at the end of session. The policy often depends on security and whether the sideboards are lockable. Either way, for clearance:

○ remove any foodstuffs and return them to the still room
○ remove any service equipment to the service area – unless restocking
○ clear out any waiter's dockets and paper rubbish and dispose of correctly
○ if a hotplate is used, unplug it
○ wipe the hotplate top while it is still warm – it is easier to remove dried-on spillages that way
○ move the sideboard and clear any food stuffs which may have fallen down the back
○ clean down the sideboard work top.

If the sideboard is lockable, the equipment can be replaced once it has been cleaned. Check that the contents of the sideboard are complete and then lock it.

Tables and chairs

The tables should now be completely clear and the room layout can be planned for the next session. Tables and chairs need repositioning according to the requirements of the next session. This may mean removing some tables and chairs – for example, after a function service – or making the room ready for breakfast service. For safety and efficiency, furniture trolleys should be used to remove surplus furniture to the storage area.

Leave dining room tidy ready for cleaning

Subject to company policy, once the positioning of the tables and chairs has been finalised, the tables can be cleaned and crumbed down. A slip cloth could be added to the tablecloth or the table could be re-clothed. This makes the restaurant look presentable.

Alternatively, the policy may be for the chairs to be placed on top of the tables, ready for the cleaning contractors to come in overnight. The arrangements could vary from session to session.

Clearing and closing down the service area
Wash up

Disposal of waste

The clear down at the end of a session must include disposing of all waste. Waste must be disposed of safely and in the correct place (see Chapter 5 pages 152–153). The reasons for this are:
- to meet the food hygiene regulations
- to prevent contamination of the service and preparation areas
- to avoid pest infestation
- to reduce accidents
- to reduce fire risks.

Food waste should be disposed of correctly in accordance with the food hygiene regulations. Broken crockery should be placed in a cardboard box and sealed before placing it in the waste bin.

Turn off equipment

All electrical equipment should be switched off, except refrigerators and other equipment which needs to stay on all the time. The reason for this is to reduce costs, to reduce the risk of overheating and fires and to extend the life of the machinery.

Clean the dishwasher

○ Turn off the dishwasher.
○ Drain and clean thoroughly.
○ Clean cutlery baskets and plate racks.
○ Remove any trapped food debris from the dishwasher filter.
○ Wash the dishwasher filter.

Clean the sink

○ Remove any food debris from the sink plughole.
○ Clean tile splashbacks.
○ Clean the sink and draining areas.
○ Spray behind the taps and clean them.

Clean the work area

○ Clean work surfaces.
○ Sweep and mop the floor.

Clean the rubbish disposal area

○ Dispose of any disposable cloths.
○ Clean the rubbish sack collar.
○ Replace the rubbish sack.

Close down the wash up

○ Collect dirty tea cloths and return to the laundry.
○ Leave the wash up area neat and tidy.

Figure 8.26 The wash up daily cleaning schedule

Wash Up Cleaning Down Schedule

Fill in details of all the items you clean

Item	Frequency of cleaning					Precaution e.g. wear gloves or goggles	Method of cleaning
	After use	Every shift	Daily	Weekly	Other		
Dishwasher	X					Gloves	1. Empty and drain dishwasher 2. Clean using metal or nylon pad, hot water and D10 around the sink, taps and plug hole. 3. Wipe down with hot water and J cloth and spray with D10 4. Spray with D10 leave for 30 seconds and wipe with disposable towel
Surface surrounding dishwasher including sink and shelves	X					Gloves	1. Ensure all crockery and cutlery is stored away correctly. 2. Clean using metal or green nylon pad, hot water and D10 3. Wipe down with hot water, clean cloth and spray with D10. Leave for 30 seconds and leave to dry naturally
Crockery and cutlery	X					Gloves	1. Clean in Dishwasher using dishwasher detergent and rinse aid 2. Store on correct shelf or in the cutlery trolley
Refuse sack holder	X					Gloves	1. Remove black plastic bag and dispose in correct wheely bin 2. Clean the bin collar in hot water and disinfectant 3. Spray with disinfectant and leave for 30 seconds; wipe with disposable cloth 4. Place bin collar back in its correct position

Hotplate

After service, turn off the hotplate. Remove the remaining crockery to the crockery store and return service dishes to store. Clean the hotplate as follows.

- Turn off the power supply.
- Remove clean equipment back to storage area.
- Remove any food and discard.
- Remove food debris and dispose correctly.
- Clean the hotplate top and dry.

Plate warmers

- Turn off the power supply.
- Remove any plates and store them correctly.
- Clean and dry the exterior sides of the plate warmer.

Silver room

The silver room receives all the cleaned stock of silverware. The stock is then stored in the appropriate sections of the silver room. For security, the silver room is locked at close down.

Still room

Still-set machine

- At close of service, turn off the machine.
- Drain away any remaining coffee from the still-set urns.
- Remove any coffee grounds and filter papers.
- Wash the filter section.
- Clean the still drainage area.
- Clean the exterior of the urns.
- Clean the steam jet.
- Drain away any water.

Hot and cold beverage containers

Empty these and clean them thoroughly, then store in the right location.

275

Electrical machinery

Most electrical equipment, such as coffee making machinery, bread slicers and dishwashers, should be switched off at end of session. The reason for this is to reduce costs, reduce the risk of overheating and fires and to extend the life of the machinery. Refrigeration units must be left on.

Refrigerated units

- Dispose correctly of any food items with today's use by date.
- Tidy the contents of the refrigerator.
- Cover, label with use by date and store any returned accompaniments.
- Bring forward existing stocks in readiness for restocking.
- Clean down the fridge door and handle.
- Check the door is tightly closed.
- Take and record temperature readings.
- Leave the fridge switched on.

Salamander

- Check the salamander is off.
- Collect and dispose of any food debris from the grill tray.
- Clean as required.

Cooking hob

- Check it is switched off.
- Clean the hob and around the switches.

Hot cupboard

- Switch off the hot cupboard.
- Empty the equipment for the hot cupboard and store.
- Clean inside the hot cupboard.
- Clean the hot cupboard exterior.

Storage of food items

○ All food items should be stored at the correct temperatures and in correct conditions.

○ All returned food items should be inspected for reuse. If to be reused, food should be covered with cling film and labelled with use by date

○ Butter returned from tables could be collected and issued to the kitchen for cooking.

○ Any unsafe food must be disposed of correctly.

Floor

The floor needs sweeping and cleaning by mopping.

Linen

Cloths should be inspected for cleanliness. If a slip cloth would cover any stains and extend the life of the cloth, order a slip cloth according to policy. Dirty cloths should be folded neatly for easy counting. Tie used napkins in bundles of ten for easy counting.

The used linen from all areas – including the restaurant, the still room and the wash up – is returned to the laundry or linen store. All dirty linen items – including tablecloths, slip cloths, napkins and tea cloths – are exchanged on a one for one basis. Stock can be replaced at the end of the session or the beginning of the next session.

Clean and crumb down the tables, add slip cloths if necessary and leave only the table number on the table.

Security

After completing the clearance of dining and service areas, the final task is to secure the area, as follows.

○ Lock the contents of the till in the safe. Remove the till drawer or leave it open so it is obvious there is no money around.

○ Lock the bar, making sure that you check that the shutters and stock are secure.

○ Lock fridges if applicable.

○ Lock or close doors and windows.

Locking up

Check all toilets to make sure that there are no customers left in them, no open windows and no other hazards such as cigarettes left burning. Once you are sure that the toilets are empty and secure, they should be locked.

You must be sure that the building is empty before you lock up. This includes both customers and staff who may still be in changing rooms. Remember to check any lifts. Once you are sure the building is empty, lock the exit doors and turn on the alarms.

Try this!

Waiters often have to deal with unexpected situations. Some examples are given below. Write down what you would do in each case.

o *Whilst preparing the restaurant for dinner service, there is a power cut. What do you do?*

o *At the start of the lunchtime session, two out of eight staff have failed to arrive for work. What is the solution?*

o *During a busy lunch session, you are laying table d'hôte covers for the reservations in the book. There appears to be a shortage of joint knives and forks. What would you suggest?*

o *Whilst serving food at a restaurant table, you break a glass on the table. To meet all health and safety requirements, what actions do you need to take and in which order?*

Test yourself!

1 How would you dispose of broken crockery?

2 Why must waste be disposed of correctly?

3 Why is it important to check stock?

4 At the end of service why must fresh food items be returned to storage areas immediately?

5 At the end of service what happens to the used linen tablecloths and napkins?

6 Clearing down areas after service is critical. Why is that?

7 List the reasons why the service areas should be left clean and neat and tidy after service.

9

Providing a counter/take-away service

In this chapter you will cover skills and knowledge in the following units:

○ 7132 – Unit 109 (1FS3): Prepare and clear areas for counter and takeaway service

○ 7091 – Unit 258: Service of food at table

○ 7103 – Unit 108: Food and beverage service skills

○ 7103 – Unit 209: Food and beverage service skills

Working through this chapter could also provide evidence for the following Functional Skills:

Functional English – Speaking, listening and communication Level 1

Functional Mathematics – Representing Level 1

In this chapter you will learn how to:

○ serve customers at the counter

○ work safely during counter service

○ prepare the counter for service

○ act in a polite, professional and hygienic manner during service

○ maintain counter and service areas

Serving customers at the counter

When a customer requires a quick and efficient service because they only have a short period of time for their drink or food, and table service will take too long, then a counter service facility is the ideal answer.

Counter service staff must be able to deal quickly and courteously with each customer so that they can be served in as short a time as possible, allowing them the time to consume their purchases.

Many establishments offering a counter service also offer a take-away service, especially in busy city centres, railway and bus stations, airports, and at sports and recreational events.

During busy periods customers often have to queue, and this can make them stressed, especially if they have little time or are late. A pleasant, courteous counter assistant who gives an attentive, efficient and speedy service can help to avoid this and make customers more likely to return.

Figure 9.1 Time is often important to customers who have chosen counter service

Health and safety

Under the Health and Safety Act 1974 you are responsible for the safety of yourself, your work colleagues and, most importantly, your customers at all times while on the establishment's premises.

Potential hazards

It is most important that you ensure the environment is free of any potential risks that may cause an accident (see pages 54–55). Some of the regular problems that apply specifically to counter service are as follows.

Marcus says

Don't spend time chatting to your work colleagues when you are looking after a customer.

Wet floors and spillages

These must be cleaned and mopped dry, and a notice displayed warning of the danger.

Hot crockery and equipment

Ensure that any items to be carried or handled by customers are at a safe temperature of between 40°C (104°F) and 60°C (140°F). Inform customers when crockery/equipment is hot. Customers should be offered a serviette when plates are hot.

Chipped and cracked crockery

All chipped or cracked crockery must be removed from service as it is not only unhygienic and could cause food-poisoning, but is also dangerous and may cause cuts to the hands and mouth.

Broken glassware and bottles

Glass is often broken accidentally by customers when carrying their purchases to the table. It is important that you clear up the broken glass immediately using strong protective gloves to pick up pieces of glass, and thoroughly sweep up all shards from the floor. Have a separate container for any broken glass to retain during service; after service, dispose of the glass in a safe manner (box, wrap or deposit it in a glass or bottle bank).

Extra care should be taken if a bottle top chips when removing a Crown Cork™ as customers often drink straight from the bottle, and may cut their lips. Do not serve the bottle or its contents to the customer, and do not throw it away. Instead, report the incident to your supervisor, who will record the damaged goods and return the bottle to the suppliers (if a deposit on the bottle has been paid). Non-returnable bottles should be disposed of as for broken glass.

Walkways

All walkways (service and dining areas) must be free of debris and obstacles to prevent the risk of tripping. This is especially important for customers who are carrying trays of food.

Poorly maintained furniture

Dining area tables and chairs must be checked daily to ensure they are in a good condition and that the legs of chairs and tables are in good repair. Tables with uneven legs, which cause the table to wobble, often result in spilled drinks and dissatisfied customers. Spilled hot drinks can scald (especially young children with sensitive skin). Do not attempt to wedge pieces of card, wood, etc. under the offending leg, as this only adds to the danger. Instead, remove the table and have the leg fixed properly.

Falling equipment and display items

Always ensure that any items stored or displayed above head height are secure and cannot fall onto staff or customers (especially if they are placed on display cabinets).

Knives and other cutting implements

All knives and sharp implements used for food preparation must be stored in their correct place when not in use (see page 51). Never put a knife or sharp implement into the washing-up water unattended (a major cause of cut fingers). Always wash and sterilise knives while holding them (using protective gloves).

Unattended items

It is unfortunate that we now live in an age of potential terrorism attacks, especially in busy public areas such as railway stations, airports, public events, etc. A high state of alertness is a must for all employees in busy areas, as they can easily spot and recognise anything unusual.

The greatest risk is from unattended packages, suitcases, bags, holdalls, boxes, etc. that have been left within the dining area. It is most important that you identify any item and report it to your supervisor immediately. Failure to do so could have disastrous consequences. While, in most cases, it will prove to be harmless, peace of mind will be assured for yourself and everyone else.

Regular announcements may be given over the public address system, and large notices displayed warning people not to leave their belongings unattended for risk of them being removed by the security personnel.

Figure 9.2 Unattended bags or packages should be reported

Counter preparation

A well organised counter area (front and rear counters) will ensure an efficient service, especially at busy periods. You will find a lot of information about preparing areas for food service in Chapter 8. Below are some things that you need to be particularly aware of when preparing an area specifically for counter or take-away service.

○ Make sure that all items are well stocked and that adequate back-up supplies are easily at hand for restocking during service.

○ All electrical equipment should be switched on in plenty of time for the equipment to reach the correct temperature before service begins.

○ Check the temperature readings of refrigerators, deep-freezes, and hot and cold display cabinets to ensure they are at the correct working temperature. Also check that all lights on the display units are working. This should be done as soon as you start duty. Any units not at the correct working temperature should be reported to your supervisor immediately.

○ Check the trays for use by customers, ensuring they are clean, dry and available in sufficient numbers. Remove any damaged trays.

○ Ensure you have sufficient serving equipment for each item of food. A different set of service implements must be used for each food item. Never use one implement for different foods because of the risk of:

– cross-contamination (see pages 160–162)

– flavour contamination (savoury ingredients contaminating sweet foods, and *vice versa*)

– ingredients to which customers may be allergic (such as nuts, dairy or garlic) contaminating other foods

– contamination by ingredients that may be forbidden to customers (on religious grounds).

○ Check and clean the dispensing systems for sugar, artificial sweeteners, butter/margarine pats, condiments, cutlery, straws and paper napkins, and make sure they are all refilled and tidy. This should be repeated on a regular basis, as the area can quickly become untidy with customer use.

○ Check expiry dates regularly and remove any items that are out of date (see page 171).

Have as many of your products as possible on display. Prepared foods are best displayed in heated or refrigerated, glass-fronted cabinets, with easily readable labels describing the products and contents. Products that cannot be displayed should be represented by photographs or poster adverts, or tent cards, again with an easily read description.

A large tariff board (price list) at the beginning and ideally again at the end of the counter will assist customers in calculating their spending and help speed things up at the till. Before each service you should check that the information on the board is up-to-date and correct. If a particular item is not available, ideally you should remove it from the board, or make a note of it so that you can inform customers.

Remember!
It is important under all circumstances when serving food to avoid cross-contamination.

Figure 9.3 Use implements when serving food

Remember!
It is vital to ensure you do not sell any foodstuffs that are past their expiry date.

Figure 9.4 Display items for sale attractively

Personal qualities

While we all tend to think that serving at a counter is easy, there are a number of important qualities that all counter staff should possess and demonstrate while on duty.

Hygiene

Under the food hygiene laws, all food handlers must follow the strict guidelines regarding both personal and food hygiene (see Chapter 2). Failure to do so can lead both you and your employers to heavy fines, possible closure of the premises or even prison.

Personal hygiene

A very high standard of personal hygiene (uniform, hair, hands, etc.) is of utmost importance, including attention to all food-handling hygiene practices (see Chapter 5, pages 139–144). You must never eat, chew gum or drink while serving, and should only eat or drink during your official breaks. Usually there is a designated area away from the counter where you can relax and have a drink or a snack.

Food hygiene

All foods on display must be kept covered and at the correct holding temperature to prevent the risk of food poisoning (see Chapter 5, pages 130–137). Hot foods must be held above 63°C (145.4°F) and cold, unwrapped foods below 5°C (41°F). Filled sandwiches, baguettes, rolls and prepared salads, wrapped or contained in sealed packages, can be held at 8°C (46.4°F) in the cold display cabinet, for sale within 24 hours of manufacture or up to 72 hours or below 5°C (41°F). All foods must be handled with food tongs (separate tongs for each food item, see page 283). Food handlers must wear disposable gloves when handling items that cannot be handled using tongs.

> **Remember!**
> All food at the point of sale (the counter) must be in a wholesome condition and fit to eat without any risk of food-poisoning.

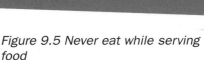

Figure 9.5 Never eat while serving food

> **Remember!**
> Your job at the counter is a very visible one. Customers will be watching your every move while you are preparing their order. Bad hygiene practices will be very noticeable and may cause the customer (and others) to leave without their order!

Attentiveness

While on duty you must always be attentive to your customers, their needs, requests and any questions they may ask. If you are not sure you have understood the order, politely repeat it back to the customer.

If there is preparation time before the food is ready, make sure you know which customer's order is next in the queue. This applies especially where hot foods are cooked to order in the kitchen.

Figure 9.6 Make sure you know which customer's order is next in the queue

Attitude and politeness

A good attitude is one of the most important personal qualities for someone working in food service. Customers will remember a helpful, polite service, and are much more likely to return and also to recommend the establishment to their friends. Here are some particular pointers to help you develop good customer service at the counter (see also Chapter 4).

o Try to avoid using abrupt terms such as 'Next?' or 'Yes?'. Instead, try 'Who's next please?', 'Yes sir?' or 'Yes madam?', in a gentle and warm manner. Finish with 'Thank you sir' or Thank you madam'.

o Always show customers where the sugar, artificial sweeteners, butter/margarine pats, condiments, cutlery, straws and paper napkins are.

o Explain to the customer if there will be a delay for any item they have ordered, to allow them to choose an alternative if they are restricted by time.

o Even if there is a long queue, you must be patient and understanding.

o Tell the customer if an item is very hot, to avoid them burning or scalding themselves.

Did you know?

Many establishments now have a ticketing system for customers who have to wait while their order is cooked/prepared.

Remember!

A list of the foods and ingredients kept at the counter can be a useful aid – especially if the selection of foods (menu) is large and your establishment is busy.

Remember!

Rule 1: the customer is always right.
Rule 2: if you think the customer is wrong, then re-read rule 1.

Remember!

Even if you are getting tired after a long shift, you must never show it to the customer.

Remember!

At the end of service, you must report any problems that occurred during the service to your supervisor. The problems should be discussed fully, and ways agreed to prevent them happening again.

Organisation

Good organisation will keep the queue moving. If you use anything, put it back where you found it. This allows you and your co-workers to access the item easily the next time, without having to look for it.

For health and safety reasons, you must also immediately clean up any spillages you make – a messy counter surface or floor is only likely to spread as equipment is placed in the spillage. Spilt liquid may contaminate other foods, or someone may slip on a wet floor and hurt themselves. Make sure you know where replenishing stock is held to ensure continuity of service.

Product knowledge

A sound knowledge of the recipes and quantities of food and beverages on offer is essential. You must be able to inform customers if a food item has an ingredient in it to which they may be allergic (such as garlic, onions, nuts, cheese and other dairy products). You should also know which items are suitable for vegetarians. Visitors from other countries, and those belonging to religions with food restrictions, will also need to ask about the contents of foodstuffs on sale. Knowing the contents of your sandwiches/baguettes, for example, will help if a customer has not seen the choice on display.

Location knowledge

Customers often think that counter staff will have a good knowledge of the surrounding area and facilities, and may ask for directions or information. If information is delivered quickly and efficiently, it will be helpful, prevent time-wasting, and give a good impression to the customer.

Good memory

As most customers will require more than one item in their order, it is important that you can remember the order until you have completed it. Large orders should be written down, especially if there will be a time lapse (while food is being cooked or prepared).

INGREDIENTS

OATS (30%)
SUGAR SYRUP, VEGETABLE OIL,
GLUCOSE, FLOUR, SUGAR,
GOLDEN SYRUP, DRIED MILK,
EMULSIFIERS, FLAVOURINGS,
SOY, RAISING AGENT, IRON,
VITAMIN B6, VITAMIN B12,
FOLIC ACID

MAY CONTAIN NUTS

Figure 9.7 Make sure you know the contents of items you are selling

Remember!

The customer may not have their reading glasses with them. They may be unable to read, or to understand the language or terminology.

Find out!

What ingredients are in the foods that you serve in your establishment? Make a note of any that may cause allergies.

Figure 9.8 A good memory for orders is important

Test yourself!

1 What is a safe temperature range for items of food and drink to be carried by customers?

2 State five potential hazards when providing a counter service, and how you can avoid each one.

3 What temperature should the following be displayed at?
a Hot foods
b Cold, unwrapped foods
c Filled sandwiches, baguettes, rolls and prepared salads (wrapped or sealed)

4 What should you do if a customer complains?

Did you know?

Many establishments now have an automated order/ billing system, where the counter staff key in each ordered item as it is given by the customer. These machines aid efficiency and service, as they produce an accurate order and bill (providing the correct keys have been pressed).

Try this!

With a colleague, practise remembering an order of five or six items. Take it in turns to give the order.

Maintaining counter and service areas

An efficient counter/take-away service depends on staff keeping on top of all the routine tasks throughout the service session. The service area must be kept clean and hygienic at all times.

Routine

During service, you must ensure:
o there is easy access for a customer in a wheelchair
o the children's high chair is in an accessible place, and is clean and serviceable
o sufficient clean service trays are available for customers
o foods prepared first are served first – replenishing foods must be placed so that the older stock is selected for service; how the new stock is placed should be agreed between all counter staff so no confusion arises about which stock is 'new'
o food presentation displays are clean and well presented so that they look appetising and pleasing to the customer's eye at all times during service

Remember!

It is important that the service area looks as attractive to the last customer as it did to the first.

Figure 9.9 Check that children's facilities are available, clean and safe

287

- portion control is maintained at all times – you must never favour one customer over another; if a customer asks for a larger portion, explain that they must be given a full second portion and charged the full amount for it
- dispensing systems for sugar, artificial sweeteners, butter/ margarine pats, condiments, cutlery, straws and paper napkins are refilled
- rubbish bins (sacks) must be emptied at regular intervals – in some areas (airports, railway stations, public events, etc.) this is also a security requirement to reduce the risk of a terrorist attack
- tables are cleared and cleaned in a quiet and hygienic manner, remembering that customers will be watching you and any bad practices will be noticed – use a clean trolley to collect trays and waste (most establishments have a purpose-built trolley); do not fill the trolley to overflowing as this may cause items to topple over when the trolley is being moved, which will be embarrassing to you, annoying to customers, and create extra work in clearing up the mess!
- tables are cleaned using a bactericidal spray – never use sprays while customers are seated at the table because it could offend, and may cause an unexpected allergic reaction
- tables, chairs and eating areas are clean and free of rubbish – always replace chairs neatly under tables.

Take-away service

A **take-away** service is often available at the counter, and requires some additional tasks and different service techniques.

- As the food and drink is to be consumed away from the premises, it must be packaged in such a way that it will keep hot/cold, and sealed to prevent spillage when it is being carried.
- Make sure there are sufficient containers, paper cups and lids, paper bags and other items (e.g. pizza boxes, baguette bags).
- Always handle any food in a hygienic manner using food tongs (or disposable gloves) to pick them up and transfer them to the packaging.

> **Did you know?**
> Portion control is important in order to give customers a consistent service – but also for stock control and profitability reasons.

Figure 9.10 Be very careful when using sprays – never spray near customers

> **Definition**
> **Take-away:** any food that is purchased in a prepared, ready-to-eat condition for consumption off the premises at another location.

- After sealing the food package or drinks lid, ensure there are no spillages. Wipe clean any spillages with a clean sheet of absorbent kitchen paper.
- Pack cold foods (salad items, rolls, etc.) separately from hot foods, as there may be some time before the customer has a chance to eat them. They will not enjoy their hot food if it has gone cold. Cold items such as salads are spoiled by becoming warm, and butter/mayonnaise in sandwiches will melt.
- Identify to the customer which containers have which order in them. This will also help to confirm that the order is correct.
- Always show customers where the sugar, artificial sweeteners, butter/margarine pats, condiments, cutlery, straws and paper napkins are.
- As always, rules of hygiene must be followed when cleaning and restocking – see Chapters 2 and 5.

Figure 9.11 Make sure take-away food is well packaged

Handling cash

There are two main methods of taking payment for foods purchased at a counter: payment of receipt of food or payment at point of exit. The majority of payments are cash-based, although more and more outlets are now taking card payments (both debit and credit cards).

Payment on receipt of food

The customer pays in cash for the items, handing the money directly to the member of the counter staff who served them. This method has the most problems.

- Handling cash will contaminate the member of staff's hands, and therefore creates a high risk of cross-contamination. When this type of payment is in operation (usually small cafés, sandwich bars, coffee bars, etc.) even more care should be taken, and food must always be handled with food tongs.
- There is a high risk of miscalculating the correct amount when a number of items are to be paid for. This can be at the business's expense, or at the customer's expense. Staff must be able to calculate accurately, in their head, or use a calculator or a suitable till/billing machine to do so. If you make a mistake, you should apologise and adjust quickly and efficiently.

Remember!
Most payments for counter/take-away service take place after the food has been served, so any delay in calculating and taking payment will result in hot food becoming cold. It is most important that you perform all payment procedures with speed and accuracy.

○ Any notes should not be put in the till until the change has been given to the customer – it is difficult to argue with a customer about the correct value of a note once it is in the till. The customer may have made a genuine mistake – or on occasion a customer may deliberately tell an unwary and busy staff member that they have paid with a £10 note and have only been given change from a £5 note. Either way, the problem can be easily solved if the note has not already been put in the till (see page 197).

Figure 9.12 Notes should be kept outside the cash box until change has been given, to avoid disputes

Payment at point of exit

This is the practice for large, busy canteens, cafeterias, etc., where customers collect their food and then move to a till which is manned full-time by one member of staff (often the shift supervisor) calculates the cost of the items on the customer's tray using the till/billing machine. The risk of inaccuracies is minimised, and this method has the added advantage of a final quality control at the point of exit from the service counter.

It is the normal, accepted practice to take payment for food that has to be cooked after the order has been taken. This ensures that customers do not leave before the food is delivered, and does not hinder the normal flow of queuing customers at busy times.

Figure 9.13 An efficient, organised counter means happy customers

Test yourself!

1 State five things that you should keep checking throughout the period of counter service.

2 What information should you give the customer as you give them their food/drink take-away order?

3 Why can handling cash be a problem at food service counters?

4 How can you assist the cashier at a food service counter?

10 Serving food at table

In this chapter you will cover skills and knowledge in the following units:

- 7132 – Unit 108 (1FS2): Provide a table and tray service
- 7132 – Unit 207 (2FS2): Serve food at the table
- 7091 – Unit 258: Service of food at table
- 7103 – Unit 105: Understand menus; and part of Unit 108: Food and beverage service skills
- 7103 – Unit 205: Menu knowledge and design; and part of Unit 209: Food and beverage service skills

Working through this chapter could also provide evidence for the following Functional Skills:

Functional English – Speaking, taking part in formal discussion, listening and communication Level 1

Functional English – Reading Level 1

Functional Mathematics – Representing Level 1

In this chapter you will learn how to:

- greet customers and identify their requirements
- offer the correct menu and dish information
- take orders, maximise the orders if appropriate and record orders correctly
- serve food hygienically and safely
- maintain the dining area during service
- dispose of all waste hygienically
- present the bill and assist customers departing

Introduction

The hospitality and catering industry is now more diverse than ever. This has an impact on the types and styles of food offered, and the way food is served. People eat out more nowadays – for a cup of coffee and a croissant on the way to work, and for lunch from a sandwich bar, café, bistro or fast food outlet. For dinner, the choice is as diverse as the industry – restaurants may serve food that is international, oriental (Indian, Japanese, Chinese, Thai), European (Spanish, French, Italian, English) or locally traditional in style, and may range from a gastronomic restaurant with a Michelin star rating to a local pub.

With such a range of options, the style of service is clearly also varied, and aims at meeting the style of cuisine, the price and the target market, based on the establishment's understanding of what the customer wants.

Generally, customers nowadays tend to want a more informal approach to service. This runs through the whole meal experience and has an impact on everything, from the way the establishment lays out tables, the style of cutlery, how they meet and greet customers, and the service itself.

This chapter explains how to greet customers, take orders and serve them, and maintain the dining area. With these skills, you can adapt to any style of service in any type of establishment.

Standards of service

Customers' expectations are high when they are dining out, whether at a high-class restaurant or an independent street café. The role of the waiter is to fulfil or exceed the customer's expectations. Waiting staff need to have good technical skills – but their **social skills** are just as important.

In order to provide outstanding customer service, the waiting staff need to understand what customers want. You need to treat any customer as you would wish to be treated yourself.

> **Definition**
>
> **Social skills** – in the restaurant, this means assisting customers, looking after their welfare, communicating well and anticipating their needs throughout the meal experience.

Your customers want you to:

- show respect
- show interest
- listen to requests
- accept problems
- enjoy serving
- provide information that is correct
- communicate successfully
- provide care
- give prompt service
- be friendly and welcoming
- be aware of hygiene, safety and security.

Marcus says

A good waiter knows and understands the menu and is able to confidently explain the details to an enquiring guest and make recommendations when asked.

Test yourself!

1 List ten different types of establishment where you might go for lunch in the UK.

2 Why is it important for waiting staff to be able to communicate properly?

3 Why might customers nowadays prefer a more informal style of service?

Greeting customers and taking orders

Greeting

Customers with a reservation

Where possible, information about customers should be obtained in advance. The best time to note any comments, special needs or dietary requirements is when the reservation is made. With advance information, the restaurant can be organised in line with customers' requests.

Depending on the type of establishment, greeting customers and showing them to their table may be the role of the head waiter, reception waiter or table waiter.

Definition

Customer requirements – information such as customers' names, number of place settings, time of arrival, type of occasion, special seating arrangements, special dietary requests, time limitations, any pre-orders for food or drinks, and requested style of service.

The greeting a customer receives gives them their first impression of your establishment. The greeting should be prompt, welcoming and make your customers feel at ease (see Chapter 4, pages 94–98). If customers' names are known, you should use them. Never leave customers waiting at the entrance unattended.

Customers without a reservation

These customers are unexpected, but very welcome in any business. Greet them immediately on arrival – with no booking, they could easily decide to go somewhere else. Ask how you can help – obtain information including the number of guests in the party and when they would like to eat, and, if relevant, whether they have any special seating requirements such as high chairs or wheelchairs.

Sometimes the requests of **chance customers** cannot be met. Perhaps the restaurant is fully booked, or one party may have taken the best tables. Wherever possible, chance customers should be accommodated in your restaurant subject to availability. Offer what is available, and show them to their table.

If there will be a delay before a table is available, inform them, offer to seat them in the bar/reception area, and offer drinks (**aperitifs**) and menus. Take their drinks order and serve it. Discuss the menu with them and take their order – the pre-order will speed the service once they have a table. Show your customers to the pre-set table once it has been relaid.

Assistance on arrival

Customers often need some assistance on arrival. Help them off with their coats, take their umbrellas, and generally settle them in. When your customers are ready, show them to their table at a pace to suit them. As the waiter, you should already know of any special requests and will have pre-organised these requirements. Offer a helping hand if any customers find walking difficult.

Identifying the host

The host is the person who is entertaining other guests, and is the spokesperson for the table. As the waiter, it is useful to find out who is the host by checking the named person on the reservations list.

Remember!
Smile!

Definition
Chance customers – customers who arrive at a restaurant without a reservation.

The host may arrive before their invited guests to meet with the head waiter and table waiter. If arriving at the same time as their guests, the host will normally introduce him or herself to the reception waiter. The head waiter may introduce the host to the waiter as the guests are being shown to their table.

As the waiter, you may be able to identify the host as they are arranging the seating plan. The host should also organise the service of food and drink for the guests by linking with the waiter. The waiter should refer to the host for further instructions throughout the service.

The bill is presented to, and usually settled by, the host.

Remember!
Do not assume that the host is a man.

Seating customers

The process of seating diners will vary from one establishment to another. Depending on your establishment's policy, the waiter should be ready to help with seating the diners. Eldest female first to youngest, then the eldest gentlemen before the youngest, and the host last. To seat customers, pull out the chair slightly and push the chair in as they sit down. After seating diners, the waiter may be required to break open their serviette and place it on their lap. Turn over glasses on the table from the right, if it is your company's policy.

Remember!
Seek help from your team to assist with seating a large number of diners at one table.

The wine waiter or the waiter should now offer customers the drinks list and take any **aperitif** order.

For more information on seating customers, see Chapter 4.

Checking and understanding the menus

You should study the menu carefully before offering it to customers – make sure that it is today's menu, that it is for the correct session (e.g. lunch or dinner), and that it is correct in content and pricing. Be aware of special offers and current promotions so that you can inform your customers. The menu must be clean and presentable.

It is usual to offer table d'hôte and à la carte menus for table service unless the customer has stated otherwise at the reservation stage.

Remember!
It is an offence against the Trade Descriptions Act 1968 to apply a false description to goods that are advertised for sale. (See Chapter 6, page 188.)

All waiting staff on any given shift must have complete knowledge of all the menus that are to be offered to customers. Before service, you may have a menu briefing from the chef. This might include explanations of any special dishes, the dish of the day, promotions, changes to dishes, reservations and level of service. This is the time to ask the chef any questions regarding the menu.

You need to be ready and able to describe any dish accurately – the method of cooking, ingredients and pricing.

Special dishes may not be written on the menu – you need to inform customers about these, and sell them to customers. These dishes must be described and sold accurately.

Presenting the menus

Have sufficient correct menus available, ready to present to customers. Menus may be presented open or closed, depending on your company's policy. Hand the menus to female diners first, then male diners, and the host last. At this stage, inform your customers of dishes that are no longer available. Describe any special dishes: the food contents, style of cooking and price.

Leave customers to look at the menu. While they are doing this, check or serve any aperitifs that have been ordered. Place butter on the table, and offer bread rolls.

One way of knowing if your customers are ready to order is when their menus are closed.

Taking orders

Order-taking provides the opportunity to assist diners in making their choice, and the chance to maximise food sales. Standing to the left of the host, to take the food order the waiter will need an order pad or hand-held device (see Chapter 6, pages 180–182). Your customers may need assistance with:
- an explanation of what is in the dish
- translation of dishes
- advice on contents of dishes
- vegetarian options*
- coeliac choices*
- requesting a dish that is not on the menu

Remember!

If there is a special offer or promotion, inform your customers – this may be one of the reasons they will want to return to your restaurant.

Remember!

The Price Marking Order states that at least a sample of the menu and drinks list, with prices, must be displayed in a prominent position outside the premises. (See Chapter 6, page 188.)

Did you know?

Sometimes the host is the only person in the party who has a priced menu. The host will settle the bill, and wants his guests to be free to order whatever they wish from their unpriced version of the menu.

Find out!

What food items can a diabetic not eat?

Try this!

Look at your menu and suggest a dish suitable for each of the three starred requests in the list alongside.

o a modification to a menu item to suit a dietary need (e.g. diabetic)*.

This is a good time for the waiter not only to sell additional food items, but also to sell the establishment.

Standing to the left of the host, check that customers are ready to order. Face customers as they make their choices, and look at them when they speak. Do not stand behind any guest who is ordering. Be patient when customers are indecisive or change their minds. Be ready to offer dish suggestions if requested.

Recording the food order

Recording the food orders correctly provides quality service to your customers. Orders may be recorded manually or electronically. Take orders following a set order of customers – this will remind you who ordered what dish for any change of cover, and act as a reminder at the point of service. Manual orders are usually recorded using the **triplicate checking system** (see Chapter 4, pages 180–181).

First food order

This first order will consist of the starter and main courses, and vegetables or additional side dishes. All orders need to be completed correctly, with table number, number of covers, date and waiter's printed name (or sign-in if using an electronic system). If taking orders manually, make sure you write neatly – others will need to read the order. Make sure the waiter's printed name on the food order is legible – the chef may need to know which waiter to speak to regarding the food ordered. In some establishments, specific abbreviations agreed in advance may be used for food orders. This is a good idea, so long as the abbreviations are understood by everyone – otherwise they may be misunderstood by the kitchen staff and the wrong order may be prepared.

If taking orders electronically, the dishes ordered are either coded or ordered by touch-screen. The completed order is then transmitted to the issue points – the kitchen for food, perhaps the bar for drinks, and a copy to the cashier for bills (in some restaurants, the waiter is also the cashier).

If the menu is à la carte, the order will also have to be priced and the time the order was taken recorded. On electronic systems, orders are automatically priced and timed. See Chapter 6 for more information on taking orders.

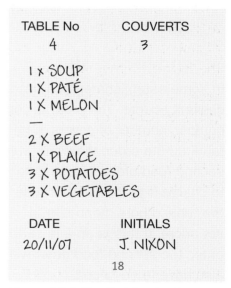

> **Definition**
> **Triplicate checking system** – a means of ordering, issuing and pricing food sold in a restaurant – a triplicate order pad produces separate copies of the order for different staff.

TABLE No	COUVERTS
4	3

1 x SOUP
1 X PATÉ
1 X MELON
—
2 X BEEF
1 X PLAICE
3 X POTATOES
3 X VEGETABLES

DATE	INITIALS
20/11/07	J. NIXON

18

Figure 10.1 The first food order

> **Remember!**
> Noticing which diners have returned their menus tells you which tables have had their orders taken, and which tables are still waiting.

Having completed the first food order, read the order back to customers to confirm that it is correct. Collect the menus from your customers, and offer the wine list or ask the wine waiter to attend the table. Now customers know what they are eating, they can decide more easily on any drinks to accompany their food.

At the sideboard, for manual triplicate orders, tear off the completed order and separate out the three copies. The top copy of the triplicate order goes to the kitchen, the second copy to the cashier, and the third copy is for the waiter for information.

Passing the order to chef

Pass the top copy of the order to the **aboyeur** or to the chef on the service counter or hotplate. Make sure the order is acknowledged by the chef by announcing 'Check on!'.

Find out!

What does the term **aboyeur** mean?

Second food order

In some establishments, a second food order is taken for the **dessert** course. The order is completed as before, with table number, number of covers, date and waiter's signature. If this is a table d'hôte order, the word '*suivant*' or '*en suite*' is written on the second food order, meaning 'to follow', and the cashier knows not to charge it to the bill (because the table d'hôte menu is at a set price). If this is an à la carte order, the second food order will also have to be priced.

As before, if three manual copies of the order are produced, the top copy goes to the kitchen, the second copy to the cashier and the third copy for the waiter's information – or the order may be passed on electronically.

TABLE No	COUVERTS
6	4

2 x MELON @ £2.75
1 X HORS D'OEUVRE @ £3.50
—
1 X GOUJONS @ £4.50
1 X MIXED GRILL @ £6.25
1 X BEEF CARBONNADE @ £5.00
1 X VEGETABLE CANELLONI
@ £3.50
+ SELECTION OF VEGETABLES +
POTATOES – INCLUDED

DATE	INITIALS
30/11/07	J. NIXON

22

TABLE No	COUVERTS
6	4

2 X CREME CARAMEL @ £3.25
1 X CHEESE @ £3.50
1 X COFFEE BAVAROIS @ £3.75

DATE	INITIALS
30/11/07	J. NIXON

23

Figure 10.2 An à la carte order

TABLE No	COUVERTS
4	3

'SUIVANT'

1 X PANNACOTTA
1 X APPLE CHARLOTTE
1 X RICE PUDDING

DATE	INITIALS
20/11/07	J. NIXON

19

Figure 10.3 The second food order

Third food order

The third order is for coffee or tea, which may be served after the meal or with dessert (this may depend on the time availability). As above, the top copy is given to the **still room**, the second to the cashier, and the third is for the waiter's information; or the order may be transmitted electronically. As above, for table d'hôte orders add '*suivant*' to the order to indicate that no further charge should be added to the bill. For à la carte orders, again each item should be priced.

Hot drinks can be ordered at other times of day, such as early morning tea, breakfast service, morning coffee, afternoon tea or late-night drinks. The top copy of the order is handed to the still room for the issue of hot drinks for service.

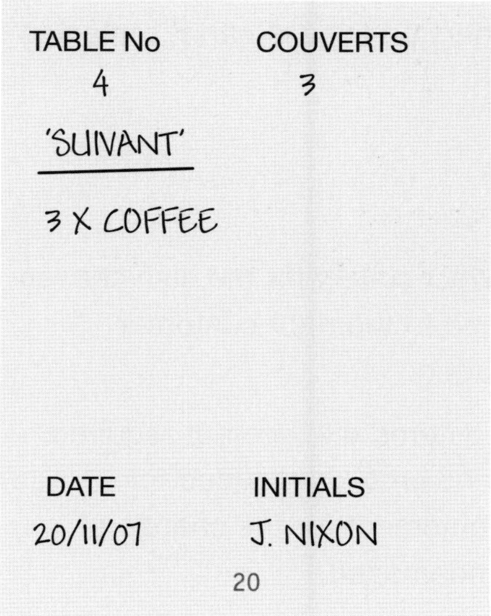

> **Definitions**
>
> **Dessert** is the service of fresh fruit and nuts.
> **Entremets** is the term for hot and cold food items offered as the sweet course.
> **Still room** – makes and issues food and beverages that the kitchen or bar may not provide in some establishments (see Chapter 8, page 245).

TABLE No	COUVERTS
4	3

'SUIVANT'
_____

3 X COFFEE

DATE	INITIALS
20/11/07	J. NIXON

20

Figure 10.4 The third food order

Test yourself!

1 Why should menus be checked before service?

2 Why is it is essential to provide accurate menu information to customers?

3 Recording the customer's order includes completing: (a) the table number, (b) the number of covers, (c) your signature, (d) the date, (e) the food order. State why each of (a–e) is important, and for whom.

4 Who should you serve first?

5 At the top of a table d'hôte order, you may see the word '*suivant*' or '*en suite*' – what does this mean?

Serving customers' orders and maintaining the dining area

Serving orders

Before serving any orders to your customers, the place settings need to be checked and adjusted to suit the dishes selected. This may involve removing and adding cutlery or, for à la carte, replacing the cover.

Changing the cover

Changing the cover:

- provides the customer with the correct cutlery for the dish chosen
- helps waiters to serve the right food to the right customer
- allows for efficient use of clean cutlery.

Changing the cover requires removing items that are not required and replacing them with the cutlery and crockery needed for customers' chosen food items. All equipment for the change of cover must be clean, polished and undamaged.

Table d'hôte

For table d'hôte lay-up, the cover needs adjusting for the starter and main course chosen by each diner. With your copy of the first order, and using a tray or salver (some establishments only), remove cutlery items from each place setting from the side on which the items have been laid. Knives are removed and added from the right, and forks are removed and added from the left. This avoids stretching across the customer. Once the cover has been changed, the food order is likely to be ready from the kitchen.

Remember!

When changing covers, move round the table clockwise – this enables the change of cover on the fork side for one guest, and the change of cover on the knife side for the next cover.

Try this!

The first food order for table d'hôte lunch for two customers:

- the female diner has ordered 1× soup and 1× fish
- the male diner has ordered 1× paté and 1× chicken.

State what equipment you will need for each cover before serving the food.

À la carte

For à la carte lay-up, the cover is changed one course at a time. This is done by removing and adding the cutlery and crockery needed by each guest to eat their chosen dish, before the course is served.

Remember!

A common mistake with à la carte service is to leave the customer with no cutlery as the next course is served. As soon as you have cleared one course, you must lay the cover for the next.

> **Try this!**
> The starter order is 1x paté and 1x minestrone soup – what adjustment to the à la carte cover will you need to make before serving this order?

Table accompaniments

Table accompaniments are often bottled condiments, which should be placed on the table prior to the service of the food they accompany. For example, cayenne pepper, peppermill, chilli vinegar and Tabasco® sauce make up the table accompaniment for the service of oysters.

Definition

Table accompaniments are not prepared by the kitchen, they are issued by the still room (see Chapter 8, page 245).

Accompaniments are offered to make an ordinary dish special. They may enhance the flavour of food (for example, horseradish sauce with smoked fish), or soften the richness or greasiness of certain foods (for example, redcurrant jelly with certain game dishes; apple sauce with roast pork). Accompaniments are served at the point of service of the dish that they accompany. So if you are serving roast pork, you follow on by offering and serving apple sauce, roast gravy, etc. (see Figure 10.5). Some establishments may also offer sage and onion stuffing with roast pork – it depends on the establishment.

Dish	Cover	Accompaniment	Comment
Hors d'oeuvre			
Hors d'oeuvre *Assortis*	Cold fish plate, hors d'oeuvre knife and fork (or fish knife and fork)	Oil and vinegar	Should look appealing, with colour contrast
Prawn cocktail (*cocktail de crevettes*)	Teaspoon, oyster fork, cocktail coupe (stemmed dish) or Paris goblet (stemmed glass), side plate	Cayenne pepper, peppermill, segment of lemon, brown bread and butter	Same service for crab or other seafood cocktail
Smoked fish, e.g. trout (*truite fumé*), eel (*anguille fumé*), salmon (*saumon fumé*)	Cold fish plate, fish knife and fork	Horseradish sauce (but not for smoked salmon), cayenne pepper, peppermill, segment of lemon, brown bread and butter	Lemon segment could be presented in lemon press

Dish (cont.)	Cover	Accompaniment	Comment
Soup (*potage*)			
Consommé (hot or cold)	Consommé cup, consommé saucer, cold fish plate, dessert spoon	Hot consommé always served with a garnish, e.g. celestine (strips of pancake) or profiteroles (miniature choux buns)	Can be served cold (*consommé en tasse*)
Purée soup (e.g. green pea soup)	Hot soup plate, cold underplate, soup spoon	Croutons	Offer croutons and sprinkle onto soup
Minestrone	Hot soup plate, cold underplate, soup spoon	Grated parmesan cheese	Offer parmesan and serve with teaspoon
Cream of tomato	Hot soup plate, cold underplate, soup spoon	Croutons	This is the only cream soup to be served with croutons
Egg (*oeuf*) dishes			
Egg in a dish (*oeuf en cocotte*)	Side plate, teaspoon	None	Always garnished from kitchen
Poached egg (*oeuf poche*)	Hot fish plate, dessert spoon and fork	None	Often served garnished
Omelette	Hot fish plate, joint fork (right of cover)	None	Omelette may be folded or flat
Farineux (includes pastas, savoury rice dishes and continental dumplings, e.g. gnocchi)			
Braised rice/ pasta/gnocchi	Hot fish plate, dessert spoon and fork	Grated parmesan	Have peppermill ready – often requested
Spaghetti napolitaine/ noodles	Hot soup plate, cold underplate, joint fork on right, dessert spoon on left	Grated parmesan, peppermill	
Fish (*poisson*)			
Mussels in white wine (*moules mariniere*)	Fish knife and fork, dessert spoon, hot soup plate, cold underplate	Brown bread and butter, cayenne pepper, peppermill	Often a debris bowl is offered for empty shells
Poached salmon (*saumon poche*)	Fish knife and fork, hot fish plate (or joint plate if main)	Lemon segment, hollandaise sauce (hot) or mayonnaise (cold)	Use cold plates if served cold
Grilled fish	Hot fish plate (or joint plate if main), fish knife and fork	Lemon segment, parsley butter (*beurre Maitre d'hotel*) or anchovy butter	

Dish (cont.)	Cover	Accompaniment	Comment
Whitebait (*blanchailles*)	Fish knife and fork, hot fish plate	Lemon segment, brown bread and butter, cayenne pepper, peppermill	Lemon segment could be presented in lemon press
Deep-fried fish in batter (*poisson a l'Orly*)	Hot fish plate (or joint plate if main), fish knife and fork	Lemon segment, tomato sauce	
Deep-fried fish in breadcrumbs (*poisson frit*)	Hot fish plate (or joint plate if main), fish knife and fork	Tartare sauce, lemon segment	Sauce offered and served to customers
Entrée			
Curry	Hot soup plate, cold underplate, joint fork on right of cover	Mango chutney, poppadoms, Bombay duck, curry tray (assorted citrus fruits, apple, onion, dried fruits, coconut), yoghurt (*raita*)	It is not usual to offer vegetables to accompany a curry dish
Irish stew	Hot soup plate, cold underplate, joint knife and fork, dessert spoon	Worcestershire sauce, pickled red cabbage	Offer and serve accompaniments
Beef			
Steak, e.g. sirloin (*entrecôte grillée*), minute steak (*entrecôte minute*), fillet, rump	Hot joint plate, steak knife and fork	English and French mustard	
Lamb and veal			
Grilled lamb (e.g. cutlet, *côtelette d'agneau grillée*; fillet, *filet mignon*)	Hot joint plate, joint knife and fork	Parsley butter	Serve grilled lamb cutlet with meat at base of plate and bones crossing at top
Mixed grill	Hot joint plate, joint knife and fork	French and English mustard, straw potatoes (*pommes pailles*), parsley butter, watercress	Consists of sausage, kidney, cutlets, tomatoes and bacon
Grilled veal (*côte de veau grillée*)	Hot joint plate, joint knife and fork	Parsley butter, straw potatoes, watercress	
Pork and chicken			
Grilled pork chop (*côte de porc grillée*)	Hot joint plate, joint knife and fork	Any listed sauce for grilled meats, English mustard	
Grilled chicken (*poulet grillée*)	Hot joint plate, joint knife and fork	*Sauce diable* (devilled sauce, with a strong pepper flavour)	

Dish (cont.)	Cover	Accompaniment	Comment
Game (*gibier*)			
Pheasant (*le faisan*)	Joint knife and fork, hot joint plate	Roast gravy, bread sauce, fried breadcrumbs, watercress, game chips	Game chips are thin, crisp chips traditionally served with roast game birds
Venison (*le venaison*)	Joint knife and fork, hot joint plate	Redcurrant jelly or Cumberland sauce	
Roast meats			
Roast beef (*boeuf roti*)	Hot joint plate, joint knife and fork	Horseradish sauce, roast gravy, watercress, Yorkshire pudding, French or English mustard	
Roast lamb (*agneau roti*)	Hot joint plate, joint knife and fork	Mint sauce/mint jelly, roast gravy, watercress	
Roast pork (*porc roti*)	Hot joint plate, joint knife and fork	Apple sauce, roast gravy, watercress	
Roast turkey (*dindonneau roti*)	Hot joint plate, joint knife and fork	Cranberry sauce, bread sauce, chestnut stuffing, bacon rolls, watercress, game chips, roast gravy	
Sweet course			
Most sweets	Hot or cold sweet plate, dessert spoon and fork		
Strawberries	Coupe (stemmed dish), underplate, teaspoon	Caster sugar in dredger, cream (double or clotted)	
Ice cream	Coupe, ice cream spoon, underplate		Serve this dish last with a mixed sweet order
Savouries			
Savouries on toast/ quiche/fritter/ soufflé	Hot fish plate, side knife and dessert fork	Condiments, cayenne pepper, peppermill, Worcestershire sauce	Small underplate for soufflé dish
Cheese (*fromage*)			
Cheese	Side plate, side knife	Condiments, butter, celery in tumbler on ice, caster sugar (for cream cheeses), assorted cheese biscuits, fruit (e.g. grapes, dried fruit), chutneys, nuts, salad garnish	All cheeses offered should be described to the customer; arrange on side plate to contrast colours

Dish (cont.)	Cover	Accompaniment	Comment
Dessert/fresh fruit			
Fresh fruit and nuts/ dessert	Fruit knife and fork, fruit plate or sweet plate, debris plate for nutshells, nutcrackers, finger bowl on underplate for rising fingers (right of cover), warm water, lemon slice and serviette, finger bowl for rinsing fruit (top left of cover)	Caster sugar in dredger, salt (for nuts)	Usually presented in fruit basket, customer selects fruit required

Figure 10.5 Some commonly served dishes, their covers and accompaniments

Service of accompaniments

The items used and service will vary according to the establishment. Some restaurants use a silver flat dish lined with paper. Sauce boats are placed on the flat, with one sauce ladle per sauce boat. To the left of the guest, check whether diners would like all the accompaniments on offer, and serve. The sauce boat lip should be facing the customers. Place the silver flat as close to the plate as possible, to avoid spillage. Fill the sauce ladle, scrape over the edge of the sauce boat, and place the sauce on the plate. Serve all accompaniments as required, turning the silver flat if necessary for ease of service.

Types of food service

There are many different styles and methods of serving food. The type of service chosen for serving food to customers is determined by several factors, including:

○ the service requested by the customer
○ the type of establishment
○ the type of customer
○ how much time is available
○ the type of menu
○ the cost of the meal
○ staffing and skills.

Definitions

Entrée – a dish of small meat cuts in a sauce. There are numerous entrée dishes that need no special service.
Ice cream spoon – a spoon the size of a teaspoon, but with a spade shaped bowl to the spoon.

Did you know?

All steaks (flambé or grilled) should be cooked to the customer's taste: very rare (*bleu*), rare (*saignant*), medium (*à point*) or well done (*bien cuit*).

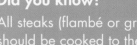

Find out!

Visit three different eating places, and list how the factors listed above apply to the type of service there. Start collecting menus.

Service	Style of service	Examples
Plate	Food ordered is ready plated	A wide range of restaurants
Family	Food is placed on the table in serving dishes, customers serve themselves	Schools, clubs, ethnic restaurants
Silver	Food is served from silver (dish) with silver (spoon and fork) in front of customers at the table	Function service, conference and banqueting, traditional restaurants
Plate/silver	The main item is plated, vegetables are silver served	Restaurants offering high-class food; presentation controlled by chef, restaurant skills match the food standard
Plate/family	The main item is plated, vegetables are family-served	Restaurants offering quick service
Table theatre	Cooking, filleting, carving, flambé, mixing salads and serving food on a trolley in front of customers at the table (this requires a high level of skill)	Traditional restaurants offering a high level of individual service
Tray (in situ)	Complete food and lay-up on a tray	Room service in hotels, hospitals and service on trains, planes and home delivery

Figure 10.6 Types of service

Plate service

In plate service, the waiter receives the food from the kitchen. A ready plated meal is ordered and served to the customer. The cover is changed and any necessary accompaniments are added to the table before service. Any dish accompaniments are served to the diner.

Plate service offers a speedy food service to customers, and allows staff extra time to look after their customers. Plate service helps food to stay hot, as it is a fast service.

Family service

As the name suggests, this is service for a group of persons who are often eating the same food from a set menu (for example in schools, clubs or ethnic restaurants). Family service can be operated in various ways:
○ all food is placed on the table for guests to help themselves for each course

> **Try this!**
> Note each time you work a new style of service – where, when, for whom, menu served, and comments.

- or for the main course, the main dish may be plated and the vegetables and accompaniments placed on the table for guests to serve themselves
- or starters may be served ready plated and the rest of the meal family served.

Family service works well in restaurants where staffing levels are low. However, the equipment used for table presentation can be expensive – vegetable dishes and serving spoons have to be of high quality, hygienic, safe and clean. Provide service cloths with the hot dishes, as there could be a safety issue if customers handle dishes that are too hot.

Hotplates may be placed in the centre of the table to keep the food hot. For this service, tables need to be larger to make space for the additional equipment. The temperature in the restaurant rises due to the tabletop hotplates remaining on tables. Some elderly guests may require assistance with service.

Silver

For information on silver service, see Chapter 11.

Plate/silver

Plate/silver service is a combination of ready plated food served to customers and silver service of vegetables and sauces. The cover is adjusted once the order has been taken. The starters are usually ready plated. The main dish for the main course is served from the kitchen ready plated. The vegetables and any sauces are silver served. In the same way, the sweet course is plated, and the sauces and accompaniments for the sweet course are served.

This combination of the two styles of service provides speed as well as personal service to customers. Waiters need to have both technical and social skills.

Table theatre

Table theatre is where the waiting staff perform tasks involving food to be served to the customer at the table. Examples are given overleaf.

Activity	Type of food	Description	Equipment
Flambé	Crêpes, fruit, meat	Alcohol is added to the dish and set alight	Flambé trolley, lighter, small pans, spoons, choice of alcohol, plates for service, ingredients
Carvery	Meat	Meat is carved from a large joint on a trolley	Carvery trolley, meat, accompaniments, carving knife and fork, plates for service
Gueridon	Meat, fish. Cream or other liquid may be added to deglaze the pan	The waiter cooks the food on a gueridon at the table. If necessary, the waiter will fillet the fish or bone/carve meat before serving	Gueridon trolley, lighter, pans, spoons, knives, forks, plates for service, ingredients
Mixing	Salads	The waiter mixes and dresses a salad at the table. The customer is given a choice of oils/dressings	Trolley, ingredients, oils etc for dressing, spoons, forks, plates for service

Table theatre is a skill which was developed in Victorian times. It varies in popularity, but it does require specialist training. The reason it is called theatre is because it should be done in a dramatic way and it is meant to draw the attention of everyone in the restaurant. You need to be very confident to do this kind of service and that only comes with a lot of practice!

Successful table theatre relies on having all the mise en place done before starting.

Definition

Gueridon: moveable service trolley or moveable side table, placed adjacent to the customer's dining table for the purposes of preparing, cooking, filleting, carving, flambéing and serving food in front of the customer.

Service of food

Service of food takes place once all covers have been adjusted in line with the customer's order.

General rules on service:
○ serve all food from the left (the side where the fork is)
○ clear all food from the right (the side where the glasses are).

The food items to be served first are governed by the following rules (in order of priority):
○ serve cold food before hot – cold food will not spoil, but hot food can lose heat
○ where possible, serve the ladies first, eldest to youngest, then the gentlemen, eldest to youngest – and the host last, irrespective of gender
○ all diners at a table should be served at the same time.

Figure 10.7 Serve from the left and clear from the right

Service at a table should not start until all the food for the course about to be served has been received from the kitchen and is on the sideboard awaiting service. There should be no delays once service at table has started. This combines with the rule about serving cold food before hot food.

Some additional rules include the following:
- clear when all the diners have finished
- serve all drinks from the right (the side where the glasses are)
- clear all drinks from the right (the side where the glasses are).

Service tips

- Be professional!
- Never use anything that has dropped on the floor – remove and replace it.
- Never use damaged equipment.
- Use a tray when possible (to collect items – not to serve to table).
- Hold salvers on the flat of the hand.
- Serve all food as soon as it is ready.
- Never touch or smell the food.
- Never serve unsafe food – this might include food at the wrong service temperature; food that is out of date (e.g. cheese board); food that has been held for too long (e.g. buffets, see Chapter 12, pages 362–363); re-used food or drink (e.g. milk returns, food returns in family service); undercooked items (e.g. grilled chicken, see Chapter 5, page 168).
- Check that silverware is clean.
- Always use a clean, dry service cloth to carry hot plates, to avoid burns.
- Use cold underplates under hot food items (e.g. soups) for ease of carrying.
- Have sufficient serving spoons for sauces (plate service), and for main courses and vegetables (family service).
- Have accompaniments ready – serve these to the customer, do not leave them on the table.
- Replenish accompaniments as they are used.
- Replace butter dishes and offer more bread.
- Keep tidying the table throughout the meal.
- Remove table accompaniments when clearing the course.
- Tidy and clean your work areas as you go.
- Be attentive – and plan ahead!

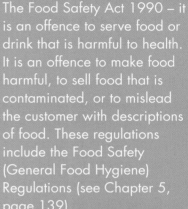

Remember!
The Food Safety Act 1990 – it is an offence to serve food or drink that is harmful to health. It is an offence to make food harmful, to sell food that is contaminated, or to mislead the customer with descriptions of food. These regulations include the Food Safety (General Food Hygiene) Regulations (see Chapter 5, page 139).

Remember!
Silverware, dishes, cutlery and flatware must be clean and at the right temperature to meet the Food Hygiene Regulations (see Chapter 5, page 139).

Remember!
A damp cloth will not help to carry hot plates – heat is transferred by water.

Remember!
Waiters' cloths or service cloths are part of the waiter's uniform, and should be carried or tucked into an apron (depending on the rules of the establishment). These must also comply with the hygiene regulations.

Collection of food from the service point

The food ordered should be ready on the hotplate or service point in the kitchen, or on a service lift. Take your copy of the order so that you can check the correct food has been prepared. Before taking any food from the kitchen, check with the chef that it is for your table, and that the order is complete and ready (for example, for a large party). The waiter should check that the food has been arranged and presented in line with the menu specification. Never serve any food if it does not look correct. Finally, check the temperature of the food to be served, and that all items needed are ready. Correct any queries before serving your customers. All the food is then served to diners at the same time, to a quality standard, with no delays.

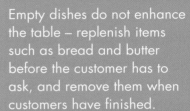

Remember!

Empty dishes do not enhance the table – replenish items such as bread and butter before the customer has to ask, and remove them when customers have finished.

Remember!

- Refer to your copy of the order to remind you who ordered what.
- The change of cover will show you who is eating what.
- Service etiquette – who are you going to serve first?

Carrying plated food

For speed of service, and to ensure that hot food is served hot, waiting staff may have to carry three plated meals at once.

How to carry several plates at once

1 Pick up one plate in your right hand.

2 Turn over your left hand and raise your little and ring fingers to form a platform.

3 Transfer the plate from your right hand to your left hand, placing it on index and middle fingers, and hold the plate with your thumb.

4 Pick up the second plate, place it on the little and ring fingers of your left hand, and balance it safely.

5 Pick up the third plate, and carry it in your right hand.

Placing plates in front of customers

Hold hot plates with a clean, dry service cloth. Keep the plate level, so that ready plated food does not move and sauce does not spill. Always think of the customer's safety and comfort.

From the left of the customer, place the plate in the centre of the place setting, with the main dish item (for example meat or fish) nearest the customer – if the cover is viewed as a clock, this is at six o'clock. Serve any accompaniments with the appropriate dishes, using sauce boats and ladles, or the correct serving spoon and fork.

In some restaurants, all food may be served to the correct diners with cloches or lids – working as a team, the cloches or lids are all removed at the same time.

Having served the food to all the diners, wait to check that they start eating. If not, it may be that they require more attention. After a few mouthfuls, check back with the diners that everything is to their satisfaction – then any problems can be dealt with straight away.

Remember!
View the customer's plate as a clock – the main dish item is placed between 3 and 9 o'clock (bottom half of the plate), potatoes between 12 and 3 o'clock (top right quarter), and vegetables between 9 and 12 o'clock (top left quarter).

Clearing from the table

Clear only when all customers have finished eating.

Place the empty tray on the sideboard. Clear from the right – take the plate with most food waste on first, placing it in your upturned left hand between the index and middle fingers. Remove the next plate, balancing it on the left hand and raised fingers (ring and little fingers). Turning away from the diners, scrape any food debris onto the first plate. Place knives under the fork arch – this helps to keep them in place and avoid dropping them. Continue until all plates are cleared. Take the plates to the sideboard and stack them on the tray. Remove the dirty plates and cutlery to the wash-up area. Now wash your hands!

Adjust à la carte covers as soon as the starter course has been cleared. Adjusting the cover at this point ensures that diners will have their utensils when the main course is served.

Service of the main course
Plate service

Plated food should be checked with the chef against your copy of the order. When the order is complete, transfer the food to the sideboard. Check who to serve first (see page 309). Serve ready plated food from the left, with the main dish item at the bottom of the plate, nearest the diner. Follow round with accompanying sauces.

Family service

If hot food is to be served, place clean hotplates at the centre of the table. For safety reasons, inform customers that the serving dishes will be hot. Check that all equipment is clean, safe and hygienic. Place all food on the hotplate, together with the correct, clean serving equipment. Place a hot food plate at the centre of each customer's place setting, from the left. The diners will now serve themselves. Remove any empty dishes as soon as possible, to allow more room and to tidy the table.

Silver service

For detailed information on silver service of the main course, see Chapter 11, page 335.

Plate/silver service

Check the food produced by the chef against your food order. When the order is complete, transfer it on a tray to the sideboard.

Check who to serve first (see page 309), and what they have ordered. From the left, place the ready plated main course at the place setting, with the main food item nearest the customer. If working in a team, the vegetable service can start once two plates have been served. Place the vegetables on a lined salver (or presented in line with your restaurant's policy), with a clean spoon and fork per vegetable. Serving from the left, offer and silver serve potatoes to the top right of the plate, and vegetables to the top left of the plate. When each diner has received the whole selection of vegetables, move to the next person, and repeat the process. Meanwhile, the sauces are served by another waiter. Working as a team, the service will be speedier, ensuring that the food is served at the right temperature.

Plate/family service

Place the hotplates at the centre of the customers' table. Check with the chef that the order is ready and complete. Collect the vegetables from the kitchen, and place them on the hotplates with

Figure 10.8 A ready plated meal

serving spoons. Collect the ready plated main courses and place them on the sideboard ready for service. Check who ordered which main course, and who to serve first (see page 309).

Serve from the left, placing each plate down so that the main course item is nearest the customer. Leave sauces on the hotplate. The customers will now help themselves to vegetables.

Clearing after the main course

Clearing at the end of the main course is as described on page 311. After the main course plates have been removed, the side plates and knives are collected. These are removed from the left – the only exception to the 'remove from the right' rule. This is because the side plate is at the left of the cover, so you do not have to stretch across the customer to remove it. After clearing the side plates, crumbing down may take place.

Crumbing down

Whether and how this is done depends on the establishment. Crumbing down is the removal of crumbs – usually from the bread rolls – from the table, before the service of the sweet course. If you are using a salver and a clean, folded service cloth, from the left, sweep the tablecloth with the service cloth to remove crumbs onto the salver.

A table crumber can also be used for crumbing down, instead of the service cloth. A crumber is a thin scraper in the shape of a thin metal strip made of aluminium, with a bevelled edge. It can be carried conveniently in the waiter's pocket. Some establishments use a larger table crumb sweeper.

Figure 10.9 Crumbing down using a table crumb sweeper

For a table d'hôte or function cover, after crumbing down, place the dessert spoon at the right of the cover (moving it down from the top of the table setting if it is already on the table), and place the dessert fork at the left of the cover, for each guest.

Using a salver, remove any accompaniments, condiments and butter dish. Clear onto a tray at the sideboard. Open and present the menus to diners for the sweet course order.

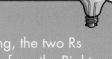

Remember!
When clearing, the two Rs are – Remove from the Right (the one exception is the used side plate).

Take the tray to the wash-up area, and remove dirty crockery and cutlery. Scrape food debris into the waste food bin, place cutlery in the cutlery wash-up containers, and stack dirty plates in size order. Wipe the tray ready for re-use.

The wash-up area requires constant attention, and the waiting staff must help by clearing. Dirty plates should be stacked in the correct sizes. Waste should be divided into the correct bins (e.g. food waste, paper waste, glass waste, crockery waste). This process is essential to reduce accidents and to meet the Food Hygiene Regulations. Now wash your hands!

Remember!
A waiter's cloth is a service cloth – always check that it is clean before use.

Service of sweet course

Having taken the sweet course order, check that the cover is correct. For à la carte service, add the cover according to the order. As above (page 298), orders (manual or electronic) are passed to the relevant departments.

Check that any accompaniments for the order are ready for service. When the order is complete, check the food against your food order, agree with the chef, and serve the sweet course to the customers. Serve from the left, and in the correct sequence (see page 308). Offer and serve sauces and accompaniments if not included in the dish.

Service of cheese

Cheese may be served instead of a sweet course, or as a further course served after the sweet course. The cover for the service of cheese is a cold side plate or dessert plate and a side knife. The accompaniments added to the table for the service of cheese are given in Figure 10.5.

Remember!
Use a different cheese knife for each cheese.

The cheese could be ready plated, and the diners are served from the left. Alternatively, the cheese may be presented on a cheese board with cheese knives. The waiter may present the cheese board and cut the cheeses selected by the diners. Cheese is cut using a cheese knife, which has a pronged end to lift the cheese onto the customer's plate. It is important to present the cheese attractively on the plate. Some establishments may use a knife and fork, or two knives, to serve cheese – this depends to some extent on the range of cheeses available and their textures.

Clearing the sweet/cheese course

Place a tray on the sideboard. Clear all plates from the right, and stack them on the tray at the sideboard. Crumb down if necessary. Using a salver or tray, remove any remaining glassware from the table.

Taking and serving coffee orders

Take the order, and pass the top copy (or electronic order) to the stillroom.

The many different sorts of coffee available in most establishments today are described in Chapter 18 (pages 552–525). Some increasingly popular types of coffee that may be ordered, such as cappucino or latte, are served with foamed milk already in the cup, so only sugar is needed on the table. These may require specific presentation, such as a tall latte glass with a long spoon. The following describes the service of coffee at table.

Prepare the coffee cup, saucer, underplate (if used) and teaspoon. Check that the customer has finished with their glass, and if so, remove it and place the complete service at the top right of the cover, where the glass was placed. If any glasses on the table are still in use, just move them slightly over to the left to accommodate the coffee service. The position of the coffee cup on the table acts as an important safety measure – when hot coffee is poured into the customer's cup, there is less risk of spillage and of the customer being injured. Place brown sugar, hot milk and/or cream on the table. From the right, pour the coffee from a coffee jug into the cup. Carefully move the full coffee cup to the centre of the place setting. Diners will add their own hot milk, cream and sugar. The order of service to customers remains the same (see page 308).

Decaffeinated coffee requested by individuals is prepared in the coffee cup and presented ready to drink. Large quantities of decaffeinated coffee would be served by jug.

Often the policy for a table d'hôte menu is to refill customers' coffee cups if required. Check the policy in your establishment. If the menu is à la carte, each coffee is charged on the bill.

Remember!
All drinks are served from the right.

Presenting the bill

Request the bill from the cashier – or, if it is your responsibility, produce or print off the bill. Check that it is correct, and adjust it if necessary. Fold the bill so the contents are not on view. Place it in a bill holder or on a bill tray or small plate, and present it to the host. When requested, collect the payment and hand it to the cashier. Return the receipted bill, card receipt and card or any change on the bill tray, and return it to the host. See Chapter 6 for more detailed information on dealing with payments. Comment cards may be presented along with the bill (see Chapter 6, pages 186–187).

Remember!
Keep a copy of any comment cards relating to your service, for your evidence.

Remember!
Be observant and ready to assist customers as they leave (see Chapter 4, page 105)

Stage of service	Action	Notes
Lay-up	Table preparation	Neat and aligned
Sideboard	Preparation	Tidy and organised
Mise en place done	Check lay-up; collect rolls, butter	Cover rolls with napkin
Customers arrive	Greet and seat Unfold guest's napkin Hand out menus	Hold chairs Move napkins onto laps Hold top of menu
Customers study menu	Serve water (if required)	
	Offer rolls Place butter dish on table if not already done	Remove napkin from rolls Place rolls on underplate from left
Customers order	Write carefully	Split checks and take to cashier and kitchen/still room; third copy on sideboard
Adjust covers	Adjust covers using service plate or salver	
Prepare for starter course	Collect starter	Check plates for cleanliness and heat Tureen and ladle at sideboard Hot hors d'oeuvres – hot plate Cold hors d'oeuvres – cold plate
Serve starter	From *left*	
Check back	Check diners have everything they need	
Clear starter from table	Stack empty plates and dishes as you go from *right*	Take dirty plates and cutlery to wash-up; scrape plates well For a la carte add cover for next course
Prepare and serve main course	Collect plated food from kitchen and put down from *left* in front of diners If plates are crested, the crest must be at 12 o'clock	Check plates are hot and clean Check service etiquette

Stage of service (cont)	Action	Notes
Silver serve	Serve from *left* main course dish bottom of plate (3–9 o'clock)	
Serve vegetables	Place vegetable dishes on underplates with spoons for customers to help themselves	Family service of vegetables
Silver serve	Use spoon and fork as required	Use salver with cloth underneath dishes Clean spoon and fork for each vegetable
Serve gravy or sauce	From *left* on underplate	Sauce boat lip towards customer; use ladle or spoon
Check	Garnishes	Ensure all accompaniments served; replenish as needed
Check back Main course clearance	Check diners have everything they need Clear plates from *right* when all diners have finished Remove unwanted items (cutlery, condiments) – clear and stack on sideboard	Use fork as bridge for knives
Prepare for sweet service	Crumb down if this is done in the establishment	From *left* use a crumber, or from *left* use open end of napkin to brush Bring down dessert cutlery from cover top to side
	Hand out menus	Write order Split up checks
	Take sweet and coffee orders	
	Readjust cover if required	Use service plate or salver to bring items needed
	Go to kitchen	Collect sweets ordered
Serve sweet	From *left* place down plates	From *left*, using cloth
Serve cheese	Adjust cover, placing side plate and side knife for cheese service Place condiments on table	Check accompaniments (biscuits, etc.) all offered from *left* Suggest Port for cheese
Check back	Check diners have everything they need	Water, etc. as before
Prepare for coffee service	Go to still room and collect coffee, milk, sugar, cups, spoons, saucers	
Prepare coffee service	Assemble cups, place on small underplates	
Clear sweet/cheese course	Remove plates from *right* and stack on sideboard	Remove to wash up

Stage of service (cont)	Action	Notes
Serve coffee	Place coffee cups before diners from *right*. Request: *Do you take sugar?* *Do you require black coffee or coffee with milk?*	Sugar, coffee, milk
Check back	Check if the customers require anything more	
	Offer second cup of coffee	If the policy of the organisation
Check back	Check if customer would like anything more	
Bill presentation	Collect bill and check it	Place folded bill on plate or in bill folder in front of host/customer
	When requested, collect payment Return to cashier Return bill, receipt and change/card Place on table, on a plate	Leave on table
Assisting departing customers	When diners get up to leave, help with chairs; assist with coats	Smile and say 'thank you!'

Figure 10.10 Traditional Formal Service Procedure

Try this!

Waiters often have to deal with unexpected situations. Here are four examples – write down how you would deal with each one.

1 You have taken the food order and adjusted the cover to suit the order. Then chef informs you that he or she cannot provide the fish requests. As a waiter, list in order the actions you would take.

2 A customer has ordered mackerel fillets. At service, the mackerel is served whole. The elderly female customer refuses the dish. Where did the service go wrong? Had the customer the right to refuse the dish? As a waiter, what should you do now?

3 The restaurant is booked for a function for exclusive use. A regular guest arrives with three other persons, stating that he has booked a table and is expecting dinner service. How will you solve this?

4 At the point of serving the customers, one customer changes their mind and requests the chicken dish instead of the beef. How are you going to handle this situation?

Remember!

To collect the following evidence: copies of food orders, copies of menus (tick the foods you have served), and notes of the number of tables served and number of diners served on each specific occasion. Keep customers' comment cards, and note your own comments on the menu. Note what you did well – and what you could have done better!

This chapter offers a lot of suggestions for cross-referencing evidence collected.

Test yourself!

1 At what stage of the meal should you:
   a serve an aperitif?
   b offer bread rolls?
   c remove table accompaniments?
   d adjust the cover for à la carte cover?
   e remove the cruet set?
   f crumb down?
   g present the bill?

2 What is the accepted order of service for a table of four customers, two female and two male?

3 Suggest and name a dish suitable for:
   a a person with coeliac disease
   b a vegan
   c a diabetic (sweet course).

4 A table of four diners have ordered 1× soup and 1× beef, 1× soup and 1× plaice, 1× grapefruit and 1× beef, 1× paté and 1× chicken from a table d'hôte menu. What cutlery should be on the table after adjusting each cover?

5 From which side would you:
   a clear glasses
   b serve soup
   c remove side plates
   d serve iced water
   e serve coffee.

6 Name four safe working practices to observe when serving food to customers.

7 Name the accompaniments to offer with:
   a minestrone soup
   b smoked salmon
   c whitebait
   d mussels in white wine
   e roast beef
   f beef curry
   g cheese.

continued

8 Name the items of equipment numbered 1–11 for the table d'hôte cover lay-up in the illustration on the right.

9 Name the items of equipment numbered 1–8 for the à la carte cover lay-up in the illustration on the right.

11

Silver service

In this chapter you will cover skills and knowledge in the following units:

o 7132 – Unit 208 (2FS3): Provide a silver service

Working through this chapter could also provide evidence for the following Functional Skills:

Functional English – Speaking, taking part in formal discussion, listening and communication Level 1

Functional Mathematics – Analysing Level 1

In this chapter you will learn:

o about the advantages and disadvantages of silver service

o how to prepare service equipment ready for silver service

o how to provide silver service in line with your service operation

o how to use service cutlery to portion, serve and arrange food

o how to silver serve safely and with minimum disturbance

o how to clear at the right time

o how to work safely during silver service

Introduction

Silver service is a formal style of serving food, item by item, to each diner at the table. It is called 'silver service' because silver dishes or 'flats', with a silver spoon and fork, were used in the past, but nowadays it is more common to use stainless steel equipment. This style of service is most often used at weddings and banquets. Sometimes the main course is plated/portioned and the vegetables are silver served.

Silver service is a very personal food service, as it allows the diner to communicate directly with the waiter at the point of service. The waiter serves up to the portion size, but within this allows the customer to choose how much or how little they would like. Waiters have the opportunity to display their silver service skills, and customers appreciate the additional level of service when dining out. Technical skills are important when silver serving – as are social skills. The combination of good social and technical skills will lead to exceptional customer service, which will be valued by your customers. Silver service is perhaps used less often nowadays than in the past, as chefs often want to position food themselves for presentation and to arrange the correct balance of food and/or sauces. Also, training can be a problem when staff are often part-time, and paid by the hour.

Figure 11.1 Silver service is a formal style of service

Advantages and disadvantages of silver service

Advantages

○ Silver service is not offered in all restaurants, so customers enjoy the special service and personal attention.

○ It is therefore a good opportunity for staff to show their skills, in terms of both the quality of food and the presentation and service.

○ Waiters can control the portions of food at the point of service.

- More portions are carried and served by the waiter, for example ten covers per waiter for function silver service – the service is quick, especially when linked with a set menu and using trained staff.
- The service can be mixed with other forms of service (e.g. plate/ silver, see Chapter 10, page 306). This allows flexibility and speed of service when the restaurant is busy or staffing levels are low.

Disadvantages

- It is expensive to offer silver service due to the high quality of equipment required (e.g. service dishes).
- The specialist service equipment is more difficult to clean, which adds to the cost.
- Trained staff are essential to silver service, but this also increases costs.
- Extra space is needed between tables, reducing the number of customers that can be served.
- The higher price charged can reduce the number of customers.

Test yourself!

1 How did silver service get its name?

2 What qualities does a waiter need to provide quality silver service?

3 Why might a restaurant manager argue against providing silver service?

4 Give three arguments in favour of providing silver service.

Preparing for silver service

The menu is an integral part of silver service, and is an important link between the waiter and the customer. The waiter will need to have copies of all the menus on offer and to study each dish. The waiter will also need to know how to serve each dish on the menu. Knowing what is to be served, and how to serve the dishes, is the key to preparing the equipment for service.

The equipment used to silver serve is usually a tablespoon and joint fork. For every item to be served, a clean service spoon and fork will be required. This is for reasons of hygiene, and to avoid cross-contamination. With some food items it is better to use different service equipment, for example, for a flat omelette use two fish knives; for a folded omelette use two joint forks. You should collect all the service equipment required for the menu to be served, and check that they are all clean and damage-free. Store items in a sideboard or on a side table.

Preparation of equipment

As all food is served from metal equipment (now usually stainless steel), the serving dishes need specialist cleaning. All service equipment is on show to the customers, and cleanliness and hygiene are paramount.

Figure 11.2 The main items of serving equipment – a tablespoon and joint fork

---

Try this!

Here is a menu – as you read through this section, list all the items you will need to prepare for a table d'hôte cover and for silver service of all menu items.

FORRESTER'S RESTAURANT

BEEFSTEAK TOMATO
STUFFED WITH PRAWNS AND AVOCADO

FRENCH ONION BROTH
WITH PARMESAN CROUTONS

DEEP FRIED BRIE
WITH CUMBERLAND SAUCE

~~~

PAN-FRIED SKATE
WITH BLACK BUTTER

STEAK AND KIDNEY PUDDING

STIR-FRIED VEGETABLES IN FILO PASTRY BASKET
WITH A SWEET PEPPER AND BASIL COULIS

FRENCH BEANS WITH GARLIC
CAULIFLOWER MORNAY
CREAMED POTATOES
BATAILLE POTATOES

~~~

VANILLA PANNA COTTA
WITH A WILD BERRY COMPOTE

APPLE CHARLOTTE
WITH FRESH EGG CUSTARD

BAKED RICE CUSTARD

Coffee or Tea

3 courses for £17.75 per person

Please note: Dishes may contain traces of nuts

For reservations please ask your waiter

Before service, check which dishes or **flats** are to be used for each food item, and make sure enough of each type are clean. Other than for weddings or banquets, where the orders are known, it is advisable to have plenty of each type available as the mix of customer orders cannot be guessed in advance. Any flats for the service of hot food need to be placed on the hotplate in time to reach the required temperature.

Definition

Flat – a tray, usually oval, made of silver or stainless steel, used to present the food to be silver served.

See Chapter 8 for more information on preparing and cleaning food service areas.

Silver dishes		Dishes with sides, used for the service of entrée-type food dishes (such as meat in a sauce). When these are used, prepare the appropriately sized underliner (see below)
Underliner/liner		A cold, usually oval, silver dish used to carry and serve very hot dishes at the table. A cold liner helps the waiter to hold and serve hot food at the table. Liners are available in various sizes to suit the size of the entrée dish. Underliners should be checked for cleanliness. The edges of the liner will need polishing to remove any smears or finger marks. Liners are also used underneath sauce boats
Sauce boats and ladles		Needed for each type of accompaniment, together with an oval liner – all need cleaning and polishing
Change of cover	Refer to the menu and have sufficient, clean and undamaged covers ready in the sideboard. Having additional cover changes prepared in advance makes for an efficient service	
Service cloth		This is part of the waiter's uniform, and should be clean to meet the hygiene regulations. There must be sufficient service cloths available for service. The cloth should be thick and dry, for carrying hot flats. Also used to carry and polish customers' plates at the table, and for removing crumbs from the table after the main course
Salvers or service plates		A round tray, lined ready for service (a service plate or a joint plate lined with a napkin may be used as a substitute). Used for removing and replacing cutlery and flatware from tables. A lined salver is more hygienic and reduces noise, spillage and scratching of the cutlery. Never carry cutlery in your hand, it is unhygienic and totally unprofessional. Check salvers for cleanliness, and line with napkins. Prepare the service plate with cutlery for cover changes
Linen	More is required for silver service. Additional linen serviettes are used for presenting food to customers before service. Serviettes are used to line salvers or trays to stop food dishes moving while serving at table. Serviettes should be replaced regularly to maintain cleanliness	
Sideboard or side table	The sideboard is prepared as for table service (see pages 239–240)	

Figure 11.3 Equipment for silver service

Silver service staff

To provide silver service, staff need to be trained to a high level. Paying attention to the following areas is vital.

Good personal organisation

This means being completely prepared for service.

Time-management skills

Use your time efficiently by working in a logical order and planning ahead. As you finish one task, be ready for the next, and continue in this way. Complete all tasks to a quality standard, so that each task is perfect first time. Clear as you go. Organise the rotation of service to several tables. Make every trip to and from the service area effective – never go empty-handed.

Exceptional hygiene

Waiters are very close to the customers when silver serving. The customer will be very aware of your service skills, so it is very important to make sure you follow best practice in hygiene (Chapter 4), and in health and safety (Chapter 2).

- Use only clean, undamaged service equipment.
- Use a clean set of service cutlery for serving different food items (see page 324).
- Use only clean, dry, thick service cloths for silver service of dishes at table.
- Change service cloths regularly to maintain hygiene standards.
- Practise good personal hygiene (pages 139–144) and wear a clean, correct uniform (pages 140–142).
- Wash your hands regularly to reduce the risk of cross-contamination, especially when clearing waste and dirty plates (pages 143–144).
- Cover any cuts and wounds with clean, waterproof blue plasters.

Outstanding social skills

Silver service is a very personal service, and your social skills will be noticed:

- have a positive attitude to customers and enjoy serving them
- treat your customers as you would like to be treated

Remember!
Check the menu and list the equipment you need, to avoid wasting time cleaning items that will not be used.

Remember!
Wet or thin service cloths are a safety hazard, especially when carrying and silver serving hot food at table.

Remember!
Think hygiene – make sure hygiene is integrated into the food service.

Marcus says
Most of our dishes are plated but if anything were silver served I would hope that the server had respect for the food that was being plated. It should look good and be handled with care. Try to avoid splashes!

- employ good organisational skills and prioritise your workload
- communicate well with your customers
- learn how to cope with the unexpected.

Thorough product knowledge

Waiters are employed to sell food, as well as to serve it. To sell the dishes on the menu, you need to know what you are selling. The waiter must know about the following, to be able to inform customers:

- contents/ingredients of any dish and cooking methods
- suitability of each dish for different diners
- suggested dishes for different dietary requests
- description of the dish and degree of cooking
- prices of dishes, as well as any promotions or special offers.

Types of silver service

Silver service may be offered as a style of service for:

- high-class restaurants
- functions
- buffet/carvery.

High-class restaurants

For restaurant table silver service, all the food is issued from the kitchen on silver flats or silver dishes. The food items are placed on the hotplate at the sideboard to keep the food hot. Plates are placed in front of all the customers. The food is served to the diners using a service spoon and fork, or other suitable serving equipment. Silver service can be used in conjunction with a table d'hôte, à la carte or function cover (see Chapter 8, pages 255–257). The restaurant is prepared as for table service (pages 252–257). It is the style of food service to the customer that differs. The preparation of sufficient and correct service equipment is the additional task at the *mise en place* stage.

Functions

Special functions offering silver service could include weddings, anniversaries, product launches, charity events, lunches or dinner dances. Function service is different from other types of service due to the advance pre-orders: a pre-selected set menu, a known number of customers, service at a set time, and a pre-agreed price per cover.

Remember!

The Trade Descriptions Act – attention must be paid to accurate descriptions of food dishes on menus. For example, *filet* of herring should be off the bone – it cannot be replaced with whole herring. An elderly customer may choose filet of herring believing it to be free of fish bones, whereas a whole herring would have to be deboned by the customer and would be unsuitable in this case. The Price Marking Order – customers must have been able to see the menu with prices before ordering. Where specials are not on the menu, prices quoted to customers must be accurate, inclusive of VAT. Customers must also be informed of any additional charges, such as service charge and/or cover charge.

Definition

Fillet or **filet** – a boneless cut of meat or fish.

Remember!

The customer is always right.

Definition

Mise en place ('in its place') – the preparation of ingredients and dishes before the beginning of food service.

The price per cover always includes the pre-selected menu, and sometimes also pre-selected wines. If this is not the case, wines and drinks may be sold as cash sales. Function service can involve large numbers of covers, and the table layout is important. The type of table plan depends on the customer's wishes, number of covers, and size and shape of the function room. The table plan could be formal or informal.

> **Definition**
> **Sprig** – a long table, placed at right angles to the top table in a formal table layout.

Formal table layout

This includes a top table, which seats the important guests (e.g. at a wedding, the bride and groom and their families). The rest of the guests are seated at long tables known as **sprigs**.

On the top table, guests are seated on only one side of the top table, looking out at the other invited guests. On the sprigs, guests are seated on both sides of the table, allowing a large number of guests to be seated together and the top table guests to be seen by all.

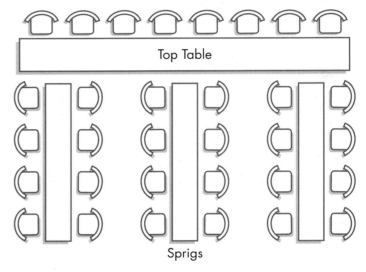

Figure 11.4 Top table and sprigs for formal banqueting layout

A table plan is displayed at the entrance to the function room. This shows the table layout with a seating plan per table, with guests' names.

On each table, the guests' place cards are placed at the top centre of each cover, facing the guest, following the table plan. This allows guests to locate their seats quickly and easily.

Figure 11.5 Typical cover

★ Top table ★		
Pete Susan Andy Jane Mary Bob		
Table 1	**Table 2**	**Table 3**
Trevor	Abdul	Rodney
Florence	Georgia	Donna
Bruce	Tim	Lawrence
Shankar	Susan	Britney
James	Archie	Ricky
Deliah	Daisy	Sam
William	Nick	George
Claire	Aleisha	Edith
Olaf	Pete	Raj
Vicent	Tony	Paula
Anushca	Jack	Anna
John	Amba	Amanda
Ron	Harry	Emma
Laura	Aleisha	Bob
Tina	Sally	Maybel
Jason	Phill	Denzil
Gary	Nataylia	Tracy
Liz	Dennis	Theo

Figure 11.6 A table plan

Informal table layout

This layout may include a top table, and will also have several tables (rectangular or round), each seating ten or more covers. The room layout is designed to be as attractive as possible.

Figure 11.7 An informal room layout

Organisation

For function silver service, a large number of pre-booked diners are silver served with a set menu. Preparation still needs to be thorough – function silver service is usually set within a certain time frame, and speed is often important.

The level of waiting staff needed is one waiter for every ten covers. The waiter will know in advance which ten customers they will be serving. Staffing is often increased by employing skilled casual staff. The organisation of any function service will differ according to the customer's specific requests and requirements.

Preparing service equipment and covers

The set function menu provides all the information needed for the preparation of service equipment and cover lay-up. The number of diners is known, so the quantity of equipment required is also known.

All covers will be the same, except for any special dietary requests. The function menu will include vegetarian options and any special diets requested, and the guests who have pre-ordered these dishes will be known by name. The seating plan will indicate where these guests are seated, and the cover can be set accordingly. The waiter must remember to silver serve any special diets without discussion with the guest.

Remember!
From the customer's viewpoint, serving special diets to the correct diners without discussion demonstrates impressive customer service.

329

Service procedures

For all functions, there are set procedures for service:

○ all diners are served the same set menu – the cover laid follows this menu

○ no change of cover is required – only the items for the set menu are laid

○ all diners eat at the same time – so customers must be served speedily

○ staff need to be silver serviced trained – waiters need to be proficient at serving

○ food must be served efficiently – so that any hot food will still be hot

○ all diners are served together – the top table is served just before the rest of the guests

○ to make this easier, waiters are given a number, and stand in number order at the hotplate to receive the food

○ at the service of main course – waiters present the dish to customers and then serve

○ all silver served food should look identical – the head waiter will brief staff on the final layout of food on the plate

○ when a course has been served, all food waiters leave the function room

○ all tables are cleared together – the head waiter gives a signal for all staff to clear.

Buffet/carvery

Buffet/carvery silver service requires customers to leave their table to select their food from the buffet or carvery. The cover is set according to the menu offered. The menu is placed on the table to help customers make their decisions before going to the buffet/carvery. This speeds up service at the buffet and reduces queues.

Roles are allocated to the restaurant staff before service begins. Waiters will either be silver serving behind the buffet or carvery, or providing service at the table. Service at table includes:

○ greeting and seating

○ inviting customers to the buffet/carvery

○ clearing tables in between courses

○ assistance for less able customers.

Did you know?

When serving at a function, the first waiters at the hotplate are the top table waiters, followed by the waiters for diners seated furthest away from the kitchen. The waiters for diners nearest the service doors are last in line at the hotplate.

Remember!

As every guest is eating the same food, the head waiter will check every sprig or table – every plate should be identical.

Remember!

For a function menu, the head waiter and/or the chef will brief waiters on how to arrange the food, stating the food layout on the plate, taking food colour contrasts into consideration.

Figure 11.8 Take care with colour contrast

Customers should be invited to the buffet or carvery by the restaurant staff at a pace to suit, so that queues are limited. For less able customers, waiters should be available to collect their chosen food and silver serve at the table.

Buffet

The buffet consists of one or more long tables with hot holding equipment and refrigerated units to present the food on offer (see Chapter 12, page 354). This speeds up the service. Depending on numbers, sometimes there are two identical buffets to help speed up the service. The serving staff who stand behind the buffet silver serve the customers their chosen food. The waiter holds the customer's plate in one hand, and with the other hand serves the selected food on to the customer's plate.

Accompaniments may be silver served at the buffet, or displayed at a table away from the buffet for customers to help themselves. For specialist dishes, cutlery is usually on the buffet table, adjacent to the dish.

Carvery

Carvery service is similar to buffet service – both require customers' participation. Carvery service allows diners to view the food before ordering. Customers generally choose from a selection of roasted meats on a heated display. Silver service staff are allocated set tasks behind the carvery before service starts.

The restaurant staff will carve the meat to order. Then, holding the customer's heated plate with a service cloth, they silver serve the meat onto the plate, also offering and serving the accompanying hot sauces and food items. The plate is then completed by silver service of vegetables and potatoes, as chosen by the customer. Sometimes customers help themselves to vegetables, etc. but are usually served the main course dish. The completed meal should appear as if silver served at the table. Customers may be given a serviette or a wooden underliner to help them carry their plate to the table. The starter and sweet courses are usually silver served to customers at their table. For more on carvery service, see Chapter 12.

Remember!

The Food Hygiene Regulations specify time limits and temperatures for displaying food (see Chapter 5, page 167).

Remember!

Separate service spoons and forks are used for each dish served, to reduce the risk of cross-contamination (pages 160–162).

Preparation checklist

Preparation of any service is dictated by the menu. As a waiter, you have checked:

o the menu
o the number of covers/bookings
o the changes of cover necessary per dish
o what cutlery changes will be necessary
o the accompaniments for each dish
o that the service dishes and flats are clean
o that the silver service spoons and forks are clean
o that other specialist service equipment is ready
o that the sideboard contents are complete
o that the tables are set as per the menu and bookings.

Test yourself!

1 What is a soup underliner?

2 What are the advantages, if any, of using an underliner?

3 In an all-female party, who should be served first?

4 Why should the silver service waiter be knowledgeable about the menu items on offer?

5 List four uses of a salver.

6 Where does a silver service waiter work from?

7 A sideboard has many uses – list them in relation to operating silver service.

Providing silver service

Silver service technique

Silver service is a skill, and to master this skill the technique must be practised. Silver service is operated by using a service spoon and fork held in one hand. The service spoon and fork are used to transfer the food ordered from a flat or dish onto the customer's plate, efficiently and with flair.

Using a service spoon and fork

1 The service fork should be held above the service spoon, with the curve of the fork nestling in the bowl of the service spoon. Hold the two together in the palm of one hand, with all the fingers holding the two handles.

2 Now insert your forefinger midway between the two handles. This acts as a lever to open the gap between the spoon bowl and fork prongs, to hold all food items securely.

3 It is possible to turn the fork the other way up to grip large, round food items such as bread rolls.

You should practise using a service spoon and fork. Practice is important for you to be at ease with handling the serving equipment.

Figure 11.9 Using a service spoon and fork

Serving food

Place the silver flat or silver dish onto your folded service cloth, and position the flat so it overhangs the customer's plate at a low level. This is for health and safety reasons – if there any spillage while serving, it will spill onto the plate – not onto the diner. The service spoon and fork filled with food should be raised slightly, and the food placed onto the customer's plate.

Try this!

To practise, start by trying to silver serve the following foods cold – and in your own time!

- A bread roll – *adjust the width of the spoon and fork, and reverse the fork.*
- A slice of plain bread – *this could be similar to silver serving sliced meat.*
- Peas, with a spoon and fork – *do not overfill the spoon, it is better to serve more times.*
- A stew dish – *fill the spoon and use the fork to hold the food in place, scrape the bottom of the spoon over the edge of the dish and serve onto the diner's plate.*

Then – try silver serving the same foods hot!

Practise at every opportunity

Pre-service checklist

Before serving at table, you will have checked that:

- table accompaniments are on the table
- the customer has the correct utensils to eat the food
- there are sufficient clean, dry, thick service cloths
- there is a clean spoon and fork for every food item to be served
- all food items and all accompaniments are ready for all customers about to be served
- you know who is eating what food (by looking at the food order) before you start to serve
- plates are clean and hot (if appropriate)
- that you know how to describe the dishes before presenting them to customers
- that you know how to serve the food attractively and uniformly.

Presentation of food on the plate

The food that you serve should appear attractive. In order to achieve this, there needs to be some uniformity. If the crockery being used is badged with a company logo or crest, the customer's plate should be placed so that the logo is top centre.

For restaurant table silver service, before serving, consider how you could serve food items to make them look attractive by placing food items with contrast of colour next to each other. (For function silver service you will probably receive instructions on this, see pages 327–330.)

Full silver service includes all courses, but depending on the establishment and the menu items, some starters may be served ready plated.

Remember!
- Service etiquette (see Service tips, Chapter 10, pages 309–310).
- The order in which to serve your customers (Chapter 10, page 308).

Did you know?

The food that you silver serve onto the plate should look as if it has been plated by the kitchen. Remember, customers eat with their eyes! The appearance of food really matters.

The main course

The main food item (which may be meat, fish or a vegetarian dish) should be placed at the bottom of the plate. All the customers on a table are served their main dish order before the potatoes and vegetables are silver served. If there are only a few customers at the table, the waiter may serve the complete choice of potatoes and vegetables from a salver to each diner before moving on to the next diner.

For more customers, several waiters will usually assist in serving the complete meal to speed up the service. This will ensure the hot food is still hot as the customers start to eat.

The potatoes are served to the top right of the plate, and vegetables are served to the top left (see Chapter 10, page 311).

Presentation of dishes

Dishes should be presented to customers before silver serving. Depending on the type of function, if the party at one table has a host, he or she should be shown the dish first for approval. This allows all customers to admire the dish and confirm that it is the dish ordered. If the dish is for service to only one customer, presentation is not needed.

> **Try this!**
> 1 If you are silver serving a selection of hors d'oeuvres, how could you place the items to maximise colour contrasts? Name the dishes served.
> 2 The main course is served with roast potatoes, creamed potato, cauliflower and carrots. Suggest the order for service of the above food to enhance the presentation of the meal.

Figure 11.10 The main food item is placed at the bottom

Figure 11.11 Add potatoes at the top right, and vegetables at the top left

The process of silver service

Taking food to the table

- Check the portion sizes of all food items before taking food from the kitchen to the restaurant. Knowing the portion size before you silver serve means that you will not give too much food to some customers and then not have enough for others. Portion control is essential to provide customer satisfaction, reduce wastage and control costs
- Check that the order is correct – compare the food for your table number with your copy of the food order. Transfer the complete food order from the kitchen to the sideboard. Keep the food hot if required.
- Check who is eating what – refer to your table order to refresh your memory. Remember the order of service.
- Placing plates at table – badged plates should be carried to the table with the badge at top centre.
- Place the plates (hot or cold as appropriate) onto all customers' place settings from the left. Remember to warn diners if a plate is very hot, before the plate is placed down.
- Present the food dishes to be served to the customer.
- Silver serve the food using a clean service spoon and fork for each food item.

Remember!
Cold before hot – serve cold food before hot food, regardless of whether diners are male or female.

Remember!
Always ask the customer if they would like what is being served – do not assume that they will want it.

Sliced meat/poultry

Place a folded service cloth in the palm of your left hand, and place the service flat on top of the cloth.

Serve from the left and lower the flat so it overhangs the customer's plate

Carefully lift the food with the spoon and use the fork to keep the food in place and serve onto the customer's plate. If the dish includes gravy or a sauce, carefully tilt the flat towards the customer and spoon any extra sauce if required. Remove dishes to the sideboard and continue service.

Figure 11.12 Silver serving sliced meat or poultry

Fish dishes

Fish dishes sometimes require service equipment other than a service spoon and fork. If the dish is a whole grilled fish served on the bone (e.g. grilled sole), serve using two fish knives spread apart to hold the shape of the fish, and then silver serve the accompaniments (see Chapter 10, page 305). Depending on the fish, the head may have to be removed at the sideboard before serving to the customer.

Did you know?
Some very experienced staff can bone the fish at the table.

Spaghetti or noodles

First change the cover, placing down a hot soup bowl and underplate. At the sideboard, cut the spaghetti strands in half with your serving spoon. Half-fill the service spoon, raise the filled spoon and serve the spaghetti into the soup bowl. Offer and serve Parmesan cheese.

Remember!
The order of service etiquette (page 308) applies to vegetable service as well.

> **Find out!**
> Which side of the cover should accompaniments be served from?

Remember!
Turn the salver so that the vegetable you are serving is nearest the customer's plate.

Other pasta/rice dishes

Adjust the cover, placing down a hot fish plate. Using a service spoon and fork, silver serve the dish from the left, then offer and serve parmesan cheese.

Vegetables

Silver service of vegetables takes place after service of the main dish item. Use a salver if possible. The complete selection of vegetables should be placed on the salver, with a clean spoon and fork for each food item. From the left, serve all the potatoes and vegetables requested to the first customer. Move round to the next customer, and repeat.

Vegetables may be silver served onto a hot side plate or crescent dish – this is placed at the top left of the cover. Add a dessert fork on the side plate or crescent dish.

Follow with the service of accompaniments.

Figure 11.13 Silver serving vegetables

Accompaniments

Place all accompaniments for the dish on a lined silver flat with a sauce ladle for each item. From the left, ask the first diner if they would like any accompaniments. If there are several accompaniments, wait for them to choose. The lip of the sauceboat should be facing the customer, not facing the waiter, so that the sauce is nearest the plate when you are ladling – otherwise you will be more likely to spill some. Fill the ladle, scrape it over the lip of the sauce boat, and spoon sauce onto the plate. Check that each customer has a sufficient quantity before moving on to the next customer.

Hot liquids

Soup

Soup can be served from individual soup tureens or from one large soup tureen.

Figure 11.14 Silver serving sauces

- For single-portion tureen service – place the diner's soup bowl and underplate onto the place setting from the left. Place the single-portion soup tureen on a silver salver. Using the handle, pour soup from the tureen into the soup bowl, pouring away from the customer.
- For large tureen service – at the sideboard, place the large tureen on the hotplate. Ladle soup from the tureen into a hot soup bowl. Place the soup bowl on a cold underplate, carry it to the table, and serve it from the left.

Remember!
For safety reasons, do not pour soup towards the diner.

Remember!
Scrape the filled ladle over the edge of the large soup tureen before filling a soup bowl, to ensure the rim of the bowl is free from drips.

Did you know?
A traditional crescent dish is used when you are serving cold vegetables with a hot main course – for example, salad to accompany a main course. Or hot vegetables with a cold main course. A crescent dish nestles into the curve of the main course plate.

Coffee

The hot coffee, hot milk and sugar are served from silver jugs and containers on a salver into the customer's cup. The coffee service is placed at the top right of the cover (see Chapter 10, page 315).

Place the salver on your left hand. Serving from the right, ask the customer if they would like sugar, and if so, how many. Add the sugar as requested – sugar is added before milk to avoid splashing the customer from a full cup when adding sugar lumps. Then ask if they would like their coffee with or without milk. Pour the coffee by tilting the coffee pot with your right hand and pouring into the cup. Then add hot milk by tilting the milk pot. At this point, move the filled coffee cup to the centre of the customer's place setting. Serve the next customer.

Depending on the policy of the restaurant or function, offer and serve second cups of coffee.

Find out!
What is the name of the coffee cup generally used for the service of coffee after lunch or dinner? How much coffee does it hold?

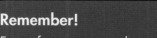
Remember!
For safety reasons – keep coffee and milk jugs on the salver, for balance.
For safety reasons – the customer's coffee cup is placed at the top right of the cover when pouring coffee.

Did you know?
You can serve a sauce around a pie to improve presentation – the diner can then mix the sauce in as much as they wish. Or – the sauce may be served first onto the plate, and the pie placed on top of the sauce.

Pies, tarts, flans and gateaux

Check the cover: a dessert spoon and fork, or a pastry fork for gateau. Place down a hot or cold dessert plate from the left.

Check the portion size before going to the table. Cut portion sizes in readiness.

Figure 11.15 The cover for a slice of tart or flan

Pies

At the sideboard, ease the pie crust from the dish with a knife, and divide up the crust. Having released the pie crust from the dish, use the service spoon and fork to lift the filling (underneath the cut pie crust) and the ready-cut portion of crust together onto the customer's plate. Offer and serve the accompanying sauce. Sauce is generally served around the portion of pie.

Tarts, flans and gateaux

The place setting is a dessert spoon and fork, and a hot or cold dessert plate. For gateau service, a pastry fork is placed on the right of the cover.

From the left, using two fish knives spread wide apart, lift the portion and place it on the customer's plate, then slide the fish knives away. Sweets that are a triangular shape should be placed on the plate with the point facing the customer. Serve any accompanying sauce.

Figure 11.16 Silver serving a pie

Puddings and spooned desserts

Puddings

The cover is a dessert spoon and fork, plus a hot or cold dessert plate. Place the hot pudding dish on an underliner, and place this on top of your folded service cloth.

Serve from the left. If serving individual puddings, use the service spoon and fork, grip the pudding from each side, and serve it onto the customer's plate. If you are taking a portion from a large pudding, use the service spoon and fork or two fish knives as scissors, and lift and serve the portion onto the plate. Offer and serve any accompanying sauce.

Figure 11.17 Silver serving a gateau

Spooned desserts

The cover consists of a dessert spoon and fork, and a small bowl or cereal bowl on an underplate.

Using a salver, present the dessert. Using the correct size of service ladle, or a service spoon and fork, serve the dessert into the bowl at the table. Serve any accompanying sauces or cream.

Figure 11.18 Silver serving a spooned dessert

Sauces

Place the sauce boat onto a lined flat together with a sauce ladle. After you have served the dessert to all customers at the table, follow round with the sauce. Fill the sauce ladle with the sauce, scrape the ladle over the sauce boat lip, and serve sauce onto the customer's plate, repeating until the customer has sufficient.

Cheese

Silver service of cheese requires a cover of a side plate and side knife, and the relevant accompaniments (see Chapter 10, page 314). Place all accompaniments on the table except fruit and salad garnish (if offered).

Before presenting the cheeses, it is important that you can describe all cheeses offered to the customer. Types of cheese may be cream, soft, semi-hard, hard or blue-veined. There are different ways to present cheese, for example in a basket, on a board, or on a trolley. A clean cheese knife should be available for each different cheese offered. A teaspoon may be used to serve some very ripe or soft cheeses to customers.

Ask the customer to select their cheese. Cut each cheese with a clean cheese knife. The cut cheese is lifted by the prong at the tip of the cheese knife, and placed on the plate. Arrange the chosen selection on the side plate attractively, to contrast taste and colour. Some restaurants with a large cheese selection may suggest to customers the order in which the cheese should be consumed – for example, starting with mild and moving on to strong or blue cheese.

The rind on most cheeses should be removed before serving to customers. For Brie and Camembert, the rind is edible and can be served with the portion.

Stilton cheese is served in a specific way. Before service, the kitchen will have marked and partially cut through the whole cheese at the correct depth from the top of the cheese, to assist the cutting process. Present the whole Stilton to the customers. Using the cheese knife, mark out and cut the top of the Stilton into a small wedge-shaped section and then slice horizontally across the whole cheese. The wedge portion is now served on to the customer's plate, using the prong on the cheese knife. If the Stilton is crumbly, serve onto the customer's plate using a spoon and fork. Remove the cheese back to the service area for correct storage, and to re-dress it for presentation for the next order.

Figure 11.19 Silver serving Stilton cheese

Additional garnishes, such as grapes, fruit and salad on the cheese board or trolley can be offered and served to the customer.

Check back

After serving each course, you need to double-check with the diners that they have everything they need to enjoy their food. Check back takes place after all food items have been silver served to all customers on the table. Any requests from customers at this stage will need to be actioned quickly to maintain the quality of the food already served at the same time as ensuring customer satisfaction.

Check back takes place before removing service dishes to wash-up.

Remember!
Service of cheese may be used to promote the sale of port to customers.

Test yourself!

1 What is the purpose of presenting a food dish?

2 Suggest the service equipment you would use to silver serve:
   a whitebait
   b fruit salad
   c folded omelette
   d croutons
   e crème caramel
   f roast chicken
   g cheese
   h minestrone.

3 Who is served first at a formal function?

4 When should table accompaniments be placed on the table?

5 Why should food to be silver served be portioned correctly?

6 How would you describe the following dishes to a customer:
   a consommé
   b hors d'oeuvre
   c panna cotta.

7 Which would be served first, vichyssoise or crab cocktail?

Clearing

The clearing of finished courses is unsightly for customers sitting at the table. Clearance should be undertaken efficiently, with the minimum of disturbance. Good hygiene is essential when clearing from the table to avoid cross-contamination. The food waste collected from the dirty plates must be disposed of immediately and correctly. Then you must wash your hands, before you carry out the next task. Professional clearance skills at table are as important as silver service skills, both to ensure customer satisfaction and to reduce the risk of accidents.

When to clear

Restaurant service

Clearance is at the end of each course, once everyone on the table has finished eating. Allow a slight gap between the customers finishing their food and the clearing of plates. If it is not obvious whether all customers have finished eating, check politely before clearing.

Function service

For function service, the waiters clear the plates at the end of each course, when the head waiter or supervisor has given the signal to clear. The signal will be given when all customers have finished eating. As function service often involves serving a large number of guests, it may be some time before clearing can take place. The timing and clearance of plates also has to fit in with the schedule of the event (such as speeches or presentations).

Buffet/carvery service

For carvery service, clearance will be as for restaurant table service. Plates are cleared when all customers have finished eating at the end of each course.

For buffet service, the customers are often invited to return to the buffet table for second helpings. Some customers will have seconds, others will move on to the next course. So each customer at a table is served as an individual, and plates are cleared when each customer has finished with their food. The waiter may have several customers eating different courses on any one table. For the comfort of the customers, clearing takes place as far as possible when customers are at the buffet.

Remember!
Customers do not want to feel pounced upon as soon as they put their cutlery down!

Figure 11.20 Give customers time!

Remember!
Clearing and tidying up the table when your customers are at the buffet table will mean minimum disturbance to them. Every time customers return to their table, their place setting should be clean and set for the next course.

Clearance skills

- Make customers aware that you are about to clear – this can be done by checking that everyone has finished their course.
- Before clearing plates from table – place an empty tray on top of the sideboard. Remove table accompaniments.
- Clear from the right of the customer – the side where the glasses are.
- Clear quietly, but with a sense of urgency – clearing is a nuisance for customers, so the waiter must be as efficient as possible.
- Clear with minimum disturbance to diners – work as a team to speed up the clearance at table.
- Having cleared the plates, stack and place them on the tray at the sideboard. Only take the tray to wash-up when it is full. This will speed up the clearance process.
- Clear only as many plates as you can manage – you need to feel confident and comfortable with the number of plates that you clear. Clearing too many plates at once may cause an accident, and then clearance will take longer.
- Increase the number of plates over time – practice, and increase the number gradually as you master the skill. Some plates are heavier and harder to clear, so adjust the number of plates to suit.
- If you drop a piece of equipment – stop clearing, return to the sideboard, and place cleared plates on the tray. Return to pick up the dropped item(s). Don't try and pick up dropped items with a stack of cleared plates on your arm – this will make matters worse.

> **Remember!**
> Work as a team – assist one another.

> **Remember!**
> Only carry the number of plates you can manage. Practice makes perfect!

Figure 11.21 Know your limits!

Standard plate clearance procedure

1 Remove plates from the right. Remove the first plate with your right hand.

2 Transfer the plate to your left hand, use your thumb to hold the plate by the rim, and stretch your first two fingers underneath the plate. The third and fourth fingers are raised to act as a stand for the next plate.

3 Separate the cutlery. Knives are usually placed under the arched bridge of the fork to secure them. Spoons and forks should be separated.

4 Remove the second plate from the right. Transfer the plate to your left hand, placing it on the raised third and fourth fingers. Place and separate cutlery onto the lower plate.

5 Remove the third plate from the right. Transfer the plate to your left hand, placing it on top of the second plate. Place the cutlery on the lower plate. Continue to remove plates.

6 On completion, place the lower plate on top of the stacked plates. Place all plates on a tray at the sideboard. Remove the tray of plates to wash-up.

Figure 11.22 Clearing main course plates

Clearance of table accompaniments

Clear table accompaniments just before clearing each finished course. This makes sure accompaniments are not still on the table long after the next course has been served. Use a salver or tray, and store them on the sideboard. When clearing table accompaniments, take the opportunity to check whether customers enjoyed the food.

Clearance of starter plates

Remove from the right, and clear as for standard plate clearance.

Clearance of mixed starter order

First clear the largest number of similar plates. If this is not applicable, clear the soup plates or soup cups first, then remove starter plates or other items.

Clearance of soup plates and underplates

Remember!
Carry only what feels comfortable.

Remember!
Clear plates indicate enjoyment. A lot of food waste needs investigating – if this is the case, ask your customers.

1 Clear the soup cover from the right.

2 Transfer the soup bowl to your left hand and hold it by the underplate. Use the same finger positions as for standard clearance.

3 Remove the second soup cover from the right. Transfer it to your left hand onto your raised fingers. The soup spoon is removed from the lower soup bowl and placed in the upper soup bowl.

345

4 The upper soup bowl, with spoons, is stacked on the lower soup bowl, leaving the underplate clear to hold the next clearance. Continue to remove soup covers.

5 On finishing clearance, place the stack of underplates under the stack of soup bowls.

6 Move to the sideboard and place crockery on a tray for wash-up.

Figure 11.23 Clearing soup bowls and underplates

Starters served in glasses

Remove covers from the right onto a lined salver. Separate the crockery, cutlery and glassware. Return glasses to bar, and the rest to wash-up.

Clearance of main course plates

o Remove the first plate from the right and transfer to your left hand.
o Holding the plate as for standard clearing, place the knife under the bridge of the fork.
o Remove the second plate from the table.
o Transfer it to your left hand, placing it on your raised fingers.
o Turning away from the customers, scrape any food debris onto the lower plate using the fork. Add the knife and fork to those on the lower plate.
o On completion of clearing, transfer the lower plate with cutlery and food debris and place it on top of the neatly stacked upper plates.

Clearance of condiments, butter etc.

Clear the condiments, butter and knife onto a salver after main course plate clearance. Put the condiments on the sideboard and take the rest to wash-up.

Remember!
Remove empty soup bowls first – leave part-filled bowls until the last clearance for that course.

Find out!
How would you clear consommé cups and underliners?

Remember!
Glassware should be carried from the table on a separate tray to meet the health and safety regulations.

Did you know?
Where possible, remove the main course plate that has the most food debris on it first.

Clearance of side plates

○ Use a lined silver salver.
○ Remove the side plates from the left.
○ On the salver, segregate plates, knives and food debris.
○ Continue removing plates from the left.
○ Remove the contents of the salver to wash-up.

Alternatively, side plates can be cleared onto the cleared main course plates. The side plates are placed on top of scraped plates, and the roll debris and knife are placed onto the lower plate. They are then removed to a tray on the sideboard. Crumb down before the ordering of sweets and desserts (see page 313).

Clearance of dessert plates

Sweets and desserts may involve a variety of dishes – bowls, glasses, cereal bowls or ramekins, all with underliners, as well as dessert plates. First clear the largest quantity of similar plates or dishes. Then clear the next type of remaining dishes. Clear dishes with underliners onto a salver. Segregate underplates, dishes and cutlery. Continue clearing, and segregate and stack. Dessert plates are cleared as for the standard plate clearance. Stack these onto a tray at the sideboard.

After clearing plates

After clearing plates from the table, check that the cover is in place for the next course (if the menu is à la carte), and that it is still correct for a table d'hôte menu. Remove the tray with neatly stacked dirty plates and cutlery to wash-up.

Clearing dirty plates at wash-up

○ Scrape all food debris into a food waste bin.
○ Segregate and dispose of other waste material.
○ Segregate dirty cutlery and place it in containers.
○ Stack dirty plates in size order.
○ Leave the clearing tray to be washed.
○ Now wash your hands!
○ Collect a clean tray to collect the next food order.

Did you know?
There is one exception to the rule about clearing from the right – you should remove the side plate from the left (the side where the plate is placed on the table). Clearing side plates from the left means that you don't have to stretch across your customers.

Remember!
Using dirty joint plates as a base to clear side plates speeds up the clearance process.

Remember!
After clearing, always check that the cover for the next course is still correct – the customer may have changed their order, or they may have used the wrong knife and fork to eat the cleared course.

Clearing glasses

Glasses should be cleared separately. Empty glasses should be removed from the table as soon as possible. Remove empty glasses from the right, holding them by the stem or (for tumblers) by the sides, and place them on a serviette-lined salver or non-slip tray. Carrying glasses on a lined salver or a non-slip tray reduces noise and movement of the glasses. Return the salver to the bar for the glasses to be cleaned. Take a new lined salver or non-slip tray to continue clearing.

Clearing table decorations

Any table decorations should be collected from the tables and stored in an allocated area. If these are to be used for another session, any flowers should be kept in a cool area with sufficient water. At the end of service at special functions such as weddings, customers often wish to take away any table flowers, decorations and menus. In this case, customers should be helped to collect these items and to carry them to their cars.

Extinguish any candles using a candle hood, not by blowing them out – this can leave candle wax on tablecloths. Check candles to be sure the flame is completely out. Move to storage area when candles are cool.

Clearance of tables after use

Tables are crumbed down, and slipcloths or clean tablecloths are placed on tables for presentation and neatness. The table could be re-laid for more customers, or for the next session.

Sideboard clearance

Unused food items may include bread rolls, and fresh rather than bottled accompaniments such as fresh mint sauce. These should be stored (labelled with a use-by date) or disposed of according to the establishment's practice – for example, bread rolls may be passed to the kitchen for use in making breadcrumbs. All paper and other types of rubbish should be removed and disposed of safely to meet the Food Hygiene Regulations.

Figure 11.24 Trying to blow out the candles may not have the desired effect

Test yourself!

1 From what side do you clear:
   a side plates?
   b glasses?
   c main course plates?

2 How should main course cutlery be cleared?

3 At a function silver service, when would you clear the table?

4 What is the purpose of crumbing down?

Safety during silver service

Accidents

Silver service involves serving cold and hot foods at the table, very close to the seated customer. By presenting the dish, you are making customers aware that you are about to serve their food. Some accidents at table are due to customers moving or turning at the wrong moment.

As a waiter silver serving food to your customers, you should always be fully prepared, using only the correct service equipment for the task. This includes the service cloth, which should be clean, thick and dry, to take the heat of the service dishes.

Waiters must take care when serving at table to avoid accidents. The priority must be the customers' safety and the safety of the staff. Accidents cause upset to anyone involved, and could damage the reputation of the restaurant and/or lead to compensation claims.

Accidents do occur, and as a professional waiter you need to manage the situation. The procedure is to first offer apologies, provide care, rectify the situation, apologise again, and proceed with the rest of the meal. Remember to inform your supervisor or line manager.

Small spillages

For example – on serving sliced meat to an elderly lady, you accidentally spill gravy on her white blouse. The procedure is to:

○ offer apologies

○ offer her a clean, damp cloth to wipe her blouse

○ a male waiter could suggest that a female waiter checks with this customer regarding the situation

○ remove her plate and any other food already served

○ when the diners are ready, restart the service with clean plates and new food

○ inform your supervisor, who may suggest that the customer sends in the cleaning bill for reimbursement, or may offer a complimentary drink or meal

○ as the customer departs at the end of their meal, apologise again

○ complete your establishment's incident or accident book (see Chapter 2, page 56), depending on the nature of any injury.

> **Remember!**
> Always apologise if you cause an accident – and cause as little fuss and inconvenience as possible.

> **Remember!**
> It is a legal requirement to complete the incident/accident book.

Large spillages

If the incident involves a large spillage on the table, it is often quicker and more pleasant for the customers involved to transfer them to a new table. If this is not possible, suggest that they sit in the lounge or bar while the table is being prepared. Always apologise to the customers, and ask other waiters to assist in the re-laying of the table, to get the job done quickly.

Figure 11.25 Teamwork clears an incident quickly

Unexpected situations

Problems with portion size

A customer may ask for more than the portion size. There can be several solutions to this unexpected situation, but all are subject to the policy of the particular establishment. You would need to inform your supervisor. This situation requires excellent social skills.

If the menu is à la carte, the answer would be 'certainly, I will get another portion straightaway', and an extra portion would be charged to the bill.

> **Remember!**
> Portion control is practised to provide customer satisfaction, as well as controlling costs and reducing wastage of food.

If the menu is table d'hôte, the answer depends on the food item requested. If the request is for more vegetables, the waiter could silver serve all diners first, and if any vegetables are left in the dish, serve them to the customer. In this case there would be no charge. If the request is for more of a main dish item, provided the dish served is as stated on the menu, the request would probably be subject to an additional charge. You should check with the chef first regarding the availability of the food item. The customer would need to confirm and agree to pay the additional price before you serve the food.

For function service, the request would be refused. Where a set menu is served to a large number of guests, it is unlikely that there will be any surplus food – and if you agree an extra serving for one customer, you may have another hundred guests requesting the same! You could confirm with the customer that the food served is as selected by their host. Suggest that if there is any surplus when everyone has been served, you may be able to bring their food request to them.

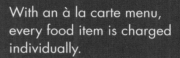

Remember!

With an à la carte menu, every food item is charged individually.

Remember!

To be in line with the Trade Descriptions Act, any weights and sizes of portions specifically stated on the menu for main dish items must be checked carefully.

Silver service checklist

(black = food service; red = drink service)

	Checklist	
1	Greet, seat, unfold serviette, offer aperitif, sell aperitif.	
2	Offer menu, serve aperitif from right, female diners first, host last.	
3	Take food order using salver, menu knowledge, collect menus.	
4	Offer wine list, take wine order, wine knowledge.	
5	Collect wine lists, adjust cover, place accompaniments.	
6	Top copy to kitchen, duplicate to cashier.	
7	Unload tray onto sideboard, present dishes, serve cold before hot.	
8	Serve female diners first, from left, serve accompaniments, check back.	
9	Clear sideboard, remove all aperitif glasses, add/change wine glasses, tray on sideboard, clear plates from right.	
10	Correct clearing, stack tray correctly, present wine.	
11	Open wine correctly, correct glasses, host's taster.	
12	Correct order of wine service, serve wine from right, adjust cover.	
13	Place accompaniments, service cutlery.	
14	Unload mains onto sideboard, present dishes to customers.	
15	Meat/main dish item bottom of plate, potatoes top right.	

16	Vegetables top left, sauces, cold before hot, ladies first, from left, re-fill wine.	
17	Clear down sideboard, re-fill wine.	
18	Clear table accompaniments	
19	Clear joint plates from right, clear side plates from left, remove butter, remove cruets, crumb down.	
20	Offer menu, take order left of host.	
21	Adjust cover, place accompaniments.	
22	Serve cold before hot, female diners first, serve from left, serve sauces.	
23	Clear from right, remove glasses from table from right.	
24	Offer liqueurs, serve liqueur from right.	
25	Take coffee order, put coffee place setting top right of cover, serve coffee from right, female diners first, offer and serve sugar, pour coffee, add milk if desired.	
26	Offer second cup of coffee (if this is your establishment's policy), present bill.	
27	Pay cashier, present change.	
28	Show diners out, help with coats, bid good-day, clear table, crumb down, re-lay.	

Test yourself!

1 How can accidents be avoided when clearing plates from the table?

2 To whom should incidents and accidents be reported? Why?

3 You have silver served all your guests at table with their main meal. A customer calls you over to inform you that the chicken is not cooked. What should you do, and in what order?

4 You are clearing at a large function. One of your guests becomes ill, and attempts to get up but falls. How will you manage this situation?

5 You have silver served the steaks, vegetables and accompaniments to all your customers. The customers have started to eat their steaks, and they complain – the underdone and the well done steaks have been served to the wrong customers. How are you going to manage this situation?

12

Providing a carvery/buffet service

In this chapter you will cover skills and knowledge in the following units:

o 7132 – Unit 209 (2FS4): Provide a buffet and carvery service

o 7103 – Unit 108: Food and beverage service skills

o 7103 – Unit 209: Food and beverage service skills

Working through this chapter could also provide evidence for the following Functional Skills:

Functional English – Speaking, listening and communication Level 1

Functional Mathematics – Analysing Level 1

In this chapter you will learn how to:

o prepare and maintain a carvery/buffet display

o use safe and hygienic practices when preparing and maintaining a carvery or buffet display

o serve and assist customers

o use safe and hygienic practices when serving customers at a carvery or buffet

o control portions when serving food to customers

Introduction

A carvery/buffet is a method of service where the food (both hot and cold preparations) is displayed artistically on a service buffet table within the dining area so that customers can see the dishes before they choose their food.

The carvery/buffet can be presented in a number of styles – the main ones are described below.

Simple **buffets** are often served in public houses, where customers are served from a hot counter and salad bar, either as self-service or by service staff. Customers then take their own meal to their table. Cutlery and condiments are usually dispensed from the buffet area.

A self-service lunch buffet is usually offered in canteens, department stores, service stations, industrial catering outlets, etc. Customers are mostly served by staff to ensure good portion control and speed of service.

Did you know?

While serving yourself at a meal has a long history, the modern buffet was developed in France in the eighteenth century and soon spread throughout Europe. The term originally referred to the sideboard where the food was served, but is now also applied to the form of service.

Definition

Buffet – a selection of light refreshments where diners help themselves, often eating standing up.

Figure 12.1 A hot buffet

A buffet or carvery may form part of a meal's menu (lunch or dinner) in a restaurant or hotel, where customers can choose the buffet meal (usually self-service) while other guests may select the set (**table d'hôte**) menu. This style may be offered in hotel restaurants. Some establishments may offer just a carvery at certain meals, with a range of roast joints of meat and poultry (and usually a fish and a vegetarian option) – these are a popular choice for a traditional Sunday lunch.

Figure 12.2 Carveries are popular for a traditional Sunday roast

A buffet/carvery is often served at large organised functions, especially those held in a hall, marquee or other venue. Because kitchen space is limited, food is usually prepared off-site and transported to the dining venue.

Definition

Table d'hôte – a set meal at a set price. The written menu will have a simple choice of between three and six choices for each course. If a buffet is offered (common on the continental mainland), this usually heads the list for each course as 'Selection from the buffet table'.

Figure 12.3 A buffet is often an efficient choice at a wedding

A buffet/carvery may provide a large range of cold foods as well as hot meats, poultry and fish dishes, along with a range of salads and hot vegetables. This style is popular on cruise liners and large hotels at lunch times.

Figure 12.4 Many cruise lines pride themselves on the quality of their buffet

Themed buffets are popular at organised functions. These may consist of two or more separate buffets offering food with a common theme (seafood, Chinese, curry, roast meat carvery, barbecue, etc.).

A finger buffet is also a popular method of serving cold food, especially at lunch time for organised functions, allowing guests to mix freely. For this style of buffet, special buffet clips to hold wine glasses may be useful. These are plastic clips that can be secured to the side of the diner's plate, with a slotted, rounded extension for holding the diner's glass (the glass must have a stem to fit into the slot). Sometimes a wine glass holder may be built into a special buffet plate or party plate.

Figure 12.5 The equipment used can make it easier for guests at a buffet

A fork buffet operates on the same principle as a finger buffet, but hot food is served (e.g. fricassée and rice, curry and rice, beef stroganoff and rice). A wine glass holder (buffet clip) is also ideal for this style of eating.

A buffet service is a popular method of service for breakfast in hotels, offering hot and cold dishes together with cereals, fruits, yoghurts, etc. Breakfast buffets are mainly self-service, but in high-class establishments they are often maintained by service staff.

Figure 12.6 Buffet service is often used for hotel breakfasts

Because a carvery/buffet service is very visual, both personal and food hygiene practices must be of a very high standard both during preparation and during the service. Presentation and customer care also require a very high standard to ensure customer satisfaction.

Test yourself!

1 What are the main advantages of a carvery/buffet service?

2 Name three occasions on which a buffet is the best choice of service, giving reasons why.

3 Why is presentation especially important for a buffet/ carvery?

Prepare and maintain a carvery/buffet display

Planning the buffet

A meeting must be held between the head chef and restaurant manager to discuss the buffet and its service. Elements to agree on include the following.

- Starting time of service, and when tables will be required.
- How many dishes are to be displayed.
- The style of dishes and methods of service (including any carving and portioning).
- Vegetarian and special diet options.
- Who will be serving (chefs, service personnel, customers as self-service).
- The surface area of the buffet table.
- What specialised equipment may be required.
- Whether any electrical equipment is to be used – this might include infra-red lamps, hot plates, **chafing dishes**, **bain-maries**, etc.

A briefing of all service personnel is then conducted by the restaurant manager, detailing the siting of the buffet, the style of service and dishes, the expected number of covers, and pre-service/service duties for each member of the team.

Remember!
A successful buffet/carvery service relies on a good liaison between the kitchen and service personnel.

Definition
Chafing dish – a large, portable food dish that is heated using candles, spirit lamps or individual spirit-jelly burners.
Bain-marie – a double boiler, used to protect foods from direct heat. A smaller container is partially immersed in a larger container of heated water. (Some people refer to a 'dry bain-marie', where electric elements heat the air beneath the dishes – but this is really a chafing dish.)

Did you know?
The word 'bain-marie' means 'Mary's bath'. It comes from medieval alchemists who invented a method of slow heating in a double-walled container filled with water.

Figure 12.7 Chafing dishes

Preparing the dining area

Check that all lights, fire doors, ventilation units, etc. are working, and that furniture is fit for purpose (especially that chair and table legs are sturdy and pose no risk to the customers).

Vacuum the carpet, sweep and polish the floor, dust and polish all furniture, polish mirrors and also any glass door windows, brass fittings, etc.

Ensure there are sufficient tables and seating, and that there is easy access for wheelchairs. Make sure that no tables, chairs or other items are blocking the fire exits.

Figure 12.8 Make sure the dining room or function room is clean before service

Set up the buffet area near the kitchen entrance, with the hot carvery section (if required) nearest to the kitchen and adjacent to an electrical power supply.

Setting up the buffet

Always allow plenty of table area for setting out the buffet. The shape of the buffet area will depend on the dining area available, the shape of the restaurant, the number of diners, etc. A large rectangular or square restaurant or dining area will offer the best choice of table layouts, especially for a long, straight single table. An irregularly shaped dining room may require two or more small buffet tables. For a large buffet, tables are often prepared with two identical service areas that mirror one another.

Carvery

Arrange this so that the hot carvery is at the beginning, followed by hot dishes (curries, ragoûts, fricassées, etc.) and any hot vegetables. Cold meats (including any being carved) and salad items should then follow. This allows for customers to be served quickly and efficiently. Sauces and condiments should be placed at the end of the buffet.

Buffet styles

A buffet table can be presented in a variety of shapes, and much depends on space available. The most popular formats are listed below.

○ A long, straight table that can allow two identical service points running from each end.

○ An angled table in the corner of the dining room, ideal where space is limited – but this restricts the speed and flow of diners.

○ A long, U-shaped table system with the centre, containing the main buffet, usually running along one wall of the dining area, with the end 'sprigs' (tables at right angles to the main table) containing the starters and desserts. This is ideal for limited space in a small dining room, with a large number of guests standing.

○ A round table situated in the centre of the dining room, with the dining tables arranged around the buffet. This is very visual, and is ideal for cold, pre-sliced buffets. This style is often tiered (two or three levels) for maximum use of the area. A square table system can also be used in this format.

Figure 12.9 Some different examples of buffet layouts – but every buffet is different!

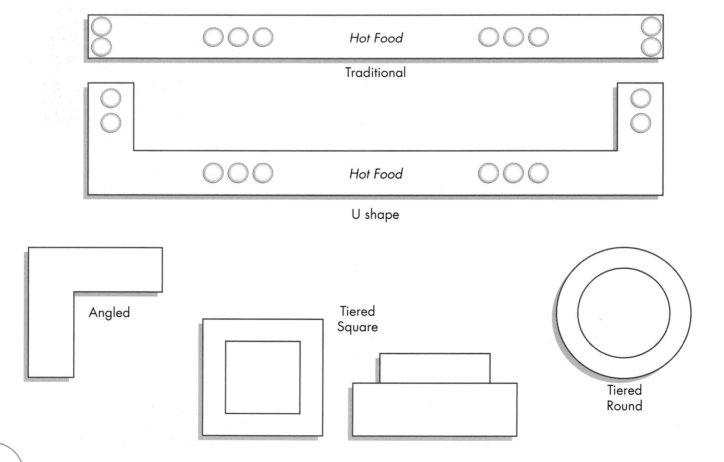

Traditional

U shape

Angled

Tiered Square

Tiered Round

Hot Food

Buffet table decoration should be tasteful, but not overpowering. Remember that any decoration should not hinder the service of the food and the removal or replenishment of salvers and dishes. The table covering should ideally reach to the floor (in the diners' visual area) and any edging should be secured firmly. Take extra care if you are using fresh flowers, as the pollen from some species can stain diners' clothes. One way of avoiding this is to use greenery with artificial flowers. Table decorations, especially for wedding breakfast buffets, are often set by outside flower-arranging specialists, and consultation with the flower arranger is advisable. Themed buffet events (sports clubs, birthday parties, business functions, etc.) often require some decorations specific to the event. Again, good liaison with the organisers can prevent possible problems during service.

Prepare the buffet table with cloths and any decorations according to the establishment's standards. This should be completed well before service so that any additions or adjustments can be made in plenty of time. Check with the head chef that the table area is sufficient for his or her needs – if possible, use the same number of empty service flats, salvers, salad and vegetable dishes that the chef will be using, to help assess whether enough space has been allowed for the chef and servers to work comfortably.

Allow ample space for storing dirty crockery, cutlery and serving dishes. Make sure there is a suitable container for waste food and dry rubbish, for transporting to the still-room.

Figure 12.10 Make sure the chef and servers have enough space

Preparing table items

Clean and polish all the crockery, glassware and cutlery required. Check crockery for chips, cracks, smears and finger marks.

If cutlery is to be dispensed from the buffet table, it is a normal practice to wrap it up together or insert it into a napkin, to assist the customer. This can speed up service. Follow your establishment's procedure and napkin folds. If cutlery is not dispensed from the buffet table, then you will need to lay up the dining tables.

Prepare any decorative items or flowers for the table.

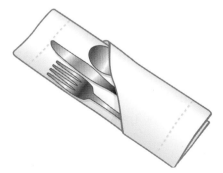

Figure 12.11 Each different establishment will have its own way of folding napkins and presenting cutlery

Preparing service equipment

Clean, polish and check any heated service equipment, such as hot plates, chafing dishes, bain-maries or infra-red lamps, and put these in position well before service starts. If spirit lamps, candle heaters or other patented heating devices are to be used, make sure there are enough refills/replacements available for a quick and speedy change when required. If any are almost used up, it is best to replace them before service. Ask your supervisor if you are unsure.

Clean and polish service spoons and forks, and any specialist service equipment (ham stands, carving boards/trays, tongs, salad tongs, perforated spoons, ladles, cake slices, etc.), ensuring that there is an ample supply of replacements available.

Switch on all heated service equipment at least 30 minutes before service. Ensure that boiling water is placed into bain-maries to speed up the heating time.

Preparing food items

Fill and polish all condiment containers. Place all proprietary sauces and condiments required for service into sauce boats or dispensers. Prepare butter portions (keeping plenty in reserve) and store these in the refrigerator. Place bread rolls and or sliced breads in baskets following the practice of your establishment. Make sure there is a good supply of bread, bread rolls, butters, sauces and other accompaniments at hand for replenishment throughout the service.

To meet food hygiene regulations, the carvery/buffet must meet certain standards, as follows.

○ If the carvery/buffet is held over a long period of service, the food must be held at a working temperature of 5°C (41°F) or lower for cold foods, or at 63°C (145.4°F) or higher for hot foods.

○ The foods on display must be protected from customers by glass screening to prevent the risk of contamination, and must be served by trained staff.

○ If the carvery/buffet is served open to customers, even if only
served for a short period of time, then on completion of service
high-risk foods must be disposed of and not re-used, under the
Hazard Analysis and Critical Control Point (HACCP) regulations
(see Chapter 5, page 171). Meats, sauces, gateaux, creams,
etc. are 'high-risk'. Salad items (lettuce, tomatoes, cucumber,
beetroot, etc.) are termed 'low risk', but if the food has not been
stored during service at the correct temperatures (hot/cold;
see above), and not screened from the public, over a standard
service period of 3 hours, then they also pose a high risk and
must be disposed of. Food handlers must demonstrate all due
diligence to ensure all food is free from contamination.

Preparing yourself

Check your uniform for stains and creases, and ensure your hair,
hands and nails are clean and tidy (see pages 142–144).

Assist in setting out the buffet items (this is usually a joint effort
between the chef and waiter/waitress), ensuring that the dishes are
easily accessible by both customers and servers.

Be ready on station at least 10 minutes before customers are due
to arrive, and check that everything is in place and ready (especially
the hot food). Identify all dishes suitable for vegetarians so that
you can assist vegetarian customers quickly and efficiently. If you
are serving, ensure that you know the portion size for each dish
(consulting with the chef).

Assisting and serving customers

Figure 12.12 A good first impression makes all the difference!

Assisting customers

It is important that you give every assistance to customers during the service. Welcome them to the buffet table with a pleasant smile and a polite greeting (Sir or Madam). Explain the procedure of service – what is available, a simple explanation of the dishes, and the choices and number of selections available (there may be a restriction on the number of dishes per customer). Also explain where they will find plates (if they are serving themselves), where they should collect their cutlery, and where condiments and sauces are situated.

If there are two identical services running, explain at regular intervals to the customers that these exist, and where each service starts.

Figure 12.13 Make sure diners know if there is a restriction on the number of food items per customer

Serving customers

Work hygienically at the buffet table. Do not lick your fingers, eat, chew or drink while serving. Do not cough, sneeze or touch your face, hair or other parts of your body at the table (see Chapter 5, page 142).

The UK is a multicultural society, and customers may have a variety of religious beliefs that include what can and cannot be eaten (**halal** for Muslims, **kosher** for Jews, **sattvic** for Hindus). When serving food, you must always use the designated serving spoon and fork to serve each dish, and never use the same equipment to serve different meats. This can cause offence to some people, especially if pork products are on offer (these are banned in Hindu, halal and kosher diets). If a large number of ethnic people are in the party, it is advisable to omit pork products altogether from the buffet.

Place the food neatly on the plate so that it looks attractive and appetising. Be prepared for customers who may ask questions regarding the ingredients contained in the dishes (especially dairy, nuts, garlic, etc., which may cause allergies). If you are unsure, apologise politely and find out from your supervisor or the chef, quickly and without fuss.

The possibility of food allergies is another reason why you should always use the correct utensils for the correct dish (see Chapter 5, page 136).

Carving meats

Make sure you use the correct knife for the type of joint (a carving knife for hot joints and a serrated ham knife for cold joints) and that it is kept sharp. A fine grained knife steel should always be at hand to 'hone' (re-sharpen) the knife during service.

Carving accessories

A variety of accessories to assist the carving joints of meat and poultry are available, including spiked carving trays/dishes, grooved cutting boards, stainless steel ham stands, etc. These are specially designed to make carving safer and to prevent escaping juices from running over the buffet table.

Definition

Halal – food that is permissible according to Islamic law.
Kosher – food that is in accordance with Jewish law.
Sattvic – food that is uncontaminated and pure (vegetarian), the Hindu ideal.

Remember!
When using a carving knife, you must always use a carving fork to hold the joint steady and with the protective guard in the upright position, to prevent any injuries if the knife slips.

Figure 12.14 Use the right knife for the right job – and keep them sharpened

Remember!
You are more likely to cut yourself with a blunt knife than with a sharp one.

Type of meat	Carving technique	Notes
Roast beef	Thinly against the grain. For fillet: thickly against the grain	
Roast lamb	For leg: thickly against the grain For saddle: thinly with the grain	For leg, cut from the outside to the bone following along the muscle line on both sides of the leg. For saddle, cut along the backbone.
Pork	Thinly against the grain	If a leg is to be carved on the bone, then carve as for a leg of lamb.
Veal	Thickly against the grain	If a leg is to be carved on the bone, then carve as for a leg of lamb.
Venison	Thickly against the grain	If a leg is to be carved on the bone, then carve as for a leg of lamb.
Baked and roast hams	Thickly against the grain	If a gammon leg is to be carved on the bone, then carve as for a leg of lamb. Cold hams are often served on a ham trivet, which is a stand with spikes to hold the meat in place.
Poultry and game birds	Breasts (suprêmes): thinly with the grain, at a slight angle	Poultry meat is more tender than butcher's meats and provided it is not over-cooked, will not be stringy or chewy. If the bird is to be carved on the bone, remove the wishbone first before roasting the bird to make carving easier.
Goose	Breasts: thickly with the grain	

Figure 12.15 Carving techniques

Did you know?

The general rule for carving meats is to slice the meat *against* the grain (cut the meat across the muscle line and following it). If you cut the meat *with* the grain (muscle line), the meat will be stringy and chewy. But there are exceptions to this – see Figure 12.15.

Try this!

Cut a piece of roasted meat as follows: one slice against the grain, and one slice with (along) the grain. Note how tender or tough each slice is.

Did you know?

Carving meat from a joint and serving it straight to the customer will ensure that each slice of meat retains its moisture (juices) much better than joints of meat that are pre-carved before service and reheated.

Whole poached fish

On large cold buffet displays, decorated whole poached fish on the bone are popular (salmon, sea trout, turbot, brill, etc.). To remove the flesh from the bones (working from the central line along the length of the fish's body), use a large service spoon and fork (so that you do not cut the bones) and separate gently. To lift off the flesh onto the customer's plate, a pair of fish eaters (fish knives) are ideal.

Portion control

Always keep to the portion control and never give an extra helping to anyone who asks – otherwise you may run out before everyone has been served. If a customer only wants one item of meat, for instance, and so requests a larger portion, explain politely that there is a strict portion control and that if there is some meat left after everyone else has been served, you will bring it to them. You can then silver serve it to that customer at the table. But you must remember that if you give one customer an extra portion because you feel sorry for them, the next customer is likely to request the same, and so on! If you find that a customer persists in requesting an extra portion, you must refer the matter to your supervisor.

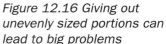

Remember!
Portions, especially for a set number of customers at a function, will be precise because the food cannot be re-used later (food hygiene laws) – any leftovers must be destroyed.

Figure 12.16 Giving out unevenly sized portions can lead to big problems

Maintaining the service and dining areas

Check with customers who are eating that everything is to their satisfaction.

Watch out for dishes that are depleted and starting to look untidy and unappetising. Remove these and replenish with a fresh dish, or have the dish topped up in the kitchen. Never transfer food from one dish to another at the table in front of customers!

Keep the buffet table clear of any food debris that has been dropped or spilt. Use a pair of tongs to remove these onto a small plate – never use your hands or fingers to pick up the debris.

Clear away empty plates and cutlery quickly and efficiently, and remove any debris (dirty napkins/serviettes, side-plates, unused cutlery, etc.).

If the carvery/buffet is at a function, if any food is left on the buffet table once all the guests have been served, second helpings are generally offered. You should visit each table (starting with the top table), politely informing diners of the facility. You must ensure there are enough clean plates and cutlery available, in case the guest's first plate and cutlery have been removed.

Clearing after buffet service

When clearing after service, it is important to remember that customers may still be present and watching you. Always work quietly and hygienically, and only remove the table linen when your supervisor has given their permission.

After all the customers have been served, it is important to remove all left-over food back to the kitchen for disposal. If 'low-risk' food has been held at the correct temperature and screened during service, it can be covered and refrigerated for later use. Hot foods should be rapidly cooled before refrigeration. It is important to remove the food immediately service is completed to reduce the risk of contamination or deterioration.

Once the buffet table has been dismantled, vacuum the area thoroughly to ensure that no food particles remain on the floor and therefore risk attracting vermin.

Any breakages that occurred during service must be entered in the breakages book and reported to the supervisor so that they can be replaced immediately.

Figure 12.17 Hold a meeting to review the service and pass on customers' feedback

After clearing up has been done, it is important to hold a debrief session with the team to discuss any problems that may have occurred during set-up and service, and how any improvements might be made. If this meeting is left until later, incidents may be forgotten. Customers' comments (both positive and negative) should also be discussed so that where praise has been given, it is passed on to the appropriate personnel (including the kitchen staff).

Test yourself!

1 List five things that the head chef and the restaurant manager must agree on before setting up a buffet/carvery service.

2 What is the best location for a buffet serving table?

3 In what order should the different foods be presented on a carvery buffet?

4 What is the correct temperature for displaying:
a hot foods?
b cold foods?

5 What must happen to the food left over from an open buffet?

6 Give two reasons why it is important to always use the designated utensils for serving each separate dish.

7 How would you carve roast pork:
a off the bone?
b on the bone?

8 What sauces would be served with:
a roast beef?
b roast lamb?
c roast turkey?

9 What is the main purpose of portion control?

13

Preparing and clearing drinks service areas

In this chapter you will cover skills and knowledge in the following units:

o 7132 – Unit 113 (1BS1): Prepare and clear areas for drinks service

o 7132 – Unit 211 (2BS1): Prepare and clear the bar area; and part of Unit 214 (2BS4): Prepare and serve wines

o 7103 – Part of Unit 109: Bar service skills

o 7103 – Part of Unit 209: Food and beverage service skills

Working through this chapter could also provide evidence for the following Functional Skills:

Functional Mathematics – Analysing and interpreting Level 1

In this chapter you will learn how to:

o maintain types of drink stock

o prepare and maintain the service area

o prepare and store drinks accompaniments

o maintain and prepare other bar equipment

o prepare the customer service area

o clear and clean the customer service area

o clean and store glassware

The importance of a well-prepared drinks service area

There are many types of establishment which serve drinks to customers, including pubs, bistros, hotels, restaurants and wine bars. Whichever type of establishment you work in, it is essential to maintain a clean, well-organised and attractively displayed drinks service area. This creates a lasting impression with your customers when entering your premises and encourages them to return.

On arrival customers will expect the area to be prepared and ready for service. The process of preparing and maintaining the service area is continuous – you will need to clear and clean the area before, during and after service. This process can be represented as a circle, as shown in Figure 13.1.

Customers form an opinion of any establishment from the professionalism of the staff. Therefore the staff must have a clean, tidy and hygienic appearance to meet both the hygiene regulations and customer expectations.

As the drinks service area consists of both public and staff areas, security is important. Check that the bar is locked when unattended and that the area is secure from unauthorised access. This is for the safety of all and helps prevent theft or damage to the premises. In the food and drink industry, the safety of all customers, visitors and staff is paramount.

Figure 13.1 Preparing and maintaining the drinks service area is a continuous process

Did you know?
Personal uniform must comply with food hygiene regulations.

Preparing, maintaining and clearing drinks service areas

The drinks service area, equipment, stock and staff must all be fully prepared *before* the customers arrive.

The order and organisation of the **mise en place** tasks that take place before service will vary according to number of staff on duty, the level of business and the time available. Managing your time will be critical to ensure completion of tasks to the required standard and on time.

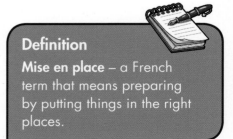

Definition
Mise en place – a French term that means preparing by putting things in the right places.

Types of drink stock

There are three main categories of drink stock:

○ soft or non-alcoholic drinks

○ alcoholic drinks

○ hot drinks with or without alcohol.

Drinks can also be classified by the method of serving. The methods of serving drinks are:

○ bottled or canned

○ draught

○ optics

○ measure

○ pourer. Sometimes drinks are poured into a measure, but experienced cocktail makers can judge the amount of drink by eye. This is called free pouring.

Classifying drinks in this way helps with stock control. The stock sheet lists every stock item by bottle size, can size, quantity per draught item (for example, pint and half pint for beer) or quantity per measure (for example, 25 ml for spirits, 50 ml for aperitifs). At the end of the session, the number of sales per item can be worked out. These figures are then marked manually on the stock sheet, or the sales figures can be retrieved electronically and the stock figures adjusted accordingly.

Soft drinks

Soft drinks include fruit juices, squashes, cordials and syrups, mineral water and carbonated drinks.

Fruit juice

Fruit juice stock is available canned or bottled or measured from a carton or other container. Canned or bottled fruit juice comes in portion size, which is usually 4 fl oz (125 ml).

When dispensing juice from cartons, check any opened carton before using. The quality of the contents must be acceptable and within the use by date. Fruit juice should be stored in the chiller unit.

Fresh fruit juice and smoothies

Producing fresh fruit juice is an expensive option, so it is often best to prepare fresh juices to order.

To make fresh juice:
- use only quality, fresh fruit
- squeeze the juice
- remove any pips
- pour into jug
- keep covered
- and chilled
- add a use by date label to meet the Food Safety Act.

The fresh fruit juice selection offered could include: orange, lemon, grapefruit, pineapple, mango, apple and tomato.

Smoothies are healthy drinks made from fresh fruit blended with fruit juice and/or milk or yoghurt. Smoothies should be made to order.

Fresh fruit and vegetables for fresh fruit juice and smoothies should be ordered to suit the drinks list. They should be classed as food items for bar use only.

Mineral water (bottled)

Mineral waters have largely replaced iced tap water. Their popularity is due to the uncertain quality of tap water and customers choosing healthy options.

Mineral waters are stocked in bottles, which can be individual portion size or large bottles. Store the bottles in the chiller unit. Mineral waters are classed according to their mineral content and whether they are still or sparkling. As mineral water is ordered for its purity, it is usually served on its own or with a slice of lemon. Sparkling mineral water or lemonade can also be used as a mixer for wine **spritzer** instead of soda water.

Carbonated drinks (bottled or draught)

Carbonated drinks are coloured liquids which have been impregnated with carbon dioxide gas, and flavoured with natural or artificial flavourings.

Find out!

How long can freshly squeezed fruit juice be kept for? Find this out, and make your use by date labels accordingly.

Definition

Spritzer – a mixture of white wine and soda water, served chilled.

Remember!

Ice is made from tap water and is not usually offered with mineral water. The reason for this is that the customer who orders mineral water instead of iced tap water will want a pure product. Only serve ice if the customer requests it.

Stock items include:

- soda water, tonic water, ginger ale, dry ginger and bitter lemon, in 4 fl oz (120 ml) bottles or cans
- lemonade, orangeade, cola and energy drinks, in 12 fl oz (355 ml) bottles or cans.

All should be stored chilled ready for service. Most carbonated drinks also have diet or low calorie alternatives.

Draught carbonated drinks can be produced to order using a post-mix drinks dispenser. A drink concentrate is mixed with mains drinking water and carbon dioxide gas is passed through the liquid. This eliminates the need for bottles and reduces costs for the organisation. Before service, check that there are enough cylinders of drink concentrate and gas for service.

Fruit squashes (bottled and measure)

Fruit squash is made from fruit pulp and juice mixed with sugar or a sweetener. Fruit squash is measured in a 50 ml measure and diluted with iced water, soda water or lemonade.

Basic stock items should include orange and lemon squash. These are stored on the display shelf at **ambient temperature**.

Syrups and cordials (bottled and measure)

Syrups are made of natural ingredients. They are very sweet and have a strong concentrated flavour. They are mainly used for their flavour, colour and sweetness as an ingredient in mixed drinks such as cocktails and in milkshakes. Because of the strong flavour, only small quantities are used. In cocktail service, syrups are measured using teaspoons or parts of a 25 ml measure.

Cordials can be used in the same way as fruit squashes to provide a long drink using tonic water or soda water. As cordials are more concentrated than squashes, use a 25 ml measure instead of 50 ml. Lime cordial and grenadine syrup are often used in this way. Lime is also used to make lager and lime.

Popular syrups (both alcoholic and non-alcoholic) include lime, grenadine, cassis, citronelle, gomme, framboise and cerise.

Coffee service often offers flavoured syrups as an additional option. The syrups used for hot drinks service have flavours that complement coffee, such as almond and caramel syrup.

Remember!

Post-mix systems do sometimes have problems, such as poor mixing of the ingredients, variations in water pressure and leakage from the system on counters and floors. For health and safety reasons, these types of machines must only be serviced by qualified service engineers.

Definition

Ambient temperature – room temperature.

Remember!

Always read the labels on the bottles, as some syrups are also available as alcoholic syrups (particularly cassis and grenadine). You may stock both alcoholic and non-alcoholic syrups within the bar.

Find out!

What is the colour and flavour of each of the syrups in the list on the left? Find out a use for each syrup.

Syrups are stored on display shelves at ambient temperature close to coffee and cocktail service points.

All bottles need wiping regularly to remove stickiness and for good presentation. Syrup and cordial bottles should be checked regularly for use by dates.

Alcoholic stock

Beer, cider, perry (bottled, draught, measure)

Stocks of bottled and canned beer, cider and **perry** should be maintained in the bottle and/or can sizes that are listed on the drinks list. Store them upright in the chiller unit.

Draught beer and cider is usually served in ½ pint and 1 pint glasses. It can also be served in ⅓ pint glasses, which is the minimum legal measure for these drinks. Draught beer is stored in casks or kegs at 12–15°C. The CO_2 cylinders should be checked before service for leaks.

Spirits (measure)

The spirits usually served include whisky, gin, vodka, rum and brandy. Stock is measured by optics or thimble measures of 25 ml or 35 ml, or multiples of these – usually single or double measures. Store any back-up stock upright on the display shelves at ambient temperature.

Fortified wines and vermouths (measure)

Fortified wines include sherry, **port** and madeira. Popular brands of **vermouth** include Martini and Riccadonna. They are stored upright at ambient temperature on the display shelves. Dry sherry should be stored in the chiller, as it is served chilled. To serve, measure using a 50 ml thimble measure or measured pourer.

Vintage ports develop a heavy sediment, known as a crust. These ports should be stored horizontally, so that the crust is on the underside of the bottle. Vintage port can be served by the glass or bottle after it has been **decanted**.

Liqueurs (measure)

Liqueurs are spirit-based drinks with the addition of flavourings and sweetener. Store them upright at ambient temperature. Wipe the bottles clean to remove stickiness. Liqueur bottles are very distinctive in shape and colour and make attractive displays, as well as promoting sales. The **measure** for liqueurs is 25 ml.

Definition

Perry – an alcoholic drink made from fermented pear juice.

Remember!

The Weights and Measures notice states the selected measure used in the establishment. This could be either 25 ml or 35 ml.

Definitions

Fortified wine – a wine that has been strengthened by adding a strong alcohol. The most common addition is brandy.
Vermouth – a fortified wine flavoured with herbs and spices.
Decanting – the separation of wine from its sediment.
Port – dark red fortified wine, originally from Portugal.

Find out!

Which country does port come from?
Why is it called port?

Wine (bottled)

All wines should be stored in numbered racks or bins. On the wine list, the wines are numbered – these numbers should correspond to the bin numbers to make the wines easy to find. Wine racks or bins allow wine bottles to be stored on their sides with the label uppermost. This is important so that the cork remains moist and provides an airtight seal to the bottle. A moist cork is also easier to remove when opening the bottle. Bottles with plastic corks and screw tops can be stored upright. Check that all chiller units are at the correct temperature.

Red wine should be placed in numbered racks behind the bar at ambient temperature. Most red wines are served at 17°C (65°F) room temperature. New red wine stock should be left for two hours to reach service temperature.

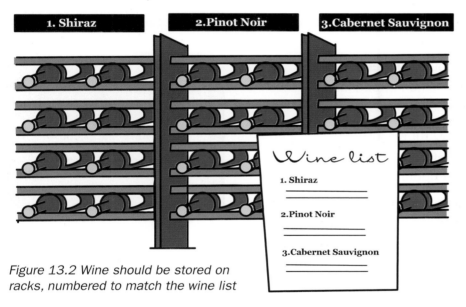

Figure 13.2 Wine should be stored on racks, numbered to match the wine list

White and rosé wines and champagnes are served chilled. The full range of wines on offer should be stored horizontally in the chiller unit. Keep them in numerical order to match the wine list. The bottle neck should face the front of the chiller unit for easy access.

Ice buckets filled with water and ice can be used to store excess stock during service. Check and adjust the temperature of chiller units. Serve dry white and rosé wines at 10°C (50°F). Serve sweeter white wines and champagne slightly colder at 7–8°C (45–47°F).

Never place white wine, rosé wine or champagne in a freezer to chill quickly as this destroys the character of the wine.

Definition

Measure – a standard unit for measuring drinks. The measures for alcohol are often determined by law – e.g. 25 ml and 35 ml for spirits.

Did you know?

Digestif is a French word that is another name for liqueurs. This is because liqueurs aid digestion, which is why they are served after a meal.

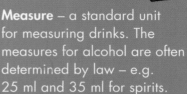

Remember!

Sudden changes in temperature damage wine. Red wine must not be placed near radiators, in the hot cupboard or in hot water to increase the temperature.

Remember!

Always use a service cloth to serve chilled wines. It is annoying for the customer to have water from the ice bucket dripping everywhere at point of service. Avoid holding the chilled wine in your hand, as this will increase the temperature of the wine.

Wine by the glass (measured)

House wines are selected to please a wide range of customers in terms of both taste and price. They are usually sold by the glass as well as by the bottle.

Red wine, white wine, rosé wine and champagne can all be offered by the glass. Whichever wine is ordered, it should be served at the correct temperature and in the right glassware. The standard measures for wine are 125 ml and 175 ml or multiples of these.

Some glassware used for wine by the glass service has a line to mark the measure, which speeds up service.

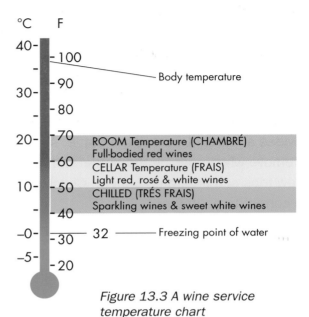

Figure 13.3 A wine service temperature chart

Dessert wine (bottle and measured)

Dessert wine is offered with the sweet course or dessert to complement the dishes. Dessert wines include sweet, luscious fortified wines, white table wines and sweet champagne served chilled.

Measure dessert wines by the glass: 50 ml for fortified wine and 125 ml or 175 ml for table wines. Dessert wines can also be served by the bottle if the customers request it.

Fortified wines that are served as dessert wines include Madeira, Marsala and sherry. These are served using a 50 ml measure.

A table may order a bottle of champagne or half a bottle of dessert wine to drink with their dessert. Serve with tulip glasses for champagne and small wine glasses for the dessert wine.

Hot drinks

Hot drinks include tea, coffee, hot chocolate and hot alcoholic drinks. When preparing for service, make sure that you have all the ingredients required for the hot drinks list, and in sufficient quantities to ensure smooth service. Check all the current stock for use by dates and quantity. Where stocks are running low, reorder as necessary.

All hot drinks ingredients should be stored covered and in dry conditions. Dairy items are stored in the refrigerator.

Remember!

Check the measure carefully when serving wine by the glass. For example, don't serve 175 ml when 125 ml is ordered.

Remember!

Under the Trade Descriptions Act, misrepresentation of products is illegal.

Hot alcoholic drinks such as mulled wine should be prepared and
stored in insulated drink dispensers to retain the temperature and
for speed of service. Check the stock required – the red wine used
to make mulled wine may not feature on the wine list, so you may
need to make a special order request.

Speciality coffees such as liqueur coffees are served in a glass
containing hot coffee, liqueur and sugar, with double cream floating
on top.

Check that you have all the ingredients in stock: coffee, sugar,
liqueurs and glasses. Store double cream in the chiller unit.

For much more detailed information on the stocks required for hot
drinks, see Chapter 18.

Preparing and restocking drinks ready for service

Preparation of drink stock levels is crucial to the smooth service of
drinks. Customers expect their ordered drink to be readily available
and served to a high standard. Factors to consider include the
quantity, temperature, glassware, garnish, presentation and speed
of service. You will only get all of these right if you have the correct
stock ready at the correct temperature.

The restocking process includes:
- checking and rotating existing stock
- ordering and reordering stock
- checking the stock received
- completing stock records
- stock storage and display
- stock availability
- substitute drinks information.

Checking existing drinks stock

Firstly you need to check the existing stock by counting to see if
you have enough supplies. Also check use by dates and remove
immediately any out of date stock. Count all existing stock using
the drinks lists and stock sheet. The stock sheet will list the
set amount of each stock item that is needed to operate a drink
service session.

> **Try this!**
> Visit a coffee bar. List all
> the syrups offered and
> the prices.

> **Remember!**
> It is illegal to serve any food
> or drink that is unfit for human
> consumption, so check use by
> dates carefully.

> **Did you know?**
> The set stock amounts are
> known as "par stock".

Stock rotation

However it is stored, all stock must be rotated so that older stock can be used first. This helps to prevent stock becoming out of date. Carry out stock rotation at stock checking and counting stage.

Organise the stock by use by date, so that the oldest stock is at the front of the storage unit. When new stock is received, it should be placed behind the existing stock.

> **Remember!**
> First in first out (FIFO) is important to avoid wastage and to ensure quality of product.

Ordering stock

The quantity of stock to order will be the difference between the existing and required stock (the "par stock" level). So to work out how many to order, take away the existing stock number from the required stock number. You might need to do this manually or your organisation may have a computerised beverage system to manage stock levels

Pre-ordered or special requests

If customers have pre-ordered drinks or have special requests, this may mean ordering some additional stock items. For example, the drinks for a wedding function are usually pre-selected, so stock orders need to be adjusted to include the drinks required.

Figure 13.4 Always check deliveries with the order form and delivery note

Requisition book

The ordering of stock is written in a book called the "requisition book". This is an internal order book used for restocking individual drink outlets. The requisition book provides two copies of the order.

Each order should be dated and list the stock items required. For each stock item, include the unit size and the quantity. Write the number required in words as this reduces the chances of error or alteration. Then give the book to the person in charge of the cellar or stores to prepare the order.

Checking stock received

When the new stock arrives, check the items and the quantities against the order. Do this with the stores person and only sign for the delivery if everything is correct.

Order

Date: 30/10/07

RESTAURANT BAR

ONE X COLOMBARD CHARDONNAY (750ml)
TWO X SAUVIGNON BLANC (750ml)
SIX X CABERNET SAUVIGNON (750ml)
THREE X RIOJA TINTO (750ml)
THREE X SHIRAZ (750ml)
THREE X ZINFANDEL (ROSE) (750ml)

ISSUER S. KNIGHT

RECEIVED BY J. NIXON
DATE 30/10/07

Figure 13.5 A page from the requisition book

If the stock does not match the order, make any corrections and sign. The stock person should then countersign the order. Both you and the delivery person should keep a copy of the signed order.

Quality checks

Always check the drink stock received for use by dates, damage, leakages and breakages.

Use by dates: All stock must be in date and there must be sufficient time remaining in order to sell. Return if necessary.

Damage: Check and inspect all stock as follows:

○ Check bottles for any chipped or broken glass and insecure bottle tops.
○ Check cans for dents or punctures.

Any stock returns should be replaced if available, recorded in the requisition book and signed for by both parties (you and the delivery person).

Wipe all bottles clean before storage. Also check cans for cleanliness.

Signing the order and receipt of goods shows that you agree with the quantity, quality and temperature of each item received. So always check carefully before you sign!

Figure 13.6 Always check new stock when it arrives and wipe bottles and cans to clean them

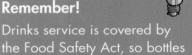

Remember!
Drinks service is covered by the Food Safety Act, so bottles and cans must be clean.

Check ...
Order stock in the correct size to match the drinks list.
Write the description of each item and the number required in words.
Check the par stock level per item and reorder by topping up the existing stock level.
Check the date of stock ordered and received.
Sign the stock order and for receipt of goods.
Adjust the quantities on the order if you return stock.
Keep a copy of the order and the receipt.

Figure 13.7 Checklist for ordering and receiving stock items

Completing stock records

Stock received is added manually onto bin cards and the drinks stock sheet or entered into the computer system electronically. For each item, the quantity of stock received is added to the quantity of existing stock to give the total stock for this item. This information informs the barperson of the stock available to sell.

Stock storage

Wipe clean all bottled and canned stock before storing. This will help reduce contamination. Then place new stock behind existing stock.

Stock that needs chilling should take priority in the restocking process, to allow for temperature adjustment ready for service.

Stock display

Drink stock should be displayed neatly and in order in display units. The labels should face the front, as this promotes the products. The stock displays act as a visual selling point and help customers to decide on their drink selection.

Stock availability

If a stock order for a drink item cannot be fulfilled due to lack of availability, it is important to remember the quantity available in stock. Before service work out an alternative stock item that could be offered if the existing stock runs out.

Substitute drinks information

Substitute stock may be a similar product but not the requested item – for example, the brand of lager requested is not available but you could suggest another brand of lager as a substitute stock item. You can only serve substitute stock to a customer after you have informed them that their choice is not available and the customer has agreed to the suggested substitute. You must also inform the customer of the price of the substitute product.

> **Remember!**
> Cleaning the tops of canned drinks reduces the risk of dirt entering the customer's glass when pouring from the can. Particularly from cans of fizzy drink which can froth over the can top.

> **Remember!**
> Under the Trade Descriptions Act, the customer must be served their named drink unless they have been informed and agreed to the suggested alternative before the point of service. They must also be told the price before purchase.

Prepare and store drink accompaniments

Ice container and tongs

Place the ice container and tongs on or next to the service counter. Make sure they are clean and polished. Fill the ice container with enough ice cubes and store with the tongs attached ready for service.

Ice buckets can also be used for bar staff to serve ice into drinks or for customers to help themselves.

Preparation of garnishes

To prepare fruit garnishes for drinks, use a clean board and a sharp knife. Have sufficient garnishes available for the drinks list. Fruit garnishes could include lemon, lime, orange and pineapple. Remove all pips from citrus fruits using the point of the cutting knife or a cocktail stick. Fruit can be cut into different shapes and thicknesses, such as slices, triangles, semicircles, slithers, zest spirals and twists.

Place each type of prepared fruit on a separate plate. Cover the plates, label with the use by date and keep in the refrigerator ready for service.

To prepare Maraschino cherries, remove the required quantity from the storage liquid and place in a glass. Add a cocktail stick for lifting. Prepare olives in the same way.

You could place extra whole fruit on the counter to make a colourful display.

Figure 13.8 Garnish preparation shows professionalism and the skills of the bar staff

Equipment and accompaniments for hot drinks

Prepare and stack the appropriate crockery, cutlery, teaspoons and napkins safely next to the hot drinks machines. Store prepared glassware for mulled wine or speciality coffees in the hot drinks section of the bar.

Store dairy items such as cream and milk in the refrigerator. Check the use by dates.

Check and restock the range of sugars offered with the hot drinks list, for example: demerara, coffee crystals, white sugar, sugar cubes and sweeteners. These can be presented in sachets, sugar sticks or in sugar bowls with spoon or tongs. Mixed brown and white sugar cubes are often presented in one sugar bowl with tongs for efficiency and attractive presentation.

Garnishes such as grated chocolate, chocolate dusting, non-alcoholic syrups and liqueurs should be ready to hand.

Snacks

All snack items require date checks and stock rotation applies as with all stock items.

Snacks such as biscuits or mints to be served with coffee should be checked for use by dates and rotated and stored appropriately. Biscuits and mints are often individually wrapped which helps cost control.

Snacks such as crisps and nuts can be sold in individual packets. They should be displayed to promote sales. Crisps, nuts, olives, gherkins and other snacks can also be served in dishes for bar counter or for table drinks service. These should be filled just before service. The snack dishes should be refilled throughout service.

For hygiene reasons, offer cocktail sticks with items such as olives.

Napkins

Check the supply of napkins before service and restock as necessary. Napkins can be made of linen or paper. The size and type of napkins should be appropriate for the type of service. Napkins provide the customer with a convenient way of cleaning their fingers when handling food and so can be offered to customers eating snacks.

Decorative items for drinks

Decorative items are used to enhance the presentation of drinks.

○ Straws of assorted colours, lengths and shapes are used in long iced drinks to prevent the ice from touching the drinker's teeth. Place two straws in the drink to allow for any damage to straws whilst drinking.
○ Swizzle sticks are used for stirring drinks and come in a range of colours and designs. They are usually plastic but can be thick glass.
○ Coasters are used underneath the glass for presentation.
○ Cocktail sticks are used for presenting drink garnishes.
○ Doilies enhance presentation under plates.
○ Parasols are used for exotic, fun and colourful presentation.

Care should be taken not to overdress drinks, which may cause embarrassment and inconvenience to the customer. Garnishes may vary depending upon the type of outlet and the associated costs.

All decorative items can be used as a display, but must be kept clean and handled as little as possible for hygiene reasons.

Prepare service and electrical equipment

Preparation of service and electrical equipment includes cleaning, checking for damage and displaying.

Bottle opener

Bottle openers are usually attached to the counter top and have a container underneath to collect the removed bottle top. This reduces the risk of cross-contamination from dirty bottle tops. The safe collection of bottle tops also reduces the risk of accidents. With a swift wrist movement the server uses the fixed bottle opener to remove the bottle top – this speeds up the service of drinks.

Cork extractor

A cork extractor is clamped onto the counter and removes corks from wine bottles. To use, insert the neck of the bottle into the cork extractor and pull the lever arm towards you. Then return the lever and the cork is removed.

Cork extractors can be decorative and must be cleaned and polished accordingly. To prepare, remove any debris and check that the clamp is tightly secured to the counter. Cork extractors are used in establishments where lots of wine is sold, for example, wine bars.

Corkscrew and waiter's friend

Corkscrews come in a variety of designs and sizes, but most require two hands to operate them. In the trade, the corkscrew known as "waiter's friend" is the favourite. The waiter's friend is a small, pocket-size, foldaway wine bottle opener. It consists of a small sharp knife to remove the wine seal from the bottle neck, a corkscrew to twist into the cork, a lever arm with a clip to remove the cork from the bottle and a clip for removing bottle tops. It looks very professional, as the cork is levered out using just one hand.

Remember!
Discarded bottle tops on the bar floor may cause accidents such as slipping, so make sure you pick them up.

Remember!
For health and safety reasons, take care when using the sharp knife on the waiter's friend. Fold the knife back once you have used it. Waiters can easily cut themselves on an open knife.

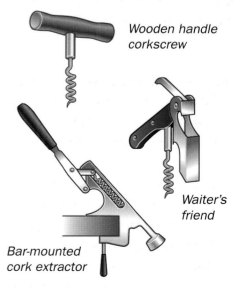

Wooden handle corkscrew

Waiter's friend

Bar-mounted cork extractor

Figure 13.9 Some of the different types of corkscrew that are in use

For health and safety reasons the corkscrew needs to be in good working order – replace if necessary. To provide a prompt wine service, it is usual to issue waiters and bar people with a waiter's friend to store in their uniform pocket before service.

Optics, measures and pourers

The measures used in the establishment must be stated on the Weights and Measures notice on display at the service point. Only the measures stated on the Weights and Measures notice may be used behind the bar. Measures used are:

- optics
- thimble measures
- pourers.

Figure 13.10 Measures used include optics, 25 ml and 50 ml thimble measures

Optics

Optics are push-up spirit measures used to serve standard 25 ml, 35 ml and 50 ml portions. They are government stamped and sealed.

To use, remove the top of the spirit bottle and push the optic into the neck of the bottle. Then turn the bottle upside down, insert the bottle into the securely clamped bracket on the display shelf. The labels must be on display and the optic measures must be full ready for service.

Thimble measures

Thimble measures are available in 25 ml, 35 ml and 50 ml sizes for measuring spirits, fortified wines and vermouths.

Thimble measures in 125 ml, 175 ml and 250 ml sizes can be used for measuring wine by the glass.

All thimble measures are government stamped. Always fill the measure right to the top and pour carefully into the appropriate glass. Check that you use the correct size measure as ordered by the customer.

Pourers

Pourers are fitted into standard size bottles for easy measurement of drinks. Pourers are not government stamped or regarded as a legal measure as they are free flow. They are used for cocktail and blended drinks service. Sizes available are 25 ml, 35 ml and 50 ml.

Remember!
Check that the optic measure is completely full before use. If not full, check that the optic is upright in its bracket. Remove the bottle from the optic if it needs replacing.

Remember!
Measures are used for non-alcoholic drinks as well. Always clean between uses. Have a dedicated thimble measure for each drink item.

Remember!
Any spillage from the measure means that the customer is getting a short measure. Under the Weights and Measures Act, this is illegal.

Glassware

Traditional glasses are clear and come in different shapes and sizes. Always make sure you use the correct glass for every drink you serve. This will enhance your service and professionalism and create a good impression with customers. See Figure 14.4 on page 417 of Chapter 14 for the full range of glasses in use.

Hygiene and safety of glassware is paramount to reduce the risk of breakages, accidents, cross-contamination and equipment costs.

Prepare for service

Always check glasses for chips, cracks, smears, marks, stains and cloudiness. Report breakages, take the broken glass out of use and dispose of safely. For safety, when you are carrying several glasses use a tray.

Make sure the shelf or bar surface is clean before you place polished glasses on it. Always hold glasses by the stem. Customers often inspect their glassware so make sure it sparkles.

Cleaning and polishing glassware

The glassware should be washed only in a glass washer at the correct temperature and then air-dried. To comply with food hygiene regulations, never wash glassware in a dishwasher. This ensures that grease or food waste does not contaminate the glassware. The glass washer is usually located behind the bar and is used solely for washing glassware.

In a restaurant, after the glasses have been washed, they are polished to add sparkle. To polish glasses, you will need a container of boiling water and a dry glass cloth. Hold the glass by the stem and place the bowl of the glass over the boiling water to steam it. Then polish the whole glass with the dry glass cloth. Hold up to the light to check there are no smears. Place the glass upside down on a tray covered with a napkin.

Use a special glass cloth to polish glasses. These are made of fine linen and are usually colour coded for bar use only. Glass cloths are used only for polishing glassware after the washing process.

Only clean, dry glass cloths must be used for polishing glassware. Plenty of glass cloths must be available to maintain hygiene at all times.

For more on cleaning and storing glassware, see pages 407–409 later in this chapter.

Alternatives to glassware

In certain situations, it is not practical to use glassware, so plastic or acrylic glasses are used instead. Most styles and sizes are available. Plastic glassware is the answer for low budget functions, outdoor events, swimming pools and for certain customers, such as children.

Carafes and water jugs

Carafes are used for serving wine which has been measured from a bottle or carton. They can be in the shape of a jug or a lipped glass container. Carafes can be used for red, white or rosé wines, so check for any stain inside the carafe, and clean until clear. Carafes should be cleaned in a glass washer and then polished to remove watermarks, as for glassware.

Prepare water jugs and place on an under plate or coaster ready for service. Water jugs are cleaned in the same way as carafes.

Other bar equipment

Drip mats and bar towels

Drip mats or bar towels are used on the counter for absorbing drips and spillages and keeping the bar top dry and slip-free. Traditionally made of towelling, they are on constant show to customers. These mats need changing regularly during service to maintain hygiene standards. Modern rubber bar mats are used in some bars and restaurants. The durable rubber mat is easily washed, more hygienic and longer lasting.

Drip trays

Drip trays are used to collect any spillages whilst dispensing draught drinks. They have a plastic base for easy cleaning and the top can be decorative in brass or stainless steel. They need to be cleaned and emptied before and during service.

Ice buckets

Ice buckets can be silver, stainless steel, or acrylic. A stand is used to hold the ice bucket and wine and is placed next to the customer's table for service. Ice buckets can also be clipped to tables, which takes up less space than the ice bucket stand.

Remember!
Hygiene regulations apply to all types of glasses.

Any ice bucket, stand or clip used will be in view of customers, so must be clean and polished. Ice buckets should be filled with a mixture of cold water and ice cubes ready for wine to be added and stored in an easily accessible place for service.

Acrylic wine cooler

This requires no ice or water. It keeps the already chilled wine at the correct temperature during service. Store on shelves when not in use.

Knives and chopping boards

Drinks service areas have bar boards for chopping fruits ready for drink accompaniments and garnishes.

A bar board is a half moon shape for cutting and displaying fruit. The central section is used to do the cutting. To cut the fruit, use a sharp knife in order to have clean-cut edges to the fruit garnishes. When cut, display the fruit on the outside of the board for easy use. Remove the centre board to be washed and sterilised and then replace it in the bar board. Clean and sterilise the knife after use and store it safely behind the bar.

Napkins and serviettes

Napkins are used to line trays or salvers to enhance presentation of drink service. There are also practical reasons for using napkins. For example, use a napkin to line a tray when carrying glassware – this will increase safety by reducing glass movement. A napkin-lined tray will also reduce noise and absorb any spillages.

Anti-slip trays and anti-skid mats

Anti-slip trays are designed with safety in mind, to reduce the movement of glasses and drinks when serving from a tray. No napkin is added.

Anti-skid mats are inserts to place in existing trays to make them anti-slip. These anti-skid mats should be checked for freshness. No napkin is added.

All types of trays are stacked ready for service. When you are using a tray, only carry the number of glasses you are comfortable with. Practise to gain confidence.

Remember!
Check the level of water and ice in the prepared ice buckets to avoid overflowing when you add the bottle of wine.

Figure 13.11 A bar board is used for cutting and displaying fruit ready for service

Wine baskets

Wine baskets or cradles need cleaning of any debris and lining with a napkin or cloth. Store alongside the red wine stock, together with under plates or clean coasters.

Drink mats and coasters

Drink mats are used to place filled glasses on, to soak up spillage and avoid unsightly glass rim stains on tables or counter tops. Drink mats are often made of pulped paper and need replacing often, so have plenty in stock before service. Dispose of damaged mats in a recycling bin.

Coasters have the same purpose as drink mats but can be made from a more permanent material, such as leather, slate, metal or wood. Drink mats and coasters are often used for advertising and promotion purposes. Clean them before and after service.

Figure 13.12 A selection of bar equipment

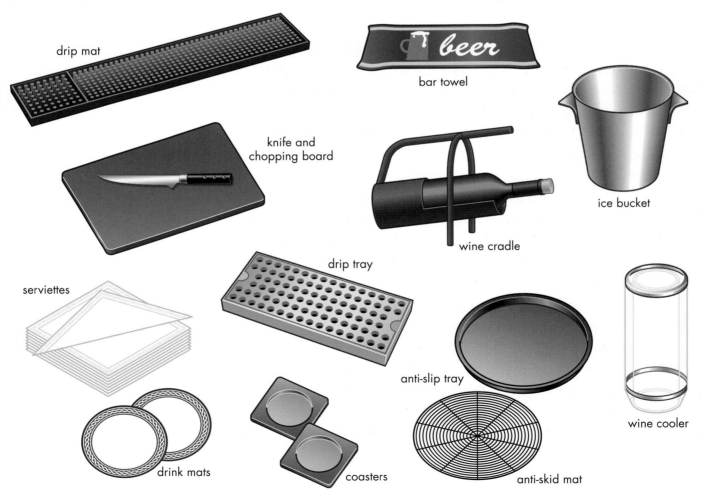

drip mat

beer

bar towel

ice bucket

knife and chopping board

wine cradle

serviettes

drip tray

anti-slip tray

wine cooler

drink mats

coasters

anti-skid mat

Electrical equipment

Check that the electrical equipment is in good working order. Then clean and prepare ready for service. If malfunctioning, report this to your supervisor. For health and safety reasons, do not attempt to repair electrical equipment yourself. Always read the manufacturer's instructions before using any new machinery.

Hot drinks production machines vary considerably. Some are plumbed in and others are table top and need filling with water. See Chapter 18 for more detailed information on hot drink service.

Machines need to be switched on early to check for working order. Some machines take a period of time to reach the right working temperature to produce the hot drinks. Fill machine with the commodities required and keep extra stock handy for refilling during service.

Cona™ Coffee machines

Check all the parts of a Cona™ Coffee machine to ensure it will be in working order to make hot drinks. Prepare the Cona™ Coffee machine ready for the first production of coffee. Switch on the machine in sufficient time so coffee has just brewed when the bar opens. The aroma of freshly brewed coffee can be very inviting for customers.

Filter coffee machines

Fill coffee jugs with the correct amount of water. Put the filter paper and coffee in position. Add water and place the jug in the correct position to collect the coffee as it is made. Switch on just before the service of coffee or opening the bar.

Water boilers

Switch water boilers on early to ensure boiling water is readily available for the service of tea and other hot drinks. Display all hot drinks commodities that require the addition of hot water next to the water boiler. All equipment required to present the hot drinks should be next to the machinery – for example, teapots, teacups, saucers and teaspoons.

Refrigerated units

The temperature of refrigerated units must be correct in order to meet food hygiene regulations. Cooling shelves, chiller units and the ice machine need checking for temperature and stock levels. You must carry out temperature checks on all refrigerated units. Record and date the temperatures and keep them in the Hygiene Health and Safety Records ready for inspection by the **EHO**.

> **Definition**
> **EHO** – the Environmental Health Officer.

Cooling shelf

Cooling shelves are made to hold 20–100 bottles standing upright in neat rows on the shelf. A cooling shelf is an open shelf that is electrically operated and cools the bottles from the bottom of the shelf. Using an open cooling shelf reduces the need to open and shut chiller units. This produces a speedier service.

The cooling shelf also displays the bottled stock, so the stock placed on a cooling shelf should be the most popular bottle sales.

Defrost regularly to avoid build up of ice and the hazard of bottles becoming stuck to the shelf. Defrost by collecting the melting ice in a container and swabbing dry. Then re-set the temperature. Stock with the full range of drinks, remembering to rotate the stock.

> **Remember!**
> Under the Food Safety Act, it is illegal to sell out-of-date stock.

Chiller unit

Clean the doors so stock can be viewed. Check the temperature. Stock with a range of chilled drinks. Leave switched on after service to allow items to be kept at the required temperature and to keep for the correct shelf life.

Ice machine

Ice machines provide a constant supply of chipped ice or ice cubes. Inspect ice machines early in the preparation session to check they are working and that ice is available. Ice may be needed by several departments, not just the bar.

You must use the ice scoop to remove ice from the ice machine. The scoop should be kept out of the machine when not being used, in the sanitiser for hygiene reasons. If you

Figure 13.13 The chiller display unit filled with stock

cannot find the scoop, never use a glass to remove ice from the ice machine. This would be a health and safety hazard, as the glass could very easily be broken.

Alternative means of providing ice

Alternative means of providing ice require early planning. Ice can be produced by filling ice cube trays and freezing. After use, trays need to be refilled with water straight away and placed in the freezer for the next batch of ice.

Alternatively, bags of ice cubes can be purchased and kept in the freezer until service time.

Prepare the customer service area

The customer area is separated from the service equipment and drink stock by the bar or service counter. The drinks counter is a focal point so it must be perfectly clean and uncluttered. A clear display is not only welcoming for customers but also helps them to make their choice.

The counter

The counter allows customers to view the display of service equipment and the shelves which store the drink products on offer. A clean and neatly organised bar encourages customers to stay longer and helps promote the sales of drink.

To prepare the counter, it must be cleaned. Use the process of
- pre-clean
- main clean
- rinse
- disinfect using a chemical allowing sufficient contact time.

For much more detail on this process, refer to Chapter 5, Food safety.

Display of menu, drinks list and promotions

Check that the drinks list, menus and promotional material are for today and are accurate, clean and undamaged. They should all be displayed in a prominent position before entry to the bar and on the bar counter. They must be opened facing the customers.

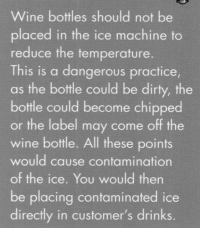

Remember!
Wine bottles should not be placed in the ice machine to reduce the temperature. This is a dangerous practice, as the bottle could be dirty, the bottle could become chipped or the label may come off the wine bottle. All these points would cause contamination of the ice. You would then be placing contaminated ice directly in customer's drinks.

Remember!
It is a legal requirement to display **sample** menu and drink list before entry to the restaurant or bar.

Remember!
Under the Price Marking Order, it is a legal requirement to display a menu and drinks list which states the prices before the point of sale.

Display shelves

Display shelves are used for displaying and storing stock. The stock on display is stored at ambient temperature.

The display shelves store drinks such as spirits, fortified wines and vermouths. Bottles to be displayed should be wiped clean and fully stocked. Some bottles should be fitted with the correct optic measure and clamped to the display shelf, with the labels facing outwards so the customer can see what they are.

Figure 13.14 The display shelves must look attractive and well-organised at all times

Display shelves should be cleaned appropriately and the bottles should be displayed tidily and attractively. Bottles should be displayed at eye level to encourage customer awareness and drink sales. They should always be stored in the same position to assist bar staff and speed up service.

Cleaning the customer service area

Cleaning should take place after service. But always carry out a check before service, and clean anything that is dirty or smeared.

Waste bin, bottle skip, etc.

Check that the waste bin is lined with a plastic liner. Keep a spare bin liner for replacing during service. Place out of sight of customers but in a convenient place for staff.

The bottle skip is for the storage of used bottles during service. It is a large, deep plastic container on wheels and is placed behind the bar.

Crates are used for storing empty returnable bottles. They should be stored safely under the bar. Clear them from the bar when full and replace with an empty crate.

> **Remember!**
> Dispose of any broken glass carefully by placing in a cardboard box, sealing the box and placing in outside metal waste containers.

Lighting, heating and ventilation

For the comfort of customers, it is important to make sure that the area is adequately lit, ventilated and at the correct temperature. So set the scene by adjusting all of the appliances to suit the time of day, the weather and the type of customers to create the best atmosphere.

Interior and exterior lighting

Having an adequate lighting level outside is important for the customers' safety. It also creates a good impression and may help to attract new business. You need to consider lighting of the entrances, car parks, fascia signs, display lights and table and room lighting. Make sure that any fascia signs are working properly.

Check all lighting and arrange for light bulbs to be replaced immediately as necessary. Check for any damage to light covers, clean lampshades and set lighting.

Heating and ventilation

Check the appliances are in working order. Report any faults and inform maintenance. For the safety of all, it is important you take faulty equipment out of use or display an "Out of order" sign, so it cannot be used in error. Replace with available alternatives for the comfort of customers. Adjust to suit the season and the weather and the known clientele – for example, for a social event for older customers in the winter, it would be a good idea to set the heating to high.

Music

Finally, adjust the music system to the right volume and play appropriate music before customers arrive.

Figure 13.15 Carry out a final check to make sure the bar area is ready for service

PRE-SERVICE CHECKLIST	
Staff appearance	
All staff are correctly dressed	
All drinks are stocked up, including:	
wines	
spirits	
liqueurs	
fortified wines	
fruit juices and carbonated drinks	
mineral waters	
squashes and syrups	
beers and ciders	
hot drinks	
Drinks service area	
Counter polished and set out with bar mats, and drinks lists and promotions	
All machines switched on and working properly	
Bottle skips and bins empty and in place	
Display shelves attractive and fully stocked	
All measures and optics ready for service	
Chiller units and cooling shelf fully stocked	
Glasses washed, dried and stored correctly	
Chipped and cracked glasses disposed of	
Sufficient cloths and napkins for service	
Bottle openers, corkscrews to hand	
All drink accompaniments ready	
All snacks ready	
Ice buckets filled and tongs and scoop available	
Maintenance items and cleaning materials out of sight	
Customer service area	
Appropriate heating, lighting and ventilation switched on	
Appropriate music playing	
Check and display menus, drinks list and promotional material in correct locations	

Figure 13.16 Checklist for preparing the drinks service and customer areas before service

Test yourself!

1 Optics are a means of measuring drink. Name other methods of measuring drinks.

2 What will be the consequences if you do not rotate the stock?

3 What are the advantages of wine bottles sealed with plastic corks?

4 Drinks lists must contain certain information. What does this include?

Unexpected situations

5 How would you deal with a power cut that occurs whilst you are preparing the service area?

6 When preparing stock for service, you discover that there is not enough stock available for the customers' pre-order request. What is the solution?

7 It is a busy Christmas lunch session and two members of staff are off sick. What would you suggest to ease the problem for the service of drinks when customers arrive?

Clearing and cleaning the customer service area

The clearing process should be maintained throughout service. Then thorough clearing and cleaning should occur at the end of service. The customer service area must always look tidy and inviting for existing and new customers.

Maintaining and clearing the customer service area

Some of the tasks listed below can only be carried out at the end of the session, but many of them can be done continuously during service. Always keep an eye out for tables that need clearing, bins that are becoming too full, spillages that need wiping up, etc. This will ensure you maintain a professional and welcoming bar area and will mean there is less work to do at the end of the session.

Clearing glassware

See page 407.

Vacated tables

When tables have been vacated by the customers, remove all finished items. Clean and clear the table ready for the next customers.

Drink stock and accompaniments

All empty drink containers, bottles, cartons and cans should be placed in the waste bins and bottle bins.

Separate these items into the containers in line with the recycling policy of your establishment. Part-used drink containers – for example, cartons of juice – should be stamped with a use by date and placed at the front area for that stock item in the refrigerator.

Figure 13.17 Empty bottles should be recycled

Drink accompaniments

Check hot drink accompaniments for use by dates and store them
appropriately. Cream and milk are stored in the refrigerator. Sugars
should be stored in sugar bowls or containers in dry conditions.
All hot drink commodities should be sealed in separate airtight
containers in dry conditions.

Hot drinks

If you have prepared hot drinks in bulk – for example, filter coffee
– dispose of everything that is left over. For cafetières, remove the
coffee grounds and wash in the glass washer. Store next to the hot
drinks section of the service area.

Ice container and tongs

Throw away all ice cubes that have been made to accompany drinks.
The ice will have started to melt and refreezing does not meet the
hygiene regulations. Clean and dry the ice container and wash and
sterilise the tongs. Replace the lid loosely onto the ice container. To
avoid a musty smell, do not fit the lid tightly on the container.

Food garnishes for drinks

If you have stored food garnishes for drinks correctly during service,
any unused garnishes can be saved to use in the next session. For
example, Maraschino cherries could be replaced in the jar.

Fruit garnishes need covering and marking with the appropriate use
by date. Store in the refrigerator. If in any doubt, dispose of the fruit
garnishes.

Decorative drink items

Decorative drink items should be discarded at the point of use by
the customer. Items such as straws and parasols are only added
to the drinks once sold, so unused stock can be stored in display
containers ready for the next service.

Completion of stock sheets

Complete stock consumption sheets, by booking out stock on the drinks stock sheet in line with the drink sales. In the same way, use the appropriate stock sheet to book out all accompaniments used. Depending on the system in place in your workplace, the stock sheets may be adjusted electronically or manually.

Service equipment

Bottle openers: To clear collected bottle tops, remove the collection container and place the bottle tops in the waste bin. Then wash the container, dry it and return to counter fixing.

Optics: Wash the optic on the outside if required. Clean optic bar if necessary

Measures: All measures should be washed in the glass washer, then air-dried and stored upside down on a napkin-lined plate.

Pourers: These can be cleaned on the outside and checked for leakages,

Drip trays: Empty drips trays, wash them in the dishwasher or glass washer, then dry them.

Drip mats: Wash plastic mats in the glass washer or dishwasher, then dry them. Return towelling drip mats to the laundry for washing.

Ice buckets: Drain of ice and water. Store them in the ice bucket stands or stack and store them on the under-counter shelf. Acrylic ice buckets should be washed in the glass washer to retain their clear appearance.

Knives and chopping boards: The bar board and knives should be washed in the glass washer or dishwasher, then air-dried and stored in the bar. Make sure that the knives are stored safely and securely.

Trays or salvers: All trays or salvers should be cleaned in the dishwasher and stacked ready for the next session.

Coasters and drink mats: Soiled drink mats should be recycled or disposed of as for paper goods.
Coasters should be cleaned according to the type of coaster. Stack mats and coasters ready for the next session.

Glass cloths, service cloths and bar mats: Collect all used and dirty glass cloths, service cloths and bar mats. Count them and return to stores or laundry.

Electrical equipment

Hot drinks machinery: If electric equipment for making and dispensing drinks is used, first unplug the machine. Remove coffee jugs and wash in the dishwasher, dry and return to the machine. Remove any used ingredients and dispose of in the waste bin. Rinse the ingredients container and return to the machine. Clean the machine and polish dry. Check that all parts of the machine have been returned to the machine. Clean the milk pipes if applicable. Clean the steam injector. Leave the machine complete and switched off.

Cona™ Coffee machine: Switch off the machine. Remove the coffee grounds and wash the coffee containers in the dishwasher. Retrieve the connecting filter. Reassemble ready for use. Wipe down the machine stand.

Filter coffee machine: Remove the used coffee grounds and filter paper and discard in the waste bin. Rinse the coffee holder. Switch off the machine. Clean the outside of the machine to remove stains.

Hot water boiler: If it is the final session of the day, switch off the boiler.

Refrigeration units

Chiller units: Check that all stock is still in date for the next session. If not, discard and dispose of correctly.
The doors should be wiped clean and any display lights turned off. The chiller unit should remain switched on. Check that the doors are tightly closed.

Cooling shelf: The stock could be moved to the front of the cooling shelf. At the end of the session, leave switched on but turn the display lights off.

Ice machine: At the end of the session, leave the ice machine switched on if that is the policy of your establishment. Clean down the outside of the ice machine. Clean the ice scoop and sterilise.

Refrigerators: The contents of the refrigerator should be checked for use by dates – discard any contents as necessary. Tidy the contents if necessary. Clean up any spillages. Leave switched on.
Refrigerators should be cleaned thoroughly approximately once a week. To do this, first switch off. Remove the fridge shelves and wash thoroughly. Rinse and dry with paper towels. Clean down the interior surfaces, door and seals with hot water and detergent. Rinse and sanitise, then replace the shelves.

Counter/bar area

At the end of the session, check the menu, drinks list and promotions and remove any information that is now out of date. Sample drinks lists and menu items should remain in a prominent position before entry to the bar.

The counter needs cleaning. First clear the counter and pre-clean, then do the main wash, rinse and disinfect (see page 349 for more details on the cleaning process). Leave the counter top clear.

Display shelves: Any spillages should be cleaned up. Check that all bottles have lids and are screwed tight. Wipe clean any bottles that need it. The bottles should be placed so labels are facing the front. Tidy up the display of bottles into the correct sections.

Waste bins: For clearance, put all rubbish in the bin. Waste bins must be emptied, washed, dried and lined with a bin liner. All waste must be disposed of correctly to meet the hygiene regulations.

Bottle containers: Put any empty bottles straight in the bottle skip. For clearance, remove empty bottles from the bar by moving the bottle container to the outside waste or recycle bins. Wash and dry the bottle container and add a plastic liner.

Broken glass: Collect all broken glassware and place in a cardboard box. Seal the box and place in the outside refuse bins.

Bar floor: Sweep the floor, then mop the floor. Leave to dry. Place a hazard sign to avoid potential accidents. Dispose of mop bucket and contents. Rinse the mop and leave to dry in a suitable place.

The customer area

Tablecloths: Soiled tablecloths should be replaced. Count the soiled cloths and return to the laundry or stores. At the end of the session, fold the dirty cloths correctly to assist counting of the cloths and for easy and neat storage.

Napkins: For clear down, dispose of all types of paper napkins in the waste bin. Count dirty linen napkins and tie in bundles of ten. Then return to the laundry or stores.

BAR CLEANING ROTA		
	Frequency of cleaning	Person responsible
Fridge	Weekly	Bar dispense
Sink and draining board	As required	"
Shelving	As required	"
Optics	Weekly	"
Bin and waste disposal	Session	"
Floor	"	"
Glasses	"	"
Salvers	"	"
Ice bucket	"	"
Waiter's friend	"	Bar dispense and wine waiter
Tea towels	"	

Figure 13.18 The bar cleaning rota should list all the cleaning tasks to be done

Cleaning the customer service area

The customer service area must meet all hygiene regulations and offer a warm welcome to customers. The area therefore requires cleaning. Cleaning takes place both before and after service.

Why do we clean?

- To remove grease, waste and dirt
- To dispose of waste which attracts pests
- To make the working environment safe
- To reduce the risk of cross-contamination
- To create an inviting environment to attract customers.

Health and safety

When cleaning always check that you are using good working practices. In order to comply with health and safety regulations, you must:

- be trained how to use chemicals
- be trained how to use correct cleaning materials for the task
- read instruction labels
- never mix cleaning materials
- display warning hazard signs as required
- take safety precautions by wearing PPE
- use the correct dilution strength of cleaning materials
- store cleaning materials in a locked cupboard and away from food rooms
- check electrical equipment for faults – isolate and report if you find a fault
- use wet floor cones as required
- clear spillages and breakages immediately.

For much more detailed information on health and safety, refer to Chapter 2.

Remember!

PPE stands for personal protective equipment. It is any device or clothing worn by the worker to protect against hazards and the environment – for example, gloves, respirators and goggles are used to protect against chemical splash.

The correct order of cleaning

The correct order of cleaning is to sweep before you dust, then dust before you vacuum clean. This is so dust and dirt do not spread to areas just cleaned. Always start at the top of a vertical surface and clean down to avoid dirtying a clean area with runs.

Floors

Sweep hard floors, then vacuum and mop with a damp mop. Leave to dry. Place a hazard sign to avoid potential accidents. Dispose of the contents of the mop bucket. Rinse the mop and leave to dry in a suitable place.

Vacuum carpets and spot clean as necessary. At the end of the session, pick up and dispose of any rubbish, such as napkins and crisp packets. Mop up any spilled drinks.

Tables

Continually clean during service once tables are vacated. Clear the table completely. Clean the table using the process:
○ pre-clean – by wiping off loose particles
○ main clean – using hot water and detergent
○ rinse – to remove smears
○ disinfect – using antibacterial spray.

Dust and shine any metal parts of the furniture. Add drink mats or clean tablecloth as necessary. Leave ready for the next customers or the next session.

Figure 13.19 Cleaning and clearing should be an ongoing process throughout service

Chairs

Check chairs for spillages. If possible, clean the chair. Remove a chair if it is badly soiled or damaged. Replace any chairs that you have removed so that there is adequate seating available.

Upholstered chairs need a regular vacuum and may need occasional spot cleaning.

Repositioning of tables and chairs

Continually reposition and tidy the furniture during service. At clear down, replace the tables and chairs in their set positions. Tables and chairs should be positioned to allow easy access for customers and service staff. The arrangement must be visually attractive.

At the end of the clearing and cleaning session, the customer and service areas should appear as at the start of the service session.

Check equipment

At the end of the session, part of your clearing up process should
be to check all equipment.

Refrigeration units

Check the temperature on all refrigeration units and record it.
Check that the refrigeration equipment is switched on. Check
that the display lights are off. Make sure that the doors to all
refrigeration units are tightly shut.

Heating and ventilation

Turn the heating down or off, or set the timer. For ventilation,
increase the fan to clean the air in the bar and then switch off.

Music

Turn off the music when the bar is closed.

Securing the area

The last thing to do after all the clearing and cleaning have been
done, is to secure the area. You may not be ultimately responsible
for this but the stages below outline the main procedure.

Cash

Remove the cash taken during the service session and lock it in
the safe. Remove the till drawer or leave it open, following the
procedure or your workplace.

Check all areas

Before locking up, check all toilets for open windows or customers
still using the toilets. Check that no cigarettes have been left burning
in the toilets. Be sure that all customers have left the area, including
any lifts. Check staff have left the changing rooms and staff area.

Locking up

Lock the bar, checking that the shutters and stock are secure. Lock
or close all doors and windows. Lock the exit doors and turn on the
alarms.

AFTER SERVICE CHECKLIST	
Update the stock sheet in line with drink sales	
Electrical equipment switched off apart from refrigeration units	
All doors to freezers and refrigeration units tightly closed	
All work surfaces clear and clean	
No taps left running and all plugs out of sinks and hand wash basins	
All equipment washed, dried and stored correctly	
Glasses are neat and tidy on shelves	
Fruit garnishes covered, labelled with use by date and stored	
Chiller lights switched off	
All rubbish disposed of correctly	
Rubbish bin and bottle skip emptied and relined	
Bar floor swept and mopped	
Dirty linen returned to laundry	
Bar locked	
Floor in customer service area clean	
Tables and chairs in correct positions	
All areas left as you would like to find them	

Figure 13.20 Checklist for clearing and locking up after service

Test yourself!

1 Why should clearing and cleaning tasks be carried out continuously during service?

2 Why should the drinks service areas be left clean and free of rubbish after service?

3 Some electrical equipment should not be turned off at the end of service. Name which ones.

4 How can you maintain security at the end of a session?

Cleaning and storing glassware

Glassware enhances the presentation of any drinks served but only if it is in perfect condition. Glassware is also very fragile. Breakages occur very easily if glasses are mishandled. It is very important that glasses are handled and stored properly to prevent injury and accidents. Caring for and maintaining the cleanliness of glassware extends the life of the glass stock. The correct storage of glassware reduces breakages and the chipping of glass rims. Glasses neatly stored on display shelves in the bar are very attractive.

It is better not to have excessive numbers of glasses stocked in the bar for service. Instead have sufficient stock that is continuously cleaned throughout the session.

Clearing glassware

As soon as glasses are empty they should be cleared. Remove the glasses from the right of the customers. Remove by holding the glassware by the stem or base. Place on tray or salver. Carry only the number of glasses you feel able to manage. Just fill the tray sensibly. Do not pick up glasses by putting your fingers inside the rim of the glass and do not stack glasses. Return the dirty glassware on the tray to the bar for cleaning.

Always have safety in mind when clearing empty glasses. Stacking glasses can cause accidents as glasses can become stuck together and separating them is difficult. Overloading trays causes accidents and breakages.

Prepare glassware for cleaning

Glasses

All dirty glassware should be carried by tray to the wash up area. It is usual to leave this tray with the glassware on it, so do not unload it. Instead, take an empty tray to collect more glasses. Inspect the glasses for cracks, chips and discard if required. Damaged glassware is kept and disposed of at the end of session.

Try this!
Collect all dirty glasses on one tray and clean glasses on another tray. It reduces the workload of the barperson as well as saving on energy costs.

Look for lipstick marks and remove these. Discard any liquid in the glasses down the sink. Place food garnishes in the rubbish bin and put glasses upside down in the glass washer racks. Stack the rack until full.

Jugs and carafes

Drain jugs and carafes of any liquids. Rinse carafes that are used for red wine to reduce the chance of staining. Discard any contents and food garnishes. Place upside down in the glass washer rack or wash by hand.

Preparation of equipment

Glass cloths

Glass cloths are fine linen cloths colour coded for bar use only. Sufficient stock of dry glass cloths should be available to complete the drying of glassware.

Glass washer

Before use, check that you understand the manufacturer's instructions and that it is in good working order.

Glass washers clean glasses perfectly, but first you will need to check and refill the detergent, rinse aid and dishwasher salt as necessary. Put the draining plug back in place and switch on. Follow the manufacturer's instructions.

Preparation for hand washing

If glasses are washed by hand, check you are suitably dressed and have personal protective equipment, particularly rubber gloves.

To hand wash you need a double sink. Fill one sink with hot water and detergent and the other with water heated to 82°C (180°F) for rinsing.

Remember!

Smoke-free legislation was introduced on 26 March 2006 in Scotland, on 2 April 2007 in Wales, on 30 April 2007 in Northern Ireland and on 1 July 2007 in England. It is against the law to smoke in any enclosed public place or workplace. "No Smoking" signs need to be placed in prominent positions at every public entrance to smoke-free premises.

Remember!

Store all cleaning materials in a secure area away from food and drink.

Cleaning glassware

In the glass washer

The glass washer is more efficient than hand washing, and allows staff more time to look after customers. Washing by machine controls the wash and cleaning process better and is more hygienic, as the glassware is handled less.

Load the machine with full racks of dirty glassware. Close the door and operate according to the manufacturer's instructions. When the cleaning cycle is complete, remove the trays and allow the glasses to air dry. Place the next full tray into the machine.

By hand

Hold the glass in one hand and totally immerse in hot detergent water, including the stem, base and handle. Check any awkward shapes for stains and use a small brush to remove them. Remove the glass from the sink, dip into the rinsing sink and place upside down on plastic matting on the draining board. Allow water to drain off before hand drying with a linen glass cloth. The sinks need to be refilled regularly with clean hot water at the correct temperature.

Checking and storing glassware

The process of washing glasses can cause damage to the glassware, so once glasses are dried, check that they are undamaged. Store glasses upside down to keep them clean and dust free. Store the same type of glasses in the set sections on the shelves. This makes the bar look well-organised and helps the bar staff to easily locate the glasses for service.

After washing, drain water jugs and remove any water marks. Store upside down as for glasses.

Try this!
Fill the glass washer tray with the same type of glasses. This makes offloading and storing the glasses quicker and easier.

Remember!
It is important to know how to wash glassware by hand. Your glass washer may not be working one day. Or just try hand washing as a learning experience.

Remember!
To comply with the food hygiene regulations, the water must be at the right temperature to kill germs.

Leave the area ready for future use

Clear down the glass washer

Empty the glass washer of all clean glassware. Drain the glass washer by removing the plug. Switch off. Clean the outside of the machine. Leave the door slightly open to avoid a bad odour developing.

Clear down sinks used for hand washing glasses

Drain the water from the sinks. Remove and dispose of any debris from the plugholes. Clean and sanitise the draining surfaces. Clean and sanitise the taps.

Bar sink

Clean the bar sink and remove debris from the plug hole. Dispose of any waste in the rubbish bin. Clean the draining board and polish dry. Clean and sanitise the taps.

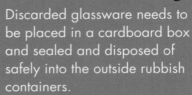

Remember!
Discarded glassware needs to be placed in a cardboard box and sealed and disposed of safely into the outside rubbish containers.

Test yourself!

1 What is the best way to carry dirty glasses?

2 What is the best way to clean ashtrays?

3 List what you should look for when inspecting glassware.

14 Serving alcoholic and soft drinks

In this chapter you will cover skills and knowledge in the following units:

- 7132 – Unit 114 (1BS2) Serve drinks

- 7132 – Unit 212 (2BS2): Serve alcoholic and soft drinks; Unit 213 (2BS3): Prepare and serve cocktails

- 7091 – Unit 259: Service of alcoholic and non-alcoholic drinks

- 7103 – Part of Unit 104: Legislation in food and beverage service; and part of Unit 109: Bar service skills

- 7103 – Part of Unit 207: Principles of beverage product knowledge; and part of Unit 209: Food and beverage service skills

Working through this chapter could also provide evidence for the following Functional Skills:

Functional English – Reading , speaking, listening and communication Level 1

Functional Mathematics – Representing Level 1

Functional ICT – Using ICT to find information Level 1

In this chapter you will learn how to:

- work within regulations concerning recent changes in bars and pubs

- take customers' orders on arrival and offer appropriate drinks

- deal with unexpected incidents

- serve alcoholic and non-alcoholic drinks appropriately

- identify and understand different categories of alcoholic and non-alcoholic drinks

- prepare , finish and serve cocktails with finesse

Recent changes in bars and pubs

Bars and pubs these days are very different from how they were even 20 years ago. All are now smoke-free environments and often offer more than just beer and spirits. For example, 20 or so years ago many pubs and bars had a very limited range of wines available and many did not offer food. Pub food is now a £6 billion a year industry and contributes 25% of the average pub's turnover.

Changes to the way that bars operate are not just down to one factor; there are many factors that have impacted on bar service. Let us consider a few.

Drink driving

The introduction of more stringent laws on drink driving forced pubs to think about the market and how they could attract more customers in to make up for shortfalls in drink sales. This encouraged more pubs and bars to increase their food sales.

Smoking ban

The smoking ban has prompted bars and pubs to improve the quality of the food on offer to encourage more families and female customers rather than just the traditional male customer.

Opening times

During the First World War the government introduced licensing laws restricting the opening hours of pubs. These laws were changed in 2003, implemented in 2005, to reflect changes in people's lifestyles and to bring the laws in line with the trading hours of other types of business. Now the restrictions on opening hours are much more relaxed and pubs can be open 24 hours a day.

Types of service

Alcoholic and soft drinks service can be offered at the bar or at the table. Bar drinks service is less formal than table service, but the service should be of the same high standard wherever the drinks are ordered. The style of service is the only difference.

Taking customers' orders

Greeting customers

First impressions are important, so make sure that you are correctly dressed and prepared for the customers' arrival. Greet your customers with a smile as soon as they arrive. This creates a good impression, is very welcoming and makes your customers feel comfortable. Your organisation may have a particular style of greeting which should be given by all staff to customers. Make sure you know what is expected in your workplace. When regular customers arrive they will expect you to recognise them and greet them by name if you know it.

For table service

Make customers feel welcome. You can do this by talking to them, offering to take their coats and to store other belongings such as bags and umbrellas. Be observant and watch customers' body language. If possible, allow them a choice of where they would like to sit. Check that the table is suitable and assist customers to their seat if required.

For bar service

If you are working behind a bar, greet your customers with a smile, even if you are busy serving a drink order to someone else. The customer will be pleased to be noticed. They will understand you are busy. It gives them time to look at your promotions and drinks list and make their choice.

Get to know your customers

People return to an establishment if they feel welcomed and have an enjoyable experience. The way you treat customers will determine how much they enjoy their visit and if they are likely to return. It is always a good idea to check the reason for their visit, so you can understand the occasion – for example, if it is a celebration.

On departure

The last impression is also important, as it is the last thing that customers remember. Be ready to help your customers as they leave. Check their table for items left behind. Assist with coats and say goodbye.

Remember!
Departure is often forgotten by staff but remembered by customers.

413

Licensing laws (England and Wales)

To control the sale of alcohol, anyone wishing to sell alcohol must have certain licences. There are different sorts of licences that allow the sale of alcohol. In order to carry out your role effectively, you must familiarise yourself with licensing hours, trades descriptions and age restrictions when selling and serving alcohol.

Premises licence

All premises where alcohol is sold need a **Premises licence**. This allows alcoholic drinks to be sold and served only at stated times and on the named premises.

Personal licence

In addition, a **Personal licence** is required. This states the named person who is legally authorised to sell alcohol on the premises. Only the licence holder and staff approved by the licence holder can sell alcohol on the premises.

Licensing hours

The licensing laws have changed over the last few years and now there are no set permitted hours. Trading could be up to 24 hours per day, but in reality most bars do not operate 24 hours a day. The Premises licence states the hours during which alcohol can be sold and drunk on the named premises. As a waiter you need to know the correct times when you can sell and serve alcohol at your workplace.

When applying for a licence, the times of opening throughout the year must be stated. Applications are made to the local authority and are subject to the approval of police, local residents and the environmental health department. The local authority will grant a licence and state the approved hours in which alcohol can be sold and consumed on the premises.

> **Definition**
>
> **Licensing hours** – the hours permitted by the local authority for the sale of alcohol on nominated premises.

Find out!

What are the licensing hours for the outlet where you work? In hotels there may be several drink outlets, but the trading times may vary for each outlet.

Under age drinking

Only customers aged 18 years or over can be served alcoholic drinks. If you are not sure about a customer's age, then you should request and check some form of personal identification. It is an offence to knowingly serve anyone under the age of 18 years with alcohol.

When must you not sell alcohol?

You must **not** sell alcohol:

- to customers under 18 years of age
- out of legal opening hours
- to a customer who is drunk, violent, quarrelsome or disorderly
- to an associate of a drunk person, if the purchase is intended to be consumed by the drunk person
- to customers who are under the influence of drugs
- to a policeman on duty
- to a known prostitute
- to those previously barred.

Identifying customer requirements

The first step when serving a customer is to identify what it is that they wish to order. You should listen carefully and check anything you are not sure of. If you take care to identify customer requirements correctly it will lead to quicker service and avoid mistakes occurring.

Special requirements

Some customers may have special requirements – for example, if they wish to smoke they will need to know where the smoking area is. The smoke-free legislation has restricted the areas where customers can smoke. On 1st July 2007 England introduced a new law to make virtually all enclosed public places and workplaces in England smoke free. The Smoke-free (Signs) Regulations 2007 states that "No Smoking" signs must be displayed in a prominent position at each entrance to the smoke-free premises.

The Trade Descriptions Act

Regarding the sale of drinks, the Trade Descriptions Act 1968 states that any wording on the drinks list, cocktail list and any promotions must not be misleading.

The description given should include:

- name of the drink
- type of drink
- contents of the drink, particularly for mixed drinks such as cocktails
- price
- alcoholic strength.

The drinks list should be displayed in a prominent position where customers can see it before they make a purchase. Any special offers and promotions should also be displayed and/or brought to your customers' attention before they place their order.

When you are working in a bar you must be careful how you describe drinks to the customer, as well as taking care to serve exactly the drink that is ordered. It is an offence to substitute or "pass off" a different brand of drink or food to the one ordered without the prior permission of the customer. Sometimes a customer may ask for the drink by a brand name, but your organisation only stocks an alternative brand. In this situation, you must ask the customer if the alternative brand is acceptable.

Price is also part of the product description and you can only sell a product at the price published on the list. This is to comply with the legislation and to avoid complaints.

When describing drinks to customers, it is important that you give accurate product-specific information. A customer may need to know specific details about the products – for example, the alcoholic content of a drink because they are driving or whether the drink contains an ingredient they are allergic to.

The Weights and Measures Act

The quantity of each type of drink served is governed by the Weights and Measures Act. This act is intended to protect customers' interests and to standardise the measurement of alcohol across the country. It also helps in determining prices and managing stock control.

A Weights and Measures notice must be displayed in a prominent position for customers to see the measures used for the prices charged.

> **Definition**
>
> **Alcohol by volume (ABV)** means the proportion of the total volume of a drink that is alcohol. It is written as a percentage, for example '11% alcohol'. The higher the number, the more alcohol is present, and the stronger the drink is.

Figure 14.1 You must inform the customer if the brand you stock is different from the brand they request

Type of drink	Legal measures
Spirits, including gin, whisky, vodka and rum	25 ml or 35 ml
Aperitifs and fortified wines	50 ml
Wine by the glass	125 ml/175 ml, or multiples of
Wine by the carafe	25 cl, 50 cl, 75 cl or 1 litre.

Figure 14.2 The legal measures for spirits, aperitifs and wines

Measures of spirits

The Weights and Measures notice will state the legal measure to be used for the sale of spirits. All spirits served must be in the stated measure or multiples of the measure. For example, a double whisky is two measures.

It is an offence for the licence holder or their staff to serve incorrect measures. Many bars use optics to dispense spirits – these ensure that the correct measure is being used. Thimble measures are sometimes used. These need to be filled to the top and carefully poured into the glass.

The Weights and Measures notice refers to the measure used for the service of gin, whisky, vodka and rum in the establishment.

Remember!
Any spillage of drink measured is short-changing your customer.

Mixed drinks and cocktails

A mixed drink is any drink made from at least two or more liquids (e.g. shandy). The Weights and Measures Act does not apply to mixed drinks.

Figure 14.3 25 ml and 50 ml measures. Can you remember what drinks these are used for?

Figure 14.4 An optic automatically fills to the correct measure after each measure is drawn out

Taking drinks orders at the table

As soon as your customers are seated at the table, the drinks waiter may need to link with the host. Here are some tips on how to recognise the host.

○ If a table has been booked it is usually in the host's name.

○ The host arrives ahead of his guests to greet them.

○ The host may meet with the waiter to discuss and arrange the drinks service before the guests arrive.

○ The host may introduce the guests to one another.

○ The host is the organiser of the occasion and will make sure the guests receive good service.

○ The host is the person who will settle the bill.

> **Remember!**
> The host may be male or female!

Presentation of drinks lists

Before presenting the drinks list to the customer, check that it is clean, presentable and accurate. Present the drinks lists as well as any special offers and promotions to the host. Allow your customers enough time to select their drinks. If nuts or nibbles are offered, place them on the table. The timing and pace of the service will vary from customer to customer. For example: some customers may prefer to wait for all their party to arrive before ordering drinks. Others may want to wait until they have ordered food before ordering drinks. Others may be limited for time, by their lunch hour, parking tickets, etc.

Drinks orders taken at the table can be recorded electronically or manually. Listen carefully to the order given. It is a good idea to make a note of who ordered which drink. This will help you when you serve the drinks to your customers.

> **Try this!**
> **Give each guest a number and place the drink ordered next to the numbered guest. In this way you will not forget who ordered what, and your guests will be impressed by your excellent service.**

When taking the order you should always try to maximise sales by upselling – for example, suggest a 175 ml wine by the glass instead of 125 ml. Suggest and promote special offers and cocktails by providing correct descriptions of the drinks. As your customers order their drinks, you should offer and confirm any accompaniments. For example, "Would you like ice and lemon with your gin?"

Make sure you clarify exactly what the customer wants. For example, if a sherry is ordered, ask, "Would you like dry, medium or sweet?". When you read back the order, you must read it exactly as requested. If a customer asked for a Bells whisky, then you must read back the order as "one Bell's whisky" not just "one whisky". If a Bells whisky cannot be served, you should offer an alternative brand instead. If the customer just requests a whisky, then any brand can be served, though you may like to check with the customer that they are happy with your selection.

When everyone at the table has ordered, repeat back the complete order to confirm that everything is correct. This is important to avoid mistakes which could affect the customer's satisfaction and reduce profits.

If you are taking the order manually, make sure you include the table number, the number of covers, the date and your name before giving a copy to the barperson. If you are recording the order electronically, check the order through the display option, adjust if required and send.

> **Remember!**
> When you have to offer substitute stock, remember to inform the customer at the point of ordering. Under the Trade Descriptions Act, it is illegal to substitute the brand of drink ordered without the permission of the customer.

Taking orders at the bar

Orders taken at the bar are usually made directly by the customer and are served at the bar. Bar orders are not written on drink order pads unless they are for hotel guests who wish to charge the order to their room bill. In this case, the guests must sign the written order and it will be manually or electronically booked to the room number.

Order of serving at the bar

Customers at the bar need to be served in the order of arrival, unless they indicate they are waiting for others to arrive. If you make a point of greeting each customer, it helps you to remember the order of arrival. Stick to serving the customers in order. If someone tries to jump the queue, you should say politely that another person is next

Figure 14.5 Check that the customer is happy with the brand of spirits served

and that you will serve them as quickly as possible. If you forget who is next, you could just ask politely, "Who is next please?"

Recording the order

Listen carefully to the order given to prevent mistakes and delays to service. If necessary ask the customer to repeat the order. If the order given is vague, for example "a Martini", you will need to confirm whether the customer wants a sweet, dry or martini cocktail. Repeat the order back to the customer to make sure you have taken the order correctly.

If the customer is undecided on part of an order, you could start preparing the order and allow the customer time to choose. If the customer is still undecided, use your selling skills and product knowledge to promote and suggest something.

Regular customers

Regular customers expect to be recognised and to enjoy a personalised service, such as when they order "the usual". However, you should not serve "the usual" automatically, but only if requested – the customer may want something different on some occasions.

Taking large orders

Taking a large order can be complicated and it can be helpful to write down the order. You should always confirm the order to avoid delays and wastage.

Figure 14.6 Always write down and confirm a large order

Dealing with unexpected incidents

Staff training should include how to deal with the unexpected. The service industry is complex and events often occur which are out of the staff's control. Most of the time your supervisor will deal with any problems. However, you need to be able to recognise whether a problem is something you can deal with yourself or whether it is something to escalate to your supervisor or manager. If you are in any doubt, you should tell your supervisor or manager. If security is available on site, alert them as well.

How to recognise and deal with a drunken customer

When a customer is very drunk there are usually some obvious signs. They may become aggressive, they may talk a lot, their speech may be slurred and they may be unsteady on their feet.

If you see a customer displaying these signs of drunkenness, you should inform your manager immediately. Stop drink service to the drunken customer, although you can still offer to serve food. You should also stop service of alcohol to any associate of the drunken customer if you think they are buying the drink for the intoxicated customer.

You should offer to call a taxi or suggest that the drunken person's friends arrange to get him or her home. On no account should you let the drunken customer drive. Most of the time it is possible for a senior member of staff to handle this, but there are occasions when you may need to call the police to assist.

How to deal with a violent, disorderly customer

In this situation, the highest priority is to ensure the safety of staff and customers. You should inform your supervisor or manager at once and also seek assistance from security or the police if necessary. Listen to the customer and remain polite. Stay calm and act as normally as possible. Do not react to the situation by becoming angry yourself.

How to deal with a non-complying smoker

If a customer is smoking in a non-smoking area you need to deal with this, as it is illegal and could cause offence to other customers. Your organisation should have "No Smoking" signs in place. Point these out and explain to the customer the smoke-free regulations which came into force in July 2007. Show them where the designated smoking area can be found and ask them politely to move to this area if they wish to smoke. If the customer refuses to comply with your request, you could call your local compliance police number for assistance.

How to recognise and deal with drugs trading

Signs that trading of drugs may be taking place include:

○ frequent trips to toilets or hidden corners
○ customers behaving oddly
○ regular change of customers
○ increased sales of water
○ customers who make little eye contact.

If you have any suspicions, inform your supervisor or manager. Keep control of the situation until your manager arrives. Call the police if necessary.

Recording of incidents or accidents

If you are working behind a bar, you should be trained to notice and report unusual situations whilst offering a high standard of drinks service. To comply with health and safety regulations, any incident or accident must be recorded in the incident or accident book. This should be done immediately after the event in order to gather evidence from any witnesses. The record should cover the following information:

○ the day, date, time and detailed location of the incident
○ customer details if any customers are involved
○ a description of the sequence of events
○ any action taken and by whom it was taken
○ any treatment given
○ staff and witness details.

The report should be signed and dated by the manager, the staff involved and any witnesses. The recording formally documents the problem for future reference or if there is an insurance claim or problem. It also records any specific accidents or incidents that may be occurring regularly. This means that management will be aware of the problem and can take action to correct it.

Test yourself!

1 List the legal measures for: spirits, wine, draught beer, fortified wine and cocktails.

2 Why must the information on the drinks list be accurate?

3 Why is it important to repeat back the customer's order?

4 When should you refuse to serve alcohol?

5 How should you deal with a drunken customer?

Serve alcoholic and non-alcoholic drinks

Preparing to serve drinks

Drinks should be prepared and served to a set standard for customer satisfaction and cost control. This set standard will be described in the drink service standards manual within your organisation.

Find out!

Where is the drink service standards manual kept in your organisation? It may be behind the bar.

For each drink offered on the special offers, promotions or drinks list, you will need to carry out the correct preparation before service. This includes making sure that there are sufficient quantities of the correct kind of glass, as well as any ingredients, garnishes and decorative items. The quantities you prepare should be enough for business levels and any customers' special requests.

Drink storage units and chillers

Drink storage units should be checked to ensure that they are in working order and at the correct temperature before service. Correct any problems if needed to ensure a quality drinks service to all customers.

Glassware

Check all glassware for quantity and type in line with the drink lists. It should also be checked to ensure that it is damage free and is clean and sparkling. Glassware should be stored ready to use. For cocktail service, chill glassware if appropriate. Some glassware may need frosting before service. Brandy balloon glasses should be warmed ready for service.

Marcus says

I would expect this area to be as clean and tidy as my kitchen. Glasses are easily broken – only carry as many as you safely can. Remember to keep your fridges well stocked: if you have to bring extra from the store room during service then they are unlikely to be at the correct temperature. Remember to put the new ones at the back of the fridge.

Glass	Image	Drinks
12 fl oz (360 ml) Worthington		Canned and bottled beer, cider, squash, cordial, etc.
2 fl oz (60 ml) Paris goblet		Liqueurs, port
Brandy balloon		After dinner brandy
Pilsner		Canned and bottled lager
Red wine		Red wine sold by the glass or bottle
White wine		White wine sold by the glass or bottle
Hock (brown stem) Mosel (green stem)		German Hock/Mosel as available
6½ fl oz (190 ml) Paris goblet		Water, spirits (single measure) Vermouth (short), mineral waters
8 fl oz (230 ml) Slim Jim		Fruit juice, cocktails
10 fl oz (280 ml) Slim Jim		Carbonated drinks (cola etc.), cocktails, spirits (double measure) Vermouth (long)
Tulip		Champagne, sparkling wine, cocktails
Cocktail		Short cocktails, e.g. dry martini
Copita		Sherry
Saucer		Perry

Figure 14.7 Types of glassware

Ingredients

All ingredients should be stored at the correct temperature. For special offers and promotions, some ingredients may be placed next to the appropriate glassware. This speeds up the service.

Garnishes

Prepare the appropriate garnishes for all the drinks on offer. Prepared garnishes need storing correctly before service. For example, cut oranges and lemons should be covered and stored in the refrigerator.

Ice

Place ice in an ice container ready for service. Check that there is enough ice available, especially for cocktail service. Check that ice tongs and an ice scoop are available.

Decorative items

Decorative items must be prepared in sufficient quantity and stored near the relevant drink ingredients.

Trays

Trays should be neatly stacked and lined if required, ready for table service of drinks and for clearing the bar area.

Water jugs

Prepare ready for service and store at the correct temperature.

Prepare till

Before service, check the till rolls and printers and replace them as necessary. Count the float and divide the notes and coin types into the correct sections of the till. The till must be secured from unauthorised access until service starts.

Serving drinks

The bar staff need to provide high standards of drinks for service at table or for bar service. The standard and content of the drink served should always be exactly the same, regardless of service style. However, the prices may differ due to additional service levels.

At the bar

At the bar the customers are able to watch every action of the barperson. This means that you should pay particular attention to hygiene and constantly clear the area as you go.

The bar is often the customers' social meeting place. Customers expect the bar staff to be interested in their conversations as well as concentrate on serving the drinks ordered. For bar service the drink ordered is served and the bill is settled either by cash or card. For card transactions, the card can sometimes be retained until the customer has completed all his or her purchases.

Regular customers

Regular customers sometimes have their order served in their own drinking glass. This glass is stored at the bar. It must meet all hygiene regulations as for any glassware used in your establishment. If the glass provided is not the usual size, the drink should be first measured in a standard glass and then transferred into the customer's own glass.

Multi-drink orders

A customer's order may cover a whole range of drinks. Drinks should be dispensed in a certain order to maintain the quality of the drinks ordered.
○ First, serve drinks such as squashes, juices, spirits and glasses of still wine.
○ Next, serve drinks that lose their head such as beer.
○ Finally, serve drinks such as lager, champagne, sparkling wines and cocktails. This is to retain the quality of the drink, such as the temperature, bubbles, head and to ensure that cocktails do not separate.

If the order is large and covers the range of drinks on offer, serve four or five drinks at a time and then repeat the process until the order is complete. This will reduce mistakes, provide quality drinks and speed the drinks service.

The running total price of the drinks should be visible to the customer so that he or she is aware of the amount to be charged.

Service of bottled wine

Bottles of wine ordered at the bar should have the cork removed at the bar. To do this, you could use a cork extractor clamped to the bar counter or a corkscrew. Fill the required number of glasses at the bar. Any left over wine in the bottle can be kept at the bar at the correct temperature or the customers may prefer to take the bottle to their table.

Table service

The drinks order is prepared by the bar staff. Drinks for table service will be poured at the bar, away from the table. Prepared drinks should be served straight away to offer a quality drinks service. The order is placed on a tray and carried to the table by the waiter. The tray can be anti-slip, but if a standard tray is used line it with a napkin to reduce the movement of glasses and to absorb spillages.

Once at the table, the waiter serves the prepared drinks by holding each glass by the stem or near the base and placing it to the right of the customer. Ladies should be served first, then the men and finally the host. If a drink has a mixer with it, such as a gin and tonic, it is usual to pour the mixer into the drink at the table. This is so the spirit is diluted to the drinker's taste. The remainder of the mixer remains in the bottle on the table.

Wine service at table

The bar staff issue glasses if glassware is not already on the table. The wine ordered must be served at the correct temperature. Bottles of wine are served and opened at the table by the waiter. The bottle is presented to the host with the label uppermost for the host to agree it is the wine ordered. The waiter removes the cork and provides a taster for the host. If the host approves the wine, ladies are served next, followed by gentlemen and finally the host.

The waiter should return to the table to refill wine glasses or clear empty glasses and take further orders. The bill for the drinks can be presented at the time of service or at a later stage. If drinks are to be charged to a hotel room, then a customer signature will be required.

Additional drinks

As soon as the glasses are empty, they should be removed to be cleaned. Ask the customer if they would like more drinks. If so, take the new order.

Types of drinks

Alcoholic and soft drinks can be divided into these six categories:

- aperitifs
- spirits
- liqueurs
- beer, cider, perry
- wine
- minerals.

Aperitifs

Aperitifs are alcoholic drinks offered before a meal to whet (or sharpen) the appetite. Most aperitifs contain aromatic herbs to stimulate the palate. These drinks can be spirit-based – for example, Campari – or wine-based – for example, vermouths such as dry martini. A vermouth is a wine which is flavoured with herbs and other ingredients. Flavourings used are orange and lemon peel, quinine, cloves, coriander, liquorice and other roots and flowers.

Digestifs

Digestifs are liqueurs or spirits consumed at the end of a meal to help you to digest your meal, although there is no proven evidence that this is the case. Examples are Drambuie, Cointreau, crème de menthe, cognac, Armagnac, Calvados, grappa, eau de vie. Digestifs are served neat, or possibly with ice.

Spirits

Spirits are drinks of high alcoholic strength made by **distillation** – for example, whisky, gin, vodka and rum. They can be served neat or with a mixer for a long drink. The legal measures for spirits are 25 ml or 35 ml measured by optic.

There are three main methods of distilling spirits:

Remember!
No order means no drinks.
No order means no money.

Did you know?
Sherry is produced in Spain and only Spanish sherry can be sold as "sherry".

Remember!
With a drinks tray full of different sherries, the colour will tell you which is dry, medium or sweet.

Definition
Neat – if a drink is served neat, it has nothing mixed with it.

Remember!
The stronger the alcoholic drink the smaller the measure.

Definition
Distillation: the separation of alcohol from a fermented beverage by a process of heating, evaporation and condensation.

The pot still

The copper **still** is filled with fermented beverage and heated so that the alcohol **evaporates**. The vapour rises to the top of the still where it cools again, **condenses** and is collected in a separate vessel. This process does not produce pure alcohol but retains about 30–40% of the original beverage and therefore its flavour. Scottish and Irish malt whisk(e)y, French cognac brandy, French Calvados and West Indian rums are all pot-stilled spirits. All pot-stilled spirits are aged in wooden casks, mainly oak. This allows the spirit to mellow, take on the oak's flavours and turn a golden brown colour. Approximately one third of the alcohol evaporates during the aging process. The lost spirit is known as 'the angel's share'!

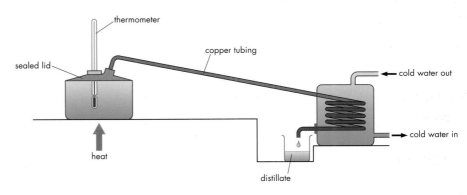

Figure 14.8 The pot still

The advantage of this type of still is that the flavour of the fermented beverage is retained. The disadvantage is that it is a labour-intensive process and may require more than one distillation depending on how pure the alcohol is required to be. Also the alcohol content in the final product is lower.

> **Definition**
>
> **Condensation:** The process by which a gas becomes a liquid when cooled.
> **Evaporation:** The process by which a liquid turns into a gas when heated.
> **Still:** The vessel used in the process of distilling alcohol.

The continuous or column still (also known as the Coffey still)

This type of still consists of two columns. In one column is a series of pipes and in the other a series of perforated and solid plates. The cold fermented beverage is fed through the pipes in the first column and high pressure steam is fed into the base of the column. The steam heats the beverage converting it into water and alcohol vapours. These vapours rise and flow into the second column where they condense back into water and alcohol. The perforated plates in the second column allow the water to fall back to the base whereas the drinkable alcohol is

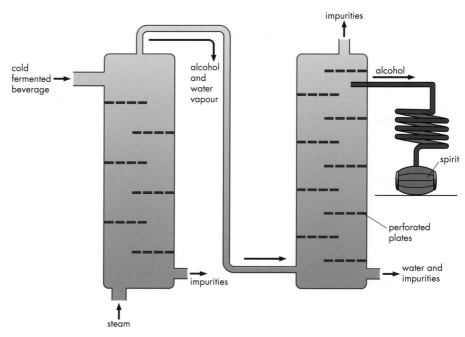

Figure 14.9 The column still

collected when it condenses on the solid plates. By adjusting the plates the distiller can produce pure alcohol.

The advantage of this type of still is that it is automatic and it can produce 100% alcohol. A disadvantage is that the flavour of the fermented beverage is lost, so flavourings need to be added.

The alembic Armagnaçais still

This is a cross between the pot still and the continuous still. It distils to an alcoholic strength between the two so that the distillate is stronger in alcohol but still retains some of the fermented beverage's original flavour.

Brandy

Cognac

Cognac is made from wine distilled in a copper still and aged in oak casks. A cognac is made from a blend of brandies from a single distillery. Quality is measured by the minimum age of the youngest brandy in the blend.

Cognac ages	
*** (Trois Etoiles)	youngest 4½ years
VS	youngest 4½ years
VSOP	4½ to 6½ years
Réserve	4½ to 6½ years
XO	youngest 6½ years
Hors d'Age	youngest 6½ years
Napoléon	youngest 6½ years

Armagnac

Armagnac is made from wine distilled in an alembic Armagnaçais still and traditionally sold in flask-shaped bottles. An Armagnac is a blend of brandies from a single distillery or a vintage brandy from a single year. Quality is measured in a similar way to cognac.

Grape brandies

In France, grape brandy is called marc. Marc is made from wine produced from the residue from wine fermentation, distilled in an alembic still and aged in oak casks for 3 to 5 years (a few for much longer). Marc is usually tempered to 40% abv.

Whisky

Whisky is the distillation of a fermented beverage made from malted cereals, water and yeast.

Scottish malt whisky

This is produced in a pot still from a single distillery, the fermented beverage being made from malted barley, Scottish spring water and yeast. The distilled whisky is clear and 70% abv. It is matured in oak casks for a minimum of 5 years for blending, and a minimum of 8 years for bottling whiskies. Malt whiskies are blended before bottling with whiskies from a number of years. The youngest whisky used in the blend will be the age used on the bottle label. Prior to bottling, the whisky is mixed with water to a selling strength of 40% to 45% abv. There are four malt whisky regions as follows:

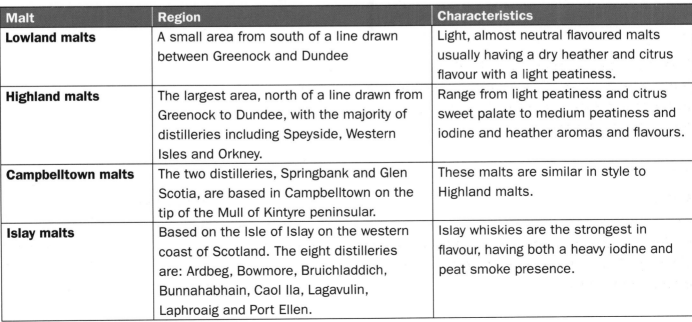

Did you know?
Other grape brandies are: grappa (Italy), bagaceira (Portugal), aguardiente (Spain) and pisco (South America).

Did you know?
Whisky is a spelling used only for whiskies from Scotland and Canada. *Whiskey* is the spelling used for whiskies from Ireland and any other source country.

Malt	Region	Characteristics
Lowland malts	A small area from south of a line drawn between Greenock and Dundee	Light, almost neutral flavoured malts usually having a dry heather and citrus flavour with a light peatiness.
Highland malts	The largest area, north of a line drawn from Greenock to Dundee, with the majority of distilleries including Speyside, Western Isles and Orkney.	Range from light peatiness and citrus sweet palate to medium peatiness and iodine and heather aromas and flavours.
Campbelltown malts	The two distilleries, Springbank and Glen Scotia, are based in Campbelltown on the tip of the Mull of Kintyre peninsular.	These malts are similar in style to Highland malts.
Islay malts	Based on the Isle of Islay on the western coast of Scotland. The eight distilleries are: Ardbeg, Bowmore, Bruichladdich, Bunnahabhain, Caol Ila, Lagavulin, Laphroaig and Port Ellen.	Islay whiskies are the strongest in flavour, having both a heavy iodine and peat smoke presence.

Blended malts

These are blends of malt whisky from different distilleries and are produced by large distillery companies. They are sold under brand names (often fictitious distillery names).

Scottish grain whisky

This is a whisky produced from an alcoholic beverage fermented from malted grains and distilled in a continuous still. The spirit is coloured with caramel and used in blended scotch whiskies. There is one distillery (Old Cameron Brig) that produces a single straight grain whisky which is cask-matured.

Blended Scotch whisky

This is a blended whisky using malt whiskies and grain whiskies and is the bulk of whisky produced in Scotland (Bell's, Famous Grouse, White Horse, Haig and Ballantine are some of the major brands). The standard blend has a higher proportion of grain whisky (30% to 40%) whilst the de luxe blends have a higher proportion of malts (50% to 60%). De luxe blends have a more peaty flavour and richer body.

Irish whiskey

Irish whiskey is produced from malted grain in pot-stills but is triple-distilled. Cask aged, it has a smooth, soft, sweetish flavour. Ireland also produces blended whiskies (malts and grain).

Canadian whisky

These whiskies are produced from malted rye grain but can be made from other cereals. Pot-stilled and cask matured, they are much smoother and milder than Scottish malt whiskies.

American bourbon whiskey

This whiskey is produced from corn (minimum 51%) and other cereals. Most bourbon sold today, however, contains 65% corn and is aged for a minimum of four years. Bourbon whiskey has a smooth, slightly smoky aroma and flavour. America also produces a range of other whiskies including: rye whiskey, Tennessee whiskey, corn whiskey and sour mash whiskey.

> **Remember!**
> By law, pot-stilled spirits must be aged for a minimum of 3 years before sale, whilst continuous-stilled spirits need only one year.

Liqueurs

A liqueur is a sweetened alcoholic beverage made either from distilled fruit-based wines, passing alcoholic vapours through botanicals (herbs) or by flavouring base spirits. Whilst most liqueurs are sweet, a small number also produce a drier version (for example: Grand Marnier and chartreuse). Some liqueur producers are now producing a range of styles/flavours (for example: sambuca and Malibu). Liqueurs have an alcoholic strength by volume of between 23% and 49% (cream-based liqueurs can be as low as 17%). There are numerous liqueurs on the market and new brands are introduced quite frequently.

The list below is of the main liqueurs and spirits.

Name (colour/taste)	Base spirit	Main flavour
Akvavit (clear/dry)	neutral spirit	aromatic seeds
Advocaat (yellow/half-sweet)	brandy	egg yolks, vanilla
Bailey's cream (white/sweet)	Irish whiskey	whiskey, cream
Bénédictine (green/sweet)	neutral spirit	herbs
Calvados (brown/dry)	apple brandy	apples
Chartreuse (green/sweet)	brandy	herbs
Cointreau (clear/sweet)	fruit spirit	oranges
Crème de menthe (green/sweet)	neutral spirit	spearmint
Drambuie (brown/sweet)	whisky	heather, honey, herbs
Eau de vie (clear/dry/sweet)	fruit spirit	named fruit flavour
Gin (clear/dry)	neutral spirit	botanicals
Glayva (brown/sweet)	whisky	herbs, spices
Grand Marnier (orange-brown/sweet)	cognac brandy	oranges
Kahlúa (brown/sweet)	tequila	coffee
Kirsch (clear/sweet)	Eau de vie	cherries
Malibu (clear/sweet)	white rum	coconut
Marc brandy (brown/dry)	grape brandy	grape
Sambuca (yellow-green/sweet)	grappa	elder, liquorice
Schnapps (clear/dry)	neutral spirit	plain and flavoured
Slivovitz (clear-pale gold/dry)	plum spirit	plums
Strega (yellow-green/sweet)	grappa	herbs
Tequila (clear/dry)	agave spirit	agave cactus
Tia Maria (brown/sweet)	rum	coffee
Vieille Curé (green/sweet)	neutral spirit	herbs
Vodka (clear/dry)	neutral spirit	plain and flavoured

Beer, cider and perry

Beer

Beer is the fermentation of malted grain, water, hops and brewer's yeast. British beers (known as ales) are made with malted barley. The process of making beer is called brewing.

The brewing process

Malted grain is milled (crushed) and mixed with hot water to extract the malt sugars. Invert sugar and caramel colouring are sometimes added. The resulting liquid is known as the **wort**.

↓

The wort is transferred to a boiler known as the **copper** or **lauter tun**. Dry hops are added and the **hopped wort** is boiled to extract the hop essences and destroy any enzymes present.

↓

The hopped wort is strained and cooled then transferred into large **fermentation** tanks. Brewer's yeast is added and fermentation takes place.

↓

Once the alcohol content has reached the required strength by volume (between 4% and 5% for most ales and lagers), the beer is filtered and stored at 0°C for **conditioning**.

↓

After conditioning, the beer is fine filtered and/or pasteurised (if it is a keg beer) or lightly filtered (if it is a cask-conditioned ale).

Cask ales

These ales are only lightly filtered after conditioning and then placed into casks. A small amount of yeast, dry hops, invert sugar and **finings** are added (known as *primings*) and the cask is sealed. The casks are **tapped** at the point of sale and allowed to produce a secondary fermentation. This produces a natural carbonation which can be controlled by the publican/cellarman. This process is known as *cask-conditioning* and when the ale is fine and bright it is ready to serve. Many cask-conditioned ales are now conditioned at the brewery and are ready for sale on delivery.

Did you know?

There are two types of brewers yeast:

○ top-fermenting yeasts for ales

○ bottom-fermenting yeasts for lagers.

Definitions

Finings – substance used to clarify beer or wine.

Tapping – a steel or brass tap is driven into the bung at the end of the barrel.

Keg ales

Keg ale is ultra-fine filtered to remove all traces of yeast, and is often pasteurised. It is then placed into metal kegs and delivered to the bar ready to drink. The beer is delivered into the glass by gas pressure in the keg pushing the beer to the pub/bar beer dispense tap.

Types of beer

Beer	Method of sale	Characteristics	ABV	How to serve
Ales	Cask-conditioned, keg, bottled pale ales, bottled Indian pale ales (IPA), brown ales and stout.	Dark colour. Bitter, sweet, malty flavour. Stouts can be either bitter or sweet.		Serve in 'sleeve-style' glasses at a cool temperature but never iced.
Lager	Draught, keg or bottled.	Mild flavour and pale colour.		Traditionally served ice cool in tall, slender glasses.
Belgian Trappiste beers	Draught or bottled.	Light brown (*blonde*) to dark brown (*brune*).	5.7%–12%	Serve at cellar temperature in squat, round glasses with celery sticks, cheese and salt.

Beer faults

Fault	Cause	Solution
Fobbing (beer comes out of pump as foam)	CO_2 left on during closing hours. Yeast deposit in pipes. Drop in atmospheric pressure.	Switch off CO_2 at night. Clean beer lines at least once a week. Always turn beer tap fully open.
Cloudiness in bottled beers	Some bottled-conditioned beers have a sediment at the base of the bottle.	Pour beer carefully, leaving sediment in bottom of bottle.
Cloudiness in keg and cask beers	Dirty pipes. Beer is too cold. Jerky pulling at pump which forces beer back into cask disturbing sediment.	Clean lines immediately. Raise cask temperature. If cask is half full, return any beer in the line to the cask and remove the cask from the line. Allow the beer to settle 24–48 hours before use.
Flat beer	Beer is too cold. Glass is greasy or has detergent deposits on it. Loss of gas in cask-conditioned ales. This can be caused by a soft spile being left in overnight, leaking connections, or the cask not being primed sufficiently.	Raise beer temperature. Always check glasses are clean. Always use hard spile at night. Check connections regularly.
Sour beer	Beer is past its use-by date. Check use by dates. Build-up of bacteria or wild yeasts in the dispensing system.	Clean beer lines regularly.

For more information on problems with beer and how to avoid and/ or solve them, see Chapter 16.

Cider

Cider is the natural fermentation of apple juice. The apples (cider apples for acidity and sweet varieties to aid fermentation) are chopped, placed between mats and then pressed to extract the juice. Cultured yeast is often added to produce an even fermentation. After fermentation, the cider is filtered and conditioned as for beers. The styles of cider are:

Types of cider

Type	Characteristics	ABV	How to serve
Draught cider, also known as scrumpy	Only slightly carbonated. Cloudy appearance. Local to cider producing areas such the West Country and Herefordshire.	6–8%	Often served from the cask at the bar from the cask's tap.
Keg cider	Clear and sparkling.	5%	It is delivered to the bar from the cellar using gas pressure.
Bottled ciders	Carbonated. Sweet ciders tend to have a darker colour, dry ones are paler.	Sweet: 2–4% Medium: 4–6% Dry: 6–8%	Range of bottle sizes.
Canned cider	Most keg ciders are also canned. They are charged with gas before canning.	5%	
French ciders	Produced mainly in north-western France. Bottled like sparkling wines with a cork and wire cage. Tend to have less CO_2 gas than British ciders.	Sweet: 2–4% Medium: 4–6% Dry: 6–8%	Traditionally served in earthenware cups.
Non-alcoholic/ low alcohol cider	Fermented ciders that have had the alcohol removed. They are sweet and carbonated.	0% or 0.05%.	

Perry

Perry is the natural fermentation of pear juice. It is made in the same way as cider. Perry was very much a local drink in the past but was made famous by the Showerings Company creating Babycham™, a sparkling perry that was marketed at young female drinkers in the 1960s and 1970s. Perry is now becoming more popular in the drinks market as an alternative to cider.

> **Did you know?**
> To check whether beer is too cold, swish a small amount round in your mouth. If there is a surge of gas released then it is too cold.

> **Did you know?**
> Most large scale cider and perry production is now done using automatic presses that cut the fruit and press it continuously.

Wine

Wine comes in many forms, including red, white, rosé, sparkling and still.

The measures for wine sold by the glass are 125 ml, 175 ml and 250 ml. Wine should be served at the right temperature, as follows.

○ Red wines are usually served at room temperature, 17–20°C, although some may be served chilled.
○ Rosé and white wines should be served cool at 10°C.
○ Sparkling and sweet white wines should be served chilled at 7–8°C.

Wine sold by the bottle for service at the table should be served correctly, as follows.

1 Change glasses if applicable, depending on the type of wine ordered.
2 Present the bottle to confirm the customer's choice.
3 Remove the foil and then the cork.
4 Check the cork.
5 Pour a small amount into a glass and offer to the host.
6 If accepted, serve all the guests first.
7 Serve the host last.
8 Refill wine glasses as required.

You can find much more in-depth information about wines and how they should be stored and served in Chapter 15.

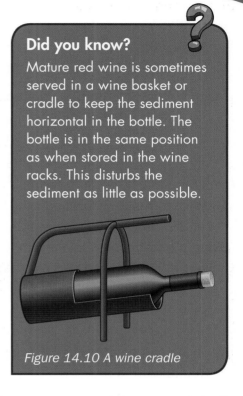

Did you know?

Mature red wine is sometimes served in a wine basket or cradle to keep the sediment horizontal in the bottle. The bottle is in the same position as when stored in the wine racks. This disturbs the sediment as little as possible.

Figure 14.10 A wine cradle

Fortified wines

Fortified wines are wines where the natural alcohol content has been increased by the addition of a spirit, usually brandy, taking the alcoholic content to between 18 and 22%. Fortified wines include sherry, port, madeira and marsala. They can be served either at the beginning of the meal as an aperitif, or as an accompaniment to food (e.g. port served with cheese), or at the end of a meal.

Sherry is produced in Spain. Dry, medium and sweet sherry are all popular in the UK. Sherry is made using a system called *solera* whereby young wine is blended with older wines, taking on the characteristics of the older wine, helping to ensure consistent quality of the end product.

Port comes from Portugal. Dry, semi-dry and white versions are available. It is fortified with a neutral grape spirit called 'aqua dente' that stops fermentation, leaving natural sugar in the wine and also increasing the alcoholic content. It is aged in barrels before bottling. Vintage port is made from a single year's grape production.

Madeira comes from the island of Madeira. It ranges in flavour from dry to sweet. It is made by adding a grape spirit to wine, but the unique part of making madeira involves heating up the wine to 60°C for various lengths of time. This unique process produces the robust characteristics of madeira.

Marsala is a sweet fortified wine, of relatively low strength (17–18%) produced in Sicily. It is made by adding brandy to wine, using the traditional solera method as for sherry. It can be served chilled with cheese, as an alternative to port.

Minerals

Minerals can be classified as:
- fruit juices
- squashes and cordials
- aerated waters
- natural mineral waters.

Juices

Fresh fruit juice requires a fruit press or squeezer to extract the juice efficiently. Fruit juice can be bottled, canned or in cartons and in all cases requires shaking before opening.

Squashes and cordials

Squashes are fruit-based drinks, which are diluted with iced water or soda water to provide a long, cool drink.

Aerated waters

Aerated waters or artificial mineral waters consist of flavoured water which is carbonated to produce a fizzy drink. Examples are tonic water, bitter lemon, dry ginger, soda water, lemonade and cola drinks. They are usually clear except for bitter lemon. Aerated waters can be served on their own or as a "mixer" with other drinks.

Try this!

When serving cola, ask the customer if they would like lemon in their drink. If they would, put two slices of lemon into diet cola drinks to distinguish them from ordinary cola.

Find out!

What is the difference between ginger ale and ginger beer?

Natural mineral waters

Natural mineral waters are obtained from the ground and are bottled at source. They come from various countries around the world. The waters are named after their source of origin, for example: Malvern, Buxton, Evian, San Pellegrino. These waters naturally contain various minerals and can be still or sparkling. They are often drunk for health reasons. No ice (made from tap water) should be served in natural mineral waters but they should be served chilled to enhance their natural flavour.

Find out!

Where are the geographical locations of the natural mineral waters named in this section?

Non-alcoholic and low-alcohol drinks

Due to stringent drink-driving laws, non-alcoholic or low-alcohol versions of traditional alcoholic drinks such as wine, beer and lager have grown in popularity. Department of Trade and Industry rules apply when describing these drinks as follows:

○ Low alcohol means a drink with an abv of not more than 1.2%

○ De-alcoholised means a drink from which the alcohol has been extracted and which has an abv of not more than 0.5%. These tend to taste more like the 'original' drink.

○ Alcohol-free means a drink from which the alcohol has been extracted and which has an abv of no more than 0.05%.

Packaging

Bottles

Beer, cider and perry are sold in a variety of shapes, sizes and capacities. Half-pint and one pint bottles are used by the major breweries and Guinness for their bottled beers and are returnable for reuse. The 500 ml bottle is now becoming popular as breweries change over to metric sizes (especially for off-licence sales ranging from 275 mls to 568 mls). Most beers are now sold in off-licences using the 'stubby' bottle (in sizes ranging from 330 mls to 375 mls). These bottles are non-returnable. Newcastle Brown Ale is traditionally sold in 500 ml bottles. Barley wines (now known as 'Winter Warmers') are traditionally sold in one third-pint 'nips' bottles. Bottled alcoholic beverages are primed with CO_2 during bottling. Most bottled beverages have a shelf life of three to six months and will have the *best-before* date printed on the label.

NOTE: if a bottle is delivered in a moulded plastic crate with slots to hold each bottle, then the bottle will be a returnable bottle and a deposit will have been paid by the licensee. All of these bottles (including damaged and broken bottles) and the plastic crate must be returned to claim the credit for them.

PET Bottles

A moulded plastic bottle made from *polyethylene terephalate* (PET) is used for 2 pint quantities of beer, cider, perry and non-alcoholic beverages. They are non-returnable and are mainly sold from off-licence outlets. PET bottles are also used in metric sizes, the most popular being the one-litre bottle. PET bottled alcoholic beverages are primed with CO_2 during bottling. PET bottles are recyclable.

Cans

Cans are the most popular method of beer and cider packaging for off-licences and small licensed premises such as restaurants and cafés. Most cans hold 440 mls, some hold 500 mls. Canned beers are primed with CO_2 during canning but some brands (Guinness and premium ales) have a 'widget' fitted at the base of the can, containing a nitrogen/carbon dioxide mixture. The widget releases the gas into the beer when the seal on the can is broken, giving the beer are creamy 'head'. There are also large ten litre 'party' cans of beer available, mainly for lager. These have a *tap* that allows the beer to retain its gas once opened. All cans are recyclable.

Did you know?

All packaged beer, cider and perry must have the net contents of the container printed on the label or packaging. Most is in metric, but beer can be in imperial pints (unless for export). The country of origin, producer's name and alcohol by volume must also be printed.

Bag-in-Box

Whilst this method of packaging is mainly used for wines, large quantities of beer, in sizes ranging from 3 to 20 litres, are also sold for parties, using this type of packaging. The beer used is usually a traditional ale and is conditioned at the brewery prior to sale. Beer has a very short life in the bag.

Poly kegs

These are ridged plastic containers used for pre-ordered off-sales of large quantities of beer from the brewery. They usually contain keg beers for immediate consumption. The poly kegs are returnable and reusable. The sizes vary from 5 to 20 litres capacity.

Kegs

The most common way of selling beer and cider in 'draught' (bulk) form. Sold in both gallons and litres and lightly pressurised at the brewery, keg beers and ciders are ready for sale as soon as the CO_2 gas supply is attached at the point of sale. Kegged beverages have a shelf life of between two to three weeks depending on the temperature at which the kegs are stored. All kegs are returned to the brewery for reuse.

Casks

These days casks are made of aluminium. They have two holes: one for the tap and one for the shive (see page 492). The names and sizes are: **Pin**: 4.5 gallons / **Firkin**: 9 gallons / **Kilderkin** 18 gallons / **Barrel** 36 gallons / **Hogshead** 54 gallons. Some casks are now being produced in litre sizes. All casks should be sealed once empty to keep them fresh and returned to the brewery for reuse.

For more information on kegs and casks, see Chapter 16.

Types of drink

Drink	Glass	Measure	Garnish	Notes	Photo
Campari	$6\frac{2}{3}$ fl oz / 190 ml Paris goblet	25 ml or 35 ml measured by optic or thimble	Ice, orange slice. Can be served with soda water or orange juice.	Campari is an Italian spirit-based aperitif.	
Dry vermouth (dry martini)	$6\frac{2}{3}$ fl oz / 190 ml Paris goblet	50 ml measured by optic	Ice & slice of lemon.	Vermouth gets its name from the German for 'wormwood', which is 'Wermut'.	
Sherry	Copita	50 ml measured by thimble measure	Serve medium & sweet sherry at room temperature. Serve dry sherry chilled.	Sherry is classified as a fortified wine. Find out what it is strengthened with.	
Spirits	$6\frac{2}{3}$ fl oz / 190 ml Paris goblet Whisky tumbler	25 ml or 35 ml measured by optic	Ice & lemon for gin, vodka and Bacardi. Often served with a mixer – e.g. tonic, water or bitter lemon.	All types of whisky are served neat unless requested with ice, soda water, iced water or ginger ale.	
Cognac	Brandy balloon	25 ml or 35 ml thimble measure	None	Serve a double cognac in a larger brandy balloon so that the cognac is spread thinly in the glass. This allows the contents to be warmed by the customer's hand.	
Liqueurs	Elgin liqueur glass	25 ml thimble measure	None, except coffee bean for sambuca.		
Liqueur frappé	Copita	25 ml thimble measure	Crushed ice, short straws.	Fill glass with crushed ice before adding liqueur. Add 2 shortened straws.	

443

Drink	Glass	Measure	Garnish	Notes	Photo
Draught beer/lager	$\frac{1}{2}$ pint or 1 pint mug or tumbler	Measure by glass	None	The 'head' does not count as part of the ½ pint or 1 pint measure.	
Bottled beer/ canned beer	12 fl oz / 360 ml Worthington glass	Measure by can or bottle	None	To serve, start by pouring the beer down the side of the glass and then straighten the glass to give a "head". $\frac{1}{3}$ pint is the minimum legal quantity beer can be sold, e.g. barley wine.	
Lager	Pilsner glass	Measure by can or bottle or by glass for draught lager	None. For lager & lime add 25 ml lime cordial to the glass before adding lager.	To serve, start by pouring the lager down the side of glass and straighten glass to give a "head".	
Cider	$\frac{1}{2}$ pint or 1 pint mug or tumbler	Measure by can or bottle or by glass for draught cider	None	Cider is an alcoholic drink made from the fermentation of apple juice.	
Perry	Champagne saucer	Measure by bottle size	None	Perry is made from the fermentation of pear juice. An example is Babycham.	

Drink	Glass	Measure	Garnish	Notes	Photo
Champagne & sparkling wine	Tulip or flute	Measure by glass or bottle	None	For table service, present wine in ice bucket on stand or coaster. For service by glass, pour slowly into glass & serve. Reseal bottle with stopper.	
Red wine	Red wine glass	Measure by bottle poured	None	For table service, present red wine in a wine basket, with the label facing the customer.	
White or rosé wine	$6\frac{2}{3}$ fl oz / 190 ml Paris goblet	Measure by bottle poured	None	For table service, present wine in ice bucket on stand or coaster. Label facing customer as wine is being poured.	
Wine by glass	Wine glass – marked	Measure by glass (125 ml, 175 ml or 250 ml), by bottle pouring or by carton dispensed by tap	None	Serve white & rosé wine chilled. Serve red wine at room temperature. Pour wine to the line on the glass. Often poured from screw-top wine bottles. To open twist the screw top clockwise.	
De-alcoholised wine	Wine glass or Paris goblet	Measure by glass 125 ml, 175 ml or 250 ml or by bottle pouring	None	For table service, present wine in an ice bucket on stand or coaster.	

Drink	Glass	Measure	Garnish	Notes	Photo
Fruit juice	5 fl oz / 140 ml Club goblet	Measure by bottle or by glass, free poured	Slice of appropriate fruit	For fresh fruit juice service, add an under plate for the glass and a teaspoon and offer caster sugar.	
Squash or cordial	12 fl oz / 360 ml Worthington glass	2 × 50 ml	Ice, slice of fruit & 2 straws	Top up with iced water or soda water.	
Tonic water & bitter lemon	$6\frac{2}{3}$ fl oz / 190 ml Paris goblet	Measure by bottle, free poured	Ice & lemon	Aerated waters or artificial mineral waters are flavoured water which is carbonated to produce an effervescent drink. Serve chilled.	
Dry ginger Soda water	$6\frac{2}{3}$ fl oz / 190 ml Paris goblet	Measure by bottle, free poured	None	Aerated waters can be served on their own or as a mixer with other drinks. For example: dry ginger for brandy & ginger; soda water for whisky & soda.	
Lemonade or cola drinks	10 fl oz / 280 ml Slim Jim	Measure by can, bottle size or free poured	Ice & lemon slice	Serve chilled. Can be served as mixers, e.g.. Bacardi and cola; lime and lemonade	
Natural mineral waters	By glass: 8 fl oz / 230 ml Slim Jim By bottle: $6\frac{2}{3}$ fl oz / 190 ml Paris goblet	By glass, free poured By bottle, size of bottle	Slice of lemon offered No ice served	Serve chilled. If served at table, the bottle should be opened at the table and poured into Paris goblets.	

Note: some establishments have their own particular choice of glassware.

Test yourself!

1 What are the six categories of drink?

2 What would you suggest if a customer wanted to order a non-alcoholic drink?

3 What do you look for when checking glassware ready for service?

4 Why is it important to check all items to be prepared before drinks service?

Preparing and serving cocktails

A cocktail is classed as a mixed drink and as such the ingredients are not governed by the Weights and Measures Act.

The cocktail list should describe the ingredients and the alcoholic strength of each named cocktail. The price should also be listed. The cocktail list must meet all the requirements of the Trade Descriptions Act and not mislead the customer.

The cocktails offered should be prepared following the requirements of the drinks standards manual. This is necessary so that the contents of the cocktail and the taste are consistent. The customer also expects the description to represent the drink correctly and that includes the alcoholic content.

Customers may request a cocktail that is not on the cocktail list. Rather than disappoint your customers, ask your manager to assist in this special request.

> **Definition**
> **A cocktail** – a mixed drink prepared by shaking, stirring or pouring a number of ingredients together.

> **Try this!**
> When you are shown how to make a new cocktail, make a note of the name of the cocktail, the glass, the ingredients, and how it was made and garnished. This could provide good evidence for your portfolio.

Preparing areas and equipment for serving cocktails

For cocktail service there is a range of specialist equipment needed as well as the standard bar preparation.

Glassware

Glassware for cocktail service varies in shape and size according to the type of cocktail to be served. The glass is selected according to the size and mixture of the drink. Cocktails can be short or long drinks. For hygiene always hold a glass by the stem and make sure that all glassware is scrupulously clean and sparkling. Less than perfect glassware can spoil the quality as well as the look of the drink.

Chilling glasses

Most cocktails are served cold and taste better served ice cold. Chill glasses by filling them with ice cubes and soda water whilst preparing the cocktail. Empty the glass just before pouring the cocktail into it.

> **Try this!**
> **You could place the glass in the chiller unit if space allows.**

Glassware used for cocktail service

Brandy balloon (8 fl oz / 230 ml) – a short-stemmed balloon bowl glass, wide at the base and narrow at the rim. The shape allows for the aroma to be trapped and appreciated.

Champagne saucer (6 fl oz / 180 ml) – a stemmed glass with a wide saucer-shaped bowl. The shape allows excess bubbles from sparkling wines to escape.

Cocktail glass (5 fl oz / 140 ml) – designed especially for cocktail service, it has a long stem for ease of holding. The long stem ensures the drinker does not affect the temperature, quality and taste of the drink. The curved bowl adds style and character.

Collins (10 fl oz / 280 ml) – a tall straight-sided tumbler for those extra long cocktails, e.g. Zombies.

Highball (8 fl oz / 230 ml) – a tall straight-sided tumbler used for long cocktails, e.g. Cuba libre, punches or Pimms.

Lowball (5 fl oz / 140 ml) – a short tumbler with sloping sides used for Bloody Mary and similar drinks.

Martini glass (5 fl oz / 140 ml) – a stemmed glass with a V-shaped bowl. An elegant glass for classics such as martinis and daiquiri.

Old-fashioned (8 fl oz / 230 ml) – a tumbler with sloping sides, for Gibson and Americano.

Paris goblet ($6\frac{2}{3}$ fl oz / 190 ml) – a short-stemmed, round-bowled standard wine glass. Ideal for black velvet and prairie oyster.

Sour glass (5 fl oz / 140 ml) – a stemmed glass with a tall, slim bowl that curves in slightly at the rim allowing sparkling drinks to retain their effervescence for longer.

Equipment

Cocktail shaker

A cocktail shaker is made of stainless steel or silver in three sections:

- the base for ingredients
- a top with a built-in strainer which fits tightly over the base
- a cap which covers the top, allowing the cocktail to be shaken.

The strained cocktail is poured from the shaker into the appropriate glass.

Mixing glass

A mixing glass is used for stirred cocktails. It is a glass jug without a handle, but with a lip for pouring. It requires the use of a hawthorn strainer to strain the cocktail into the correct glass.

Hawthorn strainer

A hawthorn strainer is made of stainless steel or silver. It is a flat, short-handled strainer with a spring coiled on the exterior. This allows for tight fitting in the top of the mixing glass or glass section of a **Boston shaker**.

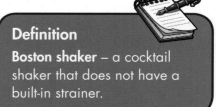

Definition

Boston shaker – a cocktail shaker that does not have a built-in strainer.

Bar spoon

A bar spoon is a spiralled, long handled teaspoon with a flat **muddler** end. The muddler is used for crushing sugar or mint as necessary.

Blender

A blender is used especially for drinks containing puréed fruits or for large quantities of a particular cocktail. A blender is used to crush ice for use in blended drinks.

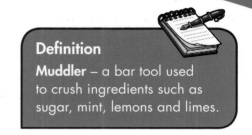

Definition

Muddler – a bar tool used to crush ingredients such as sugar, mint, lemons and limes.

Figure 14.11 Items of cocktail equipment

cocktail shaker

mixing glass

hawthorn strainer

bar spoon

blender

Measures or pourers

Measures used for cocktails are the 25 ml or 50 ml size. Measures quoted in recipes are often fractions of a measure. Measures quoted may be increased or decreased, but the ratio of the ingredients must remain constant to ensure that a standard drink is served and to allow for cost control.

Additional equipment

The following equipment should also be readily available in a truly professional cocktail bar:

- waiter's friend/corkscrew: for opening bottles
- bottle stopper: for sealing opened bottles of sparkling wine
- ice buckets: for storage of ice cubes – plentiful supply essential
- ice tongs: for hygienic dispensing of ice cubes
- ice scoop: for hygienic dispensing of large amounts of ice
- ice crusher: for easy preparation from ice cubes
- chopping board: for garnish preparation
- bar knife: for preparing garnishes, use the forked end for picking up garnishes

- canelle knife: for removing zest
- teaspoon: for measuring ingredients
- juice extractor: for fresh fruit preparation
- crown top opener: for removing bottle tops
- wine cooler: for champagne chilling
- glass cloths: fine linen for glass polishing
- bar mats: to absorb moisture and spillage from the bar top.

Remember!
For cocktail service you do not need to use full measures, as cocktails are classed as mixed drinks.

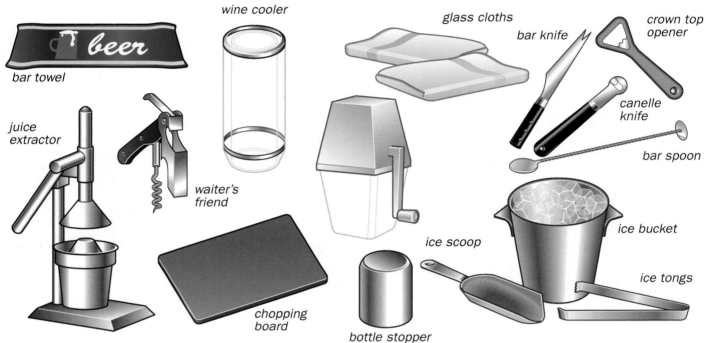

Figure 14.12 Essential equipment for the professional cocktail bar

Find out!
If you did not have an ice crusher, how else could you produce crushed ice hygienically?

Figure 14.13 Setting up the bar with the correct equipment will allow you to prepare cocktails more efficiently

Paper goods

Paper goods are used to enhance presentation of the cocktail:

○ swizzle stick: for stirring drinks
○ coasters: for placing underneath the cocktail glass
○ cocktail napkin: for the drinker's convenience
○ cocktail sticks: for presenting cocktail garnishes
○ straws: in assorted colours and lengths
○ parasols: for exotic, fun presentations.

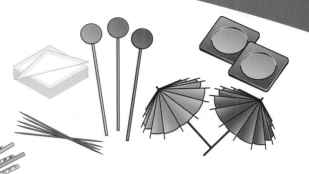

Figure 14.14 Paper goods used in cocktail service

Ingredients

Base ingredients

Most cocktails have as their base ingredient a spirit such as gin, vodka, rum or whisky or a wine or vermouth. Minerals can also be part of a cocktail or they can form the basis of the whole drink in the case of non-alcoholic cocktails.

Other ingredients

Many other ingredients are used in cocktails. Plentiful supplies of these should be on hand. In order to offer efficient service, all ingredients should be prepared before service and restocked frequently. The most commonly used ingredients include:

○ olives
○ salt and pepper
○ grated nutmeg
○ Tabasco sauce
○ cayenne pepper
○ Worcestershire sauce
○ tomato ketchup
○ angostura bitters and other bitters
○ sugar syrup
○ grenadine syrup
○ almond syrup
○ rosewater
○ caster sugar and sugar cubes
○ coffee beans
○ milk, cream and yoghurt
○ raisins
○ honey
○ tea
○ coconut cream.

Remember!
All dairy products must be stored in the chiller unit

Find out!
Pick some of the listed ingredients and find out which cocktails they are used for.

Try this!
Make a display of all the extra ingredients. It helps promote the cocktails.

Garnishes

A garnish is a colourful touch which completes the cocktail produced. Garnishes should be stored correctly to maintain quality. They should be prepared as close to the beginning of service as possible to retain their crispness, freshness and juiciness. A garnish is selected in line with the cocktail ingredients. Its purpose is to create a visual impression.

Garnishes could include:
o cocktail cherries
o lime
o lemon
o orange
o pineapple
o coconut
o apple
o mint
o kiwi
o strawberries
o cucumber.

Cocktails can be dressed with:
o fruit in the form of slices, triangles, semi-circles or slithers
o fruit zest cut into spirals or twists
o mint leaves, which can be slightly crushed to extract the mint oil and add flavour to the drink
o cucumber skin, which is best peeled to extract the delicate flavour
o cocktail cherries, which are available in a variety of colours – red is the most commonly used.

Find out!
What is zest?

Ice

Ice is used in large quantities for cocktail service in the form of ice cubes and crushed ice. Plenty of ice should be readily available for service. Ice should be stored in an ice container with tongs ready for service and replenished on a regular basis. Cocktail service demands fresh ice. Partially melted ice would dilute the drink being prepared.

For cocktail service, adding ice is part of the preparation of the drink. After the preparation of each cocktail order, the ice is discarded.

Tongs or an ice scoop must be used to pick up ice for drinks and cocktail service.

Serving cocktails

Helping your customers decide what to buy

Before you even start to prepare the drinks, you have an important role to play in making sure your customers have a good experience. Cocktails are complex drinks with lots of different ingredients, including strong spirits. Customers may need your help to decide which of the many different and exciting drinks to purchase.

You must make sure that you are totally familiar with the names of all the cocktails on your list, their strength, ingredients, the measures used and the prices. Then you will be able to advise your customers correctly and maximise sales by promoting the right drink to the right customer.

Frosting glassware

Some cocktails are served in glasses which have been "frosted" by sticking sugar or salt to the rim of the glass. To frost glassware, first dip the rim of the glass in lemon juice. Then dip it in caster sugar or salt depending on the requirements of the drink. It may be necessary to wipe the rim of the glass to tidy up the frosting and make it even.

It is usual to sugar frost cocktails that contain a neutral spirit such as gin, vodka or white rum. The use of salt frosting does not appeal to all drinkers.

> **Find out!**
> What is the name of a popular cocktail which has the glass frosted with salt?

> **Try this!**
> You can rub the cut side of half a lemon across the rim of a glass before frosting. This is an easy and hygienic way of doing it.

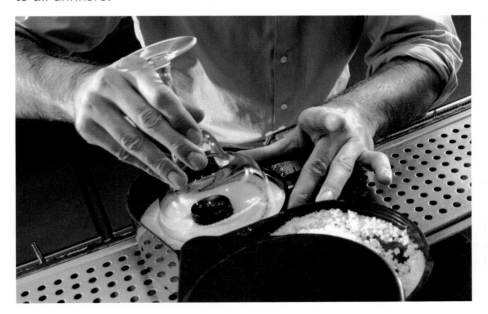

Figure 14.15 Frosting the glass gives an attractive finish to the cocktail

>
> **Remember!**
> Once there is condensation on the outside of the cocktail shaker, it is a sign the cocktail is ready.

Shake, stir or pour?

A cocktail is a skilfully blended drink prepared by shaking, stirring or pouring. It is the ingredients that determine the method.

Shake – using a cocktail shaker

If the cocktail includes fruit juice, egg, cream, milk or any cloudy ingredient, it is shaken. A cocktail needs to be shaken vigorously to blend all the ingredients together. The ice should be put into the shaker first and the ingredients on top of the ice. This is to make sure that all ingredients have a chance of mixing together. The top needs to be placed tightly on the shaker before shaking. Hold the shaker with both hands, one hand on the top of the shaker and the other hand at the bottom.

Stir – using a bar glass and bar spoon

Stir any cocktail with clear ingredients. First add ice cubes then add the ingredients. Stir vigorously with the bar spoon. Use the hawthorn strainer to strain the cocktail into a prepared glass.

Pour the ingredients directly into the glass

An example of a poured cocktail is Pimms. A half pint or pint mug is used to prepare the drink. The ingredients are added starting with the Pimms, followed by any garnishes (fruit and cucumber) and finally the lemonade. A swizzle stick is used to stir the cocktail and then straws are added.

Find out!
Pimms No. 1 is gin-based and is used for a Pimms cocktail. What are the other Pimms numbers and their bases?

Built cocktails (pousse café)

Some cocktails are built up by using ingredients of different densities. This gives the effect of several separate layers. This is achieved by placing the heaviest of the drinks in the glass first, followed by the next heaviest drink and so on until the lightest drink goes on the top. These drinks are produced for their visual impact more than for the taste of the drink. They are often served when opening a new restaurant.

Did you know?
James Bond always requests his martini to be shaken not stirred. Martini cocktails would normally be stirred except for this special request.

Did you know?
The recipe for the first gin sling was invented by James Pimms of Pimms Oyster Bar in London.

Did you know?
A cocktail that is layered so that all the colours and flavours of the drink stay separate when presented to the customer is known as a pousse-café.

Try this!
If you were opening an Italian restaurant, what colours would you suggest for a layered drink? What ingredients could you use that would give these colours?

Definition
pousse café: from the French. Literally meaning 'push down the coffee'.

Safe and hygienic working practices in a cocktail bar

Cocktail bar staff must follow the following working practices in order to work safely and hygienically in the bar.

1 You must be knowledgeable and trained to work in a safe and hygienic manner.

2 Wash your hands regularly to avoid cross contamination.

3 It is advisable not to offer cocktails using raw eggs.

4 Keep measures for non-alcoholic cocktails separate from those used for alcoholic cocktails.

5 The bar counter must be attractive and the area efficient to work in. Keep it tidy by returning bottles to their shelf position after use.

6 All equipment to be used must be completely clean to meet hygiene regulations and to ensure quality cocktail service.

7 Thoroughly wash shakers, bar glasses, bar spoons and strainers after every use.

8 You should automatically inspect any glassware before use by holding it up to the light.

9 Always use tongs or an ice scoop to pick up ice. Never use your fingers or a glass. A glass could chip within the ice container without you knowing. Your fingers could contaminate the ice.

10 The contents of cocktail shakers and bar glass must be disposed of after each mixing. The mixing of the same cocktail in a used shaker or bar glass will dilute the quality of the cocktail.

11 All ice used for the preparation of cocktails must be disposed of before the next mixing because it will have started to melt and will dilute the next cocktail.

12 Check you have all the ingredients and glassware before starting to make the cocktail.

13 Do not fill glasses to the rim. Spillages cause messy counters, tables and clothes. A completely full glass also lessens the visual impact of the cocktail.

14 Dispose of any plastic drink decorations – it is not advisable to recycle these.

Checklist for serving cocktails

Cocktails checklist	
Tables	
Prepare all glassware, ingredients and garnishes. Chill glassware as required. This provides for fast and efficient service.	
Use measures as laid out in your standards manual. This ensures the ratio of ingredients is correct. Also when a customer orders another cocktail it will taste the same.	
If you are shaking or stirring cocktails, half fill the shaker or bar glass with fresh ice using an ice scoop and then add ingredients. This will make sure no ingredients remain under the ice.	
Shake or stir vigorously – to make sure all ingredients are mixed and chilled.	
Never shake any effervescent ingredient – if you do the shaker will burst open. This would not look good with your customers watching.	
Strain drinks carefully into prepared glasses – to remove ice from the drink.	
Strain into the centre of glass to avoid spoiling frosted glasses.	
Add garnishes and serve.	
For a mixed drinks order, make cocktails last.	

Figure 14.16 Use this checklist to help you make cocktails correctly

When operating a cocktail bar, the most usual problem is a request for a cocktail that is not on the drinks list. If this happens apologise and seek help from your supervisor or manager so that the customer can be served their special request. This will provide customer satisfaction and may well be the reason your customers return.

Prepare and serve cocktails

Cocktail	Type	Ingredients	Glass	Method
Moscow mule	Shaken and stirred	o 2 × 25 ml vodka o 100 ml ginger beer o ½ × 25 ml fresh lemon juice o lemon slice o cucumber slice	10 fl oz (280 ml) Slim Jim	Half fill shaker with ice cubes. Add vodka, lemon juice – shake well and strain into chilled glass. Add slice of lemon & cucumber. Add ginger beer. Stir and serve.
Harvey Wallbanger	Shaken	o 1 × 25 ml vodka o ½ × 25 ml Galliano o 200 ml orange juice o orange slice o straws o stirrer	10 fl oz (280 ml) Slim Jim or stemmed glass	Place ice cubes in shaker, then vodka and orange juice. Shake well. Strain into glass. Add 2 ice cubes. Float Galliano on top. Garnish with slice of orange, straws and stirrer.

Pink lady	Shaken	○ 1 × 25 ml gin ○ 1 × 25 ml calvados ○ 1 × 25 ml lime juice ○ 5 dashes grenadine ○ slice of lime ○ cherry on cocktail stick	Cocktail glass	Half fill shaker with ice cubes. Add gin, calvados, lime juice and grenadine. Shake well and strain into frosted glass. Garnish with lime and cocktail cherry on stick.
Pimms	Poured	○ 1 × 50 ml Pimms ○ 180 ml lemonade ○ ice cubes ○ lemon and orange slice ○ cucumber slice & peel ○ apple slice ○ strawberry ○ mint ○ bee-borage ○ straws	10 fl oz (280 ml) Slim Jim or Pimms glass	Pour Pimms into glass. Add ice cubes and fruit. Top up with lemonade.Garnish with fruit, mint and bee-borage. Serve with straws.
Lassi	Shaken	○ 125 ml plain yoghurt ○ 1 tbsp double cream ○ 2 tbsp caster sugar ○ 1 tsp rose water ○ ice cubes ○ two fresh cherries on one stalk	Cocktail glass	Half fill shaker with ice cubes and all ingredients. Shake well. Pour into chilled glass and decorate with the cherries – one in the drink and one hanging over the rim of the glass.
Sambuca whirl	Blended	○ 1 × 25 ml sambuca ○ 1 × 25 ml light rum ○ 1 × 25 ml lime juice ○ 1 × 25 ml cream ○ 1 scoop crushed ice	Tulip glass	Blend all the ingredients together on slow speed for 10 seconds then pour into a tulip glass. Serve with straws.
Americano	Stirred	○ 1 × 25 ml Campari ○ 1 × 50 ml sweet vermouth ○ soda water ○ orange slice or lemon twist ○ ice	Old-fashioned glass	Place ice cubes in bar glass, then add Campari and vermouth. Stir well and strain into old-fashioned glass. Top up with soda and stir. Garnish with orange slice or lemon twist.
Non-alcoholic raisin and ginger punch	Shaken and Stirred	○ 100 ml apple juice ○ 100 ml ginger ale ○ 1 × 25 ml lemon juice ○ lemon zest ○ 1 tsp clear honey ○ 1 tsp raisins ○ mint ○ lemon spirals ○ straws	10 fl oz (280 ml) Slim Jim	Half fill shaker with crushed ice. Add lemon juice and zest, honey, raisins and apple juice. Shake. Pour into glass with the ice. Add ginger ale. Stir well. Garnish with lemon spriral, mint and straws.

Pousse-café	Built	o grenadine o Tia Maria o Parfait d'Amour o Blue curacao o Benedictine brandy	Liqueur glass	Pour each ingredient carefully over the back of a teaspoon into the glass. Add ingredients in equal amounts in the order stated. Serve.

Figure 14.17 How to prepare and present a range of popular cocktails

Find out!

What are the flavour and contents of each ingredient listed for pousse-café?

Try this!

Give two examples of drinks you could promote on each of the following occasions:

o *on arrival*
o *after a meal*
o *for a special occasion*
o *for a cold winter's day.*

For each of these drinks, give the glass, measure and garnish.

Test yourself!

1 What are most cocktails based on?
   a) wine b) beer c) spirit d) egg

2 What are the most important items of equipment for mixing cocktails?

3 Name three different methods of mixing cocktails.

4 Why is it important to have large quantities of ice ready for mixing cocktails?

15

Preparing and serving bottled wines

In this chapter you will cover skills and knowledge in the following units:

o 7132 – Unit 214 (2BS4): Prepare and serve wines

o 7103 – Part of Unit 109: Bar service skills

o 7103 – Part of Unit 207: Principles of beverage product knowledge; and part of Unit 209: Food and beverage service skills

Working through this chapter could also provide evidence for the following Functional Skills:

Functional English – Speaking, listening and communication Level 1

Functional English – Reading Level 1

Functional Mathematics – Representing and analysing Level 1

In this chapter you will learn how to:

o identify and understand different types of wine

o determinine customers' needs and establish rapport with customers

o present a wine list and provide product knowledge

o maximise sales through suggestion selling

o present and serve wine at correct temperature

o serve wines correctly, implementing wine etiquette

Introduction

Wine has been made and drunk by people for thousands of years. It is now a sophisticated product, produced all over the world. In the UK, sales and consumption of wines have increased dramatically. Wine is drunk not just with meals, but before meals, after meals, without meals, when celebrating or drowning sorrows, and during everyday social drinking.

Today wine is consumed in many different types of establishment – wine bars, gastro-pubs, ordinary pubs, restaurants, hotels, theatre bars and others. The types of wine offered and the method of service (for example, by the glass or by the bottle) will vary depending on the establishment.

As the trend to eat out more continues, so too does customers' interest in drinking wine. Wine is a matter of personal taste, but as there is such a great variety of different qualities and characteristics, customers have choices and may often need your help to make decisions.

Wine is the perfect partner for food, and provides an excellent opportunity to enhance customer satisfaction and your establishment's profitability. The wine list is usually chosen to complement the type of food served. Wine lists today offer customers an interesting, balanced list of familiar wines with more interesting wines that may provide a customer with new discoveries.

Your wine service skills and knowledge of wine will help you to keep your customers happy by being able to help with wine selection and service.

Figure 15.1 Customers may need help with the wine list

What is wine?

Wine is an alcoholic drink made from the fermented juice of freshly picked grapes. Because the grapes are freshly gathered, the yeast (or 'bloom') on the outside of the grape will be fresh and intact. Yeast is one of the vital ingredients of the fermentation process.

How is the alcohol produced?

The alcohol in wine is produced by fermentation. The grapes are pressed, and the sugar in the grape juice mixes with the bloom or yeast on the outside of the grape. The yeast interacts with sugars in the grape juice and this chemical reaction creates alcohol and carbon dioxide gas (as a by-product). This gas rises to the top and is allowed to escape.

Most fermentation takes place near where the grapes were harvested, so the grapes are fresh and have not been transported too far. Each wine-producing area has traditional methods and practices. This is one of the factors that give individual wines their unique characteristics. Some lesser-quality wines are blends of wine from a number of different sources.

Classification of wines

Customers may request a wine in a variety of ways – by country of origin (German, Italian, French, Californian), by type of grape (Cabernet Sauvignon, Chardonnay, Gewürztraminer), by colour, by sparkling or still, or by taste (sweet, medium, dry).

> **Definition**
> **Wine** is an alcoholic drink obtained by fermenting the juice of freshly gathered grapes.
> **Viticulture** is the process of cultivating grapes.
> **Vinification** is the process of fermenting grape juice to make wine.

Figure 15.2 The location of the vineyard affects the type of wine produced

> **Try this!**
> **I would like a German sparkling white wine – what would you recommend?**

Wine is classified by:
○ colour
○ taste (sweet or dry)
○ still or sparkling
○ strength
○ grape variety
○ vintage/non-vintage
○ country of origin.

All this information can be gathered from looking at the wine bottle, and in particular at the label. The label on the back of the bottle will often carry information on taste. The label on the front of the bottle should carry the following information:

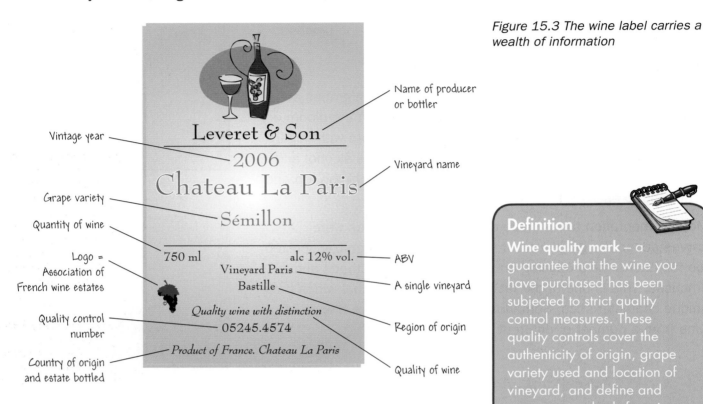

Figure 15.3 The wine label carries a wealth of information

Labels (from image):

Vintage year

Grape variety

Quantity of wine

Logo = Association of French wine estates

Quality control number

Country of origin and estate bottled

Name of producer or bottler

Vineyard name

ABV

A single vineyard

Region of origin

Quality of wine

Leveret & Son
2006
Chateau La Paris
Sémillon
750 ml   alc 12% vol.
Vineyard Paris
Bastille
Quality wine with distinction
05245.4574
Product of France. Chateau La Paris

Colour

The colour of wine is produced by the skins of the grape. The actual grape juice is colourless!

Red wine

Red wines are made from black grapes. The skins remain in the juice during fermentation.

Rosé (pink) wine

Rosé wines are also made from black grapes. The skins are removed when the colour has reached the right shade of pink.

White wine

White wines can be made from white or black grapes. With black grapes, only the juice is used, the skin is removed so there is no colour transfer.

Definition

Wine quality mark – a guarantee that the wine you have purchased has been subjected to strict quality control measures. These quality controls cover the authenticity of origin, grape variety used and location of vineyard, and define and approve standards for wine production and certification. Wines are classified into categories, from the cheapest table wines to quality wines of distinction. Each category has to meet exacting standards to be awarded certification for that category. The quality marks can be abbreviated (e.g. for French wines, AC or AOC for *Appellation d'origine contrôlée*) and are prominently displayed on wine labels. The quality mark is proof to the customer that the wine in the bottle is as described on the label.

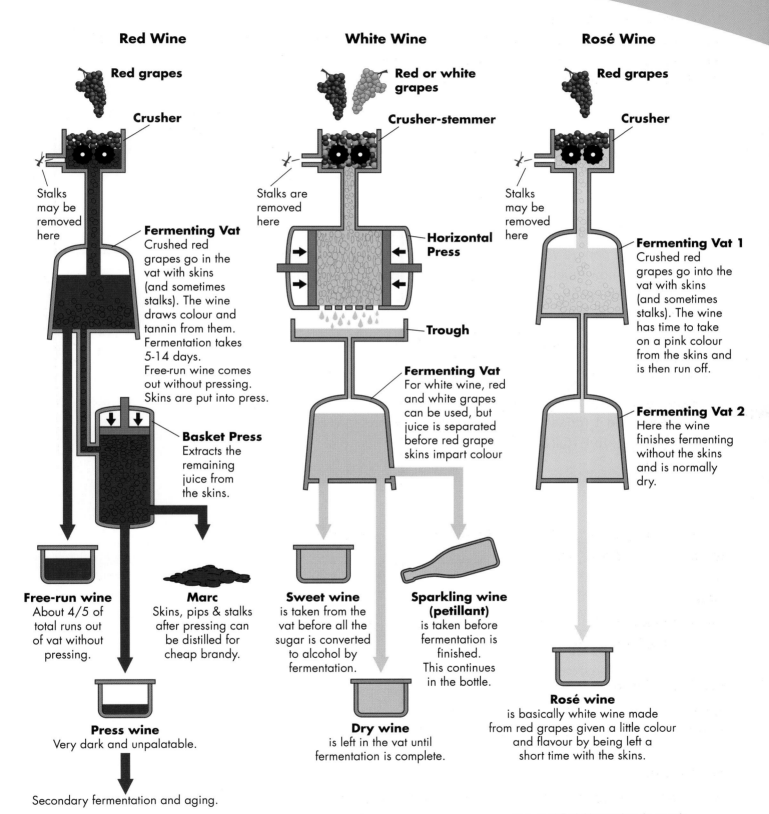

Red Wine

Red grapes

Crusher

Stalks may be removed here

Fermenting Vat
Crushed red grapes go in the vat with skins (and sometimes stalks). The wine draws colour and tannin from them. Fermentation takes 5-14 days. Free-run wine comes out without pressing. Skins are put into press.

Basket Press
Extracts the remaining juice from the skins.

Free-run wine
About 4/5 of total runs out of vat without pressing.

Marc
Skins, pips & stalks after pressing can be distilled for cheap brandy.

Press wine
Very dark and unpalatable.

Secondary fermentation and aging.

White Wine

Red or white grapes

Crusher-stemmer

Stalks are removed here

Horizontal Press

Trough

Fermenting Vat
For white wine, red and white grapes can be used, but juice is separated before red grape skins impart colour

Sweet wine
is taken from the vat before all the sugar is converted to alcohol by fermentation.

Sparkling wine (petillant)
is taken before fermentation is finished. This continues in the bottle.

Dry wine
is left in the vat until fermentation is complete.

Rosé Wine

Red grapes

Crusher

Stalks may be removed here

Fermenting Vat 1
Crushed red grapes go into the vat with skins (and sometimes stalks). The wine has time to take on a pink colour from the skins and is then run off.

Fermenting Vat 2
Here the wine finishes fermenting without the skins and is normally dry.

Rosé wine
is basically white wine made from red grapes given a little colour and flavour by being left a short time with the skins.

Figure 15.4 How wine is made

465

Taste

White, rosé and fortified wines

○ Dry – when all the sugar in the grape juice has been used up by the yeast during fermentation, the wine is dry.

○ Sweet – fermentation stops at 15% alcohol, at this stage if some sugar remains, the wine will be sweet. Sweet is a term used for white and rosé wines, and for **fortified wines** such as Sherry and Madeira.

Red wines

There are very few red wines that are naturally sweet. The flavour or taste of red wine can be very complex. It is often described on wine lists in terms of how much 'body' the wine has. 'Body' describes a sensation in the mouth of lightness or fullness, and is used to define the quality of the wine in the mouth. The range is from soft- to full-bodied.

Tasting guides

Tasting guides may appear on wine lists. For example, white wines may be numbered 1 (driest) to 9 (sweetest); red wines may be coded A (softest) to E (full-bodied).

> **Definition**
>
> **Fortified wine** is wine with the natural alcohol content increased by the addition of spirit, usually brandy. The added spirit increases the alcoholic content to between 18 and 22%. Fortified wines include Sherry, Port, Madeira, Marsala and Malaga.

Types of wines

White wine grapes

Grape variety	Flavour/characteristics	Region	Serve with
Chardonnay	Lemon zest, butter, green apples, pineapple, mango, buttered toast, vanilla and spices. Oaked and unoaked versions produced.	Produced worldwide. The principal white grape variety of Burgundy and Champagne in France. Oaked chardonnays of Premier and Grand Cru grades from the Côte d'Or and Chablis are the best in the world.	Seafood, poultry, cheeses, smoked fish, snails, frogs' legs and tripe.

Grape variety	Flavour/characteristics	Region	Serve with
Sauvignon blanc	Gooseberries, asparagus, cut grass, limes, green apples, nettles and passion fruit. Mainly unoaked in the New World regions.	Produced world-wide. The only grape variety used for Pouilly-Fumé and Sancerre (Loire Valley, France) and the principal white grape in Bordeaux, France.	Seafood, rice dishes, soups, salads, herb-flavoured dishes, soft cheeses, grilled and smoked fish.
Chenin blanc	Peaches, apricots, pears, honey, pineapple, citrus, flint and sweet apples. Often has an aroma of wet wool/lanolin. Both dry (mainly New World) and sweet (Loire Valley) versions produced.	Produced in Vouvray, Savennières and Coteaux-du-Layon (Loire Valley, France), South Africa, California, Argentina and Australia.	Foie gras, terrines, shellfish, white meats, poultry, soft cheeses and fruit pastries.
Muscadet (melon de bourgogne)	Lemon juice, green apples, pears, pineapple, melon, mango and toast. Famous for its Sur-Lie (bottled off its lees) process. Most Muscadet wines are unoaked.	Produced only in the Pays Nantais region of the Western Loire.	Oysters and shellfish, fish in butter sauces and chicken breasts.
Pinot grigio/ pinot gris	Apples, honey, nuts, nougat, butter, sap and citrus. Light in style and colour (with the exception of Alsace) and with soft acidity. Noted for its perfumed 'musk' and smoke aroma.	Produced in Alsace (France), Northern Italy, Germany and Eastern Europe with plantings now in the New World.	Rice dishes, salads, poultry, pasta, white fish, soft cheeses, vegetarian dishes and cream soups.
Riesling/Rhine riesling	Honeysuckle, sweet apples, slate, peaches, passion fruit, pineapple and limes. Both dry (mainly New World), medium dry and sweet (Germany, Austria and Australia) versions produced. Often has aromas of roses (young Rieslings) and of petrol (especially aged Rieslings).	Produced principally in the Mosel Valley (Germany) and in Alsace (France). Also produced in Austria, New Zealand, Australia and California (USA).	

Grape variety	Flavour/characteristics	Region	Serve with
Sémillon	Apricots, honey, grassy, nettles, citrus, lanolin, mango and marmalade. Noted for its sweet wines where the grapes are affected by noble rot which concentrates the sugar in the shrivelled rotted grapes.	Principal grape for Sauternes and Barsac (Bordeaux) and blending grape for Bordeaux white wines. Also grown in the New World (especially Australia).	Pâté de foie gras, terrines, blue-veined and soft creamy cheeses, rich puddings and fresh fruits.

Red wine grapes

Grape variety	Flavours	Region	Serve with
Cabernet sauvignon	Plums, blackberries, cherries, blackcurrants, mint, including when oaked: vanilla, tannins, cigar-box, chocolate, coffee, truffles and liquorice. Mainly oak-aged. Noted for its ability to undergo long ageing in excellent vintages.	Principally used as a 'blending grape' in Bordeaux and most wine-producing countries but is the principal grape in the Haut-Médoc (Bordeaux, France). Also produced as a single (varietal) grape wine in the New World.	Roast red meats, offal, game, cheeses and dishes with butter and cream.
Pinot noir	Cherries, redcurrants, blackcurrants, raspberries, strawberries, plums, blackberries, prunes, wild mushrooms and leather.	The exclusive grape used in the Côte d'Or, Burgundy (France), the principal red grape in Champagne, also used as a single (varietal) grape in Alsace (France) and the Eastern Loire Valley (France). Also grown in Germany (as the Spätburgunder), New Zealand, California (USA) and South America.	Poultry, lamb, fungi, oily fish, offal and cheese.
Merlot	Cherries, blackberries, raspberries, strawberries, plums, soft tannins, chocolate, liquorice and leather. Noted for its soft, silky texture and easy drinking.	Principal grape variety in Pomerol, Saint-Émilion and used as a 'blending grape' in the regional Bordeaux appellations. Also produced world-wide as a single variety and in blended wines.	Red meats, poultry, game, offal, cheeses and lightly spiced foods.

Grape variety	Flavours	Region	Serve with
Syrah/shiraz/sirah	Black cherries, blackberries, plums, black pepper, chocolate, liquorice, star anise and leather. Noted for is sweet, spice and black pepper aroma.	Principal grape of the Côte-Rôtie, Hermitage, Crozes-Hermitage and Cornas (Northern Rhône Valley). Used as a blending grape in the Côtes-du-Rhône and Châteauneuf-du-Pape (Southern Rhône Valley). Also produced world-wide under various spellings including Shiraz and Sirah (USA). Main red grape variety of Australia.	Game, roast red meats, spiced casseroles, cheeses and smoked foods.
Grenache/garnacha	Plums, damsons, raspberries, bitter chocolate, spices, linseed oil, truffles, coffee and liquorice. Noted for its 'jammy' flavours – especially in the New World.	The main grape variety (there is also a white version) in Châteauneuf-du-Pape (Southern Rhône) and in southern France. Also produced in Spain (as Garnacha and in Australian blends.	Game, rich red meats, spiced foods, offal, cheeses and cured meats.
Tempranillo	Plums, blackberries, cherries, raspberries, redcurrants, blackcurrants, vanilla, chocolate, prunes and coffee. Can be tannic when young but ages well and for long periods especially when oaked.	A main grape for Rioja in north-eastern Spain and for many other regions in Spain under various names. Also grown in Portugal where it is known as the Tinta Roriz/Aroganez and is used in Port wines. Also grown extensively in the New World.	Game, spicy stews, chorizo sausage, herb-flavoured dishes, cured meats and strong cheeses.
Sangiovese	Bitter cherries, strong tannins, plums, violets, herbs, prunes, leather, tobacco and farmyard. Noted for its gum-numbing tannins when young.	The main grape for Chianti (Tuscany) and most regions in central and southern Italy, where it has many regional names. Also grown in the New World.	Pasta, cheeses, grilled meats, poultry and game.
Nebbiolo	Plums, prunes, violets, pitch, blackberries, chocolate, strong tannins, raisins, truffles, liquorice and coffee. Noted for producing long lived wines.	The exclusive grape for north-western Italy including the famous wines of Barolo, Barbaresco and Valtellina. Has many names in the area including: Chiavennasca and Spanna. Is being planted in the New World.	Truffles, rich buttered and creamed pasta dishes, braised rice dishes, cheeses, cured meats and polenta.

Still or sparkling

Still wines

The process of making wines begins with fermentation. Carbon dioxide is produced as a by-product of fermentation. This is allowed to escape, so while the wine is being produced it will be bubbling, but once fermentation has finished the wine is still, with no bubbles.

The still wine is now stored in tightly sealed vats or casks and left for some time. This allows the sediment (mainly the dead yeast) to settle to the bottom, where it is visible as a thick, beige-coloured layer.

The wine is then siphoned to leave the sediment behind, and then bottled. Less expensive wines are ready to drink at this point, but better quality wines are left to mature for varying lengths of time to develop the flavours in the wine. Wine can be matured in bottles or casks.

Sparkling wines

Sparkling wine is produced from still wine. Once the first fermentation has finished, extra sugar and yeast is added to produce a second fermentation which usually takes place in sealed tanks. The carbon dioxide produced is trapped into the wine. The wine is left to settle then filtered and bottled straight from the tank. The bottled wine now contains its characteristic sparkling bubbles, but the alcoholic content is not increased.

Strength

The strength of wine is measured in terms of the volume of alcohol it contains. This is known as alcohol by volume (ABV).

The alcoholic strength of table wine is 10–14%, whereas the alcoholic strength of fortified wines such as Sherry or Marsala is usually between 18 and 24%.

Grape variety

The grape variety used to make the wine is usually featured on the wine label, and may be included in the name of the wine. Alsace wines are named according to the grape variety (Riesling, Sylvaner, Gewürztraminer, etc.). New World wines tend to include the grape

Did you know?

The most famous sparkling wine is Champagne. Only wine from the Champagne region of France is allowed to carry this name. Champagne must be produced by *Methode Champenoise*.

Definition

Methode Champenoise – the second fermentation takes place in the bottle, after a mixture of wine, liquid sugar and yeast is added to the wine. Other sparkling wines may have *Methode Champenoise* on the label to indicate that they are produced by the same secondary fermentation method.

Figure 15.5 Sparkling wine does not contain more alcohol – but it can be more fun!

variety as part of the name, for example 'Whispering Mills Merlot'. Customers are now increasingly asking for wines by grape variety, such as Pinot Grigio, Merlot or Chardonnay. On wine lists, the grape variety is usually listed underneath the name of the wine, followed by a description of the wine. This can help both the customer to choose, and the waiter to make suggestions.

Vintage/non-vintage

Vintage wines are made from the grapes of a single harvest. They will have the year printed on the label. Vintage wines are not declared every year, only when wine-producing conditions are perfect.

A non-vintage wine is a blend of wines from more than one year. Non-vintage wines are usually less expensive than vintage, and the taste is more predictable.

Country of origin

Wine lists often group wines according to their country of origin. This can be helpful, for example, if a customer wishes to link their wine with their chosen food. As a waiter, you could suggest a Spanish wine to go with Spanish food, for example a Rioja with paella.

Information on preparing service areas, equipment and stock for wine service is covered in Chapter 13. Additional information about specialist equipment for serving wine is given in the following two sections of this chapter.

Test yourself!

1. Name two types of fortified wine.

2. How does Champagne differ from other sparkling wines?

3. List three grape varieties as featured on your wine labels.

4. How would you describe a vintage wine?

5. White wine can be made from black grapes: true or false?

Remember!
Champagne is a sparkling wine – but sparkling wine is not Champagne. Remember the Trade Descriptions Act! (see page 472).

Did you know?
Countries other than France also produce sparkling wines – for example, Italy produces Asti Spumante, Spain produces Cava and Germany produces Sekt.

Figure 15.6 A vintage wine is not necessarily old – it is a wine made from grapes grown in a single specified year

Remember!
If a vintage noted on your wine list is no longer available, and you substitute it with another year, you must inform the customer at the point of ordering. This is a requirement under the Trade Descriptions Act.

Determining customers' needs

In order to sell wine successfully, you need to know what you are selling and serving. Customers expect you to be able to answer their questions and to give them good advice on which wines to choose. If they have a good experience, they will buy more wine, and they will come back next time and bring their friends!

Wine lists

A key tool for selling wine is the wine list. This can be simple or very detailed, depending on the type of establishment. Wines are usually listed under headings to help the customer to choose.

> ### Definitions
> **New World wines** – wines produced outside Europe, in particular in Australia, Argentina, Canada, Chile, New Zealand, South Africa and the US.
> **Old World wines** – wines produced in the traditional wine-growing areas of Europe, including France, Germany, Italy and Spain.

Information on wine lists should be similar to that on the right. Legal requirements are also covered, including the Trade Descriptions Act 1968, the Price Marking Order 2004, the Weights and Measures Act 1985 and the Weights and Measures (Intoxicating Liquor) Order 1988.

Much of the information on the wine list will be as given on the wine label (see Figure 15.3, page 464).

> ### Try this!
> Check every wine on your wine list, and describe each one according to colour, taste, strength, whether still or sparkling, grape variety, vintage and country of origin.

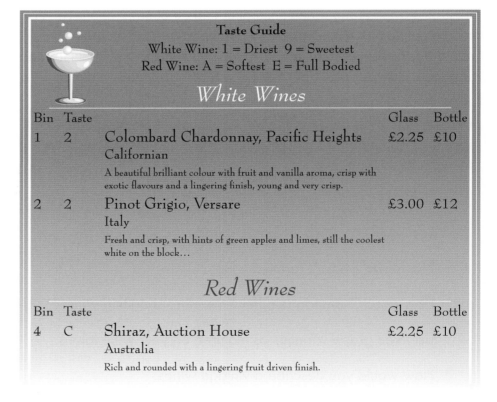

Taste Guide
White Wine: 1 = Driest 9 = Sweetest
Red Wine: A = Softest E = Full Bodied

White Wines

Bin	Taste		Glass	Bottle
1	2	Colombard Chardonnay, Pacific Heights Californian	£2.25	£10
		A beautiful brilliant colour with fruit and vanilla aroma, crisp with exotic flavours and a lingering finish, young and very crisp.		
2	2	Pinot Grigio, Versare Italy	£3.00	£12
		Fresh and crisp, with hints of green apples and limes, still the coolest white on the block…		

Red Wines

Bin	Taste		Glass	Bottle
4	C	Shiraz, Auction House Australia	£2.25	£10
		Rich and rounded with a lingering fruit driven finish.		

Figure 15.7 The wine list is a chance to offer customers an interesting choice

Principles of wine tasting

In order to advise customers on which wines to choose with their meal, you need to understand how to taste and appreciate wine yourself. The process of tasting begins at the moment when the cork is removed from the bottle. You should examine the cork. The information on the cork should match the information on the label.

Start by pouring a small amount of wine, usually into an over-sized glass. Hold it up to the light to check that it is clear and to check the colour. Tilt the glass and then put it upright again. With better quality wines, the liquid should run down the side of the glass in streaks called 'legs' or 'tears'.

Next, cover the glass and swirl the wine around to coat the inside. Remove your hand and put your nose into the glass and inhale. This process releases the full intensity of aroma from the wine. By now you should know if the wine is not going to be good to drink.

Finally you should taste the wine by taking a mouthful and washing it around your mouth and teeth. Some people suck air through the wine as they do this. You should always spit out the wine after tasting.

You will be looking for taste characteristics such as dryness or sweetness, acidity, fullness of flavour, how long the taste lasts on the palate, texture in the mouth. When tasting red wine, the tannin leaves a bitter coating in the mouth and on the teeth. This is caused by the grape skins, pips and stalks. If the wine was matured in oak, you may get undertones of oak in the flavour.

You should practise recording your impressions of the wines you have tasted. Although the description of a wine is very personal, there is a common range of words used to describe the flavours or undertones within the wine. For example, white wines are often described as flowery, light, citrus; red wines might be full bodied, with berries, spicy, smoky, oaky.

Matching wine and food

The combination of well prepared food and well chosen wines often provides the greatest satisfaction to customers. The customer can, of course, drink whatever they like to accompany their meal, but there are times when help is needed. The following guidelines may be useful if you are asked to suggest wines to go with food.

General principles

○ Always consider the occasion.
○ Listen carefully to the customer's expressed tastes.
○ Champagne can be served at any time.
○ Dry before sweet.
○ White wine before red wine.
○ Young wines before old.
○ White wines with white meat or fish.
○ Rosé wines with pink food, such as salmon.
○ Red wine with red meat.
○ Red or fortified wine (e.g. port) with cheese.
○ Wine is less commonly served with spicy foods (but some German wines, for example, do complement spicy foods).
○ No wine with egg dishes.
○ Wine must complement the food, not overpower it.
○ The quality of the food and wine should be equal.

If you are devising a menu with a wine for each course, for example for a function, the wines offered should improve in quality with each course, the main course being accompanied by the best quality wine. The type of occasion should be central to your wine choices. Always provide suggestions for customers who may not want alcohol with their food, perhaps including an alcohol-free wine.

		Amuse Bouche
2002	*St Aubin 1er Cru Les Combes*	*Russian Style Soup with Cabbage,*
	Marc Colin	*Beetroot & Lamb Tongue*
	Côte-de-Beaune	...
	France	*Assiette of Smoked & Marinated Fish with*
Smooth, buttery, well balanced not oaky		*Winter Salad*
		...
		Pressed Ham Hock Terrine with Foie Gras
		Served with Pickled Cucumber Julienne
1996	*Chateau Fourcas-Hostens*	...
	Cru Bourgeois	*Pan Roasted Fillet of Beef with Truffle*
	Listrac-en-Medoc	*Mash Potatoes*
	Bordeaux	*Served with Mustard Cream, Buttered*
	France	*Cabbage & Semolina*
A classic Bordeaux blend of Cabernet Franc, Cabernet Sauvignon and Merlot, fruity and not too tannic		...
2002	*Muscat de Jau*	*Apple Croustade with Honey & Rosemary,*
	Rivesaltes	*Soured Cream flavoured with Passion Fruit*
	France	...
A sweet, smooth, aromatic, fresh grape taste to complement dessert		*Freshly brewed coffee & Petit Fours*

Figure 15.8 For a function, the menu may list a different wine with each course

Suggested appropriate wines to accompany different courses

Aperitif	white port, vermouth bianco, dry sherry, dry madeira
Hors d'oeuvre	dry sherry or dry madeira
Soups	dry sherry
Pasta dishes	Italian red wine, e.g. Chianti
Fish course	medium white wine
Shellfish	dry white wine or champagne
Salmon dishes	rosé wine
White meat	medium white or rosé wine
Red meat	red wine – quality to match dish
Game	high quality, robust red wine
Sweets	champagne, dessert wine
Cheese	fortified wine, red wine
Coffee	cognac, Calvados, Armagnac

These are guidelines, but as a waiter you should consider the cooking methods and any garnishes of the food that may affect the choice of wine you suggest.

Maximising sales of wine

Any staff presenting the wine list, making recommendations and serving wine must be thoroughly familiar with the wines available. Wine waiters and bar staff need to be able to 'sell' the right wine to the right customer. Customers will return more often to establishments where the staff are helpful

Some customers may require more information than is on your wine list. In order to advise them, you will need to be familiar with the characteristics of the wines offered. If the information on the label (see page 464) doesn't help you to answer the customer's question, then you should ask for help from your supervisor or someone more senior than you.

Personal selling is the best promotional tool. You should always balance the needs of your customer and the needs of your organisation. Aim to satisfy both by promoting and selling the right drink to the right person at the right time. Here are some ideas to help you do this:

○ check the availability of wines before selling them, so you know what you have in stock to sell

○ check which wines are on special promotion

Definition

Hors d'oeuvre – a light, appetising course to stimulate the appetite. May be a variety of small items for the customer to select from, e.g. a cold assortment of meats, fish, vegetables, salads, eggs, or a single hors d'oeuvre such as avocado pear, melon, fruit cocktail, oysters or smoked fish.

Try this!
What wine would you suggest to accompany strawberries?

Find out!
In your establishment, who should you refer customer queries to if you can't answer them?

Remember!
Keep a photocopy of your wine list, with descriptions of each wine, with you for service (see Figure 15.7, page 472).

- use tent cards on tables to highlight any special promotions
- maximise sales by suggesting 175 ml instead 125 ml glasses
- refill glasses regularly from bottle sales, to encourage customers to order a second bottle
- link food with wine – for example, suggest a dessert wine with sweet service, or port with cheese
- offer champagne with breakfast for hotel guests.

> **Try this!**
> Check every wine label on your wine list – the more you know about your wines, the more you are likely to sell.

Establishing a good relationship with the customer

If you have a good relationship with your customers, you will almost certainly sell more wine. Make sure you are there to greet customers when they arrive. Talk to them, make them feel welcome and offer them help as required.

Get to know your customers. Try to find out if the party has a host. If so, make a link with the host and help them to entertain their guests. Try and establish the reason for the visit. Is it a special occasion? If not – make sure you make it special.

Present the wine list at the appropriate time, which might be straightaway on arrival, or when the food has been ordered. You will need to be observant to know when to do this. As you present the wine list, remind your customers of any special offers or promotions.

If your customers are dining, check the food order and have in mind the wine(s) you could recommend to accompany the food order. Make suggestions linked to the food and occasion if requested, and allow customers decision-making time.

Offer glasses of wine at 125 or 175 ml or multiples, or half-bottles or larger bottles of wine such as a **magnum**. If appropriate, you could offer some wines that are not listed, often bin ends from an old wine list. This can make customers feel very special, and if it happens to be a good match for their requirements then they will be very impressed. Remember to offer alcohol-free or low-alcohol wines for customers who do not wish to drink alcohol. If a customer asks for a particular wine that you do not stock, suggest a suitable alternative.

Figure 15.9 Make your customers feel special!

> **Definition**
> **Magnum** – a double-sized bottle equal to two standard bottles of wine.

476

Prices

Restaurant and wine bars generally price their wines in relation to the price of a meal. Except in the most expensive restaurants, or for a special occasion, customers rarely buy wine for a meal that is more expensive than the meal itself. Some wines are priced to suit the average price of a meal. Wine bars generally sell bottles of wine over the bar, so staffing levels are lower than restaurants, and this may be reflected in their wine prices. Pubs carry a range of stock, and the prices charged can vary a lot. Naturally, wines are priced to sell. If you are asked for advice, you should suggest wines within the price range of the food order.

Try this!
Try to serve every wine on your wine list. Keep a record of all the wines you have served – you could photocopy the wine list and add comments. This will be useful evidence.

Taking the wine order

If wine is being ordered with food, the wine order should be taken after the food order. Link with the host if applicable. If the order cannot be fulfilled, offer alternatives. Check that you have covered all customers by reconfirming the order. Check when the host would like the wine to be served, especially if it is to accompany a meal.

Test yourself!

1 A customer has asked for help in deciding on a wine to accompany her lunch – what factors would you consider before recommending any wine?

2 A bottle of wine has been ordered and issued to you for service. What information will be on the label?

3 As a wine waiter, you are employed to sell as well as to serve. How can you maximise sales?

4 If you were asked to describe a certain wine to a customer, list the characteristics of wine that you would refer to.

5 Wine can be sold to a customer in various quantities – can you list them?

6 Two customers are dining – one has ordered a veal dish and the other a fish dish. They would like to order wine, but want to buy one bottle between them. What would you recommend?

Presenting and serving wines

Your customer's wine order can be recorded manually or electronically (see Chapter 6 for more information on the different types of ordering and recording systems). You should check that the order is recorded correctly. In a restaurant, the barperson should check that the order will be ready in time. The waiter will link the service of wine with the food service (see Chapter 10, page 309).

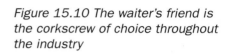

Figure 15.10 The waiter's friend is the corkscrew of choice throughout the industry

Preparation of equipment for table service of wine

Check there is sufficient space at the table for service of the wines ordered. If not, prepare and place a side table next to the customers' table.

You will need service cloths, a waiter's friend, a tray or salver with napkin, coasters, and an order pad and pen or handheld terminal (see Chapter 6, page 182). Service cloths are worn folded over the arm by restaurant staff for serving drinks at table, it also protects their uniform. Service cloths must be clean and should be replaced regularly to maintain hygiene standards. They are used when presenting, opening and serving wine. For chilled wine service, the cloth is folded and clipped to ice buckets ready. The cloth is then used to remove the bottle, to catch the water drips, then hold and pour the wine. The service cloth also maintains the correct temperature of the chilled wine when pouring.

Collect your glassware

Check glassware for smears, chips or cracks, and that there are the right quantity and type for each wine ordered. Glassware is carried to the table upturned on a napkin-lined salver or a non-slip tray. Glassware is always lifted by the stem.

Remember!
Knowing the number of covers will help the barperson to issue the right number of specialist glasses for your order.

Remember!
Always have a handheld terminal, or order pad and pen, ready for further wine sales – second bottles, dessert wines, fortified wines, or just 'upselling'.

Remember!
Lift glasses up to the light to check for any defects, and to ensure they sparkle, before taking glassware into the restaurant. Always have one extra glass per wine sold ready as the host's taster glass for second-bottle sales.

Place glasses on the table

Place the glasses on table from the right of the customer. Glasses should be positioned at the top right of each cover in order of use, first glass on the outer right, second glass to the left of it, and so on.

Collecting the wine order from the dispense bar

Red wine

Red wine should generally be served at room temperature, although there are a few exceptions to this. It should be issued on a side plate with a doiley or coaster to catch any drips, to avoid any stains on customers or tablecloths. If it is a mature red wine, serve it in a wine cradle. If the red wine is very old, it may need **decanting**.

Find out!

Name the French red wine available for service on the third Thursday in November every year. How would it be prepared for service? How does it differ from the service of red wine generally?

White wine and rosé wine

White wine should be served chilled. It should be issued in an ice bucket, with a stand or underplate, and a service cloth. The service cloth is used throughout service to catch drips from the wine bottle as the waiter removes it from the ice bucket, and to hold the bottle when serving so the temperature of the wine is not increased while serving the wine. This cloth remains with the ice bucket for use throughout service, so there is no chance of a wet service cloth being used to serve hot food and causing an accident.

Sometimes a wine cooler or a wine bag is used instead of an ice bucket. These are used dry.

On collection of the wine order, you should check:
○ is it the correct quantity and type? (see the label)
○ is it at the correct temperature?
○ is it presented with the right service equipment?

Remember!

The customer always drinks from the outside right-hand glass to the inside right-hand glass, in line with the sequence of service of wine.

Definition

Decanting – separation of wine from its sediment in the bottle.

Figure 15.11 How to decant wine

Remember!

Use a thick service cloth when serving wine to catch the water drips and to ensure the heat of your hand does not change the wine temperature. Keep your service cloth attached to the ice bucket for that use only.

Carry red wine to the table as it was issued – if it is in a wine cradle (used for expensive wines in some restaurants), keep it horizontal so as not to agitate the wine contents, or, if the wine is issued upright, keep it in that position, presented in a service cloth.

Carry white and rosé wines in the ice bucket. If the bucket has a stand, place it to the right of the host; or if it does not have a stand, place the ice bucket on a plate on a separate service table next to the host. It can also be clipped onto the table as mentioned earlier.

> **Try this!**
> Try placing or removing glasses from the left (only do this when customers not present). Now you know why you serve and clear glasses from the right!

Opening and service of wine at the table

Opening red, white and rosé wine

Check that the correct glasses are on the table for the wine. Present the wine label uppermost to the host for approval. Once it has been approved by the host, place red wine bottles upright on a plate with a doiley, or keep in the cradle. For white and rosé wines, present using a service cloth to catch water drips and place the bottle back in the ice bucket.

- Cut the foil at the neck of the bottle with a neat, clean cut, and remove the cut top.
- Wipe the top of the bottle. Close the knife section.
- Open the corkscrew and pierce the centre of the cork. Turn the corkscrew so that one screw turn is visible.
- Clip the lever arm onto the rim of the bottle neck, and with an upward lift, ease out the cork.
- Wipe the bottle neck with a clean cloth.

Remember!
All wine is served from the right of the customer and all glasses are placed or removed from the right.

Remember!
Turn the corkscrew until only one more screw turn is visible, then remove the cork. If the corkscrew is turned too much, pieces of cork will be floating on the wine. (If the wine has a plastic cork, floating cork will never be a problem.)

Remember!
If wine is of great quality, it may be served in a wine cradle or basket. In this case, you should open the bottle as above, but keeping the bottle horizontal in the cradle. After opening, present the cork to the host.

Remember!
For personal safety reasons, close the knife section of your waiter's friend immediately after use.

Etiquette of serving wine

Standing to the right of the host, with the bottle in a service cloth and the label facing the host, pour a taster (small amount) into the host's glass. Wait for his or her approval. If the wine is approved, proceed to the right of the host and serve the ladies first, eldest to youngest, then the gentlemen, eldest to youngest – and the host last, irrespective of gender. A glass of wine should be poured to two-thirds full.

Serving red wine

- Pour a taster into the host's glass.
- If the wine is approved, serve the ladies first, eldest to youngest.
- Then serve the gentlemen, eldest to youngest.
- Serve the host last.
- Refill glasses as needed.
- Provide a second bottle as requested.

Find out!
What are corks made from?

Find out!
List the disadvantages and advantages of plastic corks.

Serving white and rosé wine

Follow the instructions for serving red wine and return the wine bottle to the ice bucket to retain the temperature.

Opening sparkling wine

Place a tulip or flute glass to the right of the cover. Take the wine to the table in the ice bucket with a service cloth. Present the bottle to the host, label uppermost. The bottle should be held in a service cloth to catch water drips. Place the bottle back in the ice bucket, to keep it at the right temperature, and to make it easier to open.

Remember!
When pouring wine, hold the bottle with the label facing the guests while pouring. The guests often don't know what wine has been chosen by the host – the label will inform them.

Remember!
For health and safety reasons, you should always point the neck of the bottle away from any customers while removing the cork from a sparkling wine bottle.

Remember!
If the top of the stopper cork was accidentally snapped off while opening a bottle of sparkling wine, immediately return the bottle to a safe, secure cupboard or store room to allow removal of the cork naturally – the pressure of the bubbles in the wine will eventually remove the cork now that it is no longer secured by the muzzle. Do not attempt to remove the broken cork with a waiter's friend, for safety reasons.

- Remove the foil cover to expose the muzzle securing the stopper cork.
- Holding a service cloth over the cork with one hand, untwist the wire muzzle.
- Holding the cloth tightly in place over the cork, raise the cork upwards and twist the bottle. Never twist the cork.
- Ease the cork out slowly in a controlled way, with little noise.

Serving sparkling wine

Sparkling wine should be served immediately after opening. Sparkling wine is very **effervescent** and should be poured slowly into the glass, which should be filled to two-thirds full. After all glasses have been filled, return the wine bottle to the ice bucket to keep it cool.

Refilling glasses

You should continually check the level of wine in your customers' glasses – this encourages more sales. When the glasses need refilling, hold the wine in a service cloth with the label facing the guests, check if each guest would like more wine, and pour. The order of service remains the same (page 481). If the wine bottle being served is emptied, it is usual to check with the host if another bottle is required.

Serving a second bottle of the same wine

If a second bottle of the same wine is required, record the new order immediately. When it is ready, collect the wine from the collection point. Place a clean taster glass for the host. Open the second bottle as before, and offer the host a taster. If the host approves the second bottle, remove his new taster glass and proceed to refill guests' glasses in the order of service as before, with the host last.

Hold the wine at the temperature required until further refilling is required. You should continually monitor the customers and offer more wine to all guests when necessary. Remember to give them the chance to decline if they wish to.

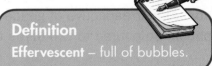

Definition
Effervescent – full of bubbles.

Remember!
Sparkling wine should be poured more slowly due to the bubbles, so each glass is half-filled and then slowly topped up to two-thirds full. See Chapter 13, page 377 showing wine service temperatures.

Remember!
All glasses are placed and removed from the right of the customer. All drinks are served from the right of the customer.

Remember!
From time to time, you should check to see whether the ice buckets are still cold enough.

Figure 15.12 Ladies first ... host last

Serving a second bottle of a different wine

Record the new order. Remove (from the right) any empty, finished glasses and place (from the right) clean glasses on every cover. Collect the new order and serve as appropriate for the type of wine.

Monitor customers carefully, and refill glasses as required. Offer a second bottle once the first is finished.

Serving wine by the glass

Table wine can be sold by the glass in measures of 125 or 175 ml, or multiples of these measures. When a customer orders a glass of wine, it is usual to suggest 175 ml, giving the customer a chance to agree or otherwise.

The wine is measured and served at the right temperature, but is usually served in a standard wine glass, which may be lined according to the measure. Lined glasses speed up service, reduce spillage and ensure accuracy of measure. If the wine bottle has a screw top, replace the top to retain the quality of the wine and to avoid spillages.

Dessert wine

Dessert wines are served with the sweet course. Dessert wines include port, Madeira, Marsala, and Muscat wines. A 50 ml measure is usually served in an appropriate glass. A 125 ml glass of sweet table wine can be offered as an alternative to a dessert wine.

Glass quantities per bottle

A standard bottle of sparkling wine will serve eight glasses.

A standard 75 cl bottle of wine will serve six glasses, with an average serving of 125 ml.

For smaller or larger bottle sizes, the number of glasses per bottle will increase or decrease *pro rata*.

Find out!

What should you do with a bottle of wine that has the cork pushed down into the wine? How are you going to salvage the wine?

Problems with service of wine

While serving wine, you will be faced with unexpected situations. Handling and managing these situations will provide learning opportunities for developing skills. If you record your experiences, it will be evidence for your portfolio and also useful for your future career. Figure 15.14 lists some common problems and the best way of handling them.

Figure 15.13 Wine that is corked or tastes vinegary must be replaced

Problem	Reason	Best way of handling
Cork is pushed inside the bottle.	Careless opening.	Apologise, remove the bottle and replace it with a new one of the same type. Start opening the wine again.
Customer rejects the wine because there are crystals in it.	These crystals are formed by extreme temperature fluctuations during storage or transport of the wine.	The crystals do not affect the taste of the wine but if the customer is unhappy, replace it with a new bottle.
Customer rejects the wine because it has a musty or corky smell.	The wine is 'corked' due to a fault with the cork.	Apologise and replace the bottle.
Customer complains that the wine tastes 'vinegary'.	The wine has been stored incorrectly. Bacteria has turned the alcohol into vinegar.	Apologise and replace the wine. Wine should be stored horizontally in racks (bins) to keep the corks moist and ensure they keep a perfect seal.
Customer complains that there are bits of cork floating in the wine.	Careless opening.	Remove the bottle and start opening a new bottle. Replace the customer's glass as well.
On opening the bottle, the cork snaps in the bottle.	Brittle cork.	Step back from the customer's table, place the corkscrew hard against the inside neck of the bottle and carefully turn the corkscrew a few turns. Avoid piercing the end of the cork. Clip the lever arm to the top of the bottle and lift upwards.

Figure 15.14 Handling problems

Try this!

Log the unexpected situations you experience while serving wine, and the solutions you applied.

Test yourself!

1 What action would you take if someone who looked under 18 years old asked for a large glass of white wine? (see Chapter 14).

2 List the occasions when you can refuse to serve alcohol (see Chapter 14).

3 What equipment would you need to prepare and serve a bottle of Champagne?

4 Why do some red wines need decanting?

5 You are required to serve a glass of white wine to 100 guests – how many bottles would you need to chill before service?

6 One guest at the table does not want to drink wine because of the alcoholic content. What could you suggest as an alternative?

7 When would you open a bottle of red wine that has been ordered to accompany the main course?

8 What types of wine would you find in these glasses?

16

Cellar work

In this chapter you will cover skills and knowledge in the following units:

o 7132 – Unit 215 (2BS5): Maintain cellars and kegs; Unit 216 (2BS6): Clean drink dispense lines

o 7103 – Part of Unit 207: Principles of beverage product knowledge

Working through this chapter could also provide evidence for the following Functional Skills:

Functional English – Reading Level 1

Functional Mathematics – Representing and analysing Level 1

In this chapter you will learn how to:

o maintain the safety and security of cellars

o prepare kegs and gas for use

o clean drink dispense lines

Maintaining cellars

The cellar plays an important part in the day-to-day operations of any licensed premises, and must be well maintained and organised to ensure the smooth running of the business during each working day.

The main purpose of a cellar in catering establishments is to store drinks in a safe and hygienic condition. Drinks are classed as 'foods' for hygiene purposes, so the food hygiene regulations (see page 139) apply to all storage areas used for drinks.

Drinks can come in bottles, or may be served from large storage vessels via dispense lines or pumps. These dispense lines and pumps use pressurised gas cylinders or pressurised **kegs** to deliver the drinks.

Figure 16.1 A beer dispense system in the cellar

Cellar security

It is important that the cellar is secure (locked) at all times when not in use, and that access is restricted to designated staff responsible for the contents and day-to-day management of the cellar area. The contents of the cellar are mainly high-value goods (alcoholic drinks). The licensing laws restrict who can have access to them.

Definition

In the past the term **cellar** meant an underground storage room – but modern cellars can be situated either above or below ground.

Definition

Keg: a metal, straight-sided container for kegged (pasteurised) beers. Kegs are fitted with a 'spear' and two-way valve head for attaching to the beer line's broaching head (see page 501).

Figure 16.2 It is important to keep the cellar secure

Remember!

The cellar stock is a major portion of the business's assets and income. Security is of the highest importance. A complete record of all purchases and issues of cellar stock must be kept, and any discrepancies should be reported to your superior immediately.

Health and safety in the cellar

A cellar has many hidden dangers, especially from carbon dioxide (CO_2) and nitrogen (N) gases, which may build up from leaks in casks. It is therefore extremely important that anyone who enters the cellar must notify a work colleague (or even a customer) before entering the cellar. If no-one is available, then you must not enter the cellar until there is someone to inform.

> **Remember!**
> Carbon dioxide and nitrogen gases have no smell – within two to three breaths you could be rendered unconscious!

Requirements for a cellar

Any cellar used for storing drinks must be constructed to provide a satisfactory level of hygiene, and kept clean and free of any waste or rubbish. It should be well lit, but not by direct sunlight.

Temperature

There are two temperatures that are important in a cellar. The first is the **ambient temperature**, which is the temperature of the walls, plant and drinks stored in the cellar. This should be constant and have little or no variation with each temperature check. The second is the **air temperature** – this will vary according to the amount of warm air entering the cellar when the doors are open, and the body heat generated by the workers in the cellar. The air temperature will quickly return to the normal range when the cellar is vacated and locked.

Cellars should be kept at a constant temperature of between 12 and 15.5°C (54 to 60°F). It is important that the temperature within the cellar is constant, to maintain the quality of the products stored in it. Beers (kegged and bottled), together with any wines stored in the cellar area, require this constant temperature range to prevent spoilage.

Higher temperatures will produce off, 'cooked' flavours in both beers and wines. In beer, high temperatures can cause the onset of further fermentation and bacterial contamination.

Lower temperatures can cause such problems as **hazes** in beers, and prevent the **cask**-conditioning process from being completed. In wines, long storage in cold conditions can cause the **precipitation** (crystallisation) of natural **tartaric acids**, making it taste flat and producing unsightly white particles in the otherwise clear wine.

> **Definitions**
> **Haze:** a condition of the beer when it is cloudy and not bright. Usually caused by dirty pipes or disturbed casks (cask ales), or from the beer being too cold (keg and cask ales).
> **Cask:** an oval metal cask that has the keystone (tap) hole at the base of one end and the shive opening at the top.
> **Precipitation:** the crystallisation of a tartaric acid due to very low temperatures.
> **Tartaric acid:** a natural edible acid found in most white wines that gives the wine its fresh 'mouth-watering' taste. When wines are stored for long periods at very low temperatures the acid may precipitate into white crystal deposits which can cause the wine to become 'flabby' because the acidity has been lost. These crystals when crushed into a powder is known as cream of tartar (used in cooking processes).

Humidity

A cellar should have a constant **humidity** level of between 45 and 65%, especially if bottled wines are stored in the cellar area. In the past, when wooden casks were used, if the humidity level was too low the casks would dry out and leak. Nowadays it is necessary to prevent the corks in wine bottles from drying out. Humidity gauges are available to give an accurate reading of the cellar's humidity, and humidifiers can be used to control the humidity levels within the cellar.

A cellar that is too damp will encourage the growth of moulds. **Impervious** walls will help avoid the risk of dampness. Cellar walls are often painted to make them impervious.

> **Definition**
> **Humidity:** the moisture in the cellar air. Too high a humidity reading (above 85%) will cause dampness.

> **Definition**
> **Impervious:** a surface (e.g. a cellar wall) that does not allow water to pass through.

Figure 16.3 Maintaining the right humidity level is important

Ventilation

Free movement of fresh air will reduce the risk of a build-up of carbon dioxide and nitrogen gases from leaks in casks. It will also reduce the risk of mould, wild yeasts and bacterial growth, and prevent a build-up of stale air.

Usage of the cellar

A cellar should be used only for storing drinks and the equipment used for the safe dispensing of the drinks. It should have a secure area for wines and spirits – these are high-value commodities, and storing them in a secure area will reduce the risk of theft.

Easy access must be provided for the delivery of casks, kegs and bottle crates.

> **Marcus says**
> A large proportion of a restaurant's capital can be tied up in wine and beverages; until the wine is sold the revenue will not be realised. A poor selection of wine may never be sold, so it is vital that the stock is monitored, that the list available to the guest is fully stocked and that the buyer is buying wine that the customers want to drink!

Equipment

Every cellar has a range of essential equipment available for its daily operation. Every piece of equipment must be easily accessible to everyone who has to work in the cellar.

All cellars should have the following items.

Instruction notices	should be sited above each relevant item of equipment in clear, step-by-step, easy-to-read lettering, and covered in protective plastic film
Tools	spanners, screwdrivers, pliers, etc. on a 'shadow tidy', which should be placed at the entrance/exit to the cellar
Thermometers	a wall-mounted thermometer to check the cellar's air and ambient temperatures (recorded twice per day), and a hand-held thermometer for checking beer temperatures
Barometer	to check humidity and atmospheric pressure
Vice	a small vice for maintaining equipment
Torch	hanging at the cellar entrance, with spare batteries and bulb in a box in the cellar cupboard
Spares	a set of clean washers, **reducing valve** (for keg beers), cask taps, spiles, keystones, shives, corks, filters (for cask ales) stored in the cupboard
Scotches	for securing traditional ale casks while conditioning and during dispensing
Brushes	of various sizes for cleaning beer lines and equipment

Definition

Reducing valve: a brewery-set gas pressure-reducing system fixed between the gas bottle and the beer keg.

Scotch: wooden wedge used to hold the casks in place on the **thralls**.

491

Punch	for broaching the **shive** (for cask ales)
Bucket	stainless steel or plastic with lid (for cask ales)
Funnel	stainless steel with filters (for cask ales)
Mallet	a wooden or rubber mallet (for cask ales)
Dipstick	for checking cask content of cask ales
Scales	for checking content of beer kegs
Sink with hot and cold running water	for washing equipment
Clean glasses	for checking the clarity of cask-conditioned ales before putting on line
Cleaning equipment	a mop (with spare heads), galvanised bucket, scrubbing brush and swabs stored in a cupboard, ideally in a separate area near the cellar
Bleach, detergents and sterilisers	for general cleaning of cellar and equipment – must be stored outside the cellar

Definitions

Shive: a wooden 'biscuit-like' disc with a grooved centre that is placed into the top opening of a beer cask. The grooved centre is 'punched out and a spile fitted when the beer is 'conditioned' in the cellar.

Thrall: the wooden frame on which cask-conditioned ales are held. The casks are held in place on the thrall with scotches. Also known as **stillage**.

Checklist

To ensure that the cellar is well maintained, and for health and safety reasons, an inspection checklist should be drawn up for daily or weekly inspections.

> **Try this!**
> **Find out if there is an inspection checklist for your own place of work.**
> **If not, try making one.**

Cellar safety

Health and Safety while working in a cellar environment is of extremely high importance. The safety of yourself, any other employees, and visitors must always be a priority. Safety equipment and clothing, including heavy-duty rubber gloves, protective goggles, hard hats, heavy-duty steel-capped shoes and leather aprons are recommended to be worn when performing manual duties within the cellar area.

The Health and Safety at Work Act requires that all businesses have a Health and Safety Officer (a member of the business's staff) who is responsible for implementing all health and safety issues on the premises. He/she is also responsible for advising staff on all health and safety issues.

Did you know?
Under the provisions of the Health and Safety at Work Act 1974, it is the responsibility of all employees to ensure their own safety and the safety of others.

Figure 16.4 Safety equipment and clothing should be available to cellar workers

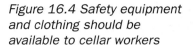

Remember!
Accidents are caused mainly by human error, carelessness or negligence – by not following proper procedures.

Frequent cellar accidents are caused by:

o falling equipment, casks, kegs, gas cylinders, crates, etc.

o cuts from broken glass

o slipping on wet floors

o tripping over items left on the floor

o electric shocks from faulty switches and equipment

o gas-pressure injuries due to failing to turn off the supply before changing kegs

o injuries to the head through knocking on low ceilings and doorways

o falling cellar trap-doors

o asphyxiation from carbon dioxide and nitrogen gas leaks

o tampering with the internal workings of pressurised kegs.

If an accident occurs, it must be recorded in the Accident Record Book (date, time, description of accident, who was involved, and action taken), and also reported to your supervisor (see page 18).

There are many areas of potential danger.

Figure 16.5 It's easy to hit your head in a cellar

High-pressure gas cylinders

All gas cylinders must be secured to the cellar wall using straps, chains or clamps, to prevent the risk of them falling and rupturing or causing injury. The cylinders are charged to a working pressure of 660 lbs per square inch (p.s.i.) and are available in 7, 14 and 21 lb standard sizes (although larger capacities are also available). Ensure that those on-line are also secured to the wall and correctly fitted to the pressure reducing valve. Check for leaks at all joints and connections within the line using neat detergent around the joints/seals.

Risk of gas leaks

The carbon dioxide and nitrogen gases used in the beer-dispensing process are odourless. Although these gases are inert (non-explosive) and non-toxic, they are both heavier than air and can build up in a cellar by pushing out the air from below – this can eventually cause **asphyxiation**. Good ventilation of all cellars is of utmost importance to prevent any gas build-ups from leaking cylinders, pipes and fittings.

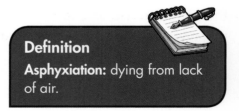

Figure 16.6 Gas cylinders must be secured

Definition
Asphyxiation: dying from lack of air.

Pressurised beer kegs

All beer kegs are pressurised, and must be treated with care when handling them (moving, attaching to dispense lines, attaching to gas cylinders, etc.).

- Even when they are empty, the kegs are still pressurised. You must never attempt to remove the **extraction spear** fitted inside the beer keg.
- If you think the keg is faulty, do not try to fix it. Instead, remove it from the line and report it to your supervisor. It will be returned to the brewery.
- Always move kegs by rolling, using a trolley, fork-lift or hoist. Never try to lift and carry them on your own. If a new (full) keg is accidentally dropped while moving it, report the incident to your supervisor and have the keg checked to ensure it is safe to use.

Figure 16.7 Beer kegs must be moved with care

Wet surfaces

Spillages and water from daily floor cleaning can create a potential slipping hazard if they are left unattended. Always clean up and mop dry any spillage, and notify any staff of its presence by using a clear sign (e.g. Danger – Wet Surface).

Falling crates

Incorrect stacking of beer and soft drink crates can cause the stacks to topple over. Examples of incorrect stacking are:

- placing newly delivered full crates on top of crates of empty bottles or on empty crates, making the stack top-heavy
- stacking differently shaped crates together
- stacking crates on an uneven surface.

Always stack crates as follows:

- stack the same size and shaped crates
- ensure the guides at each corner on the top and bottom of the crates are slotted in correctly
- only stack together crates that are all empty; or all full with empty bottles; or all full with full bottles – never stack a mixture of these
- do not over-stack crates – four to five crates per stack is a maximum; any more makes handling (especially full crates) difficult and dangerous.

> **Definition**
>
> **Extraction spear:** a hollow tube attached to the keg's spear head valve (onto which the broaching head is connected). It is fitted with a spring-loaded valve that is opened by the keg's internal gas pressure which pushes the beer up the spear into the beer dispensing system. On no account must you ever attempt to remove an extraction spear from a keg (full or empty)!

Figure 16.8 Stacks that are top-heavy, wrongly shaped, on an uneven surface – and a safe stack

Falling kegs and casks

Do not attempt to stack empty kegs or casks unless they are in proper racks. They can easily topple if they are touched accidentally.

Back injuries through incorrect lifting

A great deal of lifting and moving of heavy kegs, beer crates, gas cylinders, etc. is required within the cellar area. All staff must follow the guidelines for safe lifting (see page 66) and always use the correct equipment (trolley, hydraulic lift, fork-lift, etc.) for moving heavy items, where these are provided. Never attempt to lift on your own something that may cause you injury.

Trap doors

Trap doors can fall back if they are not properly secured. The entrance must also be fenced off, with caution signs in position, to prevent pedestrians falling down into the cellar.

Low beams and other hazards

Low beams and doorways are often present in the cellars of old buildings. Ensure that well positioned, highly visible warning notices are sited to warn people of the low beams and any potentially dangerous suspended object.

> **Remember!**
> You must always tell someone you are going into an underground cellar, why you are going, and how long you think you will be down there. They can then check on you if you take longer than usual.

Try this!
Identify as many hazards as you can in Figure 16.9.

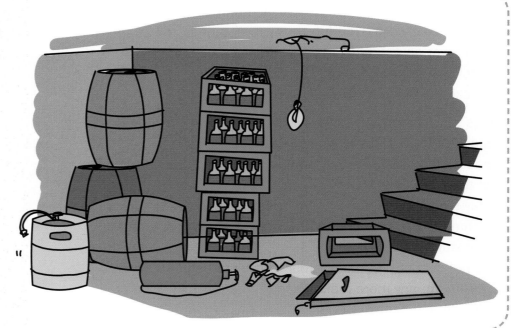

Figure 16.9 How many hazards can you see?

Major gas leaks

A major gas leak can be caused by a pipe fracturing or bursting, or a **pressure release valve** rupturing (this is set at 2500 lb p.s.i. (pounds per square inch)). It can also happen when a fault occurs in the **reducing valve** or **keg-extraction mechanism**.

If there is a major leak, you must:

o turn off the gas supply if you can do so without entering the cellar

o inform all staff and evacuate the area

o call for assistance

o do not let anyone enter the cellar under any circumstances until you are sure it is safe to do so

o open all outside doors and windows to ventilate the area.

Minor gas leaks

If you suspect a leak, you must immediately:

o ventilate the cellar by opening all doors and cellar flaps

o prevent anyone else from entering the cellar

o turn off the gas cylinder/regulator valve upstream of the leak, preferably at the cylinder tap

o spray the cellar floor with water (carbon dioxide is very soluble in water)

o report the leak to your supervisor.

Remember!

Gas (carbon dioxide and nitrogen) leaks are a major hazard in a cellar, especially an underground cellar. Leaks, both minor and major, can occur through faulty or poorly maintained equipment, or shoddy working practices by cellar staff.

Figure 16.10 A pressure release valve

Definitions

Pressure release valve (also know as the Bursting disc): a pressure-release system fitted to a gas cylinder to prevent it bursting. The disc will rupture if the pressure within the cylinder rises high enough to cause the cylinder to burst. If the pressure release valve does rupture, there will be a sudden loud hissing noise and cloud of white vapour as the gas escapes. The cylinder may fall over.

Extraction mechanism: a general term for the keg's extraction spear and broaching head system.

497

Dispense systems

Check for faults in the dispense system. Check that all nuts and seals are tight and listen for hissing sounds. Any suspected leaking joints and seals should be painted with liquid detergent (undiluted). If bubbles appear, a leak is present. Tighten any nuts until the bubbling ceases. If the bubbles persist, turn off the gas at the cylinder and replace the washer(s), reconnect and turn on the gas. Check, again using detergent, that the leak has been repaired.

Remember!
Carbon dioxide causes a feeling of a shortness of breath and breathing more quickly. If you feel this on entering the cellar – leave immediately and warn others.

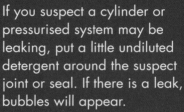

Did you know?
If you suspect a cylinder or pressurised system may be leaking, put a little undiluted detergent around the suspect joint or seal. If there is a leak, bubbles will appear.

Figure 16.11 Any suspected leaking joints or seals should be painted with undiluted liquid detergent – if bubbles appear, there is a leak

Building maintenance

- Door and cellar flaps – must be in good order (able to be opened and secured in accordance with security requirements).
- Steps, stairs, rolling ways and walkways – should be clean and in good order, free from waste, rubbish and any obstruction.
- Hand rails – should be secure and in good order.
- Walls and ceilings – must be kept clean (and painted to provide an impervious surface).
- Wall attachments – all equipment fittings attached to the walls (beer lines, cylinders, meters, regulators, etc.) should be in good order.
- Notices – check that all notices (warnings and instructions) are in the correct place and in good condition (immediately replace any that are missing or damaged).
- Cellar tidy – check that all tools are in place.
- Shelving – should be impervious, clean and in good condition with ridged, well maintained wall brackets.

- Floors, gulleys, drains, thralls/stillages – must be clean and free from waste and rubbish (such as used keg seals, corks, **spiles**, filter papers, water and beer residue).
- Sink and drainer – keep clean and free from waste, with no dirty equipment around. A daily disinfecting of the waste-water outlet to kill any build-up of yeasts and bacteria is necessary to prevent contamination, especially if cask-conditioned ales are present.
- Lighting – all should be in working order and providing adequate illumination. Check switches and spare bulbs/tubes.
- Electrical equipment – check this is working correctly, and that switches and cables are not damaged. The immediate area should be clean and free of rubbish.
- Cellar cooling – the thermostat should be set to the correct setting and the thermometer in the correct position, confirming the correct temperature.
- Buckets, mops, brushes and cleaning materials – should be clean, in good repair and properly stored in the allocated cupboard.
- Kegs, casks and crates – check all kegs, casks (on **thralls** and with scotches secure) and crates to ensure they are stored correctly. Make sure **gyle labels** and best-before dates are in correct rotation, so that stock does not go out of date. Full bottle crates should be easily accessible, and empty kegs, casks and crates should be placed ready for collection.
- Beer dispense systems – check that all connections are properly connected for cask and kegged beers, including kegged ciders and speciality beers (e.g. draught Guinness). Ensure there is a new cask or keg ready for change-over when the original is empty.
- In-line cooling systems – there are two main types of in-line cooling system for cooling beers and other drinks on tap. The first is a refrigeration unit, usually sited in the bar – the drink flows through fine tubes surrounded by coolant. The unit's temperature is set by a temperature-control switch. Each drink will have its own unit. The second method is known as the 'python', and consists of a large central pipe through which temperature-controlled cold water (the coolant) passes. The various drink lines run alongside the central tube, the whole being wrapped in an insulated sleeve. The water temperature is set by a temperature-control switch. With the python system, a number of drinks can be cooled in one line. Make sure the temperature is correct at the outlet (beer tap) and adjust accordingly.

Definitions

Gyle label: a brewery system of either a dated label (for casked ales) or plastic cap (for kegged ales) that is often colour-coded and identifies the days and dates when the ales/beers were brewed and kegged/casked. The colour coding aids identification in darkened cellars (and was useful in past times for those who could not read).

Spile: a small 'peg' that fits into the hole created when the 'shive' has been punched to allow the cask ale to 'work' during cellar conditioning. There are two types of spiles: a soft 'porous' spile which allows excess carbon-dioxide to escape while the beer is being 'conditioned' and a hard spile which is used to retain the carbon-dioxide within the cask after the beer has been 'conditioned'. Spiles should be changed daily to prevent any risk of contaminating the beer in the cask.

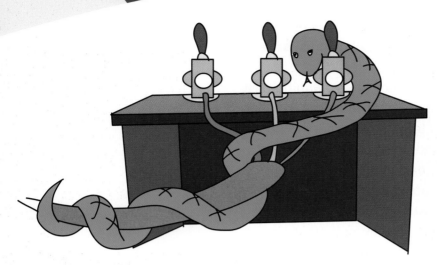

Figure 16.12 The python system of in-line cooling

o Spiles – all spiles used in conditioning and dispensing casks should be changed daily.
o Wines and spirits – check that storage is securely locked, products are in the correct position, and wines are properly stored. Check that the stock matches the stock/bin cards.

Stock checks

Stock should be checked according to the establishment's policy. Ideally this should be carried out on a regular basis using a random selection of six to twelve items.

Test yourself!

1 Name the Act that states that a health and safety officer must be appointed.

2 What actions should you take if an accident occurs?

3 What is the best way to stack crates?

4 What is the best way to move kegs or barrels?

5 How should gas cylinders be stored, and why?

6 What should you do if you suspect there may be a leak in the dispense system?

Preparing kegs and gas for use

When changing an empty keg to a full one, the following procedure must be followed.

○ Check that the new keg is full and the gyle label (keg's spear-head plastic cover) is in place and within the best-before date (by checking against the brewery's colour-code system chart).

Figure 16.13 A new, intact keg

○ Turn off the gas supply to the keg, either at the gas bottle tap (recommended) or at the in-line supply tap (between the gas bottle and the keg).

Figure 16.14 Turning off the gas supply

○ Release the **broaching head**. (The method depends on the type of head in the line – some are lever-operated, others require pushing down and twisting to unlock.) Make sure you know how to release the broaching head efficiently before attempting this operation, as you risk not only getting very wet from escaping beer, but also potential injury from the escaping beer if the release is not completed smoothly. Safety goggles should be worn while changing kegs.

○ Remove the empty keg and replace with the new one (if not already in place). Place the empty keg ready for returning to the brewery.

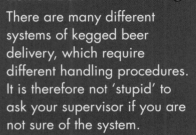

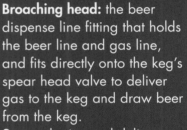

Definitions

Broaching head: the beer dispense line fitting that holds the beer line and gas line, and fits directly onto the keg's spear head valve to deliver gas to the keg and draw beer from the keg.

Spear: the internal delivery system of a beer keg, which is fitted to the head valve.

Spear head: the external fitting to a pressurised keg to which the broaching head is attached. The spear head must never be removed even when the keg is empty, as the keg is still pressurised.

Figure 16.15 A broaching head fitted to a pressurised washing bottle

o Remove the plastic gyle cap from the spear head on the keg and connect the broaching head firmly to the keg. Once again this must be achieved in one clean operation to minimise any beer escaping (the new keg is already pressurised). Check that the broaching head is seated correctly and not loose.

o When you are satisfied that the keg has been broached correctly, turn on the gas supply and ensure that the beer is flowing correctly at the bar tap.

Figure 16.16 Always wear protective goggles when changing kegs

Cleaning dispense lines

Keg beer, lager and cider

Beer and cider lines from the keg to the bar tap must be cleaned at least once a week to ensure that the beer remains clear and bright. Yeast deposits will eventually build up inside the pipes and restrict the flow, as well as contaminating the beer and cider.

As the beer dispense system involves high-pressure gas cylinders, it is most important that you are fully aware of the cleaning procedures before attempting to clean any beer/cider pressurised lines. Many instances are recorded of cellar/bar staff being injured through insufficient training on the cleaning of beer dispense systems (especially when leaving the gas tap on while disconnecting and changing cleaning bottles).

There are many different cleaning systems in operation, and it is important that you become fully familiar with the one used in your establishment. As each manufacturer's cleaning solutions will be different, it is most important that you read carefully the instructions on the side of the container and leaflets enclosed with any cleaning materials you use (especially indicating quantities). Never exceed the recommended measure. If you cannot find any information on quantities, dilution ratios and use ranges, then ask your supervisor. Never guess – this could have serious consequences. If you use cleaning materials at insufficient

Did you know?

Some kegging systems (e.g. Guinness) have their own internal gas supply within the keg. These kegs, when empty, only require the broaching head to be removed from the empty keg and fitted to the new keg. You must ensure that there is no external gas supply to these kegs. If in doubt, ask your supervisor before attempting to change kegs.

strength, cleaning will not be completed correctly. If you use cleaning materials at too concentrated a strength, damage will be caused to the beer delivery system.

> ## Find out!
> How many dispense systems are used in your place of work? What types of system are they? How is each one cleaned?

Cleaning agents

All cleaning agents must be handled as follows.

Keep a record of all chemicals used for cleaning and where they are stored. The record should also state the quantities in stock. This record is important not only for stock control, but also for the Fire Officer's information. If there is a fire on the premises, the Fire Officer will need to be aware of what toxic chemicals are held, and if they are explosive or toxic when in contact with a naked flame or heat.

Store all cleaning agents in a separate, lockable store cupboard outside the cellar, and keep it locked at all times when not in use.

Always read the manufacturer's label and instructions carefully before handling any cleaning agents.

Always handle chemical cleaning agents wearing protective rubber gloves.

Never transfer and store a cleaning agent in any container other than the one it was supplied in by the manufacturer. It is an offence under the health and safety laws to store toxic and corrosive chemicals in unmarked containers or in containers designed specifically for other items (especially food items).

After taking a cleaning agent out of its container, always replace the lid immediately and never leave the container unattended.

It is most important to isolate (turn off) the gas supply whenever you disconnect the broaching head from the keg or pressurised cleaning bottle. As there is always a small risk of you forgetting to turn off the gas, you should always wear protective goggles when cleaning beer dispense lines. If you do accidentally release the broaching head before turning off the gas (or releasing the cleaning bottle's pressure release valve), do not try to replace the broaching

> ### Remember!
> If you suspect that any part of the dispense system is not as it should be, you must report it to your superior immediately. Remember – the system operates on high-pressure gas, and the risk of serious injury from faulty equipment is always a real possibility. If in any doubt – do not use it.

> ### Remember!
> Your employer must provide you with personal protective equipment for use when carrying out hazardous tasks (see page 50).

> ### Did you know?
> Serious injuries and deaths are caused each year through toxic cleaning chemicals being placed in drinks bottles (for example, bleach stored in lemonade bottles or disinfectant stored in cola bottles).

head, but leave and, if possible, turn off the gas at the cylinder. If this is not possible, vacate the cellar and call for assistance.

The basic manual method used to clean the lines is as follows, using two pressurised cleaning bottles. (This procedure is also used for carbon dioxide/nitrogen mixes.)

○ **Turn off the carbon dioxide gas at the cylinder.** An isolation switch or tap built into the gas supply line between the keg and gas cylinder may be available, but ensure it is the nearest one to the gas cylinder. If in any doubt, always turn the cylinder off at the cylinder head.

○ Remove the broaching head from the keg.

○ Prime the washing bottle with water and cleaning fluid, mixed according to the manufacturer's instructions.

○ Make sure the pressurised cleaning bottle is secured and cannot be knocked over. Connect the broaching head to the washing bottle (with the bottle's pressure valve tightened).

> **Remember!**
>
> If you realise that you have forgotten to put the cleaning fluid into the pressurised cleaning bottle, and you have already turned on the gas – stop, and remember that you must turn off the gas and release the pressure using the pressure release valve before you remove the broaching head and bottle's top!

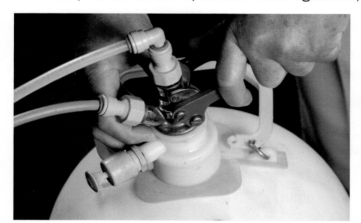

Figure 16.17 Fitting the broaching head to the water-rinse bottle

Figure 16.18 Closing the pressure valve on the pressurised washing bottle

○ **Turn on the carbon dioxide gas cylinder.**

○ Open the beer dispense tap at the bar to draw the cleaning fluid through. Allow it to stand as per the manufacturer's instructions.

○ **Turn off the carbon dioxide gas cylinder.**

○ Release the pressure from the washing bottle and remove the broaching head.

○ Fit the broaching head to the water-rinse bottle (this bottle can be the one used for washing,

Figure 16.19 Opening the beer dispense tap at the bar to draw the cleaning fluid through

but it must be rinsed thoroughly before use with fresh, clean water). Fill with clean water before the head is fitted and the pressure valve tightened.

○ **Turn on the carbon dioxide gas cylinder.**

○ Open the beer dispense tap at the bar and draw the clean water through. When the water runs clear and bright, smell and taste to ensure no cleaning material remains in the system. Some manufacturers supply a testing kit for this purpose.

○ **Turn off the carbon dioxide gas cylinder.**

○ Release the pressure in the water rinse bottle and remove the broaching head.

○ Connect the broaching head to the keg.

○ **Turn on the carbon dioxide gas cylinder.**

○ Open the beer dispense tap and draw beer through, tasting for quality.

Figure 16.20 Connecting the broaching head to the keg

Cleaning cask ale dispense systems

Cask-conditioned ales are used less frequently than keg beers because they are more difficult and expensive to maintain, and have a limited shelf life. However, cask-conditioned ales are becoming more popular with modern beer drinkers. The high-profile Campaign for Real Ale (CAMRA) has been successful in demanding their inclusion in many pubs' beer list tariffs.

Unlike keg beers, cask-conditioned (draught) ales have very little carbon dioxide present, and are delivered to the bar tap either by suction or pump action using a **beer engine**.

As live yeasts are present in cask-conditioned ales, the beer lines will become contaminated more frequently than for kegged beers/ciders, and therefore require more frequent cleaning.

The ale's condition should be checked daily at the bar tap outlet and at the cask in the cellar. If '**fobbing**' or any sign of a haze is present (especially at the bar tap), then the line must be cleaned immediately.

To clean the beer line, the following procedure must be followed.

- Ensure you have a sterile stainless steel or ridged plastic bucket, funnel and filter paper to hand.
- Turn off the flow at the cask tap.
- Unscrew the line fitting and allow the beer in the line to flow into the bucket (this then returns to the cask through the shive using the filter paper and funnel).
- Place the end of the line into a container of cleaning fluid and cold water according to the manufacturer's instructions.
- Draw the cleaning fluid into the system using the hand pump mechanism at the bar until the cleaning fluid appears as per the manufacturer's instructions.
- Drain the cleaning fluid from the line and discard.
- Place the end of the line into a container of fresh, clean water and draw through the system using the bar hand pump mechanism until all the cleaning fluid is removed.
- Drain the water from the line.
- Reconnect the line to the cask tap and turn on the tap.
- Finally draw the ale through the system until it runs clear and smell and taste before serving.

Remember!

It is most important that you check that the whole dispense system is free of any cleaning agent by testing the system (by sight, smell and taste). This will ensure that the beer will meet not only the food hygiene and health and safety requirements, but also the high product quality expected by the customer. Beers contaminated with cleaning agents can cause an allergic reaction, nausea, sickness and diarrhoea.

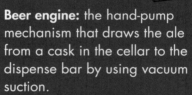

Definitions

Beer engine: the hand-pump mechanism that draws the ale from a cask in the cellar to the dispense bar by using vacuum suction.

Fobbing: a term used for the foaming of beer at the pump, which can be caused by over-gassing of the ale in the keg/cask, dirty pipes, etc.

Test yourself!

1 What is the broaching head?

2 Why might a keg have no external gas supply?

3 Describe the steps involved in cleaning the dispense lines for keg beer, lager or cider.

4 Describe the steps involved in cleaning the dispense lines for cask ale.

17

Receiving and storing drinks

In this chapter you will cover skills and knowledge in the following units:

○ 7132 – Unit 219 (2BS9): Receive, store and issue drinks stock

Working through this chapter could also provide evidence for the following Functional Skills:

Functional English – Speaking, listening and communication Level 1

Functional Mathematics – Representing and analysing Level 1

Functional ICT – Using ICT, finding and selecting information

In this chapter you will learn how to:

○ receive drinks deliveries

○ store and issue drinks stocks

Receiving drinks deliveries

The supply and sale of drinks (especially alcoholic drinks) is controlled by the liquor licensing laws, therefore all movement of drinks must be recorded, from the manufacturer to the consumer (customer).

Figure 17.1 An accurate paper trail is important when receiving, storing and issuing drinks

To ensure an accurate record is kept of the drinks during their journey from manufacturer to consumer, a series of forms is used to show their passage from one agency to the next (both internal and external).

The storage of all drinks must be in a secure area because:
○ alcoholic drinks must be stored so that no-one under the age of 18 years has access to them unsupervised
○ the value of these commodities is high, so access must be secure and the cellar open to authorised personnel only
○ spirits contain a high proportion of alcohol (on average 40% by volume), which is highly inflammable – therefore the storage area must meet Fire Safety Regulations
○ drinks are classed as a foodstuff, so the storage area and their storage must meet the food hygiene regulations – the regulations apply especially to draught casked ales and kegged beers and cider, because they will be exposed to the air and through delivery systems during dispense (see Chapter 16).

Keeping accurate records will ensure that theft and illegal transactions are kept to a minimum, and can be quickly investigated if drinks go missing.

It is therefore most important that correct procedures and documentation are strictly followed during any handling of all drinks delivered to the establishment (receiving, storing and dispensing).

Health and safety

Health and safety while working in a cellar environment is of extremely high importance, and the safety of yourself, other employees and visitors must always be the priority (see Chapter 16).

Safety equipment and clothing, including heavy-duty rubber gloves, protective goggles, hard hats, heavy-duty steel-capped shoes and leather aprons are recommended when performing manual duties within the cellar area (see page 493).

Any visitor to the cellar area must also wear the appropriate protective clothing (especially a hard hat), and be made aware of all potential hazards while in the area. They should be restricted to a 'safe' area, and accompanied by an authorised member of staff who has access to the cellar at all times.

The Health and Safety at Work Act requires that all businesses have a Health and Safety Officer (a member of the business's staff), who is responsible for implementing all health and safety issues on the premises. He/she is also responsible for advising staff on all health and safety issues.

Frequent cellar accidents that occur during deliveries are caused by:
○ falling cellar trap doors
○ trapped fingers and toes (from dropped items)
○ back injuries from lifting heavy items
○ injuries to the head through knocking on low ceilings and doorways
○ falling equipment, casks, kegs, gas cylinders, crates, etc.
○ cuts from broken glass
○ slipping on wet floors
○ tripping over items left on the floor
○ electric shocks from faulty switches and equipment.

If an accident occurs, it must be recorded in the Accident Record Book (date, time, description of accident, who was involved, and action taken) and also reported to your supervisor.

Remember!
When dealing with valuable stock items, it is most important that everything is accurate. If you are in any doubt, or suspect a problem, you must inform your superior immediately.

Did you know?
Under the provisions of the Health and Safety at Work Act 1974 (HASAWA) it is the responsibility of all employees to ensure their own safety and the safety of others.

Remember!
Accidents are mainly caused through human error, carelessness or negligence, through not following proper procedures.

Checking deliveries

Drinks sales are an important part of our industry, and account for about 60% of income through sales. Not only are the drinks themselves of high value, but many of the containers are returnable and will have a charge levied on them (crates, bottles, and now casks and kegs). Even damaged crates, bottles, casks and kegs are returnable, and will normally be credited as if they were returned undamaged.

Figure 17.2 Drinks are a valuable commodity!

Whenever drinks ordered are delivered, it is important that a competent member of staff is present to check and receive the delivery.

If you have been given the task of receiving a delivery, it is a measure of the trust that has been placed in you by your employer to ensure the drinks delivered are correct, in good condition and well within the best-before, use-by and sell-by dates. Once the drinks have been signed for, any discrepancies or damage will become the responsibility of your establishment – so it is essential that everything is checked thoroughly!

Never take anything for granted. If you suspect that something is not right, then check it thoroughly. This can include manufacturers' sealed cartons, and every crate of bottles (even when the top crate looks full and correct). If you are unsure, check with your supervisor.

Remember!

If you are returning empty beer casks, you must ensure that both the '**keystone**' and '**shive**' openings are sealed with clean corks to keep the cask 'sweet' and prevent contamination from bacteria and wild yeasts.

Definitions

Keystone: a grooved disc situated in the base of one end of a beer cask into which the beer tap is placed.
Shive: a wooden 'biscuit-like' disc with a grooved centre that is placed into the top opening of a beer cask. The grooved centre is 'punched out' and a spile fitted when the beer is being 'conditioned' in the cellar.

Preparation

To ensure speedy and efficient receipt of the delivery, you must prepare the cellar as follows.

- All **chargeable containers** should be placed ready for removal, complete with documentation. This will normally include:
  - chargeable empty containers
  - any stock or containers returned due to damage – broken bottles, crates, etc. can be returned to the brewery and a credit received for them.
  - any faulty beer and cider kegs, casks, etc.
  - any empty carbon dioxide gas cylinders (if supplied by the drinks company).
- Clear and clean specific areas ready for the incoming stock (kegs, casks, bottle crates, etc.) to prevent it getting mixed up with old stock.
- Ensure the access to each storage area is free of obstructions and rubbish, and is not wet and slippery (if it is – mop and dry it).
- Ensure warning signs and barriers for the public are ready for positioning at open cellar trap doors.

> **Definition**
>
> **Chargeable containers:** bottles, crates, kegs and casks that have had a 'deposit' levied on them by the brewery and is refundable when the containers (including damaged items) are returned to the brewery.

Receiving the delivery

Before unloading begins, check the delivery note against the order form to ensure no additional, unwanted items have been included.

Figure 17.3 Receiving the drinks delivery

If the **drayman** or delivery man is new to your establishment, show them where the items are to be placed before unloading begins. Warn them about any possible dangers specific to your cellar.

Never try to lift or carry anything that may cause you an injury. Always use the correct equipment (a trolley, truck or cart), or seek assistance. If you do attempt to lift a crate, you must follow the correct procedures (see page 66):

- wear strong protective gloves
- check there are no obstacles in your path (the route along which you are going to carry the item)
- do not try to lift too much weight at any one time
- spread the weight of the item evenly between your hands
- bend your legs at the knees
- keep your back straight and your head/neck straight
- try to lift in one movement.

Check all items for damage, correct amounts and contents, and best-before dates. Check each item individually against the order to ensure the right things have been delivered in the right quantities. Check the gyle numbers (see page 501) for kegs and casks. Kegs and casks should be weighed to ensure they are full.

Check wine, spirit and liqueur bottles for intact seals, brand names, and vintages as detailed on the order form.

In addition to drinks, other items may be included in the delivery. For example, a delivery might include glassware (purchased or hired), which must be checked to ensure the number is correct and that no glasses are chipped, cracked or the wrong style (e.g. goblets mixed in with flutes). Also check that the glasses are clean and in a hygienic condition.

Carbon dioxide gas cylinders must be secured immediately on delivery and not left for securing later (see page 494). Check that there are no leaks (using a little neat detergent if necessary; see page 498). Leaks may happen during transportation of cylinders, especially if the drayman is careless. Reject any cylinders that are leaking.

If any items are dropped or damaged during delivery, make a record of how they were damaged and who was responsible. Ask the delivery man to read and sign the report as a true record of events, for any insurance claims.

Definition

Drayman: someone who delivers drinks.

Did you know?

Back injuries from lifting incorrectly, and from lifting very heavy objects, are one of the most common industrial accidents.

Figure 17.4 An example of a gyle label

Figure 17.5 Dropped or damaged items should be recorded carefully

Record any items you reject, on your copy of the order form, giving the reason for rejecting them. You should obtain a cover note from the delivery man for all rejected items.

Check the credit note for all container returns to ensure it tallies with your documentation.

After the delivery

After the delivery has been completed, ensure that the cellar trap doors are properly closed and locked, and the area is made safe with any debris, spillage/breakages cleared away.

All items should be stored in the correct place and secured properly. New stock should be placed behind old stock, so that older stock is used up first (first in, first out – see page 159).

Any old stock nearing its best-before, sell-by or use-by date should be brought to your supervisor's attention – a special offer promotion could be advertised to ensure the stock is sold before it becomes out of date.

Check that all new stock (especially crates) has been stacked correctly and safely. Some common mistakes include placing newly delivered, full crates on top of crates of empty bottles, or on empty

Figure 17.6 If use-by dates are carefully tracked, special promotions can help avoid wastage

513

crates, making the stack top-heavy; stacking differently shaped crates together; and stacking crates on an uneven surface (for the correct way to stack crates, see page 495).

Return all completed documentation to your supervisor, and report any missing, damaged or incorrect supplies immediately.

Find out!

The person who controls the delivery of drinks stocks will vary, depending on the size and type of organisation. Who is the person responsible for this in your place of work?

Documentation

The importance of an efficient and accurate record of the movement and storage of all packaged drinks (especially alcoholic drinks) and related items (gas cylinders and chargeable containers) cannot be over-emphasised.

In addition to ensuring that no pilferage takes place, accurate records will be required for:
- stock checks
- re-ordering supplies
- accounting and taxation
- use by the fire officer, in case of fire (what spirits and other flammable items are on the premises, and where they are located)
- avoiding over-run of sell-by or best-before dates.

Basic forms

In a large catering establishment, the number of forms required will be greater than those required for a small pub or café. The number of forms increases with the number of different staff handling the drinks between the time of ordering and the point of sale. The basic forms include:
- requisition form
- order form
- delivery note
- invoice
- statement
- payment.

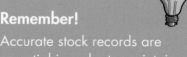

Remember!
Accurate stock records are essential in order to maintain stock levels and to identify when new stock needs to be ordered.

Requisition form

Each department and drinks dispensing outlet (bar, restaurant, coffee shop, room-service mini-bars, etc.) will require new drinks stock to replenish sold items. The request for stock will be made on a requisition form. In large establishments, there may be a separate 'control' office which will process all orders. In smaller outlets, it may be the same person creating the requisition and then drawing up the order.

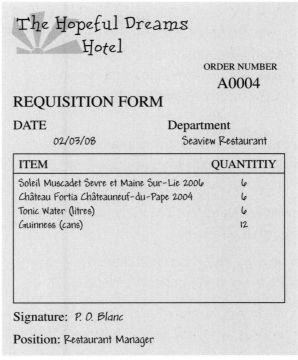

Figure 17.7 The requisition form

Order form

All drinks to be purchased will first be recorded on an order form, and the order sent by post or electronically by email, or dictated over the telephone to a telesales operator.

It is important that you have a copy of the order with you when checking incoming drinks orders.

The delivery driver (drayman) will have your order, accompanied by a delivery note.

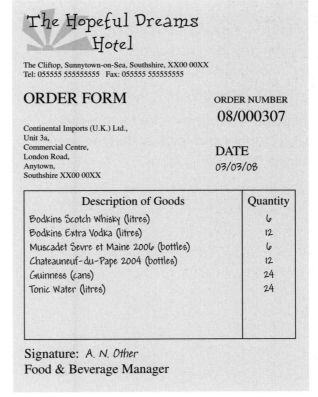

Figure 17.8 The order form

Delivery note

This form is the wholesaler's copy of the original order form, and contains the details of the order. It will include whether the items are in stock and therefore in the delivery, or out of stock (and therefore not delivered).

The delivery note will also include a container credit note (either as part of the delivery note itself, or separately) for all containers delivered.

Delivery and credit notes do not normally have the cost of the goods recorded on them.

At the end of a delivery, the customer signs the delivery note to say that the delivery has been accepted. This then goes back to the wholesaler.

Continental Imports (U.K) Ltd

Unit 3a, Commercial Centre, London Road, Anytown, Southshire XX00 00XX
Tel: 1234 98765432   Fax:12345 98765432

DELIVERY NOTE

ORDER N°
08/000307

The Hopeful Dreams Hotel,
The Cliftop, Sunnytown-on-Sea,
Southshire, XX00 00XX

Account N°
532189

DATE:
04/03/2008

Product Code	Description	Size	Quantity	Check
S0055	Bodkins Scotch Whisky	Litre	6	
S0057	Bodkins Extra Vodka	Litre	12	
W0032	Muscadet Sevre et Maine 2006	Bottle	Out of stock	
W0051	Chateauneuf-du-Pape 2004	Bottle	12	
B0018	Guinness	Cans 440	24	
N0012	Tonic Water	Litre	24	
		Total	78	

Signature: _____

Print Name: _____

Figure 17.9 The delivery note

Invoice

The invoice is sent to your establishment after the signed delivery note has been received back by the supplier. It details how much your organisation will have to pay the supplier for the goods delivered.

For small businesses, it is common for the delivery note, container credit note and invoice all to be included on a single form (the invoice).

Continental Imports (U.K) Ltd

Unit 3a, Commercial Centre, London Road, Anytown, Southshire XX00 00XX
Tel: 1234 98765432   Fax:12345 98765432

INVOICE

Invoice N°
08/000334

The Hopeful Dreams Hotel,
The Cliftop, Sunnytown-on-Sea,
Southshire, XX00 00XX

Account N°
532189

Invoice Date:
03/04/2008

Product Code	Description	Size	Quantity	List price	Net price	Check
S0055	Bodkins Scotch Whisky	Litre	6	12.95	77.70	
S0057	Bodkins Extra Vodka	Litre	12	12.50	150.00	
W0032	Muscadet Sevre et Maine 2006	Bottle	0	0.00	0.00	
W0051	Chateauneuf-du-Pape 2004	Bottle	12	16.95	203.40	
B0018	Guinness	Cans 440	24	1.32	31.68	
N0012	Tonic Water	Litre	24	0.96	23.04	
		Total	78	Gross price		511.32
				Discount 5%		25.50
				Net Price		485.82

Signature: _____

Print Name: _____

Figure 17.10 The invoice

Statement

A statement is a document that is issued at regular intervals by suppliers to their customers, often at the end of each calendar month. The control section will check all invoices against the statement, and if all is correct the account will be settled according to the terms of credit.

Continental Imports (U.K) Ltd

Unit 3a, Commercial Centre, London Road, Anytown, Southshire XX00 00XX
Tel: 1234 98765432   Fax:12345 98765432

STATEMENT

Statement Date
31/03/2008

The Hopeful Dreams Hotel,
The Cliftop, Sunnytown-on-Sea,
Southshire, XX00 00XX

Account N° :
532189

Date	Invoice Number	Goods	Balance
03/04/2008	08/000334	485.82	485.82
11/03/2008	08/000396	621.97	1083.50
18/03/2008	08/000427	392.16	1475.66
25/03/2008	08/000503	441.74	197.40

Terms of Credit: 30 days

Current	30 days overdue	60 days overdue	90 days overdue	total
£1917.40	£00.00	£00.00	£00.00	£1917.40

Figure 17.11 The statement

Payment

Different organisations have different arrangements for paying suppliers. In large organisations, the control department may check all invoices against a monthly statement, and if all is correct the account will be settled according to the **terms of credit**. Smaller organisations may not have credit terms with suppliers.

Storing and issuing drink stocks

Chapter 16 describes in detail the correct methods of storing drinks in cellars. Special attention must be paid to safety, hygiene and security.

We have seen how deliveries are received – now we will look at the importance of maintaining drink stocks at the right levels, and how drink stocks are issued.

Maintaining drink stocks

In addition to the set of basic forms required for the ordering and delivery of goods from the wholesale supplier/retailers (pages 515–517), a number of internal documents are used for controlling all stock on the premises, covering the period from when the stock is delivered to when it is sold.

As with ordering and delivery, the number of forms necessary to ensure maximum control of the drink stocks will depend on the size of the establishment. A large hotel with multiple departments and a large staff will require a larger number of forms to make tracking the drink much easier as it passes between various sections.

Figure 17.12 Large establishments will require a large number of forms to track sales

For a small establishment, issues will usually be recorded in a cellar stock record book, being entered (and signed for) by the member of staff drawing the stock during the working day. At the end of trading, the issues may be transferred, together with any receipts for the day, to the appropriate bin cards.

While these documents may be computerised, many establishments still use paper-based records within departments, as this prevents the risk of fraud. (Fraud might be possible by re-entering/changing the computer files – although this practice is becoming more difficult with modern computer programmes that automatically back up all entries.)

Figure 17.13 Smaller establishments will have a simpler system

Find out!

What types of document are used in your organisation to track drinks issues?

Basic forms

The full list of cellar documentation is as follows:

○ goods received book – for all goods received, including crates, bottles, etc.
○ container account book – all charged containers are recorded in this book
○ cellar stock record book – all cellar stock receipts and issues recorded
○ **bin cards** – for all individual items
○ requisition book – each department should send in a request for new stock
○ cellar transfer book – all issues and returns for the day are recorded, then entered in the cellar/stock record book
○ bar record book – each bar will have a book to show stock issues and receipts
○ off-sales book – records all off-sales (take-away), as these are not consumed on the premises and therefore command a lower price.

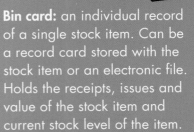

Definition

Bin card: an individual record of a single stock item. Can be a record card stored with the stock item or an electronic file. Holds the receipts, issues and value of the stock item and current stock level of the item.

Stock-taking

As the value of drinks stock is high, and many items have a limited shelf life, accurate stock checks are an important routine in any catering establishment.

Because most drinks items are 'packaged' in units (bottles, cans, tetrapaks, etc.), and are sold in these units, it is easy to identify if sales tally with deliveries and stock held. Stock checks will identify any discrepancies, but must be accurate – and ideally carried out at random to discourage any potential opportunist thief.

A regular and complete stock check should be carried out on a monthly basis (while still carrying out random checks on a random selection of stock items). Most businesses will conduct quarterly, half-yearly and annual thorough stock checks by professional independent stock-checkers.

If you are required to conduct a stock check, you must check everything – including all crated bottles, and that they are full. This includes checking that seals have not been broken, that crown corks are intact, and that bottles are full.

Double-check any discrepancies and report them to your supervisor.

Figure 17.14 The stock check

Test yourself!

1 How might drinks stocks be documented in (a) a large hotel and (b) a small café?

2 What is a bin card?

3 What should you list when carrying out a stock check?

18

Preparing and serving hot drinks

In this chapter you will cover skills and knowledge in the following units:

- 7132 – Unit 217 (2BS7): Prepare and serve dispensed and instant hot drinks; and Unit 218 (2BS8): Prepare and serve hot drinks using specialist equipment
- 7103 – Unit 110: Hot beverage skills
- 7103 – Unit 208: Service of hot beverages

Working through this chapter could also provide evidence for the following Functional Skills:

Functional English – Speaking, listening and communication Level 1

Functional English – Reading Level 1

Functional Mathematics – Analysing Level 1

In this chapter you will learn:

- about hot drinks and their ingredients
- how to prepare the work area for service
- how to prepare equipment for service
- how to prepare and serve hot drinks

Hot drinks

Hot drinks can be served either as an accompaniment to food, or on their own. Coffee or tea are often served at the end of a meal in a restaurant. Many bars also serve hot drinks throughout the day.

The main types of hot drink served in the UK are coffee, tea and chocolate.

Within these broad categories, there is a great variety. For example, look at the two cups of coffee pictured on the right.

Figure 18.1 Coffee, tea and chocolate are the main hot drinks consumed in the UK

Figure 18.2 Coffee can be served in very different ways

The equipment, ingredients and skills used to make these two cups of coffee are very different. The mug of instant coffee is quick and easy to serve. The espresso is made using specialist equipment and freshly ground, high-quality coffee beans. In this chapter you will learn how to prepare and serve a range of hot drinks using the appropriate equipment and techniques.

Ingredients

You need to know a bit about where these drinks come from, and the ingredients you are using. This will help you to make good quality drinks. You will also be able to give your customers information about the drinks you are serving.

Coffee

Coffee was first discovered over 1500 years ago in Ethiopia and introduced into Europe in the seventeenth century via Turkey, reaching England by 1650, when the first coffee house was opened in Oxford.

The London Stock Exchange and Lloyds of London were both originally coffee houses. Stockbrokers met over coffee in Jonathan's Coffee House in Exchange Alley, and ship-owners and marine insurance brokers met in Edward Lloyd's Coffee House in Lombard Street.

Coffee contains high quantities of caffeine, which stimulates the respiratory and nervous systems. This is why many people say they need a coffee to wake them up in the morning!

Coffee owes its range of flavours to a number of factors: the plant variety, its origin (where it is grown), how it is processed and how it is blended and roasted. As such it is very similar to wine: you may choose a grape variety such as chardonnay or shiraz, and then choose the origin, for example France or South Africa. Such choices open up a world of different flavour possibilities.

Figure 18.3 Coffee beans growing on a plantation

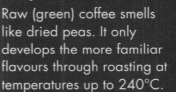

Did you know?
Raw (green) coffee smells like dried peas. It only develops the more familiar flavours through roasting at temperatures up to 240°C.

Variety

While there are over 60 different species of coffee bush (*Coffea*), just two of these are mainly used, either individually or blended together:

○ *Coffea arabica*: known as arabica coffee, it has a light citrus flavour and accounts for 75% of the world's coffee

○ *Coffea canephora*: known as robusta coffee; this has a rounder, more earthy flavour.

Origin

Different climates, soil conditions and altitude all influence the flavour of coffee. For example, Brazilian coffee generally has a soft wheat flavour, whilst Kenyan coffee has a citrus lemony flavour.

Processing

The fruit of the coffee plant is called the *cherry*. Coffee beans are actually the pips found inside the coffee cherry. Processing means extracting the beans from the coffee cherry. There are two main processes for doing this: the 'dry' or 'natural' process and the 'wet' or 'washed' process.

Dry processing dries the coffee cherries in the sun and then separates the brittle outer cherry skin from the beans. Dry processed coffee is generally sweeter, with a richer body and sometimes an earthy flavour.

Wet processing separates the coffee beans from the outer cherry skin first and then soaks the beans in water to dispose of the sticky pulp (mucilage) that surrounds them before they are finally dried. Wet processed beans tend to have a more citrus flavour and a lighter body.

Roasting

Up until this point the beans are still green. It is the roasting process that changes the beans into the more familiar brown colour and flavour. The roaster may choose to roast a coffee from a single origin or create a blend or recipe of beans of different varieties or origins. The longer the beans are roasted, the more bitterness is developed in the flavour and the natural citrus flavours of the beans are diminished. The resultant beans are what we grind to make the many varied coffee drinks.

Coffee is brewed by mixing roasted, ground coffee beans with hot water (see page 542). There are many different ways of doing this, and many different styles of coffee can be ordered.

For the best results, coffee needs serving fresh. This means protecting the beans from air which oxidises the oils in the beans and creates a stale flavour. Staleness can be prevented by good stock rotation and careful resealing of opened packaging. Once beans are ground, they oxidise more quickly and so need using as soon as possible.

Coffee is available to catering establishments in many forms, as coffee bags, pre-ground coffee, instant coffee and fresh beans.

Tea

Tea is the dried and processed leaves from the tea bush (*Camellia sinensis*), which is grown in tropical regions of the world. Although tea comes from one main plant variety, it can be served in a variety of different styles with a variety of different flavours. These are caused by differences in climate, altitude and soil conditions where the tea is grown, giving rise to such differences as the fragrant Darjeeling teas and the more pungent Assam teas, from neighbouring Indian regions. Variety is also dependent on how the tea is processed, giving rise to the four main types of tea: white, green, black and oolong.

Figure 18.4 Harvesting tea leaves

White tea

When tea is plucked it is just the new leaves at the tip of the shoots that are prized. White tea gets its name as it uses mainly the unfurled leaf bud at the end of the shoot which has tiny white hairs on it.

Once collected, the leaves are withered (left to wilt, reducing the moisture content), then steamed to stop **oxidation**. The leaves are rolled, often by hand, before being dried. The final tea made with these leaves is a pale white wine colour with a light delicate flavour.

Green tea

Green tea follows a similar process to white tea although more of the young leaves are used rather than just the unfurled bud. The tea retains its green colour as it is not allowed to oxidise. It is steamed, rolled and dried. The final drink can be slightly darker in colour than white tea but still has a fragrant light flavour.

Black tea

Black tea develops its darker colour and more pungent flavour because it is allowed to oxidise.

The picked tea is withered, allowing the leaves to be rolled without breaking the surface of the leaf.

The rolling process follows one of two main styles: Orthodox or CTC (Cut, Tear, and Curl).

The orthodox method treats the leaves with more care than the CTC method. The green leaves are put into a rolling machine which squeezes and rolls them, breaking the cell structure which starts the chemical process of oxidation.

The CTC method is often used for larger scale manufacturing. It produces smaller leaf particles often associated with tea bags, where quick brewing is desired. The leaves are minced by the rollers of the CTC machine, speeding up the oxidation process.

With both methods, the tea darkens in colour and produces a deeper flavour and caffeine, until the oxidation process is halted by drying.

Did you know?
Over 75 million cups of tea are drunk in Britain every day!

Definition
Oxidation — an enzyme reaction that turns tea leaves brown. It is the same process that causes an apple to turn brown if you cut it in half.

Did you know?
Tea bags for commercial use can now be obtained in 2, 4 and 6 cup bags.

Oolong tea

Oolong tea is half way between green and black tea. It is semi-oxidised. The leaves are withered and then bruised by being shaken in baskets. This starts the oxidation process around the edges of the leaves only. The leaves are dried when the required balanced of oxidised and non-oxidised flavours has been developed.

Most teas are now sold in individual portions (tea bags) that allow for easy portion and quality control. Many specialist teas are still sold in loose-leaf form (in packets) and require the appropriate equipment to serve them, including a tea strainer.

Tea also contains caffeine as well as other healthy elements including vitamins, minerals and trace elements, especially when taken with milk.

Tea is brewed by mixing dried tea leaves with boiling water (see page 548). Whether you are using tea bags or finest leaf tea, the same degree of care should be followed to ensure the customer enjoys their cup of tea.

Figure 18.5 A nation of tea-drinkers

Chocolate

Chocolate was first introduced to Europe in the seventeenth century.

Cocoa, the vital ingredient in making chocolate, comes from the beans at the centre of the melon like pods that grown on the cocoa tree. Two main varieties exist: *Criollo* that gives the prized refined floral fruit flavours, and *Forastero*, that gives a more earthy flavoured chocolate. A third variety, *Trinitario*, is a crossbreed of the two.

The largest cocoa-producing areas are Ghana and the Ivory Coast in Africa. These produce about 70% of the world's production. Other key countries include Venezuela, Papua New Guinea, and Indonesia.

When the cocoa pod is cut from the tree, it is split open to reveal the beans at the centre, covered in a sticky mucilage. The beans are covered by banana leaves and left in the sun until the mucilage ferments and drains away. They are then spread out on concrete patios in the sun and left to dry to about 6% moisture. Just like coffee, the beans are then roasted to develop the flavour. A winnowing machine is used to remove the shells, leaving cocoa nibs.

The nibs are then ground down to produce cocoa liquor, which looks like a chocolate version of peanut butter. Using a machine invented by Van Houten, the liquor is pressed. This separates off the melted cocoa butter leaving a cocoa presscake (a cake of compacted cocoa powder).

Chocolate is finally produced by mixing the cocoa butter (for finer chocolate), or other vegetable oils into the cocoa powder. Sugar, milk powder, and other flavouring such as vanilla may also be added in. The chocolate is then 'conched' in a machine that kneads it at temperatures between 60°–75°C. This makes it smoother.

Finally the chocolate is 'tempered'. The chocolate temperature is reduced to 40°C to allow the cocoa butter to crystallise. The liquid chocolate is then poured into the moulds that make our bars.

Cocoa powder, from which chocolate drinks are made, has no sugar added. When sweetened with sugar, the powder is known as drinking chocolate. Hot chocolate is the national breakfast drink in Spain.

Hot chocolate drinks are easy to make using cocoa powder made into a paste with a little cold water and topped with boiling/steamed milk (see page 550).

Water

The secret of producing any hot drink is in the quality of the water used to brew it. The water we draw from our fresh water supply will vary from region to region, mainly differing between soft and hard waters. Hard water is found in the counties of Kent, Hampshire and Sussex, and in other limestone and chalk areas of the country.

Figure 18.6 Hard water causes white scaly deposits

○ Hard water is water drawn from sources that have limestone-based, chalky soils. The limestone is easily dissolved in the water as it passes through the soil when it rains.
○ Soft water is drawn from sources with heavy, granite-based soils with no limestone.

You can tell if the water in your area is hard by the white, scaly deposits left on the insides of kettles, boilers and saucepans after water has been boiled in them a few times.

Hard water slows down the infusing time by blocking up the pores of the tea leaves and coffee grounds, almost doubling the time it takes for the tea or coffee to brew. Water softeners are available to remove the limestone and other minerals from hard water. In hard-water areas, regular descaling of equipment (especially nozzles, filters and taps) is necessary to prevent blockages.

The majority of bottled mineral waters are classed as hard waters, and are not suitable for brewing tea or coffee.

Whenever we use water to brew a hot beverage, it must be freshly drawn from the cold water supply and brought to a rapid boil (tea) or 89–96°C (coffee). Water that has been boiling for a long time, or reboiled, will be flat and lifeless (notice how the dissolved air and oxygen bubble and escape when the water boils).

Ice

Iced teas and coffees, popular on the European mainland and in the USA, are now gaining popularity in the UK. Also, chocolate drinks may be allowed to go cold, then sweetened, topped with whipped cream and grated chocolate, and served as iced chocolate.

The ice is usually produced using small, table-top ice machines that can produce small ice cubes at −1°C. These melt very quickly and should only be added to drinks at point of serving.

Ice for drinks is classed as a 'food', and therefore comes under the Food Hygiene Regulations. Make sure the ice machine is cleaned daily, and do not leave ice scoops in with the ice, to prevent cross-contamination.

Figure 18.7 Iced tea is a refreshing drink

Milk

On mainland Europe, people usually drink their tea and coffee without adding milk. The British rarely drink their tea without milk, and half of them take milk with their coffee.

The style of milk available varies from rich full-cream milks to skimmed milk. The choice of milk will affect the flavour of the tea or coffee:

- full-cream milk (approximately 4% fat) – entire milk, which can be very rich when produced from Guernsey and Jersey cows
- semi-skimmed milk (approximately 2% fat) – with half the fat removed
- skimmed milk – with all the fat removed
- pasteurised milk – heat-treated to destroy harmful pathogenic bacteria (all milk for commercial sale is treated this way)
- homogenised milk – pressure-treated to emulsify the fat through the milk; does not affect the milk's flavour and ensures the cream is evenly distributed through all the milk
- sterilised ultra-high temperature (UHT or long-life) milk – heat-treated to destroy all bacteria, which alters the milk's flavour; does not require refrigeration until the container is opened, when it must be then treated like fresh milk
- powdered milk – skimmed and sterilised milk with all the moisture removed, must be reconstituted with cold water before use
- creamer: in either powder or liquid form, made from vegetable fat and vegetable protein.

Individual portions are a popular method of dispensing milk (UHT and creamers) in either 20 ml pots (liquid) or 5 g paper sleeves/sachets (powdered). These require no refrigeration and are subject only to best-before dates.

Milk for coffee should be heated to a maximum of 70°C. At a higher temperature the milk sugars start to cook and alter their flavour.

Full-cream milk should be heated to order, and not left standing on the hot plate in the pot as it will quickly form a skin and film of liquid fat.

Milk for tea service should be removed from the refrigerator an hour before service to allow it to reach a temperature of about 10°C, to prevent it cooling the tea in the cup too much.

Figure 18.8 Milk is available with different levels of fat content

Figure 18.9 Pre-packaged milk portions are easy to store

Remember!

Do not store milk near strong-smelling foods such as onions, garlic, melon, vinegar-based products, etc., as the milk will absorb these aromas and pass them into the hot drink.

Cream and ice cream

Iced drinks and some hot coffee and chocolate drinks may be topped with a portion of cream or ice-cream as a part of the recipe. Fresh cream may be either poured gently over the top of the coffee to float on the top (Irish coffee), or whipped until it thickens and then piped or spooned on the top. A popular method used in many establishments is the use of cream dispensers (aerosol-style sprays of UHT or artificial creams that can be piped by spraying directly onto the hot drink).

> **Remember!**
>
> All creams (fresh and synthetic) are classed as high-risk foods and must be stored in a refrigerator, even during service. Fresh cream must also be covered when not in use.

Sugar

Sugar is an important accompaniment to hot drinks – it not only sweetens the drink, but also gives the drinker a boost of instant energy. There are a variety of sugars available for serving with hot drinks, including:

- granulated sugar – the old method of serving loose sugar in a bowl, now often served in sugar shakers or individual sachets
- cubed sugar – a popular method of serving sugar for hot drinks as the cubes dissolve in the drink rapidly; these offer good portion control
- demerara sugar – popular with coffee drinkers, as it adds extra flavour to the coffee
- sugar crystals – served either loose or on individually wrapped sticks for stirring
- syrups – sugar in liquid form, used mainly to sweeten iced drinks
- artificial sweeteners – branded products that are a sugar substitute, aspartame and saccharine are the main ingredients; have both styles available in case a customer is allergic to one or the other.

Figure 18.10 Sugar comes in many different forms

All these styles of sugar are now offered in individually wrapped portions, which allows for cost and portion control and reduces the mess associated with loose sugar.

Dusting powder

Dusting powders are used to decorate the top of hot and cold drinks with a creamy or foamy head, such as cappuccino coffee. Most establishments have their own recipe and mixtures, and proprietary brands are also available. Powdered drinking chocolate is often used.

Test yourself!

1 What is the raw ingredient of coffee, and how is it brewed?

2 What is 'hard' water?

3 Should tea and coffee be made using bottled waters?

4 What is UHT milk?

5 Why is it a good idea to provide sugar in individually wrapped portions?

Preparing the work area and equipment for service

Whenever a customer enters your establishment, they will expect to see a clean, well organised area (see Chapters 2, 4 and 5). Customers will quickly observe:

o cleanliness and tidiness of the tables and chairs

o cleanliness of the floor

o neat and tidy layout of the service counter/bar area

o presentation and neatness of staff and uniforms

o hygienic practices of staff

o hygienic storage of any food and drinks on display

o promotional information on products available.

Figure 18.11 Cleanliness is all-important

It is therefore extremely important that all these areas are clean, tidy and presentable, not only at the beginning of service, but continuously throughout service.

Attention to these details is the responsibility of every member of staff on duty and not one individual (see Chapter 3).

Proper preparation is the key to providing good quality drinks and an efficient service. You must prepare the work area, the equipment and the ingredients.

Remember!
No customers – no job!

531

Preparing the work area

It is important that your working area is clean and organised to ensure a smooth and efficient service, especially at busy times.

- Check and refill all containers with ingredients where necessary.
- Have sufficient back-up supplies that are easily accessible.
- Test all machinery before service commences, to ensure it is working correctly.

Check that you have supplies of all drinks in stock before service, and make a note of any that are temporarily out of stock, reporting the low stock level to your supervisor.

Have all your **mise en place** (preparation) ready before service begins. Check and clean the sugar, artificial sweeteners, butter/margarine pats, condiments, cutlery, straws and paper napkin dispensing systems, and make sure they are refilled. This should be repeated on a regular basis, as the area can quickly become untidy from customer use.

If you are offering a wide range of hot and cold drinks, it would be impossible to recite all the drinks (and food) you have on offer to each customer! To prevent you having to explain your menu, a comprehensive list of drinks (known as the tariff, as it includes prices) should be displayed in a prominent position near the service area and on each table. This should include any promotional material for branded products, and may include pictures of the drinks or food in the style that the establishment serves.

Ensure that all promotional material is clean, undamaged and, most importantly, up-to-date. Well placed promotional material will not only be eye-catching, but will help to ease service and increase sales.

Make sure your uniform is clean and your personal appearance (hair, fingernails, breath, etc.) is presentable (see page 46).

Remember!
You must always ensure that adequate stocks of all ingredients and branded products are available before you open for business.

Definition
Mise en place: getting everything ready before starting service.

Why not try our new milkshake?

Figure 18.12 A tent card on each table is a good method of advertising your products

Preparing the equipment

Crockery

Crockery used in hot drink service includes cups, saucers, pots,
lids, jugs, cafetières and bowls. The following checks should be
made.

- Look for damage (chips, cracks, missing handles) – remove
  damaged items from circulation and record the damage in the
  breakages book so that replacements can be ordered.
- Check that lids fit pots securely.
- Check for cleanliness (tea/coffee stains, lipstick, smears).
- Make sure there are sufficient items available for service.
- Warm the cups.

Stainless steel/silver plate

Metal items used in hot drink service may include pots, jugs, bowls,
strainers, lemon squeezers, salvers and spoons.

Wash stainless steel equipment (pots, jugs, bowls, salvers,
teaspoons) in hot water and detergent, rinse and polish with a
clean dry cloth.

Check silver plate items for signs of tarnishing. Polish with a
branded silver-cleaning agent or cloth to remove the tarnish, then
wash and polish as for stainless steel.

> **Remember!**
> Make sure you always use
> the appropriate cleaning
> materials (see page 145).
> **Never** store cleaning materials
> in an unmarked container (see
> page 50).

Hot drinks machines

Hot drinks are often prepared ready for service in the
still-room, although an espresso machine may be sited
behind the service counter or bar. Hot drinks machines
include vending machines, espresso machines, automatic
filter machines and water boilers. You should never attempt
to use or clean any hot drinks machine until you have been
shown how by an experienced operator or supervisor.

Figure 18.13 Always read the
manufacturer's instructions

Each manufacturer's machine will work differently, so it is important
to read the instructions carefully before attempting to clean the
machine. To ensure that equipment will operate efficiently during
the service period, each item must be thoroughly cleaned and
checked for signs of wear and damage. Once your supervisor is
confident that you can do this, strip down and clean all parts as

> **Remember!**
> Most hot drinks machines
> work under high pressure. The
> combination of hot steam and
> inexperience could lead to
> serious burns and scalding.

recommended in the manufacturer's instructions for daily cleaning, making sure that the parts are rinsed free of any detergent used for cleaning.

Reassemble and check that the unit is working correctly.

Vending machines

Automated vending machines are found in a variety of shapes and sizes, from small table-top units to large free-standing ones. Some vending machines are coin-operated and are designed for self-service use 24 hours a day.

Many cafés, canteens and bars have automated vending machines behind the counter for dispensing a variety of hot drinks, which allows for quick, accurate portion and quality control.

For any vending machine to operate efficiently it must be clean, well maintained and topped up with ingredients regularly.

Figure 18.14 An automated vending machine

Daily routine

o Switch off power at the mains before opening the door of the vending machine.

o Check to see there are no leaks or visible malfunctions before commencing your tasks – report anything unusual to your supervisor.

o Dismantle, wash and clean the mixing system (according to the manufacturer's instructions), making sure all 'dry-powder' feeding tubes are thoroughly dried before reassembling.

o Top up the ingredient containers, making sure there are no air pockets in the mix (tap the containers to remove any air pockets).

o Close the door and clean the outside of the vending machine using an antiseptic swab over and around the operating buttons.

o Switch the vending machine on and test to ensure it is operating correctly.

Bean grinders

The best coffee is produced from freshly ground coffee beans – once ground, the volatile oils that are part of the coffee's aroma start to evaporate and oxidise, giving a stale flavour. Many establishments use either pre-ground or vacuum-packed coffees, but a growing number of establishments now grind their own coffee beans.

Originally, coffee grinders were hand-operated and often produced an uneven grind. Modern machines grind each individual portion to the exact size instantly, which provides for ultimate freshness and accurate measures.

Make sure the grinder is placed in a dry area and away from steam (as the beans will absorb moisture and clog up the grinding mechanism). Clean the machine after each shift and always ensure that there are sufficient beans in the hopper.

Espresso machines

The espresso machine works by passing a measure of hot water through a pre-measured portion of finely ground, roasted coffee packed into a filter held in the handles of the machine. The coffee grounds are only used once, and are emptied into the 'knock-out box' after each brew. Many machines can be programmed to deliver a portioned quantity of water. Traditionally this is 25–30 ml when producing a single espresso (using the single-filter handle, which holds 7 g of coffee), or 50–60 ml when producing a double espresso (using the double-filter handle, which holds approximately 14 g of coffee).

The best espresso coffee has been brewed from the finest freshly roasted and ground coffee beans. Stale beans and grounds produce stale coffee with little aroma or flavour.

Before service you must:
o check that there is sufficient water (water gauge)
o empty and clean the knock-out box of any spent coffee grounds
o make sure the filter handles are clean
o make sure the steam wand is clean (and cleaned after every use to prevent a build-up of dried milk)
o check the pressure on the pressure gauge (under normal operation, the pressure in the boiler will be 1 bar, and the pressure used to extract your espresso will be 9 bar)
o ensure sufficient cups are on the warming plate (rims uppermost to prevent customers burning their lips from very hot rims)
o finally, test the system to ensure it is working correctly.

Figure 18.15 An espresso machine

Did you know?
The espresso machine was invented by Luigi Bezzera in 1901, and is now one of the main coffee-making systems used worldwide.

Automated filter machines

Filter or drip coffee is often referred to by customers as 'regular' coffee. It is a long, black coffee drink, which can have milk added if the customer requires.

The filter machine showers hot water (at about 96°C) over ground coffee held in a paper filter, which sits in the filter pan. The water filters through the coffee, extracting the flavour, and drips into a flask or jug underneath. The process takes about 5 minutes.

When making filter coffee:
○ Ensure that the filter paper is correctly located in the filter pan.
○ Put the ground coffee evenly into the filter. 'Gold Cup Standard' recommends that 55g of coffee is used per litre of water, although less coffee than this is commonly used in the UK.

The coffee can be pre-prepared, but should not sit for longer than 30 minutes on a hot plate, as it will develop a stewed taste.

Figure 18.16 An automated filter machine

Urns

There are times during a very busy service when it is not possible to meet demand by making individual hot drinks (canteens, outdoor functions) and a large quantity of pre-brewed tea or coffee is required. For this purpose an insulated stainless steel urn is used. Most urns are designed so that the tea or coffee can be brewed in them. The urn has its own heating element (electric), a filter insert and a tap for dispensing the hot beverage.

Blenders

Electric blenders are required when mixing/blending iced coffee (or chocolate) with ice cream to form a smooth, creamy drink. Blenders are also used for mixing fruit smoothies, which are becoming very popular.

Figure 18.17 A tea urn

Electric blenders consist of a glass or stainless steel jug fitted with a set of two or four sharp rotating blades at its base. The ingredients to be chopped or blended are placed in the jug. After the safety lid has been fitted, the jug is attached to the electrical base of the unit and switched on. Always switch a hand blender off before removing it from the liquid mixture.

While the blender is working, it must remain firmly on the table or counter with the lid secured. Always switch off the blender before removing it from the base, and take care when cleaning inside the jug – always use a long-handled cleaning brush.

Electric hand blenders have the blades situated at the base of the blender (in a protected housing). Place the blender in the container with the ingredients to be blended. Always ensure the blender is fully submerged in the liquid before switching on.

Steamers

The use of steam to heat liquids is an efficient and quick method in modern catering establishments. Steam wands can be found attached to espresso machines (see above) or to fixed hot-water boilers. The steamer consists of a narrow, high-pressure tube with an end cap of fine holes, which forces the steam out at high pressure. The nozzle must be fully immersed in the container of liquid before the tap is turned on, and not removed until the tap has been turned off.

You must **not** fill the container completely full of cold liquid, as the condensing steam will add approximately 15% more volume by the time the steaming cycle has completed.

To prevent clogging of the injection holes and a build-up of congealed milk solids on the tube, regular cleaning in a container of water (using the steaming process) should be carried out, with a final clean at the end of service.

Figure 18.18 Take great care when using a steamer

Cream whippers

These are a modern method of whipping small amounts of cream using a single whisk attachment on a small hand-held electric motor unit. Before using, you must scald the whisk attachment to sterilise it (remember that cream is classed as a high-risk food). The whisk must be fully submerged in the cream before switching on.

Domestic, hand-held, general-purpose electric whisks can also be used for whipping larger amounts of cream, but the whisk attachments must be sterilised before use.

Kettles and boilers

The kettle is the traditional method of boiling freshly drawn, cold water for brewing tea. The capacity of the average domestic kettle is metric 1.5 litres (imperial 4 pints), but metric 500 ml (imperial 1 pint) units are usually used in hotel bedrooms, while 3 litre (8 pint) units are used in catering establishments.

Most kettles are heated by electricity. The heating element is in direct contact with the water in the kettle's heating chamber. An alternative method is by direct contact with a gas flame or the solid cooking surface of a stove.

Water boilers are large units with a capacity of 10 litres (3 gallons) or more. These are either free-standing mobile units heated by electricity, or fixed units heated by gas/electricity as part of a water-heating system in the service area.

Before daily use

- Kettles and boilers must be checked for leaks from outlet taps, furring of heating elements (in hard-water areas) and worn or damaged electrical leads and plugs.
- Always site the unit in a safe position with no trailing leads, and where no-one is likely to burn themselves accidentally by touching the hot sides.
- Any stale water from the previous session should be removed and discarded, and freshly drawn, cold water placed in the chamber, before switching on the kettle or boiler.

During service

- Make sure the water is boiling rapidly before brewing tea.
- Check the water content regularly. This may be done by checking the capillary gauge on the side of the boiler or, if a gauge is not fitted, by lifting the lid to look inside. Remember there will be very hot condensed droplets on the lid's underside, and these can scald if they contact your skin.
- When topping up, add a little freshly drawn, cold water at a time, so that the boiler or kettle reaches boiling point much more quickly. Once it has reboiled, a further small amount of freshly drawn, cold water can be added.

Thermometers

Under the Food Hygiene Regulations, all equipment used for the
storage of food must be checked at regular intervals to ensure
the equipment is operating at the correct minimum temperature.
Every time the temperature is checked, it must be recorded. If the
temperature is other than normal, it must be reported immediately
to your supervisor – and no ingredients should be served from that
unit until you are given permission by your supervisor to do so.

Dishwashers

An automatic dishwasher is an important piece of machinery for any
busy food service establishment, to ensure that a constant supply
of clean, hygienic crockery and cutlery is always available.

Like all machines, a dishwasher is only as good as the person
operating it. Dishwashing is an important part of the daily routine,
and you must always:

- make sure you have read and understood the operating
  instructions
- check that the machine is free of dirty water and is clean before
  switching it on
- check that all cleaning fluid containers have sufficient fluid in
  them, and that you know where the replacement fluid is stored
- ensure all parts are clean and in place before you switch on the
  machine
- when the water has reached its operating temperature (as shown
  on the machine's temperature dial), run the machine (empty) to
  check that it is operating efficiently
- make sure you remove any debris from the items to be washed,
  and stack the holding trays correctly
- at the end of the shift, switch off the machine, drain out the
  water and clean everything thoroughly
- leave the machine's doors open to allow good circulation of air
  while not in use.

*Figure 18.19 Load the dishwasher
carefully and keep it clean*

Refrigerators and freezers

Remember that refrigerators used to store milk for beverages
should not be used to store strong-smelling foods, as these aromas
can be absorbed by the milk. Even if the food has been wrapped in
clingfilm, the aroma can still pass through.

All dairy products (milk, cream, butter, yoghurt and eggs), together with dairy-based foods (gâteaux, mousses, etc.), should be stored in a refrigerator specifically assigned for them.

Melon slices, strong cheeses, smoked foods, vinegar-based products (pickles), fish and raw onions (often in salads, rolls and sandwiches) are the main foods that give off strong flavours. These products should be stored in a separate refrigerator.

Always smell the milk before using (especially before service commences) to ensure it is not sour and has not absorbed any strong odours.

Figure 18.20 Dairy products should be stored in a separate fridge

During service

At busy times, it is most important for all serving staff to be able to locate ingredients and equipment quickly and efficiently. A well organised service area will operate smoothly when under heavy demand. A busy service area relies on teamwork, and everyone must follow these basic rules.

- When you use something, clean it and place it back in its original position.
- If you spill anything, clean it up immediately to prevent any further mess or an accident.
- Always replace lids and tops on containers and bottles after use to prevent accidental spillages.
- Any breakages or spillages must be reported to your supervisor and will have to be recorded in the breakages/accident log. All breakages and spillages will incur a cost to the business, and should be investigated to ensure they do not happen again.

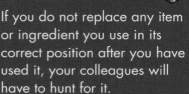

Remember!

If you do not replace any item or ingredient you use in its correct position after you have used it, your colleagues will have to hunt for it.

Taking a drinks order

Counter service

It is important that you are fully aware of the entire range of hot and cold beverages that your establishment offers.

While the majority of customers may order a standard cup of tea or coffee, many will want a speciality version of the basic drink (espresso, cappuccino, latte, Americano coffee). You must listen carefully to their order to ensure accuracy, and repeat the order back to the customer if you are unsure.

If a customer has ordered a drink you have not heard of, or have
not made previously, apologise and ask a colleague or your
supervisor for assistance. If a customer requests a drink that you
do not have available, apologise and offer the alternative that
is nearest in style:

Table service

Offer the drinks list first to females in the party (senior first). Stand
back and allow them a few moments to study the list, but be
available to assist if required.

You may wish to take orders using a salver to rest your check
(order) pad on. This makes writing out the order much easier.

As for counter service, if a customer has ordered a drink you have
not heard of, or have not previously made, apologise and ask a
colleague or your supervisor for assistance. If a customer requests
a drink that you do not have available, then apologise and offer the
alternative that is nearest in style.

> ## Test yourself!
>
> 1 Why do you need a
>   thermometer when
>   serving hot drinks?
>
> 2 What products need
>   to be refrigerated
>   separately, and why?

Preparing and serving hot drinks

When preparing any hot drink, you must be aware of the rules
regarding the safe practices required when handling hot liquids.
Burns caused by scalding and by touching hot containers
are commonplace in service areas – and are mostly due to
carelessness. You must always observe the safety rules, not only
for your own safety, but for the safety of your colleagues working
around you, and of customers.

Safety rules

- Always check that equipment is fully serviceable and in good
  working order.
- Keep your work area free from unnecessary clutter and allow
  plenty of room in which to place hot items of equipment.
- Make sure no-one is too near the boiler or steamer before you
  use it.

- Always use **dry** tea cloths or gloves to handle hot containers. Never use a wet or damp cloth to handle hot items – the moisture will quickly absorb the heat and scald or burn you.
- Always make sure your way is clear before moving hot containers of liquid around.
- Never rush with hot containers of liquids.
- Always put hot teapots in a place where all staff expect them to be.
- Always hold the teapot close to the hot-water tap when filling it with boiling water, to prevent splashing. Use a dry cloth to hold the pot – the handle can become hot very quickly as the pot fills with boiling water.
- Always check the boiler's pressure gauge/water level gauge at regular intervals. If you suspect something is wrong, warn others not to use it, and report it immediately to your supervisor.

Remember!

There should always be a kettle close at hand in case the boiler breaks down, so that a service can still be offered.

Brewing coffee

There are many methods of making coffee – but there are some basic rules which you should always follow.

- Always use freshly drawn, cold water. Always empty the kettle and fill it with fresh, cold water for each brew.
- Make sure your brewing equipment is perfectly clean and spotless – coffee has a high oil content and residue can quickly become rancid.
- Make sure the brewing equipment is in good working order.
- Always operate the brewing equipment following the manufacturer's instructions – do not cut corners.
- Always warm any equipment that you are going to use – this includes the coffee cups.
- Always use freshly ground coffee (or if pre-ground, from a freshly opened packet).
- Use the correct size of coffee grind for the style of brewing.
- Use the correct style of blend for the time of day. Do not use the same style of coffee for breakfast as for dinner.
- Do not guess quantities – always use a measure (55–60 g/litre).
- Never pour boiling water on the coffee grounds. The temperature of the water should be a maximum of 96°C (boiling water extracts the bitter oils from the coffee grounds).
- Never use stale boiled water – it will only produce flat, insipid coffee.

Marcus says

If you are serving filter coffee, remember there is nothing worse than stewed coffee. The fresher the better!

- If the water is hard, allow a longer infusion time. With hard water, it is better to use infusion methods rather than filter methods.
- Do not leave the brewed coffee (infusion methods) on the coffee grounds longer than the recipe or instructions recommend, as the coffee will become too strong and bitter.
- Do not brew the coffee too early. It should be brewed just before it is required, to preserve its freshness.
- Do not allow coffee to boil after it has been brewed. This causes the coffee to become bitter.
- Do not reheat coffee after it has gone cold. This causes the coffee to become bitter.
- Always make coffee in batches, do not brew the whole meal's requirements in one go (unless it is for a function).
- Store your coffee beans/grounds in a cool place and in an air-tight container to retain freshness.
- Do not store ground coffee for too long unless it is vacuum-packed and unopened. Once the packet is opened, use as for freshly ground coffee.
- Store away from smells.

Figure 18.21 Don't boil or reheat coffee – this makes it bitter

Grinding coffee

Roasted coffee beans must be ground before they can be used to make the brew. Grinding opens the coffee bean's cell walls, allowing water at the brewing stage to extract the cell's contents.

Because grinding opens the cell walls, ground coffee should be used as soon as possible (and never kept longer than 10 days).

Coffee is ground to different grades of fineness, which suit the many different methods of brewing. The fineness of grinding required will be directly related to the water contact time associated with the method of brewing selected.

The most suitable grinds for some common methods of brewing coffee are given below.

Method	Grind
Automatic filter/filter drip	Fine to medium
Jug	Coarse
Turkish/Greek	Pulverised
Plunger-pot method (cafetière)	Medium
Vacuum method (Cona™)	Medium-fine or fine
Espresso	Very fine
Neapolitan (flip-pot)	Medium
Percolator	Medium
Al fresco	Medium

Figure 18.22 Different grades of fineness for different styles of coffee

When brewing coffee, always follow the instructions for the specific brewing method. Experiment with different blends to find the one that suits you best.

Brewing methods

Automatic filter

As with any machine, the manufacturer's instructions should be followed (see page 52). Place a clean filter in the filter holder and charge with a measure of freshly ground coffee (60 g/litre). Make sure the coffee grounds are spread evenly in the filter. Place the filter in its slot on the machine, and place a clean jug under the filter. When the 'ready' light is illuminated, pour a full jug (to line) of freshly drawn, cold water into the water chamber. This begins the brewing process (taking approximately four to five minutes).

When the coffee has been made, discard the old filter and spent grinds, recharge with a new filter and fresh coffee grounds, and repeat the process.

Jug

This is one of the oldest methods of making coffee. Use a heat-proof jug made from a material that will not affect the coffee's flavour. Warm the pot before adding coarsely ground coffee, add the hot water, stir, and allow to infuse for four to five minutes. Pour through a strainer.

Turkish/Greek coffee

This is the original coffee-brewing method. These coffees are brewed in a special, long-handled, saucepan-like pot known as an *ibrik* (Turkey), a *briki* (Greece), or a *kanaka* (Arabia). The coffee is traditionally drunk very sweet from small (*demi-tasse* size) cups, accompanied by a glass of iced water. A heaped teaspoon of pulverised, dark-roasted coffee is added to a measure of freshly drawn, cold water that has been brought to a rapid boil in the pot. The brew is then reboiled with a teaspoon of sugar for 10 seconds, removed from the heat, and the grounds allowed to settle for 10 seconds. The coffee is then decanted into the coffee cup.

Figure 18.23 Greek coffee

Plunger pot (cafetière)

A modern version of the jug method, which consists of a (usually glass) jug (of various capacities from one to two cups up to 20 cups) with a disc plunger to hold back the grounds from the brewed coffee. Medium-ground coffee is used (25–30 g per 500 ml water). Near-boiling water is added, and the water and grounds are stirred before the plunger is put in place. Allow four to five minutes for infusion before pushing down the plunger. This method is ideal for allowing customers to judge for themselves the strength of the coffee they prefer. The pot and filters must be cleaned before the pot is re-used.

Vacuum (Cona™) method

This consists of two heat-proof glass or stainless steel bowls (the lower one in the shape of a coffee pot, the upper one funnel-shaped) held together by a rubber seal. Cold water is placed in the lower bowl; upon heating, the boiling water is drawn up (through expansion) from the lower container into the upper one, holding the coffee grounds where infusion takes place. After the heat source has been removed from the bottom container, a vacuum is created which draws the infused coffee (liquid) back into the bottom container (the grounds are retained in the top unit by a special glass stopper valve).

Neapolitan (flip-pot)

This is a two-tiered machine popular in Italy for brewing coffee. Freshly drawn, cold water is placed in the bottom half of the machine, and medium ground coffee is placed in the filter in the middle. The water is heated over a heat source. When the water boils, the machine is removed from the heat and completely inverted to allow the water to run through the coffee grounds into the lower compartment, which also has a spout for pouring.

Percolator

Medium-ground coffee should be placed in the coffee 'basket' and cold, freshly drawn water added to the pot. Turn on the heat and allow the brewing cycle to complete (usually indicated by a red light). Do not add more water to create another brew from the spent grounds. Clean and repeat the process for the next brew.

Al fresco

This is a very simple method of brewing coffee when no conventional brewing equipment is available. A measure of freshly drawn, cold water is placed in a clean, grease-free saucepan (or other suitable heat-proof container) and brought to the boil. The pan is then removed from the heat, and a portion of medium ground coffee is stirred in and allowed to infuse for three to four minutes. The coffee is then gently decanted off the grounds into warmed cups.

Coffee cartridges

These are modern, pre-measured plastic cartridges charged with a measure of ground coffee (of different strengths, to choice) with a fine mesh filter on the top and base of the cartridge to retain the grounds. The cartridge is placed over the top of a warmed coffee cup, and a measure of hot water (96°C) is poured into the cartridge and allowed to filter into the cup. A lid is usually placed over the top while the water is filtering and this is then used to hold the spent cartridge.

Coffee bags

These are individual, one-cup bags (in the same format as tea bags), or large pre-measured bags for automatic filter machines.

Pre-ground beans

For convenience and portion control, most coffee manufacturers produce their coffee in vacuum-packed, pre-ground quantities. The style of coffee (roast and size of grind) will be included on the packet, together with the quantity of brewed coffee that can be made and what brewing methods are suitable.

Instant coffee

This is freshly brewed coffee that has been either heated, roller-dried or vacuum freeze-dried. There are now a vast array of high-quality instant coffees that can be used to make single cups or large pots. Allow one level teaspoon of powder or granules to 150 ml very hot water.

Decaffeinated coffee

Decaffeinated coffee is now available either as an instant coffee, or as whole roasted beans or freshly ground coffee. It is brewed by using any of the brewing methods described above.

Speciality coffees

There are a large number of different styles of coffee available. The main styles are as follows.

○ Espresso: usually 25–30 ml of strong, black coffee brewed in an espresso machine and traditionally served in a small 2–3 fl oz coffee cup.

○ Ristretto: an intense espresso drink, allowing only 15–20 ml of water to flow through the coffee. A favourite with Italian coffee drinkers in the mid-morning.

○ Americano: hot water with an espresso added into it (so resembling a filter coffee), served with or without milk or cream.

○ Latte: literally means milk in Italy (in the UK, we shorten the original Italian name *caffé latte* or *latte macchiato* for ease). Refers to an espresso topped with a lot of steamed milk and a thin foam cap.

○ Doppio: a double espresso.

○ Mocha: similar to a latte, but with chocolate syrup or cocoa powder.

○ Cappuccino: an espresso coffee topped with steamed milk and finally topped with one-third foamed milk. A dusting of powdered chocolate may be added to the top.

○ Irish coffee: place a sugar cube in a warmed glass, fill it two-thirds with hot, strong coffee and stir to dissolve the sugar. Add a measure (25 ml) of Irish whiskey and top with double cream. There are many other versions using differed spirits and liqueurs.

Definition

Decaffeinated coffee: is coffee from which the caffeine has been removed – usually before the beans have been roasted.

Figure 18.24 Decaffeinated coffee is becoming increasingly popular

547

French	English	Spirit or liqueur
Café Irlandais	Irish coffee	Irish whisky
Café Français	French coffee	Cognac or brandy
Café Russe	Russian coffee	Vodka
Café Jamaique	Jamaican coffee	Dark rum
Café Calypso	Calypso coffee	Tia Maria
Café Caraïbe	Caribbean coffee	White rum
Café Mexicaine	Mexican coffee	Tequila
Café Italienne	Italian coffee	Grappa
Café Écossaise	Scottish coffee	Scotch whisky
	Highland coffee	Malt whisky
	Bonnie Prince Charlie's coffee	Drambuie
	Monk's coffee	Bénédictine
Café Hollandaise	Dutch coffee	Jenever
Café Anglaise	English coffee	Dry gin
Café Normande	Normandy coffee	Calvados
Café Aztec	Aztec coffee	Kahlùa
Café Scandanave	Scandanavian coffee	Kümmel

Figure 18.25 There are a wide variety of coffees with spirits added

Brewing tea

Tea is an important hot drink in the UK, and tea drinking forms a major part of our daily routine. It is important to follow the rules of tea brewing and service – always follow the procedure practised by your employer.

There are many speciality teas available, including Earl Grey, Chinese teas, breakfast teas and **tisanes**. If your establishment offers any of these, make sure you have been shown exactly how they are brewed and served.

Even if you are using tea bags, the same degree of care should be followed to ensure the customer enjoys their cup of tea.

Ingredients:
- freshly drawn, cold water
- good quality tea/tea bags
- fresh, cold milk
- sugar cubes
- lemon slices (with pips removed).

Definition
Tisane: a herb tea or infusion.

Did you know?
Tisanes have become a popular substitute for tea and coffee because they are caffeine-free. The main flavours include camomile, mint and various fruit teas.

Equipment:

o kettle or boiler
o silver salver and doily (depending on the style of establishment)
o teapot (stainless steel or china)
o milk jug
o hot water jug
o sugar bowl
o sugar tongs
o tea strainer (for loose tea)
o slops bowl (for loose tea)
o teacup and saucer
o teaspoon.

Method

o Fill the kettle with freshly drawn, cold water and bring it to a rapid boil.
o For black tea, boiling water is needed to extract the flavour from the leaves. Cooler water will not draw out the flavour and can leave a film on top of the drink. Green and white tea should be brewed with cooler water about 80°–85°C.
o Warm the teapot, hot-water jug and teacups.
o Place the tea (one teaspoonful per person) or teabag (one teabag per person) in the warmed pot.
o Take the pot to the boiling kettle, and pour the boiling water onto the tea (do not use more water than required).
o Allow the tea to infuse (pass into the water) for around two to five minutes for black tea and up to ten minutes for some white teas. Smaller particles used in tea bags will brew faster than larger leaves. The hardness of the water will also affect how long the tea takes to brew. Stir with a spoon before service.
o Fill the hot-water jug with boiling water.
o With all types of tea take the leaves out of the water once brewing has finished, or serve the tea straight away if this is not possible. This prevents the tea from stewing.

Figure 18.26 There can be a ritual element to drinking tea

Did you know?

For many tea drinkers a certain degree of ritual is important, where a set procedure is an important part of the whole experience. In Japan, the tea ceremony takes three hours!

Service of tea

Place a warmed cup and saucer on the right-hand side of the customer with the cup handle at three o'clock and the teaspoon lying across the right-hand side of the cup.

Pour the milk in first (this prevents the milk being 'scalded', which alters the flavour). But if the customer requests that the milk is poured in after the tea, or requests no milk, you should follow their instructions.

Offer sugar, and finally place the teapot, hot-water jug, milk jug, sugar bowl and tongs on the salver to the right-hand side of the customer (with all the handles pointing at three o'clock). If loose tea has been used, a tea strainer and slops bowl should also be included.

> **Try this!**
> Make two cups of tea – one with the milk poured in first, and one with the milk poured in last. See if you can taste the difference!

Making hot chocolate

Hot chocolate can be made with a number of different products: drinking chocolate powder, chocolate syrups or actual pieces of chocolate. Different products can vary greatly in the amount of cocoa solids used in them. This can greatly affect how much of a product you need to make a drink. When using proprietary brands of chocolate drink, always follow the manufacturer's instructions.

Chocolate powders normally have milk powder mixed in, so it is possible to complete the drink using just hot water, although hot milk is commonly used for a richer result. Place the powder into the bottom of the cup and add a splash of hot water to start it dissolving. Add either hot water or hot milk and stir thoroughly to ensure all the powder is dissolved.

Steamed milk drinks

When steaming milk, never fill the container completely full with cold milk – the milk's volume will increase by up to 15% by the time it reaches 95°C, due to the steam converting into water as it condenses.

Most establishments have a milk-steaming facility, which enables a variety of hot milk-based drinks to be served. Heating the milk using steam prevents the milk from burning (which often happens when it is heated in a pan). However, over-steaming will cause the milk to become watery as the steam condenses into the milk.

Making iced drinks

Iced tea and coffee, popular in continental Europe and the USA, are now gaining popularity in the UK. Canned tea is now widely available, but iced coffees should be made from freshly brewed coffee.

Once brewed, allow the coffee to cool quickly (do not add ice to hot coffee as this will water it down – instead, stand the pot in a bowl of iced water). Never use stale coffee that has been kept hot for a long time, as it will be flat and bitter. Cover and store the cold coffee in a refrigerator. Sweeten with sugar syrup and pour over ice in a tall glass.

Test yourself!

1 List five important safety rules when preparing and serving hot drinks.

2 Why should coffee not be kept too long, or reheated?

3 When making tea, should the milk always be poured in first? Explain your answer.

Appendix

Applying for a job

Jobs in the catering industry are advertised in a range of places:

○ the local jobcentre
○ local newspapers
○ trade magazines
○ specialist recruitment agencies
○ online via any of the above.

Full time Bar staff – Immediate Start

Location: Brighton town centre

Salary: £12,000 per year

Benefits: Meals on duty, uniform supplied

We are looking for bar/waiting staff for a recently opened restaurant which has already had some fantastic reviews.

If you are outgoing, passionate about good service, looking to join a company that is food orientated and want to work in a good team environment and learn new skills, please send your CV in the first instance to:

Mrs J. Baker, The Lobster Pot, Green St, Brighton, BN1 1JJ

Sample job advertisement

Writing a CV

When applying for a job you need to be able to tell your prospective employer certain information about yourself. All potential employers will want to know the same basic information to decide if they want interview you. You can impress employers by having these details prepared already on a document called a Curriculum Vitae (CV).

Curriculum Vitae

Lesley White
18 Orton Close, Haverford, Westham W45 6PQ
Tel: 01234 567 89   Date of Birth: 30.2.90

Education and qualifications
2007–2009   Portsmouth Hospitality College
             NVQ Levels 1 and 2 in Professional Cookery
2001–2007   Secondary School Porth Heath
             6 GCSE subjects at Grade C and above including:
             Mathematics   Grade B
             English   Grade B
             Science   Grade C

Additional qualifications
December 2007   Basic Food Hygiene Certificate
December 2007   Basic Health and Safety Certificate
July 2006   Duke of Edinburgh Bronze Award

Part-time employment
2007–2009 Kitchen assistant The Grill Room, Portsmouth
2005–2007 Washer-up   The Crown Hotel, Porth Heath

Interests and achievements
Member of college football team
3rd place in Level Two Live Cookery Competition at Portsmouth Hospitality
College, July 2009

Referees
Mr M Blake   Mrs H Black
Head Chef   Course Tutor Level 2
The Grill Room   Professional Cookery Dept
Portsmouth   Portsmouth Hospitality College
P56 7TY   P89 5EF
Tel: 0123 456 7890   Tel: 0123 654 9876
Email: m.blake@thegrillroom.co.uk   Email: h.black@portsmouthhospcat.ac.uk

Sample CV

Remember!
Your CV should:
o never be longer than two sides of A4 paper
o be typed
o be clearly laid out
o be factual
o use bullet points rather than long sentences
o be quick and easy to read
o only include relevant information that will help your application
o be spelled correctly.

Your CV should contain:
o **Personal details**: your full name and if you wish your date of birth and nationality.
o **Contact details**: a full address, home and mobile telephone numbers and an email address if applicable.
o **Qualifications**: school GCSE pass grades and any higher qualifications, any catering qualifications, e.g. NVQ Level 1 in Professional Cookery and Basic Hygiene Certificate.

Sending a covering letter

When sending a CV either by post or email you need to include a covering letter. This must be clear, correctly laid out and easy to read.

Your address

18 Orton Close
Haverford
Westham
W45 6PQ

Name of person applying to with their full job title and address

Mrs J Baker
The Lobster Pot
Green St
Brighton
BN1 1JJ

20 September 2009 ← Date the letter is written

Always include title and surname

Dear Mr Brown

Vacancy for Bar staff ← Title of job applying for

I am interested in applying for the position which I saw advertised in the latest copy of Caterer and Hotelkeeper. I have read the reviews of your restaurant in Restaurant and the Brighton Argus and am very keen to learn more about the business. Please find enclosed a copy of my CV as requested which I hope you will find of interest.

Say which position you are applying for and, if appropriate, where it is. State where you saw the advertisement, or how you found out about the vacancy.

I enjoy working as a member of a team and would like to improve my craft skills to the highest level that I can. I am keen to work hard and am very reliable and punctual.

Point out your strengths which may not be evident from your CV. Make sure you sound enthusiastic in your letter.

Add a closing paragraph.

I do hope you will consider my application for this position. I look forward to hearing from you.

Yours sincerely

Sign your name and then print it clearly underneath

Lesley White

Lesley White

If you have used the person's name at the beginning, end with yours sincerely. If you have put Dear Sir end with yours faithfully.

Sample covering letter

The interview process

If an employer is interested in your application and thinks you may have the skills and experience they are looking for they may ask you to come in for an interview. Interviews are held to allow:

- both the applicant and the employer to meet each other
- both parties to ask questions about the job
- both parties to be impressed by the other
- the applicant a test shift in the dining room or behind the bar to see if they have the necessary skills.

Preparing for an interview

If you take the trouble to prepare for an interview it will show on the day. First, find out the best way of getting to the location and how long it is likely to take. Assume there will be delays and allow half as long again to get there, e.g. if the journey should take 30 minutes allow at least 45 minutes.

Decide what you are going to wear several days in advance. Make sure your clothes are clean, ironed and not in need of repair e.g. buttons missing or damaged hem. Find any certificates or information you have been asked to take with you.

Read over the information about the job. This may be only the advertisement but you may have been sent a job description or information about the company. You need to be familiar with these to ask and answer questions.

Find out about the business. Look on the internet or in the catering press. Find out some facts about the organisation that you find interesting and will be able to remember, e.g. some special drinks or cocktails on the menu or special promotions they have had recently. If you can, use this information to ask or answer questions.

Think of some questions to ask at the interview and write them down in a small notebook. Take the notebook with you and do not be afraid to look at it if you are asked whether you have any questions. You are showing the employer that you have come prepared.

Try this!
Prepare your CV and ask a friend, family member or your tutor to check it for you. Collect a range of job advertisements from the catering press that appeal to you. Keep them in a scrapbook to remind you of what to look for when the time comes for you to apply for a full-time job for real!

How to impress an interviewer

Follow these simple tips to impress the person interviewing you:

- Arrive in plenty of time so you are not hot and flustered.
- Make sure you look as smart and professional as you can. Check you have clean shoes, tidy hair and ironed clothes.
- Use positive body language, e.g. walk tall, look at your interviewer and smile, try not to sit with your arms folded, and have your hands relaxed in your lap.
- Have a firm handshake – not limp and not superman style!
- Listen carefully to what is being said to you and ask if you do not understand or did not hear properly.
- Speak clearly and not too quickly.

Top marks!

Try to imagine the effect of your appearance or behaviour on an interviewer. What they want is someone who can work effectively in their team and produce good quality work. If you look scruffy or are not polite they will not think of you as that person.

After the interview

Take some time to reflect after an interview.

- Think about what you did well during the interview so that you can make sure you do it again if necessary.
- Consider what did not go so well and how you can stop that happening in the future.
- Remember any questions you found difficult and make sure you know the answers for next time.
- If you are successful make sure you know when and where you start work.
- If you are not successful this time do not be too upset, get ready to try again.

Test yourself!

1 List three places where jobs may be advertised.

2 What is a CV?

3 Give three tips for writing a good CV.

4 What is a covering letter?

5 Why should a covering letter be written?

Try this!
Ask your Careers Advisor or a family friend to give you a mock interview. Use details of the type of job you hope to apply for one day. Dress appropriately and have your copy of your CV with you. Be prepared to answer questions about yourself and the job you would like to do.

Investigate!

Find out where your local Careers Advisor is based and how to get there. Look for jobs you are interested in on the internet, in the catering press and in the local newspaper.

Research the company advertising the position to find out how big it is. Does it have branches all around the country? Abroad? Does it run a training programme?

Try this!

When you are preparing to apply for a job you have to consider the skills you have developed and can use well. You then have to consider if there are any other skills you need for your ideal job. How are you going to get these skills? Prepare a table to show:

- *the skills you have now*
- *the skills you would like to have in the future*
- *ways of learning the skills that you need*
- *the dates that you managed to achieve these skills*
- *if the skills you gained were as useful to you as you had hoped.*

This exercise can only be completed over a long period of time as you need to be able to acquire new skills and find out their value to you before you can finish this task. You need to keep the table with your CV and refer to it each time you look at new jobs you may like to do!

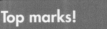

Top marks!

When preparing your personal development plan look at the qualifications you hope to obtain and the skills required by the job to make sure they complement each other.

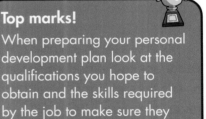

Formal learning

If you are already studying a course a formal learning plan can be very useful. It will:

- help you order the reading and coursework that you need to complete
- allow you to set realistic targets to achieve these stages in your studying
- help to train you in time management
- help you to keep your learning on track so that you can achieve your ambition.

What you need to set up a formal learning plan

You will need a diary and a notebook, in which you can record:

- your long-term aims – what you want to achieve finally
- your short-term aims – the achievements you need to fulfil your long-term aims

○ the formal short-term aims that you may have set for you by your workplace or college, e.g. passing your Intermediate Food Hygiene examination, or completing a project on different types of wine.

In the diary, set yourself some realistic target dates such as:
○ the date you have to take your Food Hygiene examination
○ the date by which you should start revising for the examination
○ the date you should hand in your project
○ a series of dates by which you should have various sections of your project researched, prepared and produced.

By planning your learning in this way, you are giving yourself the best chance of fulfilling all your ambitions. You are also demonstrating to your employer and others that you can be organised, conscientious, focused and reliable. By completing the learning experiences, you acquire knowledge and skills which can be used to help you later in life.

> **Definition**
> **Appraisal:** an assessment of performance providing feedback.

The importance of feedback

Feedback is defined as 'information provided about the quality or success of something'. In the workplace, feedback usually takes the form of:
○ customer opinion about the quality of a meal (often from a customer service questionnaire)
○ the result of an **appraisal** of an employee by a supervisor or manager.

Feedback will often result in a change or reward, for example:
○ A negative customer comment about a dish may mean it is removed from the menu.
○ A positive appraisal may mean an employee is considered for promotion.

Feedback may be the result of an appraisal

Test yourself!

1 Name three ways in which you could improve your work performance and further your career.

2 What could happen if you had a bad appraisal interview with your manager?

3 What do you need to set up a formal learning plan?

Glossary

Aboyeur: the person who takes orders from the dining room and passes them to the kitchen staff.

Alcohol by volume (ABV): the proportion of the total volume of a drink that is alcohol. It is written as a percentage, for example '11% alcohol'. The higher the number, the more alcohol is present, and the stronger the drink.

Ambient temperature: room temperature.

Aperitif: a drink served either in a bar or restaurant before a meal is served, intended to stimulate the appetite.

Appraisal: an assessment of performance providing feedback.

Bacterium: a single bacteria, which is a single-celled organism.

Bain-marie: a double boiler, used to protect foods from direct heat. A smaller container is partially immersed in a larger container of heated water.

Beer engine: the hand-pump mechanism that draws the ale from a cask in the cellar to the dispense bar by using vacuum suction.

Beverage: usually indicates a non-alcoholic drink, often hot, such as tea or coffee.

Bin card: an individual record of a single stock item. Can be a record card stored with the stock item or an electronic file.

Body language: communication that takes place between people from the movements of their body and facial expressions.

Boston shaker: a cocktail shaker that does not have a built-in strainer.

Broaching head: the beer dispense line fitting that holds the beer line and gas line, and fits directly onto the keg's spear head valve to deliver gas to the keg and draw beer from the keg.

Buffet: a selection of light refreshments where diners help themselves, often eating standing up.

Carbonised paper: paper treated so that if you write on the top copy, the writing appears on the following sheets as well. Saves writing out multiple copies of the order.

Cask: an oval metal container for holding alcoholic liquids, especially beer.

Caustic: a substance that will stick to a surface and burn chemically – used for heavy-duty cleaning.

Cellar: in the past this meant an underground storage room, but modern cellars can be situated either above or below ground. Usually used for storing beer and/or wine in a licensed premises.

Chafing dish: a large, portable food dish that is heated using candles, spirit lamps or individual spirit-jelly burners.

Chance customers: customers who arrive at a restaurant without a reservation.

Change of cover: the additional cutlery or flatware required by the customer to eat a menu item.

Chargeable containers: bottles, crates, kegs and casks that have had a deposit levied by the brewery on them, refundable when the containers (including damaged items) are returned to the brewery.

Check (or **docket**): a copy of a customer's food or drink order. It is used to communicate information to restaurant staff, for example in the kitchen or bar, to the waiter or cashier. It is also used to control food and drink stocks issued.

Cocktail: a mixed drink prepared by shaking, stirring or pouring a number of ingredients together.

Complimentary: something that is given as a free gift.

Condensation: a coating of tiny drops formed on a surface by steam or vapour.

Confidential: private or personal.

Cover: a place setting at table. There are different types of cover for different menus.

Cover charge: a minimum charge placed on a customer's order. It is used to avoid tables being blocked with diners ordering very little over a long period.

Credit card: a card that allows the customer to pay for goods on credit, and settle the bill with the credit card company at a later date. Interest will be charged by the credit card company if the bill is not settled in full each month. Examples of credit cards are Barclaycard and American Express.

Customer requirements: information such as customers' names, number of place settings, time of arrival, type of occasion, special seating arrangements, special dietary requests, time limitations, any pre-orders for food or drinks, and requested style of service.

Data Protection Act (1998): law governing the collection and storage of personal information about people.

Debit card: a card that allows the customer to pay for goods without using cash, provided they have sufficient funds in their bank account. If the customer does not have enough money in their account, the payment will not be authorised.

Decanting: the pouring of wine to leave its sediment in the bottle.

Demi tasse: a French term, meaning 'half cup', which describes the small cup used for serving strong after-dinner coffee, or espresso-style coffee.

Dessert: strictly speaking, a term for the service of fresh fruit and nuts.

Dilute: to add extra liquid (usually water) to make a solution weaker.

Documented: when a detailed record of information is made.

Dormant: not active or growing.

Drayman: someone who delivers drinks.

Due diligence: taking every possible precaution to avoid a food safety problem.

Dysentery: a food-borne disease causing mild to severe diarrhoea and fever. It can be fatal.

Effervescent: describes a liquid which is lively and full of bubbles.

EHO: Environmental Health Officer.

Empathise: to be able to imagine what another person is thinking, e.g. a customer

Entrée: a dish of small meat cuts in a sauce.

Entremets: hot and cold food items offered as the sweet course.

Excrement: solid waste matter passed out through the bowel.

Extraction mechanism: a general term for the keg's extraction spear and broaching head system.

Extraction spear: a hollow tube attached to the keg's spear head valve (onto which the broaching head is connected). It is fitted with a spring-loaded valve that is opened by the keg's internal gas pressure which pushes the beer up the spear into the beer dispensing system.

Faeces: solid waste substance from the body.

Family service: a style of service in which the food is placed in the centre of the table for people to serve themselves.

Fillet or **filet:** a boneless cut of meat or fish.

Finger stall: a plastic tube that fits over a dressing (bandage or plaster) on an injured finger to protect it. It is secured by an elastic strap around the wrist.

Flambé: a French term used to describe cooking at the table in the restaurant and briefly setting fire to the dish using alcohol.

Flat: a tray, usually oval, made of silver or stainless steel, used to present the food during silver service.

Float: a small amount of cash, including coins of all denominations. The float is put in the till at the start of the day's trading so that cash customers who do not have the correct money can be given change.

Fobbing: a term used for the foaming of beer at the pump, which can be caused by over-gassing of the ale in the keg/cask, or dirty pipes.

Fortified wine: wine with the natural alcohol content increased by the addition of spirit, usually brandy. Fortified wines include Sherry, Port, Madeira, Marsala and Malaga.

Gueridon service: food partially prepared or cooked within the restaurant itself, usually on a trolley beside the guest's table.

Gyle label: a brewery system of either a dated label (for casked ales) or plastic cap (for kegged ales) that is often colour-coded and identifies the days and dates when the ales/beers were brewed and kegged/casked.

Halal: food that is permissible according to Islamic law.

Hazard: something that could be dangerous.

Haze: describes a condition of beer when it is cloudy, not bright. Usually caused by dirty pipes or disturbed casks (cask ales), or from the beer being too cold (keg and cask ales).

Hors d'oeuvre: a light, appetising course to stimulate the appetite. May be a variety of small items for the customer to select from, e.g. a cold assortment of meats, fish, vegetables, salads, eggs, or a single hors d'oeuvre such as avocado, melon, fruit cocktail, oysters or smoked fish.

Humidity: the moisture in the air. In a cellar, too high a humidity reading (above 85%) will cause dampness.

Ice-cream spoon: like a teaspoon, but with a spade-shaped bowl to the spoon

Impervious: does not allow water to pass through it. In a cellar, walls have an impervious surface to prevent damp and mould.

In house: on the premises.

Inedible: not fit to be eaten.

Inert: a substance that will not react chemically with any other substance.

Keg: a metal, straight-sided container for kegged (pasteurised) beers.

Keystone: a grooved disc situated in the base of one end of a beer cask into which the beer tap is placed.

Kosher: food that is in accordance with Jewish law.

Licensing hours: the hours permitted by the local authority for the sale of alcohol on nominated premises.

Lip-reading: a technique of being able to identify spoken words by looking at the shapes made by the mouth of the person who is talking.

Magnum: a double-sized bottle equal to two standard bottles of wine.

Measure: a standard unit for measuring drinks. The measures for alcohol are often determined by law: e.g. 25 ml and 35 ml for spirits.

Methode Champenoise: in the process of making sparkling wine, a method of secondary fermentation which takes place in the bottle.

Micro-organism: a very small life form, which cannot be seen without a microscope.

Mise en place: a French term meaning 'in its place' – the preparation of ingredients and dishes before the beginning of food service.

Monitoring: regularly checking condition and progress.

Muddler: a bar tool used to crush ingredients such as sugar, mint, lemons and limes.

Neat: if a drink is served neat, it has nothing mixed with it.

New World wines: wines produced outside the traditional wine-growing areas of Europe, in particular in Australia, Argentina, Canada, Chile, New Zealand, South Africa and the USA.

No sale: when the till is opened without a transaction taking place – no goods are bought and no money is paid.

Non-toxic: not poisonous or harmful.

Organism: any living animal or plant.

Over-ring: when the wrong amount is keyed into the till.

Pasteurised/Unpasteurised: has/has not been heat treated.

Pathogen: an organism that causes disease.

Petty cash: a small amount of cash that is stored in a cash box for small expenses.

Plankton: a layer of tiny plants and animals living just below the surface of the sea.

Precipitation: the crystallisation of a tartaric acid due to very low temperatures.

Pressure release valve (also known as the 'bursting disc'): a pressure-release system fitted to a gas cylinder to prevent it bursting. The disc will rupture if the pressure within the cylinder rises high enough to cause the cylinder to burst.

Reducing valve: a brewery-set gas pressure-reducing system fixed between the gas bottle and the beer keg.

Regulator valve: an alternative name for the 'reducing valve'.

Reservations list: a list of all the bookings for a particular service session. In table service settings, the reservations list provides the waiters with the name of the customer, the number of covers, the time of arrival and any special requirements.

Sattvic: food that is uncontaminated and pure (vegetarian) according to the Hindu ideal.

Scotch: a wooden wedge used to hold brewery casks in place.

Service area: this is the meeting point of the kitchen staff and the food service staff.

Service charge: an extra charge placed on a customer's bill to cover the cost of the waiting staff. The charge may be a fixed amount, or a percentage of the total bill.

Shive: a wooden 'biscuit-like' disc with a grooved centre that is placed into the top opening of a beer cask. The grooved centre is punched out and a spile fitted while the beer is 'conditioned' in the cellar.

Sideboard: the waiter's work station. It holds all the equipment needed to provide an efficient food service to customers. It is sometimes called a 'station'.

Smoulder: to burn slowly with a small red glow and little smoke.

Social skills: in the restaurant, this means assisting customers, looking after their welfare, communicating well and anticipating their needs throughout the meal experience.

Spear head: the external fitting to a pressurised keg to which the broaching head is attached. The spear head must never be removed, even when the keg is empty, as the keg is still pressurised.

Spear: the internal delivery system of a beer keg, which is fitted to the head valve.

Spile: a small 'peg' that fits into the hole created when the 'shive' has been punched to allow the cask ale to 'work' during cellar conditioning. There are two types of spiles: a soft 'porous' spile which allows excess carbon-dioxide to escape whilst the beer is being 'conditioned' and a hard spile which is used to retain the carbon-dioxide within the cask after the beer has been 'conditioned'.

Spores: cells produced by bacteria and fungi.

Sprig: a long table, placed at right angles to the top table in a formal table layout.

Spritzer: a mixture of white wine and soda water, served chilled.

Still room: found in some establishments, the still room makes and issues food and beverages that the kitchen or bar may not provide.

Swab: a sterile piece of cotton used to take a sample for chemical analysis.

Table d'hôte: a set meal at a set price.

Take-away: any food that is purchased in a prepared, ready-to-eat condition for consumption off the premises at another location.

Tartaric acid: a natural edible acid found in most white wines that gives the wine its fresh taste.

Terms of credit: some organisations have an agreement with their suppliers whereby they do not need to pay invoices immediately, but can pay them within a certain period, for example 30 days. The time allowed is the 'terms of credit'.

Thrall: the wooden frame on which cask-conditioned ales are held.

Tisane: a herb tea or infusion.

Toxin: a poison produced by bacteria.

Triplicate checking system: a means of ordering, issuing and pricing food sold in a restaurant.

Triplicate order pad: a notepad for writing down customers' orders, made from carbonized paper so that there are three different-coloured copies – for example, in a restaurant, one copy would go to the kitchen, one to the cashier and one would be kept by the server.

Upsell: to suggest higher priced products to a customer in order to increase revenue.

Vermouth: a fortified wine flavoured with herbs and spices.

Wine quality mark: a guarantee that the wine purchased has been subjected to strict quality control measures. These quality controls cover the authenticity of origin, grape variety used and location of vineyard, and define and approve standards for wine production and certification. For example, *Appellation d'origine contrôlée* or *AOC* for French wines.

Wine: an alcoholic drink obtained by fermenting the juice of grapes.

Z-reading: provides a read-out of all sales and transactions. At the start of the day, this should be zero. If the till read-out is not zero, this indicates that the previous trading session has not been completed.

Index

City & Guilds

Hospitality & Catering
Skills for a Brighter Future

There's lots of exciting new ingredients available in our hospitality and catering range of support resources to aid tutors and learners achieve success!

Candidate Logbooks

We've produced premium logbooks for learners of our Level 2 NVQ Diploma in Food and Drink Service and Professional Cookery Candidate (7132) qualifications.

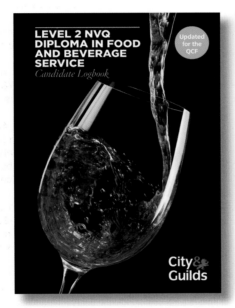

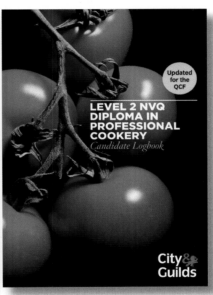

- Packed with colourful, high quality pictures with contributions and forewords from top names in the industry
- Case studies, career advice
- Stylish, easy-to-use recording forms
- Top tips from industry experts to inspire and engage learners.

Revised editions will be available from summer 2010 (incorporating the new standards and mapped to the QCF) – *keep an eye on our web pages for more information.*

Visit **www.cityandguilds.com/publications** for more information, or contact **learningmaterials@cityandguilds.com**